Imagining America

Imagining America

Influence and Images in
Twentieth-Century Russia

Alan M. Ball

ROWMAN & LITTLEFIELD PUBLISHERS, INC.
Lanham • Boulder • New York • Oxford

ROWMAN & LITTLEFIELD PUBLISHERS, INC.

Published in the United States of America
by Rowman & Littlefield Publishers, Inc.
A Member of the Rowman & Littlefield Publishing Group
4501 Forbes Boulevard, Suite 200, Lanham, Maryland 20706
www.rowmanlittlefield.com

PO Box 317
Oxford
OX2 9RU, UK

British Library Cataloguing in Publication Information Available

Library of Congress Cataloging-in-Publication Data

Ball, Alan M.
  Imagining America : influence and images in twentieth-century Russia / Alan M. Ball.
    p. cm.
  Includes bibliographical references and index.
  ISBN 0-7425-2792-1 (cloth : alk. paper)—ISBN 0-7425-2793-X (pbk. : alk. paper)
  1. Soviet Union—Civilization—American influences. 2. Soviet Union—Relations—
United States. 3. United States—Relations—Soviet Union. I. Title.
  DK268.3.B3128 2003
  303.48'247073—dc21

                                                                                2003011208

Printed in the United States of America

♾™ The paper used in this publication meets the minimum requirements of
American National Standard for Information Sciences—Permanence of Paper for
Printed Library Materials, ANSI/NISO Z39.48-1992.

For Colleen

~

Contents

~

Preface

As the Soviet era drew to a close, the Snake Brothers, a rock group from the Ukrainian city of Lvov, introduced a song titled "America":

> When midnight replaces the bright day
> And everybody is resting after work
> I haven't yet closed my eyes-ey-ey
> In my dreams I'm flying to New York.[1]

Performed partly in English, the song satirized contemporary idolization of the United States along with shabby conditions in the Soviet homeland that could give rise to such yearning. Its refrain—"America, you say to me 'welcome' / I say, Oh-yea, America / Will I ever sail to your shore?"—captured a disposition common not only in the Soviet twilight but also a century earlier, when subjects of Tsar Nicholas II emigrated by the millions to the New World.

Russian fascination with America in tsarist times passed easily through the Bolshevik Revolution and flourished thereafter. Spellbinding images of American bounty, common among the general population in the 1920s, co-existed with the interest of futurist intellectuals in an America brimming with cars, skyscrapers, and the energy of youthful iconoclasm. American jazz and movies soon held sway in Soviet cities, and even the leaders of the Communist Party spoke freely about positive features of bourgeois America that occupied a place in their imaginations. Along with the exploitation that they expected in any capitalist country, prominent officials saw in America—more than in Germany, France, or England—advanced technology and an energetic devotion to sweeping industrial challenges on a scale similar to those awaiting the builders of Soviet socialism. Late in the decade, when party leaders chose to industrialize in earnest, they did so with vital technical assistance and equipment from hundreds of American companies.

Before long, though, Stalin's government restricted the circulation of American popular culture and stressed that the Soviet Union, now reaching socialism, would soon outstrip the United States altogether. Soviet pride in industrial achievements bolstered these claims, as did Cold War hostility, which also worked to limit technological and cultural transfers from the United States. Once the Soviet Union equaled America's superpower status in the 1970s, any thought of the United States playing an important role in the construction of a new Russian society had long vanished.

Then, to the world's amazement, the Soviet Union crumbled at the end of the 1980s and disappeared altogether in 1991. Suddenly the Russian people faced an event similar to that confronted some seventy years before—the birth of a nation whose leaders promised an end to oppression and stagnation wrought by the preceding regime. More than ever, America seemed a repository of products, methods, and institutions that Russians could study or enjoy openly. In the realm of popular culture, a vast Russian appetite for American TV, movies, music, and apparel emerged from the shadows of Soviet life and recalled the attraction of American jazz and movies in Soviet cities during the 1920s. Moreover, the underlying popular image of an affluent America, widespread in Russia by 1917, survived dogged Soviet criticism and surfaced in robust condition during the century's closing decade.

Meanwhile, Russian officials and publicists looked to the West for assistance in constructing a new society. Like Lenin and Stalin, they hoped to obtain advanced technology to spur economic growth, but they also sought guidance in the formation of Western economic and political institutions loathed by Bolshevik revolutionaries. Scarcely had the 1990s commenced than Russia seemed awash not only in American products but also in U.S. advisers striving to implement such reforms as privatization of state enterprises, a new constitution, and a new judicial system, to name just a few of the ventures that would have been inconceivable less than ten years earlier.

The reforms did not bring general prosperity, however, and the passing years witnessed growing discontent with American prescriptions for Russia. Along with standard Soviet-era condemnation of the United States, critics voiced dismay over American society in terms that had flourished among Russian intellectuals during the nineteenth century and owed nothing to Marxism. America's hand did not vanish in this climate, but the euphoric hopes of reformers early in the 1990s seemed remote and naïve. Thus, at the dawn of the twenty-first century, America's example as well as its opponents are still much in evidence—new variations of longstanding phenomena.

The American angle of this study furnishes a useful vantage point from which to compare Soviet and Russian efforts to transform society. In each instance, leaders began these quests while facing a United States in ascendance—a robust newcomer to such preeminence in the 1920s and the world's lone superpower seventy years later, following the collapse of the Soviet Union. More to the point, the Kremlin's lodgers saw across the ocean a nation that led the world in matters of importance to them, after 1917 and again after 1991. Both fledgling governments also inherited a population with widespread positive (and often fanciful) notions about opportunities and wealth at hand in America. As a result the United States became a measuring stick of power and prosperity, a country whose unique role in Russian imaginations has confronted officials with the challenge of accelerating toward certain features of this "model" or promoting alternatives said to be superior. In either case, comparison with the American example proved impossible to avoid.

Long before the Snake Brothers held forth, Alexander Pushkin conceded that his heroine in *Evgeny Onegin* "knew our language only barely, / Read Russian magazines but rarely."

> In her own language she was slow
> To make her meaning clear, and so
> She wrote in French, be it admitted
> I cannot help it, it is true:
> To speak milady's love, but few
> Have thought our native language fitted.[2]

French seemed even more essential to Pushkin's Tatyana in the early nineteenth century than English does to well-educated young Russians of our day, a reminder that every aspect of America's recent influence and image in Russia finds an approximation in other locations and eras. For hundreds of years Russian rulers, aristocrats, and intellectuals looked more to Europe than to North America for guidance not only in language and culture but also in such areas as industry and administration.

Nor was Russia alone in following foreign practices. The heavy reliance of tsarist authorities and the Soviet Union on Western expertise in industrialization, for example, should not obscure the fact that other industrializing nations, including America, also depended on skills and financing supplied from abroad. Later, when American influence surpassed others' impact on

Soviet Russia and the subsequent republic, this by itself did not distinguish Russia from many lands that either sought or could not resist economic techniques, political reform, and popular culture from an ever more robust and self-assured United States. Even the gap between criticism of America by some Russian intellectuals and the vistas of American abundance more prevalent in the general population resembles divergent assessments of the United States voiced regularly outside Russian borders.

Following World War II, the loss of confidence widespread in western Europe boosted the magnetism of America's example there just as it did in Russia nearly fifty years later. In 1945 and again in 1991 the United States had weathered formidable challenges—first the conflict with the Axis powers and then the Cold War—and appeared more successful than ever to debilitated nations whose institutions had forfeited the respect of many of their citizens, especially the young. In each period America became what some have called a "reference society," a country whose prosperity, power, or modern culture (depending on the priorities of the observer) made it appear worthy of study and emulation. Foreigners recognized a sharp contrast with their own nations. Awed descriptions of American supermarkets penned by European travelers in the 1950s resemble the reaction of Boris Yeltsin on his tour of Houston in 1989, while people in liberated Europe showed the same craving for American popular culture (largely unavailable during the war) as did Russians when controls collapsed at the end of the 1980s.

Not everyone welcomed America's heft in western Europe or Russia, of course, and concerns went beyond the cultural laments of intellectuals. In Great Britain and France, resentment surfaced after the war over the nations' diminished empires and depreciated status in the growing shadow of the United States. Similar disaffection festered in Russia during the 1990s, following the evaporation of the Soviet superpower amid talk of a second "American century." If prosperity had not returned to western Europe in the 1950s, and had fear of the Soviet Union not persisted, grievances over America's global swagger might have reached a louder crescendo in domestic politics than the occasional applause won by Charles de Gaulle for defying the United States. No European politician could get far in a period of increasing affluence by saying "American measures have made your lives worse." Had better times not commenced, though, this assertion might have grown louder, as it did in Russia at the century's close.

Despite these parallels, however, America's role in modern Russia does not simply duplicate previous tsarist experience with Europe, nor does it copy American influence in other countries. European examples may have captivated tsarist administrators and intellectuals at least as much as practices from the United States drew top-level attention in the Soviet and post-Soviet periods. But nothing in the era of European predominance approached the allure of American popular culture throughout the Russian population. During most of the Romanov dynasty's three hundred years, only a small number of Russians revealed an interest in the West or sought anything from it. Then, in the twentieth century, came the birth in the United States of entertainment with international appeal, rapidly spread around the globe by new technologies of mass communication. The most determined efforts of Soviet officials could not remove (and, in the long run, simply whetted) appetites for products from the American cultural machine. Nor could Bolsheviks extinguish the popular fascination with America that had previously influenced the choice of destination made by millions of immigrants and that survived Russia's transformation from a peasant realm to a nation of urban, well-educated citizens. No European state had ever attracted such interest from ordinary Russians beneath the summit of tsarist society.

American influence on Soviet Russia stands out as well for reasons associated with the inevitable rivalry between two large countries each convinced that it alone offered the best model for other lands. Both nations cast themselves as leaders of crusades bent on the eventual demise of the other's system, and both became superpowers atop mammoth nuclear arsenals. This atmosphere dramatized almost any interaction between the two titans and imparted gravity to perceptions of influence. Regarding popular culture, for example, countries elsewhere may have absorbed more from the United States and done so earlier, but the stakes seemed higher in the Soviet Union. Washington, D.C., came to view American amusements and consumerism as weapons against communism, while Soviet officials pronounced their ideals endangered by this bourgeois contamination. To some, the confrontation suggested desperation characteristic of sixteenth-century Protestant and Catholic adversaries fighting to save their populations from damnation and struggling to extend their own paths of salvation to those less fortunate. In this light, the tenacious appeal of American popular culture in Soviet Russia meant more to both sides than it did in any other country, for the consequences associated with success or failure were momentous.

I welcome another opportunity to thank colleagues who have shared their time and advice on this enterprise over the years. At different stages of the process Samuel Baron and Richard Stites read the entire manuscript and offered thoughtful suggestions combined with encouragement sufficient to preserve my morale. Both have done so while I toiled on previous books as well, and I am grateful to have benefited from their counsel for so long. Many other people—Mark Beissinger, Jennifer Cahn, Julia Friedman, David Krugler, Yale Richmond, Vladimir Shlapentokh, and Lewis Siegelbaum— furnished comments on portions of the venture or supplied information re- garding sources that I would not likely have stumbled across on my own. In the final stage of the process, I have been fortunate to obtain at Rowman & Littlefield the guidance and support of Mary Carpenter, who buoyed me with her belief in the project. Ably assisted by Laura Roberts and Lynn Weber, she has seen the task through with good humor and sure-footed ease.

Notes

1. For complete lyrics see Sabrina Petra Ramet, ed., *Rocking the State: Rock Music and Politics in Eastern Europe and Russia* (Boulder, Colo.: Westview, 1994), 264–65.

2. Alexander Pushkin, *Eugene Onegin: A Novel in Verse*, trans. Walter Arndt, 2d. ed., revised (New York: Dutton, 1981), 73.

INTRODUCTION

~

The Land of the Benzine Pegasus

There is apparently much truth in the belief that the wonderful progress of the United States, as well as the character of the people, are the results of natural selection; the more energetic, restless, and courageous men from all parts of Europe having emigrated during the last ten or twelve generations to that great country and having there succeeded best.

—Charles Darwin

I must see America. I think one can feel hope there. I think that there the life comes up from the roots, crude but vital. Here the whole tree of life is dying. It is like being dead: the underworld. I must see America. I believe it is beginning, not ending.

—D. H. Lawrence

Describing passions felt when gazing upon a lover, John Donne found a parallel in the discovery of America.

> O my America! my new-found-land,
> My kingdome, safeliest when with one man man'd,
> My Myne of precious stones, My Emperie,
> How blest am I in this discovering thee![1]

Three hundred years later, Salvador Dalí compared the allure of America to his anticipation of a different pleasure. In France, as he leafed through issues

1

of *Town and Country* and *The New Yorker*, with Cole Porter's "Night and Day" playing on a phonograph, he savored images of the United States "with the voluptuousness with which one welcomes the inaugural fragrances of a sensational meal. . . . I want to go to America," his mind raced on such occasions, "I want to go to America."[2]

For centuries, inhabitants of diverse nations have regarded America as a land of promise—the harbinger of something new, perhaps, or the preserve of something elemental—in any case a territory enticing or reassuring by its very presence. These impressions might bear little resemblance to America seen firsthand, and they encountered scathing rebuttals from disillusioned travelers and other critics concerned about America's hold on prevailing imagination. It did not matter. No one could dam the flood of eager, desperate, or curious hopes that fed Europe's resilient notions of the New World. The earliest works of artists and writers concerned with America often contrasted an allegedly innocent, unspoiled land with an exhausted Europe whose best days lay in the past. America represented a return to uncorrupted nature or an opportunity to create something new and vibrant, free of whatever qualities the author disliked in the Old World.[3]

Looking back no further than the eighteenth century, we find the Abbé Galiani, a well-known figure among the philosophes in Parisian salons, informing a friend in 1776 that "the epoch has come of the total fall of Europe, and of transmigration into America. All here turns into rottenness, —religion, laws, arts, sciences,—and all hastens to renew itself in America." This observation, he added, was not meant as a joke or a casual prediction. He had stuck to his forecast for twenty years and saw it coming true. "Therefore, do not buy your house in the Chausée d'Antin; you must buy it in Philadelphia. My trouble is that there are no abbeys in America."[4] The outbreak of the American Revolution prompted Guillaume-Thomas Raynal, a radical voice of the Enlightenment, to present America as Europe's likely successor: "To the extent that our Peoples, one after the other, weaken and succumb, the population and the agriculture of America will increase; the arts, brought there by our efforts, will soon be born; the country arisen from Nothing, burns with zeal to make a spectacle upon the face of the earth and in the history of the world."[5]

America stirred imaginations beyond France and the Enlightenment's domain of reason. Romantics, too, could find appeal in visions of primordial nature. Mysterious forests, rivers leading deep into unknown territory, and exotic natives all roused their fancy. So did thoughts of the New World as a sanctuary from political or economic distress at home. On into the nineteenth century, then, America continued to flourish in European reveries.

Goethe, for one, declared in 1819, "if we were twenty years younger, we should sail for America," and he later addressed an enthusiastic verse to the new republic across the Atlantic.

> America, with thee life's better,
> Thou'rt free from our old Europe's faults;
> Thee no ruined castles fetter,
> Cumber no basalts.
> No useless tradition.
> No purposeless strife,
> Hinder the fruition
> Of thy pulsing life.[6]

Another prominent German, the philosopher Georg Wilhelm Friedrich Hegel, described America as "the land of the future, . . . the land of desire for all those who are weary of the historical lumber-room of Europe."[7] He pictured vitality across the ocean, and similar transatlantic contrasts occurred to others. For Percy Bysshe Shelley, young America became a bird soaring over the doomed nations of the Old World.

> That land is like an Eagle, whose young gaze
> Feeds on the noontide beam, whose golden plume
> Floats moveless on the storm, and in the blaze
> Of sunrise gleams when Earth is wrapped in gloom;
> An epitaph of glory for the tomb
> Of murdered Europe may thy fame be made,
> Great People! As the sands shalt thou become;
> Thy growth is swift as morn, when night must fade;
> The multitudinous Earth shall sleep beneath thy shade.[8]

The most influential observations on the United States in the nineteenth century, and perhaps any century, flowed from the pen of Alexis de Tocqueville, who published the first volume of *Democracy in America* in 1835. His findings ensured that America would not appear as a paradise to European readers. He tempered enthusiasm—"choose any American at random, and he should be a man of burning desires, enterprising, adventurous, and, above all, an innovator"—with misgivings or criticism about numerous aspects of life in the United States.[9] American politicians left a lackluster impression, and he judged any democracy, including the United States, deficient in the patient attention necessary for a successful foreign policy. Slavery, too, he decried in America, predicting that race relations would bedevil the new republic in years to come. More broadly, he identified a "tyranny of the majority" arising from conformity imposed by a public that was not always wise. Freedom of speech could not protect unorthodox opinion from citizens as zealous as any autocrat in combating challenges to prevailing norms. Indeed, he saw the nation threatened by the spread of a narrow-minded cultural consensus that inclined the American people to stifle eccentricity and genius, to say nothing of dissent.

Nevertheless, Tocqueville did find much to admire in America, especially when compared to Europe. He gave the advantage more often to the United States in matters ranging from the character of women and relations among family members to equality of opportunity and political freedom. "Where else," he asked, "can we find greater cause of hope or more valuable lessons?"[10] Certainly, American lawmakers could be uninspiring and democracy as a whole inefficient. Tocqueville even granted that an enlightened autocrat would run the United States more adroitly. "Democracy does not provide a people with the most skillful of governments," he explained, "but it does that which the most skillful government often cannot do: it spreads throughout the body social a restless activity, superabundant force, and energy never found elsewhere, which, however little favored by circumstance, can do wonders." "What good is it to me," he inquired in another chapter, "if there is an authority always busy to see to the tranquil enjoyment of my pleasures and going ahead to brush all dangers away from my path without giving me even the trouble to think about it, if that authority, which protects me from the smallest thorns on my journey, is also the absolute master of my liberty and of my life?"[11]

Tocqueville's fascination and hope for the United States outweighed his numerous misgivings, and *Democracy in America* helped steer many European minds in the same direction. A country of dynamism and innovation had begun to grow in foreign imaginations, promoted by Tocqueville with such comments as "the American lives in a land of wonders; everything around him is in constant movement, and every movement seems an advance." Newness and improvement were two sides of the same coin to the American, and "nowhere does he see any limit placed by nature to human endeavor; in his eyes something which does not exist is just something that has not been tried yet."[12]

While Tocqueville's voice rang loudly for years to come, European intellectuals late in the century found their thoughts drawn less to America as a land of incipient democracy and more to images of American factories and technology. Sixty years after *Democracy in America*, a second Tocqueville would sooner have published *INDUSTRY in America* to examine the accomplishments most readily associated with the United States by that time. "The industrial progress of the United States is so striking," declared a prominent Russian scholar in 1904, "that some easily frightened European publicists even speak of the impending, inevitable industrial enslavement of Europe by America."[13] Acknowledgment of American technical superiority grew ever more frequent as the years passed. Henry Nevinson, a journalist returning from New York to Great Britain shortly after World War I, combined disapproval of some American qualities ("grotesque exaggeration is called humor, and people gape in bewilderment at irony") with a farewell to technical achievements little known in his "ancient" London. "Good-bye to central heating and radiators, fit symbols of the hearts they warm! Good-bye to frequent and well-appointed bathrooms, glory to the plumber's art! . . . Good-bye to the long stream of motors—'limousines' or 'flivvers'! . . . Good-bye America! I am going home."[14] During a journey in the opposite direction, to New York in 1915, the artist Francis Picabia declared simply, "Upon coming to America it flashed on me that the genius of the modern world is in machinery." Two years earlier, a visit to America convinced France's most fashionable dress designer, Paul Poiret, that the science fiction of such authors as Jules Verne and H. G. Wells was "surpassed by the reality."[15]

With each decade, there seemed less doubt to Europeans that America had already reached the future awaiting others. Whether the prospect of this destiny moved an observer to despair or rejoice, the image of America as trailblazer gained prominence relentlessly in the European mind. In 1888 the English politician and diplomat James Bryce asked readers of his book on the United States to conclude that "America has in some respects anticipated European nations. She is walking before them along a path which they may probably follow." The twentieth century saw Europe prepared to offer more of these conclusions and with less reserve. Jean Cocteau, upon learning of Klaus Mann's impending journey to America, informed his fellow author: "You'll see New York? It's like visiting a fortune teller."[16] The English writer Mary Borden provided a similar briefing by advising in her article "The American Man" that Americans "be watched by everyone interested in the future of mankind, for the scaffolding of the world of the future is reared against the sky of America." Even in the realm of fashion, scarcely the zenith of American influence, F. Scott Fitzgerald found London's Bond Street tailors modifying their cuts to suit the New World and remarked that "the style of man" had "passed to America."[17]

Much of America's futurist image stemmed from—and contributed to—the flowering of modernism. Contemporaries sensed that something new was jostling the traditional world off the stage in the early twentieth century, and even scholars who date the origins of modernism back to the nineteenth century generally accept that the pace of change accelerated in the first decades of the twentieth. If one hesitates to go as far as the French writer Charles Péguy—who remarked in 1913 that "the world has changed less since the time of Jesus Christ than it has in the last thirty years"—it is still possible to agree that by the 1920s the world had changed more during the preceding twenty-five years than it would over the next three generations.[18]

But what is—or was—modernism? What new outlook or developments were so incompatible with nineteenth-century convention? Here, consensus often seems remote, partly because of the diverse subjects (including science, technology, fine arts, popular culture, and politics) and settings (America, England, France, Italy, and Russia, to name a few) that crowd the discussion. In addition, modernists contradicted each other avidly, as one would expect in any venture composed of so many exuberant and iconoclastic figures. Amid the cacophony, however, certain accents made themselves heard. Whether eager or alarmed, accessible or arcane, they catch the ear across a wide body of modernist work. Several of these themes deserve our attention, for they figured prominently in foreign images of the United States.

Modernism's most obvious feature is a sharp break with customary (Western) ways, often illustrated by references to Picasso's experimentation with African prototypes and Einstein's challenge to Newtonian physics. Here, in the domain of theoretical science and the fine arts, the new approaches did not gain the comprehension of many people early in the century. But other innovations did. Much of what came to seem modern at this time emerged under labels that contained the word "mass": mass entertainment, mass advertising, mass media, mass production. All of these endeavors possessed features that distinguished them from techniques of the past, and they all relied on the attentiveness of multitudes. Indeed, for some contemporaries, the very essence of modernism *meant* involvement of the masses. Relativity theory and jazz, in other words, subverted tradition along a scale of public participation that ranged from negligible for Einstein's work to frenzied in the case of jazz. Breakthroughs at one end were unintended (and too difficult to grasp) for popular consumption, while those at the other end required mass participation as never before. Aspects of modernism associated with America clustered almost invariably toward the "mass" end of this spectrum.

Also, a good deal of modernist thought and action sprang from the era's technological advances, which were linked more often to the United States than to any other nation. Automobiles, airplanes, telephones, radios, phonographs, and movies transformed life before the eyes of millions, offering new means of conveyance and communication that altered the human sense of time and distance. People, ideas, pictures—almost anything—could travel anywhere, it seemed, and much faster than before. Traditional limits imposed by space and time appeared irrelevant or archaic, as they would again with the interactive computer revolution at the end of the twentieth century. So much could be done so rapidly that an awareness of velocity penetrated deep into society. According to an American advertising writer in the 1920s, the pace of everything had accelerated: "quick lunches at soda fountains . . . quick cooking recipes . . . quick tabloid newspapers . . . quick news summaries . . . quicker novels . . . quick-drying furniture paint . . . quick-smoking cigarettes . . . quick-service filling stations." This was not a theme confined to the bustling streets of New York. When Robert and Helen Lynd published their classic study of "Middletown" USA (Muncie, Indiana) in 1929, they noted that a mania for speed had reached the heartland too. "Auto Polo next Sunday!!" announced a local amusement park. "It's motor insanity—too fast for the movies!"[19]

Whether insanity or inspiration, nothing could match the automobile as a symbol of the modern age. "Why on earth do you need to study what's changing this country?" a resident of Middletown asked the Lynds. "I can tell you what's happening in just four letters: A-U-T-O!"[20] Here, remarked a Russian futurist in 1915, stood the twentieth century's "benzine Pegasus," a creation whose speed, power, and promise of independence captured imaginations far and wide. Kaiser Wilhelm, speaking in 1906, hailed "the century of the motor car," while years later the literary critic Roland Barthes described cars as "the cultural equivalent of the great Gothic cathedrals."[21]

Many modernists found them exhilarating. Francis Picabia purchased scores of automobiles and even had a racing car placed at the top of a large tower he owned in the south of France. There the vehicle was attached by means of a long rod to a pivot, allowing Picabia to zoom round and round, as in a centrifuge.[22] No one reached a state of ecstasy faster by car than Filippo Tommaso Marinetti and other Italian futurists, for whom the unprecedented opportunity to chase a whim at breakneck speed promised emancipation. Their manifestos contain numerous passages of elation over the power of the new machines, as in this excerpt from 1909: "We say that the world's magnificence has been enriched by a new beauty; the beauty of speed. A racing car whose hood is adorned with great pipes, like serpents of explosive breath—a roaring car that seems to ride on grapeshot—is more beautiful than the *Victory of Samothrace*."[23]

The *Winged Victory of Samothrace*, sculpted around 200 B.C., could not divert modernists from their cars, but winged *machines* sometimes did. If cars provided a sense of liberation, a means to smash old restrictions on mobility, how could one resist the enchantment of flight? To be sure, automobiles enjoyed many advantages over airplanes. Cars were easier to obtain and operate, and they did not require special locations for takeoff and landing. Their very ubiquity guaranteed their status as a prime symbol of the new age. Yet automobiles could never soar through the clouds or across oceans. Both this novelty and the risk associated with flying gripped witnesses like nothing else in those days. For the most zealous futurists, flying could assume a near-mystical significance, and it also provided Marinetti another club with which to smash the hold of classical tradition. "Sitting on the gas tank of an airplane," he wrote in 1912, "my stomach warmed by the pilot's head, I sensed the ridiculous inanity of the old syntax inherited from Homer. A pressing need to liberate words, to drag them out of their prison in the Latin period! . . . This is what the whirling propeller told me, when I flew two hundred meters above the mighty chimney pots of Milan."[24]

Three years earlier, the French aviator Louis Blériot had flown over the English Channel to Dover, touching off tumultuous acclaim in London and especially Paris. The editor of Le Figaro could now conceive of "the day when man can, by the action of his will alone, pass in a few hours beyond all horizons across all the oceans and above all the rivers. . . . Within the foreseeable future, the conditions of human life will be profoundly changed." Meanwhile, a crowd of one hundred thousand gathered around a Parisian train station to greet the hero of the skies upon his return.[25] As the jubilant throng testified, an aviator's exploits captivated people far beyond Europe's small circle of futurists. The blend of audacity and technology—and its dissemination almost immediately to a mass audience by new communications equipment—distinguished the modern age.

The link between technology and modernism signified more than an interest in speedier transportation. A modernist outlook reflected awareness that technology had created new rhythms of life, evident whether or not a machine stood in view. Human beings themselves, some thought, were acquiring mechanical characteristics. Commuters shuttling back and forth according to railway timetables, workers as appendages of machinery on the new assembly lines, office jobs increasingly dependent on typewriters and governed by the capacity or schedule of a machine somewhere else—all this suggested a new sort of life for more people than ever before. As concern for regularity, precision, and efficiency dictated routines in more work places, the image of a worker as a human machine took hold of artistic imaginations. These observations focused on the city, brimming with cars, factories, and trains along with brilliant displays of electric lights that could ignore the laws of nature and turn night into day. The very pulse of urban life—the pace, the noise, the impersonal routine—resembled the "personality" of a machine more than that of a human being.

One could realize all this, and even produce works of "modernist" form—paintings that distorted traditional notions of the human body, prose that mimicked abrupt, hectic urban rhythms, or sculptures of "humans" with features of machines—while expressing alarm at the new society. By no means did all modernists share Marinetti's zeal for the machine age. In the fine arts they pictured the mechanical, urban world with despair as well as euphoria, thereby revealing another broad spectrum of modernist opinion. Marinetti and his followers capered at one end, while T. S. Eliot and Ezra Pound offered images of desolation at the other. For some modern artists, contemporary life appeared regimented, stifling, and ultimately sterile. It could even be menacing, as in Jacob Epstein's sculpture *The Rock Drill* (1913–14), a scarcely human figure whose lower body assumes the form of a pneumatic drill. Here, Epstein explained, "is the sinister armoured figure of today and tomorrow. Nothing human, only the terrible Frankenstein's monster into which we have transformed ourselves."[26] Some people embraced first one pole and then the other, or even tried to grip both at the same time, uncertain whether to applaud or lament the changes around them.

Broad disagreement on these issues did not prevent intellectuals from concluding with near unanimity by the 1920s that America had become the modernist nation par excellence. They might be enthusiastic or curious, contemptuous or worried, but few questioned the link between modernism and the United States. Never had American energy and innovation towered as they did now over a Europe drained by the carnage of World War I. While many in Europe had viewed the United States in distinctive terms long before their nations' armies eyed each other across no man's land, the Great War's influence on the belligerents and on modernism itself soon enhanced America's futurist image and its global influence.

This ascendancy had seemed a good bet even before European statesmen steered their continent over the brink in 1914. During the last quarter of the nineteenth century, some foreign economists who studied the United States were already predicting an "American peril." By century's end, commentators who took up the theme chose verbs in the present tense, as the American economy overtook its European competitors. As late as 1880 Great Britain's industrial sector accounted for 23 percent of the world's manufacturing output, more than the share of any other nation. The United States had already climbed to second place, with a total of 15 percent, and continued to expand production at such a rate as to eliminate within a few years the considerable gap that remained with Great Britain. By 1900 the American share of global manufacturing stood at approximately 24 percent, well above the British at roughly 19 percent. Andrew Carnegie's enterprise alone was producing more steel than all of England in 1901—when the even-larger United States Steel Corporation bought him out. Along with America's economic growth, the nation's military vigor during the Spanish-American War altered Europe's image of the transatlantic newcomer. Fifteen years earlier, few officials in London, Paris, or Berlin would have ranked the United States beside Europe's great powers. In the twentieth century's early light they saw things differently.[27]

World War I, then, did not account alone for America's surge, but it accelerated the process so dramatically that by the 1920s the nation's economy functioned on a different scale altogether from that of any competitor. "Let me predict," declared President Woodrow Wilson as he anticipated a place for the United States in the League of Nations, "we will be the senior partner. The financial leadership will be ours. The industrial primacy will be ours. The commercial advantage will be ours. The other countries of the world are looking to us for leadership and direction."[28] According to the historian Paul Kennedy, wartime disruption retarded the European economy by several years compared to its likely position if peace had prevailed. In contrast, the conflict stimulated production of nearly everything from steel to movies in the United States, prompting the American economy to surpass total European output as early as 1919.[29] Here was an economic behemoth distinguished not just by size but by leadership in new industries and products (including petroleum, electrical energy, cars, and movies) and in the new assembly-line method of production. As never before, American preeminence in both scope and modern technique focused attention on the nation's industry, prompting another scholar to argue that "the war made the American economy and the way it worked not *a* model but *the* model for the rest of the world."[30]

At the same time that World War I rushed America into view as an economic colossus, it spurred wider recognition of much that had characterized modernism before 1914. The sheer scale of the slaughter—and the pointlessness of it, as year after year dragged on with little change except in the body count—defied the nineteenth-century sense of civilization. Of what use were traditional notions of honor, glory, and justice in explaining the massacre? How comforting now was the Liberal-Enlightenment belief in progress, with Europe leading the world to ever loftier accomplishments? "The war," observed Allan Bullock, "swept away the old order of European society and finally destroyed its values in a way which everyone could see."[31] The collapse of traditional ideals and assumptions occurred first at the front, where random yet massive death administered the most severe jolt to the senses. Few soldiers had experienced anything before 1914 that could make sense of the ordeal. On the home front, too, though the war's effect was less abrupt, social and political norms lost some of their grip, leaving civilians in positions they would not have anticipated in 1913. As millions of men departed for the army, women faced greater independence (and burdens) at home, as well as opportunities (and pressure) to spend more time outside the home in volunteer or production work. Society was changing, and accustomed restraints wilted. This could take many forms, including an increase in casual sexual relations—not only between soldiers and civilians near the front but also among civilians back home. In short, writes Modris Eksteins, the war served as a "battering ram" for the old moral code.[32] Things that had mattered a great deal seemed trivial or hopeless from new vantage points created by the military inferno.

The fine arts revealed this without delay as painters, composers, and writers distorted or rejected established rules of composition with abandon. A few had done so before 1914, of course, as anyone acquainted with Picasso or the Ballet Russe could testify. But far more artists and patrons alike found such forms meaningful in the aftermath of the war—and that is the crucial point. The war had prepared people to accept, even demand, new ways of explaining their circumstances or denying the possibility of such an explanation. What better way to present themes of despair, disgust, disorientation, or protest than to reject established norms of presentation? Jarring, brooding, dissonant works could no longer be dismissed as irrelevant to human experience. The war had shown otherwise, and much that had been confined to the fringe world of artistic modernism won approval more readily by the 1920s.

In broader society as well, the relaxation of inhibitions and the discrediting of traditional authority continued after the armistice in 1918. Customary principles of etiquette and decorum could not regain their sway. The old order's legitimacy had crumbled, giving way to a "craving for newness," as Eksteins phrased it.[33] In politics, both communism and fascism gained followers at the expense of the established liberal center, while in other spheres, spasms of riotous, sometimes deliberately shocking behavior inspired the label "Roaring Twenties." Exuberance over the new and disgust with the old could share channels of expression ranging from the technofuturism characteristic of Marinetti to borrowings from cultural traditions outside Western experience. The "primitive" or exotic had never seemed so appealingly uninhibited, most famously in the case of jazz played by touring groups of black American musicians all across Europe. Whether aroused by a new dance craze or a new Leader, crowds swarmed down paths explored earlier by lone eccentrics. In shattering society's deference to formerly unquestioned observances, then, the Great War rushed many of modernism's alternatives to the mainstream.

Once this occurred, two impressions encountered little disagreement in Europe. First, America was the premier modernist nation—not just different or unique, as it had always seemed, but modernist in a twentieth-century sense of the term. Second, among the contradictory impulses thrashing about under the label of modernism, America stood for those laced with optimism. If some observers viewed the age's machinery and urban rhythms with apprehension, America did not care. Its modernism was popular, technological, and confident, eager to embrace mass cultural forms such as jazz and movies that were new to the twentieth century. Modernism confined to absurdist introspection in the fine arts and moods of despair or rage, often feeding on trauma left by the war, found more fertile soil in Europe. America had not left the war mangled and shaken. On the contrary, by accelerating American economic hegemony and spotlighting the decisive nature of American military involvement, the war glistened as a victory, not a slaughter, in the United States. More certain than ever of its advantages over a depleted Europe, America had come of age. Looking back on this period in 1930, by which time his enthusiasm had cooled, Bertolt Brecht recalled the power of Americans on the European imagination:

> What men they were! Their boxers the strongest!
> Their inventors the most practical! Their trains the fastest!
> . . . .
> So we imitated this renowned race of men
> Who seemed destined
> To rule the world by helping it to progress.[34]

"We were the most powerful nation," wrote F. Scott Fitzgerald. "Who could tell us anymore what was fashionable and what was fun?"[35]

The brazen energy of jazz, movies, skyscrapers, advertising, and cars saturated European impressions of the United States in the 1920s. Countless travelers and journalists featured these subjects in reports sent home, often in tones of awe or fascination produced by an apparent glimpse of the future. When Hemingway's friend Harold Loeb scoured Europe shortly after World War I in quest of literary contributions for his journal, he met authors captivated by this new America. "For half an hour," during a conversation with the French writer Blaise Cendrars in Rome, "I listened to praise of skyscrapers in the city of fountains, of jazz in the home of the opera, of advertising in the country where Dante had done a superlative job on hell—all in vociferous broken English." At about the same time, Edmund Wilson observed that American expatriates in France "discover the very things they have come abroad to get away from—the machines, the advertisements, the elevators, and the jazz—have begun to fascinate the French at the expense of their own amenities." Viewed from Paris, America's "skyscrapers seem exotic, and the movies look like the record of a rich and heroic world of new kinds of laughter and excitement."[36]

Nothing about the United States, whether ominous or exhilarating, appeared subtle to outsiders. This had long been true of American advertising, which Europeans regarded with amazement (at best) in the nineteenth century. "Americans are great masters of advertisement, and their ingenuity in this regard goes to bizarre lengths," concluded a Russian traveler in 1889, as had many visitors before him.[37] Only in the 1920s, however, did American advertising enter what its historians have termed a golden age, as revenue shot from less than $700 million in 1914 to nearly $3 billion in 1929. More important for our purposes, advertising in the United States had never seemed more modern to Europeans than in the decade following World War I. Most new products of the age—cars, radios, movies, refrigerators, and so forth—figured prominently in advertisements, which themselves often reached consumers through new technology (even skywriting airplanes) and employed techniques derived from contemporary art and psychology. With more fervor than ever, advertising executives promoted their expertise regarding things new: the latest fashions, crazes, and moods. They told people that technology was splendid and innovation even better. As a historian of the era put it, "advertising men were modernity's 'town criers.' They brought good news about progress."[38]

They also brought warnings that no family could be truly happy without a car, or a second car, according to General Motors advertisements that expressed concern for the "marooned" housewife in 1928. Here was a contraption that few Americans had glimpsed before the Chicago World's Fair of 1893. Even then, the handful of gasoline-powered vehicles on display were German and attracted little attention in the shadow of the mammoth exhibits of railroad technology in the exposition's Transportation Building. Before long, though, Americans caught the automotive fever. Vehicle registrations jumped from 4 percent of the nation's households in 1912 to 50 percent in 1923, prompting Warren Harding to remark that "the motorcar has become an indispensable instrument in our political, social, and industrial life." By the end of the decade New York City alone contained more cars than all of Europe, and America's annual production (4.5 million vehicles) surpassed that of France (211,000), Britain (182,000), Germany (117,000), and all other countries combined.[39] The United States had become the land of the automobile, one of the modern age's preeminent symbols, and Europeans could not fail to note the contrast with their own countries. Ilya Sheinman, a Soviet engineer heading home from a visit to America in 1929, viewed western Europe through new eyes.

> London gave me the impression of a city which had been flattened out some-how. There were no tall buildings of the American type. Everything was terri-bly patriarchal. The houses were of some sort of affected, antique architecture. The big, dark cars were stunningly awkward; tall and short, they recalled old carriages. . . . [They] gave no impression of movement, of a continuous urge to move ahead, which distinguished them sharply from American automobiles.[40]

Sheinman's remark indicates that skyscrapers as well as cars had engrossed him in the United States, and his reaction resembled that of other travelers. Ever since buildings of unprecedented height rose above the streets of Chicago and New York toward the end of the nineteenth century, Europeans had identified skyscrapers with America. As early as 1899, the German hu-mor magazine *Kladderadatsch* published a cartoon that showed a row of dwellings representing the great powers: quaint, diminutive structures for the European states alongside a colossal American skyscraper. No other symbol more immediately suggested both America and the future, and it remained in the 1920s among the handful of images employed by artists as shorthand de-vices for rendering a scene "modern." "Look at the skyscraper!" enthused Marcel Duchamp on a visit to New York in 1915, during which he pro-nounced traditional culture "dead." "Has Europe anything to show more beautiful than these?" Not in the opinion of Helene Deutsch, one of Freud's students, who journeyed to the United States and declared skyscrapers "the most beautiful architecture that one can imagine." "AMERICA IMPOSING REALLY NEW WORLD," she telegraphed to her son. "EVERYTHING GI-GANTIC MAD TEMPO."[41]

Meanwhile, another nation emerged from the war amid buoyant pronounce-ments about the future. Its leaders shed no tears over demolished tradition, for they were revolutionaries. Vladimir Lenin and his Bolshevik (Commu-nist) Party seized power in Russia in November 1917 and set about building socialism in a new state they soon named the Soviet Union. While Ameri-can ebullience of the day stemmed from such factors as a short, victorious war and economic preeminence, no such advantages befell Soviet Russia. World War I had been a ghastly defeat, followed immediately by enormous territorial loss, civil war, economic ruin, and social collapse. Yet, for the Bolsheviks, the conflict also represented opportunity. By maiming the old regime, World War I initiated a collapse that eventually brought Lenin's party to power. The worse things got, Lenin observed before 1917, the better the chance to make a revolution and build an entirely new society. Far from agonizing over a crumbling past, the young Soviet state presented itself as a country of destiny, a land in which the rest of the world could glimpse its socialist future under construction. Even the darkest moments of civil war did not smother Bolshevik optimism about the years to come, as Lenin demonstrated in his "Letter to American Workers" of 1918: "Slowly but surely the workers [in many lands] are moving to communist, Bolshevik tactics, toward the proletarian revolution, which alone can save dying culture and dying humanity."[42]

Thus, self-assuredness rang loud after the war in the Soviet Union as well as the United States, as each nation's elite expected to pioneer a future superior to the traditional European world. By itself, this was not new. Visions of Russia and America rising to prominence, whether as rivals or as sharers of a special destiny, entered some Western minds before the turbulent events of the twentieth century. Walt Whitman, writing in 1881, noted that Russia and America appeared "so distant, so unlike at first glance . . . and yet in certain features, and vastest ones, so resembling each other." He pointed to the size of each country and their similar tasks of fusing people of diverse race and tongue into single national identities. Much remained to be done, but this work must be "agreed on all hands to be the preparations of an infinitely greater future." The "deathless aspirations at the inmost centre of each great community, so vehement, so mysterious, so abysmic," Whitman concluded, "are certainly features you Russians and we Americans possess in common."[43]

A number of Russian travelers in America during the first half of the nineteenth century shared the opinion of P. A. Chikhachev, who concluded from his journey that "Russia and the United States are two states before whom is unfolding the most sparkling future."[44] Some of these Russians, together with a larger contingent who never crossed the Atlantic, acquired their views (or had them confirmed) upon reading Tocqueville's *Democracy in America*. Though banned for decades by the tsar's censors after publication in 1835, copies circulated among educated Russians without much difficulty. Those with access to the book encountered not only Tocqueville's assessment of America but also his conclusion that Russia and the United States "alone march easily and quickly forward along a path whose end no eye can yet see."[45]

To be sure, more European voices predicted a remarkable future for America alone, rather than in step with Russia, and even Tocqueville forecast that

Russia's future dominance "of half the world" would be one of despotism, in contrast to a gentler American supremacy in the other hemisphere. As for the possibility that Russia would leave *all* nations behind, including America, the corps of prophets shrunk essentially to a handful of Russians of Slavophile bent. By midcentury the most prominent member of the intelligentsia to defend this conclusion was Alexander Herzen, who argued that the age-old communal instincts of Russia's peasant majority would permit the country one day to welcome socialism. For the West, saddled with a large bourgeoisie intent on suppressing the toiling majority, it was too late. Herzen had read Tocqueville a decade earlier, in 1838, and even then could not accept the conclusion that Russia and America carried jointly the seeds of the future: "But where in America is the start of a future evolution to be found? It is a cold and calculating country. Russia's future, however, is without limit—I believe in her progressiveness."[46]

Herzen's faith notwithstanding, a problem faced those who expected Russia—either alone or in tandem with America—to shine one day over the hulk of Europe. Unlike America, whose power and prosperity grew in breathtaking fashion as the twentieth century approached, Russia fell farther behind. Although the defeat of Napoleon had inspired predictions of imminent Russian glory, the shock of the country's humiliation in the Crimean War (1853–56) and the Russo-Japanese War (1904–1905) made it increasingly difficult for Russophiles to extol anything concrete beyond the country's size. Belief in Russia's eventual rise to the global vanguard continued to rest mainly on assertions regarding such intangible qualities as the uniqueness of Russian civilization and its mission one day to astonish the world. As the nation staggered to defeat in World War I, however, the day when peasant Russia would inspire industrial giants seemed ever more remote.

In July 1917 D. H. Lawrence wrote: "I believe America is the new World. Europe is a lost name, like Nineveh or Palenque. There is no more Europe, only a mass of ruins from the past."[47] Millions of Europeans might have agreed with Lawrence on the ruin of Europe, three years into the Great War, and many shared his image of America. Few would have thought to include Russia in the "new World" that Lawrence imagined rising above European rubble. But scarcely four months later, Lenin and the Bolsheviks launched their revolution and set out to build the world's first socialist state. Here, indeed, was something new—newer than America. Even westerners alarmed at the prospect of sparks from Russia bursting into flame across Europe could recognize the novelty of the Bolsheviks' venture. No longer was Russia a nation of the future in only the most abstract sense. As the Bolsheviks clung to power during the civil war and then began to pour the foundation for socialism, spellbound eyes followed their progress from elsewhere in Europe. They watched from America, too, where numerous liberals and socialists now found less reason than ever to regard the New World as progressive. If the United States remained a model of the future for many of the era, it was certainly not *the* model any longer.

As early as 1919 the muckraking author Lincoln Steffens remarked on his return from Soviet Russia: "I have been over into the future, and it works." Four years later, on the sixth anniversary of the Bolshevik Revolution, the *Nation* editorialized that "the virility of Russia may hold out the best hope for civilization" in a world "sick with the diseases that breed from capitalist-imperialism." Lincoln Colcord, a liberal journalist writing at the end of 1918, saw in the Soviet Union "a foreshadowing of the next step forward in the machinery of democratic government, bringing our present machinery, a heritage from a past era, abreast of the new industrialized world."[48] Perhaps no one in the United States detected a brighter light in the East than Eugene Debs, the leading American socialist of his day:

> Monumental in its glory, it stands alone. Behold its sublime majesty, catch its holy spirit and join in its thrilling, inspiring appeal to the oppressed of every land to rise in their might, shake off their fetters and proclaim their freedom to the world!
>
> Russia! Russia! Thy very name thrills in our veins, throbs in our hearts and surges in our souls! Thou art, indeed, the land of miracles, and thy humble peasants and toilers stand forth the world's triumphant liberators![49]

Indeed, who could react with indifference to Russia's revolutionary transformation? Confronting the millions around the world who regarded Bolshevism as a menace, there massed similarly large numbers intent on following the Soviet example to new and better societies. From Europe and every other continent, enthusiasts (and a smaller share of those with misgivings) journeyed to Moscow for a look at the future and returned home to spread the news. Among them traveled the Mexican poet and historian Rafael Ramos Pedrueza, who toured Soviet Russia for six months in 1928 and then published an account titled *The Red Star*. After departing the USSR, wrote Ramos Pedrueza, "everything I observe in capitalist Europe seems antiquated, conventional, passé, like costume jewelry or the 'attitudes' of affected actors on some immense stage . . . and I have the certainty of a person who is leaving a New World to return to the Old World."[50] Previously, Europe had been the Old World only in comparison to the United States; now the continent's traditional powers appeared archaic when viewed from the east as well.

For much of the artistic avant-garde of Europe and even America, the young Soviet state shone with the promise of a new culture—of proletarian values or machine rhythms, perhaps, and at any rate pulsing with a vitality vanished from bourgeois society. In Weimar Germany, creators of the decade's bracing artistic atmosphere often revealed a passion for innovations they associated with Bolshevik Russia. Amid these enthusiasts stood the theatrical director Erwin Piscator and his circle of left-wing acquaintances, all enchanted by the Soviet beacon and determined to replicate its glow in their work. But, explained Piscator's wife, he and his friends continued to find inspiration from another land as well, and in this they were scarcely alone in Berlin of the 1920s: "Everything that was useful, effective, expedient, operative, performing properly and instrumental for productivity was called American. Even time had an American tempo and was valued as such." Through their American reveries swirled a "land of plenty, its material genius, with its prosperity, its slogans, and the great god—the machine." In short, they idealized the Soviet Union *and* the United States from afar and drew from the images of both countries in their artistic labors. "It is impossible to understand the complexity of Epic Theater," Piscator's wife concluded, "without taking into account this capture of the imagination by America, while, at the same time, the period was idealistically entangled with the new Russia."[51]

If sympathy for the Soviet cause did not prevent radicals in Berlin from admiring America, could a similar combination of sentiments exist in Moscow? More than distance separated the two cities, after all, and America might seem faded from the vantage point of the "world's first socialist state." The United States was modern compared to other capitalist realms, but how long could its futurist image survive in the glare of the new socialist sun? For the practical Bolshevik, who distinguished between American exploitation of labor and American technology, how much of the latter could be tapped without risk of the former? And what picture of the United States should the party present to the Soviet public? As officials pondered these issues, they recognized that their country's peasant majority remained fertile ground for images of the United States every bit as extravagant in their way as the notions current in Piscator's circle. From the beginning, then, party leaders wrestled with their own ideas about America while contending with fantastic popular notions of the land across the sea. So it was in 1917, and so it would remain for the rest of the Soviet Union's existence.

Notes

1. John Donne, "Elegie XIX: To His Mistris Going to Bed," in *Complete Poetry and Selected Prose*, ed. John Hayward (London: Nonesuch, 1990).

2. Salvador Dalí, *The Secret Life of Salvador Dalí* (New York: Dial, 1942), 327.

3. Gilbert Chinard, "The American Dream," in *Literary History of the United States: History*, ed. Robert Spiller et al., 192–215, 3d ed. (New York: Macmillan, 1963).

4. Charles Sumner, *Prophetic Voices Concerning America* (Boston: Lee and Shepard, 1874), 106.

5. Jan Willem Schulte Nordholt, *The Myth of the West: America as the Last Empire* (Grand Rapids, Mich.: Eerdmans, 1995), 73. This did not mean that Raynal was always enthusiastic about life in the New World. See C. Vann Woodward, *The Old World's New World* (Oxford: Oxford University Press, 1991), 7.

6. Anna Hellersberg-Wendriner, "America in the World View of the Aged Goethe," *Germanic Review* 14, no. 4 (1939): 276; Albert Bielschowsky, *The Life of Goethe*, vol. 3 (New York: Putnam's Sons, 1908), 220.

7. Richard Ruland, *America in Modern European Literature: From Image to Metaphor* (New York: New York University Press, 1976), 30.

8. Percy Bysshe Shelley, *Laon and Cythna*, in *The Complete Works of Percy Bysshe Shelley*, ed. Neville Rogers, 4 vols. (Oxford: Oxford University Press, 1975), 2:252.

9. Alexis de Tocqueville, *Democracy in America*, ed. J. P. Mayer and Max Lerner (New York: Harper & Row, 1966), 370.

10. Tocqueville, *Democracy*, lxxxviii.

11. Tocqueville, *Democracy*, 84, 225.

12. Tocqueville, *Democracy*, 370.

13. P. G. Mizhuev, "Zarozhdenie velikoi respubliki," *Russkaia mysl'*, no. 4 (1904): 125.

14. Allan Nevins, ed., *America through British Eyes* (New York: Oxford University Press, 1948), 396–97.

15. Robert Hughes, *The Shock of the New* (New York: Knopf, 1981), 51; Ann Douglas, *Terrible Honesty: Mongrel Manhattan in the 1920s* (New York: Farrar, Straus & Giroux, 1995), 186.

16. Marcus Cunliffe, "European Images of America," in *Paths of American Thought*, ed. Arthur M. Schlesinger Jr. and Morton White (Boston: Houghton Mifflin, 1963), 499; Ruland, *America*, 79.

17. Mary Borden, "The American Man," *Spectator*, 30 June 1928, 958; F. Scott Fitzgerald, *The Crack-Up* (New York: New Directions, 1956), 14.

18. Hughes, *Shock*, 9; Malcolm Bradbury and James McFarlane, eds., *Modernism, 1890–1930* (Atlantic Highlands, N.J.: Humanities, 1978), 33; Douglas, *Terrible Honesty*, 192–93.

19. Roland Marchand, *Advertising the American Dream: Making Way for Modernity 1920–1940* (Berkeley: University of California Press, 1985), 3–4; Robert S. Lynd and Helen Merrell Lynd, *Middletown: A Study in Contemporary American Culture* (New York: Harcourt, Brace and Company, 1929), 258.

20. Lynd and Lynd, *Middletown*, 251.

21. Vladimir Markov, *Russian Futurism: A History* (Berkeley: University of California Press, 1968), 379; Modris Eksteins, *Rites of Spring: The Great War and the Birth of the Modern Age* (New York: Anchor, 1990), xiv (regarding Barthes), 88 (regarding Wilhelm).

22. Hughes, *Shock*, 51.

23. Filippo Tommaso Marinetti, *Marinetti: Selected Writings* (New York: Farrar, Straus and Giroux, 1972), 41.

24. Marinetti, *Marinetti*, 84.

25. Robert Wohl, *A Passion for Wings: Aviation and the Western Imagination 1908–1918* (New Haven, Conn.: Yale University Press, 1994), 57–58.

26. Hughes, *Shock*, 48.

27. Ernest R. May, *Imperial Democracy: The Emergence of America as a Great Power* (New York: Harcourt Brace, 1961; Chicago: Imprint, 1991), 6, 182–83, 263–64, 267; Paul Kennedy, *The Rise and Fall of the Great Powers: Economic Change and Military Conduct from 1500 to 2000* (New York: Random House, 1986), 194, 202, 243; V. Motylev, "Istochniki ekonomicheskogo prevoskhodstva Soedinennykh Shtatov," *Bol'shevik*, no. 12 (1928): 36.

28. Donald W. White, *The American Century: The Rise and Decline of the United States as a World Power* (New Haven, Conn.: Yale University Press, 1996), 22–23.

29. Kennedy, *Rise and Fall*, 244, 328.

30. Douglas, *Terrible Honesty*, 182.

31. Bradbury and McFarlane, *Modernism*, 70.

32. Eksteins, *Rites*, 225.

33. Eksteins, *Rites*, 257; Doeko Bosscher, Marja Roholl, and Mel van Elteren, eds., *American Culture in the Netherlands* (Amsterdam: VU University Press, 1996), 46.

34. Bertolt Brecht, "Late Lamented Fame of the City of New York," in John H. Zammito, "Art and Action in the Metropolis: The Berlin Avant-Garde, 1900–1930" (Ph.D. diss., University of California at Berkeley, 1978), 815–16.

35. Fitzgerald, *Crack-Up*, 14.

36. Harold Loeb, *The Way It Was* (New York: Criterion, 1959), 67; Thomas J. Saunders, *Hollywood in Berlin: American Cinema and Weimar Germany* (Berkeley: University of California Press, 1994), 3; Virginia Carol Hagelstein Marquardt, "Louis Lozowick: Development from Machine Aesthetic to Social Realism, 1922–1936" (Ph.D. diss., University of Maryland, 1983), 29.

37. Olga Peters Hasty and Susanne Fusso, eds., *America through Russian Eyes: 1874–1926* (New Haven, Conn.: Yale University Press, 1988), 63.

38. Marchand, *Advertising*, 1–2, 6, 9.

39. Marchand, *Advertising*, 161; Peter J. Ling, *America and the Automobile: Technology, Reform, and Social Change* (Manchester, England: Manchester University Press, 1989), 95–98, 127; Douglas, *Terrible Honesty*, 17; Kennedy, *Rise and Fall*, 327.

40. Mark Hale Teeter, "The Early Soviet de Tocquevilles: Method, Voice and Social Commentary in the First Generation of Soviet Travel Publitsistika from America (1925–1936)" (Ph.D. diss., Georgetown University, 1987), 231.

41. May, *Imperial Democracy*, 266; Hughes, *Shock*, 175; Le Corbusier, *Toward a New Architecture* (New York: Payson & Clarke, 1927), 57–58; Marchand, *Advertising*, 242; Marcel Duchamp, quoted in Merrill Schleier, *The Skyscraper in American Art, 1890–1931* (New York: Da Capo, 1986), 64; Helene Deutsch, quoted in Douglas, *Terrible Honesty*, 129.

42. V. I. Lenin, *Polnoe sobranie sochinenii*, 5th ed. (Moscow: Izdatel'stvo politicheskoi literatury, 1977), 37:64.

43. Walt Whitman, *The Correspondence, vol. III: 1876–85*, ed. Edwin H. Miller (New York: New York University Press, 1969), 259.

44. V. Shestakov, "Russkoe otkrytie Ameriki," in *Vzaimodeistvie kul'tur SSSR i SShA XVIII–XX vv.*, ed. O. E. Tuganova (Moscow: Nauka, 1987), 21. Hans Rogger, "Amerikanizm and the Economic Development of Russia," *Comparative Studies in Society and History* 23, no. 3 (July 1981): 393.

45. Tocqueville, *Democracy*, 378.

46. Hans Rogger, "America in the Russian Mind—or Russian Discoveries of America," *Pacific Historical Review* 47, no. 1 (February 1978): 34.

47. Ruland, *America*, 37.

48. Lincoln Steffens, The *Autobiography of Lincoln Steffens* (New York: Harcourt, Brace and Company, 1931), 799; *Nation* 117 (7 November 1923), 501; Lincoln Colcord, "Soviet Russia and the American Revolution," *Dial* 65 (28 December 1918).

49. Eugene V. Debs, "The Soul of the Russian Revolution," *Call Magazine*, 20 April 1918, 1.

50. Rafael Rámos Pedrueza, quoted in William Richardson, *"To the World of the Future": Mexican Visitors to the USSR, 1920–1940* (Pittsburgh: University of Pittsburgh, Carl Beck Papers, 1993), 16.

51. Zammito, "Art and Action," 350.

PART ONE

THE EARLY SOVIET ERA

CHAPTER ONE

~

Soviet Americanism

The technology of America, joined with the Soviet organization of society, would produce communism, or in any case, conditions of life approaching it.

—Leon Trotsky

I will give you the whole of the broad Russian soul for a couple good American tractors.

—Vladimir Mayakovsky

"America is rather like life," E. M. Forster once observed. "You can usually find in it what you look for."[1] When Bolsheviks looked, they required little effort to detect distress. Capitalism without oppression and poverty would not be capitalism. But just as Karl Marx also described capitalism as an improvement over history's earlier periods, Bolsheviks found reasons to praise some of America's achievements. In the *Communist Manifesto*, Marx and Engels presented a capitalist class that industrialized whole nations, harnessing productive power beyond the dreams of previous generations. Industrial society soon undermined archaic forms of existence—including "the idiocy of rural life"—and fashioned a world in its own image. These deeds yielded economies productive enough, for the first time in history, to bestow prosperity on the entire human race. Nothing of the sort happened under capitalism, of course, because the wealthy cared only for their own profits. But they had created the essential industrial means that, once seized by enlightened hands, would build a socialist future.

The *Communist Manifesto* did not spotlight one capitalist country as more advanced than the rest, but the Bolsheviks did. Time and again, party leaders and lesser functionaries distinguished America from European capitalist lands antiquated by remnants of musty tradition. The stifling hand of the feudal past did not grip the New World as it did the Old, they contended, and thus the United States possessed a vigor unmatched in Europe.[2] Nowhere did American supremacy seem greater than in engineering and industry, especially mining, metallurgy, and machine building. The more modern the industrial branch—automobile and tractor production, for example—the more likely that preeminence would be associated with the United States. Apart from specific products, Bolsheviks perceived American assembly-line techniques in enormous factories as best suited for industrializing their own country. "In the scale of its economy, in the methods of production (mass production, standardization, and so forth)," remarked Anastas Mikoyan, commissar of trade in 1930, "America is the most appropriate for us."[3]

If America stood out among capitalist nations as the prime exemplar of modern industrial practices, one American—Henry Ford—surpassed all others as the pioneer of techniques coveted by Soviet officials. In 1925 Felix Dzerzhinsky, head the of the Supreme Council of the National Economy (and the secret police), informed two of his deputies on the Council that "it is essential to engage in the study and adoption of Ford's methods in practice. . . . Perhaps it would be worthwhile to recruit from abroad practitioners, organizers of Fordism." Soviet authorities did not confine such advice to each other, beyond public earshot. Slogans posted at many sites around the country urged factory managers and workers to "Do it the Ford way because it is the best way." According to a *New York Times* correspondent on the scene in 1928: "Cheap mass production is a Soviet goal, more precious from the practical standpoint than world revolution—Ford in Soviet eyes is the archmogul of that achievement. 'Fordizatsia'—'Fordisation'—has become one of the 'words of power' with which Soviet orators spellbind auditors."[4]

Needless to say, the Henry Ford promoted by Soviet officials was the Ford of efficiency and especially assembly-line mass production—not the Ford who rose from humble origins to become a capitalist millionaire. Soviet newspapers assured readers that Ford's industrial methods themselves were not capitalist and could be imported without fear of duplicating Ford's exploitation of the proletariat. As long as workers remained the chief beneficiaries of their own labor, they should welcome gains in productivity. The press sometimes praised skillful Soviet workers as "Russian Fords" and saluted successful factories in the manner chosen by a report in the newspaper *Izvestiia*:

"In the shop International the manufacturing processes of electrometers have been fordized so successfully that the output is now 15,000 a year."[5] *Pravda* recommended that heads of economic enterprises study a Russian translation of Ford's writings, and during the 1920s his *My Life and Work* and *Today and Tomorrow* appeared in numerous Russian editions. These volumes often included Soviet prefaces such as the one contributed by N. S. Lavrov to a translation of *My Life and Work* in 1924. Professor Lavrov (who reportedly delivered some 1,500 lectures on the principles of Fordism) argued that the automobile maker's techniques could serve the Soviet Union despite Ford's own hostility to socialism. *My Life and Work* contained some far-fetched claims, Lavrov observed, but they should not prevent readers from studying the volume for guidance on the organization of production. "For us, these questions are of vital, extreme significance. The development of industry and reduction of the prices of goods have become the task of the day. To solve these problems correctly, familiarity with Ford's book is urgently essential."[6]

Meanwhile, Bolsheviks pointed to other features of America that helped make it uniquely suitable as a guide to modernization. The United States was a large country that had recently settled and developed a sprawling frontier, the very task that Soviet officials now saw before them. It stood to reason that techniques successful in America were more appropriate for the Soviet Union than were methods favored in small European nations. Stalin's interest in the role that gold prospecting played in colonizing the American West, for example, included hope of a comparable course of events in Siberia.[7] When contemplating foreign trade, officials might even echo Walt Whitman's views on similar American and Russian (now Soviet) national characters. This comparison occurred to a prominent Bolshevik, Valerian Osinsky, during his visit to the United States in 1925. "It is much more difficult for a person from the USSR to do business abroad with a German, a Frenchman or an Englishman than with an American," Osinsky concluded, because "in the national character of the American there are very many points of contact with ours."[8]

While most Bolsheviks, if pressed, might grant some resemblance between ordinary Russians and Americans—blunt simplicity, perhaps, or impulsive geniality—they regretted the absence in Russians of other traits thought to be distinctively American. Newspapers praised the efficiency and initiative of Americans, including those working in the Soviet Union (frequently Russians who had emigrated to America years before and then returned after 1917). *Pravda* supplied numerous illustrations, including a group of miners from America whose "exceptional energy" allegedly inspired Soviet workers in neighboring mines to boost their productivity.[9] Over much of the 1920s

Soviet publications called for the creation of "Russian Americans," a labor force possessing "American" energy and competence. In 1923 a newspaper for workers published an article titled "Russian Americans" that set out to describe these formidable beings.

> They are people who know how to work with such force and resolve as old Russia never knew. "Americans" [that is, Russians working in an American manner] are those who think over a task carefully before beginning it. But having begun it, they work without doubt or hesitation, with unshakable faith in our creative powers; with a sober appreciation of these powers they see the job through to the end. "Americans" do not whine about "objective" conditions.[10]

Karl Radek, a prominent figure in party circles, praised the efficiency of American famine-relief personnel in Soviet Russia at the beginning of the 1920s. In a speech, he described their diligence as a model for a new generation of Soviet workers, whom he dubbed "American Russians." According to an American who heard these remarks, Radek divided people on the streets of Moscow into two categories. The first "slouches along in a dull stupid manner, dressed in dirty boots and wearing usually an oriental cap." The second "are men who walk smartly and energetically through the streets going straight about their business. This second type is now generally called 'the American type' and we look to these new 'American' Russians for the future of Russia."[11]

Appeals to "work like an American" cast the United States as the pinnacle of efficiency, and no American better personified this quality than Frederick Winslow Taylor (1856–1915). Raised in comfortable circumstances, Taylor abandoned an intention to enroll at Harvard and turned instead to factory work. He also studied engineering, bookkeeping, and accounting (while finding time to win the doubles title at the U.S. Open Tennis Championship in 1881), and by 1906 his reputation had elevated him to the presidency of the American Society of Mechanical Engineers. This prominence stemmed from the system of labor efficiency that he devised and promoted with the faith of a missionary. Jobs could be dissected into various components that in turn leant themselves to "scientific" scrutiny, he believed, as in his analysis of coal shoveling:

> The coal, as it is unloaded over the side of the car, leaves the shovel while the latter is turned almost upside down. It is not thrown, for instance, as most laborers would throw dirt into a cart—that is, keeping the dirt always over the shovel and shooting the shovel out in the air at an angle of about 45 degrees in a comparatively straight line. In unloading coal, the men at Midvale bring

the shovel up through a curved path, and I think in the average case, when the coal leaves the shovel the bottom of the shovel would be rather higher in the air than the coal. This, of course, means that the coal is raised very considerably above the top of the car as it goes over the side of the same; I should say on an average a foot to eighteen inches.[12]

Having analyzed a task, Taylor recommended that certain aspects be modified or eliminated, and he specified the length of time in which a competent worker should be able to complete the operation. Based on such calculations he advocated a scale of piece rates designed to reward employees who worked at the pace deemed feasible by his analysis, and put less money in the pockets of those unable to keep up.

Taylor believed that his system would so increase production as to benefit workers as well as owners. "Scientific management," he informed Congress in 1912, would enable management and labor to "take their eyes off of the division of the surplus as the all-important matter, and together turn their attention toward increasing the size of the surplus until this surplus becomes so large that it is unnecessary to quarrel over how it shall be divided." But he felt little sympathy for workers unable to cope with the new routines and tempos, as he made clear in an essay titled "Shop Management": "A certain percentage of them, with the best of intentions, will fail in this and find that they have no place in the new organization, while still others, and among them some of the best workers who are, however, either stupid or stubborn, can never be made to see that the new system is as good as the old; and these, too, must drop out." Taylor's best-known remark—"In the past man has been first. In the future the System must be first."—revealed a flinty streak that elicited condemnation and ridicule. "No tyrant or slave-driver in the ecstasy of his most delirious dream," thundered the American Federation of Labor, "ever sought to place upon abject slaves a condition more repugnant to commonly accepted notions of freedom of action and liberty of person." *Life* carried a cartoon in 1913 depicting an "Efficiency Crank" interrupting two lovers with this question: "Young man, are you aware that you employed fifteen unnecessary motions in delivering that kiss?"[13]

Nevertheless, Taylor, his close associates, and ultimately hundreds of "efficiency cranks" (including Charles Gilbreth, best remembered from his memoir *Cheaper by the Dozen*) ensured the adoption of "scientific management" techniques throughout much of American industry during the 1920s. When a pair of scholars surveyed historians of business and economics in 1977, seeking their opinions on the most important contributors to managerial thought and practice, Taylor received more votes than anyone else, including John D.

Rockefeller, Andrew Carnegie—and Henry Ford. After World War I the rep-
utations of Taylor and Ford soared in Europe as well as the United States. Few
promoters of industrial expansion—entrepreneurs and government officials
alike—believed that they could ignore the promise of assembly lines and scientific management.[14]

Not long after the Bolsheviks proclaimed their new regime, various Soviet
authorities and intellectuals sought to apply Taylorist methods in fields ranging from the fine arts to the military. Anyone who thought that a venture
could be enhanced by rational order might find Taylor's legacy appealing, but
nowhere did his name shine brighter for Soviet leaders than in the realm of
industry. Here they faced an unskilled pool of potential factory workers—
peasants who lacked not only technical experience but even the most basic
sense of industrial discipline: punctuality, repetitive precision, and so forth.
The methods of Taylor and Ford, which had harnessed a largely rural and immigrant labor force in the United States, struck Soviet observers as a promising means of achieving similar gains in production from their own rough-
hewn population.[15]

Among those convinced that Russia needed Taylorism was Aleksei
Gastev, a factory worker and poet of Bolshevik sympathies who welcomed
the Revolution as an opportunity to hasten the spread of machine culture.
Russia's economic disarray and crude workforce moved him to advocate discipline and meticulous training—which, in turn, made him an early and zealous convert to Taylorism. Soviet authorities shared his desire for a skilled
proletariat and lent support in the 1920s to the Central Institute of Labor,
which Gastev had founded in Moscow at the beginning of the decade. Here
Gastev hoped to prepare a corps of instructors who could then train many
more workers around the country.[16] His methods, described in the report of
a Ford Motor Company delegation that toured the institute in 1926, revealed
the influence of Taylor "in a beautiful building in the very center of
Moscow":

> [Here] the students learned to use a hammer by holding onto one which was
> mechanically moved up and down while the student's arm was strapped in a
> device to insure the proper distance being maintained between his body and
> the hammer. [Here] all beginners worked one minute and then on a mechani-
> cal signal laid down their tools and rested one minute; then at certain inter-
> vals lined up to go through gymnastic drills and then were allowed to smoke
> cigarettes. Small cabinets were rigged up with various devices such as for ex-
> ample a filing stand where every movement of the student was kept track of in
> an adjoining office through a maze of electric contacts and recorded on a strip
> of paper.[17]

The Ford delegation regarded Gastev's institute as "a circus, a comedy, a crazy house" and "a pitiful waste of young people's time," an assessment that would have wounded Gastev had the report crossed his desk. His respect for Taylor and Ford found voice in numerous forums, including a letter sent to the Ford Motor Company in June 1928. "Esteemed Mr. Ford!" Gastev began, "your ideas, as an organizer of production, are now recognized around the world. Here we are studying in most careful fashion everything connected with your production work." In *Pravda* he could emphasize that every worker contained the potential of a Henry Ford, while elsewhere he praised Taylor as "the undisputed founder of the science of the organization of production." His essay "How to Invent" maintained that "all the great people who developed the principles of the scientific organization of labor were inventors" and then drove home the point in the next sentence: "Taylor was an inventor, Gilbreth was an inventor, Ford was an inventor."[18]

Gastev formulated a vision in the 1920s that swept beyond the efficient work processes dear to Taylor and Ford. His dream centered on a machine culture that would yield not just industrial productivity but also a sense of dignity and community for workers. No longer mindless automatons endlessly repeating a single motion, they would feel themselves part of a creative process and derive satisfaction from recognizing their vital role in shaping a new society outside the factory. Machinery would not only yield a more comfortable life for workers, it would fulfill them as they acquired confidence in their ability to advance a worthy purpose. In 1930 Gastev explained that "socialist industrialization, after a certain period of saturation with the latest achievements of capitalist technology," would develop a superior alternative to industrialization conducted by the bourgeoisie. "This will be not only the mastery of machine technology, but a revolution of machinism [*mashinizm*] itself, carried out by the proletariat that has risen against capitalism." Thus he hoped to combine American efficiency and technical acumen with a broader social transformation made possible by the Russian Revolution. "Take the Blizzard of the Revolution in the USSR," one of his books advised, "add the American Pulse of Life, and We'll Regulate Work with the Precision of a Chronometer." The result of this "Soviet Americanism," he argued elsewhere, would turn his homeland into a "new, flowering America."[19]

Borne on the wave of the Soviet Union's industrialization drive of the 1930s, Gastev's network expanded to some 1,700 training stations by 1938 (from which half a million workers had graduated since 1921). However, Stalinist authorities desired narrow vocational instruction rather than the social metamorphosis championed by Gastev in the 1920s. The impressive number of graduates, in other words, departed with some technical skills but little trace of the exalted machine culture that had inspired Gastev. In 1938 the government closed his institute and arrested him on charges still unclear. He was apparently executed a few years later.

Creating a "Russian American" in the 1920s did not mean designing an exact duplicate of a Yankee who happened to speak Russian. Nor did emulating American assembly-line techniques or purchasing American industrial equipment imply Soviet respect for the United States in other realms. American technical proficiency and industrial productivity, yes, but not exploitation, racism, or greed. How, then, to avoid these abuses if, as Marx maintained, nations could reach socialism only after a lengthy capitalist period had yielded an industrialized economy with a skilled workforce? Lenin and the Bolsheviks had made their "socialist revolution" in an overwhelmingly peasant country, long before anything resembling Russian capitalism had run its course. Consequently, they found themselves struggling to sprout socialism in the 1920s without the preconditions that traditional Marxism required from a prior era of capitalism. For Bolshevik theoreticians, however, the situation offered certain advantages. They could industrialize and create a modern working class themselves, without the remorseless exploitation that would have accompanied the process were it conducted by robber barons presiding over a period of capitalism. To get started, they planned to study production methods in the most advanced nations of the day, above all the United States, and then employ these techniques to attain a goal loftier than anything imagined by the bourgeoisie.

Thus Gastev did not stand alone in recommending a combination of American technical prowess and proletarian enlightenment. During the Soviet Union's first decade nearly all party leaders, including Lenin, Stalin, and Trotsky, urged that Marxist revolutionary energy unite with American efficiency to establish socialism. Nikolai Bukharin, "the greatest and most valuable theoretician in the party" according to Lenin, predicted in 1923 that "Soviet Russia will become a new America, in the proletarian rather than the bourgeois sense of the word." To build the new socialist state, he explained, the party required people who possessed "desirable features of the old Russian intelligentsia—namely a grounding in Marxism, breadth of vision and theoretical acumen—but combined with an American practical grasp of things. . . . We need Marxism plus Americanism."[20]

The following year, shortly after Lenin's death, Stalin gave a series of lectures in which he sought to explain Leninism to an audience at one of the party's institutions established to train officials. *Pravda* circulated his remarks a few months later, and they reappeared in many editions thereafter under the title *Foundations of Leninism*. This was no casual chat, improvised and then disregarded, for Stalin meant the work to stand as a basic guide to the wisdom of the Soviet Union's founding father. In his concluding section, he noted that the socialist cause required "a special Leninist style of work" characterized by two traits: "Russian revolutionary sweep" and "American efficiency." The first quality supplied the vision and zeal necessary to break free of tradition and cherish socialism. "Without it, no movement ahead is possible." But vision alone might not lead beyond idle dreaming unless one knew how to work, and here Stalin looked to the United States. "American efficiency is that indomitable force that neither knows nor recognizes limits, that clears away all obstacles with its efficient persistence, that cannot but carry through any task to the end, even a minor job, and without which serious constructive work is impossible." By itself, American efficiency might not rise above "narrow and unprincipled pragmatism," but inspired by Russian revolutionary fervor it could become the tool of socialism. "Only such a combination gives us the finished type of Leninist worker, the style of Leninism in work."[21]

Stalin regarded Leon Trotsky, hero of the Revolution and civil war, as his greatest rival, while Trotsky made no secret of his contempt for Stalin—a relationship leaving few pronouncements that both leaders could embrace sincerely. Yet Stalin's well-publicized espousal of American efficiency and Russian revolutionary vision did not prevent Trotsky from endorsing a similar formula. In the summer of 1924 Trotsky declared that in the area of science and technology "we desperately need to resemble the Americans more closely. To put the shoes on Bolshevism in an American manner—that is our task—to put on the technical shoes with American nails." He concluded with a comment that left no doubt as to the stakes: "If we Americanize our still-weak socialist industry, we will be able to say with tenfold confidence that the future is completely and finally ours. Americanized Bolshevism will triumph and crush imperialist Americanism."[22]

Appeals to blend American expertise with Soviet revolutionary zest caught the eye more often in the 1920s than in the following decade.[23] The country industrialized at an extraordinary rate in the 1930s, and word soon spread from Moscow that socialism was at hand. Instructions to learn from America seemed less appropriate in this climate of triumph. To be sure, the old prescription reappeared from time to time, as in comments by the head of the Soviet film industry in 1935. He praised a character in the Soviet film *Pilots* who "combines American efficiency with Russian revolutionary sweep." How much better is this "Stalinist, a loyal son of Lenin's party," than another character who "laughs at discipline and self-control, regarding them as cowardly, but cannot manage prolonged struggle or persistent achievement of goals."[24] Two years earlier a Soviet economic newspaper had asserted that "only in the country of the dictatorship of the proletariat, where Bolshevik sweep is combined with American efficiency, was it possible to create in three or four years" the nation's colossal industrial enterprises. Here the point was not a need to acquire certain American aptitudes but a claim that this had already been done, as in Vyacheslav Molotov's assertion that the key to the recent success of the Dnieprostroy hydroelectric project lay "in the adoption of American mechanization of the building work and in our own Bolshevik energy."[25]

Further achievements would soon inspire pronouncements that the Soviet Union had mastered its lessons and now matched or even surpassed its teacher in one respect or another. What did not change was America's role as a measuring stick. From the beginning, comparison had colored such phrases as "American tempo," "American efficiency," and "Russian American." In technical and industrial respects America was the gauge, a country whose standard of production must be reached before the Soviet Union could celebrate socialism's victory. Moreover, Bolsheviks hoped that, as they approached their goal, America's distinctive image as a new and advanced society would pass to them. This expectation lay behind phrases designating the Soviet Union as the "second" or "new" America—in Bukharin's case the "new proletarian America," for Gastev a "new, flowering America"—that would soon overtake the original America and leave it far behind. Even a *Pravda* article on tractor production, with the humbling title "Why Is It Possible for America but Not for Us?" referred in 1925 to the Soviet Union as a country with the agricultural potential to be a "second America," richer than the first.[26] It was only a matter of time.

America remained the preeminent standard of comparison during the 1930s, as the Soviet humorists Ilf and Petrov confirmed in a popular account of their American travels in 1935–36. "We want to catch up with technical America and to outstrip it," they declared after recounting their experiences.[27] No longer did it appear audacious to anticipate success, for the United States lay mired in the depression while their Soviet homeland raced from one industrial project to the next. The thought of learning from America lost its awe, as evident in remarks by Soviet engineers sent to study manufacturing techniques in Henry Ford's factories. They planned to apply their knowledge back home in a manner to surpass their American teachers—"to fool 'dear' Henry."[28] A similar combination of respect for American methods and confidence in Soviet development characterized an article titled "Notes on American Efficiency," which appeared in *Pravda* in 1935. "Of course we should not blindly follow and copy America," concluded the author, after several laudatory paragraphs on American industrial procedures. "We have already sufficiently developed our own creative work. But America must be for us that standard by which we constantly check our technical achievements." There were still things to learn from America, in other words, but "we are now on the way to building the world's most advanced technology."[29]

While Bolshevik leaders found the United States useful as an example of the diligence and expertise required to industrialize their nation, America's appeal in the Soviet Union did not rest solely with those intent on producing steel and tractors. Poets, painters, filmmakers, and architects also contemplated the United States, and they did so in a manner that shared only a portion of the perspective favored by officials. With a cheeky verve that would be muffled or extinguished during the Stalinist decades to come, the artistic avant-garde of the 1920s argued over methods and theory in diverse endeavors. Their creations often revealed imaginations that harbored an interest in America, especially those aspects of the United States linked to modernism.

The Bolshevik Revolution did not give birth to Russian modernism—or futurism, the label often used after 1917 for all avant-garde views in the fine arts. The kaleidoscopic array of suprematists, cubists, constructivists, and others had developed much of their outlook in the preceding years, as had a group of Russians who proudly called themselves futurists even before World War I. Though rarely politically minded themselves, many accepted the Revolution's demolition of the old regime as an opportunity to sweep away traditional culture. With the Bolsheviks in power, some futurists even claimed the sole right to create a new communist culture for the society under construction. Party leaders welcomed expressions of support from nearly any group of intellectuals willing to stay in the country, but they had no intention of placing the futurists in charge of Soviet culture. Lenin and his colleagues possessed more traditional tastes in the arts, as Lenin freely acknowledged: "I cannot force myself to consider the works of Expressionism, Futurism, Cubism, and similar 'isms' as the highest manifestations of the artistic genius. I do not understand them. I do not experience any joy from them."[30] Futurists thus received official scoldings as often as subsidies, but they remained free to present their views for roughly a decade.[31]

Like modernists elsewhere in the 1920s, Russian futurists scattered opinions between several sets of conflicting poles. Machines, cities, and electricity thrilled some. Others regarded the urban industrial landscape with dismay and favored primitivism's fascination with tribal or pagan practices deemed more vibrant and elemental than nineteenth-century Western customs.

Meanwhile, balancing those who preferred arcane creations stood colleagues determined to engage a broad audience, preferably with new technologies of mass communication. An individual might assume different positions between these poles at one moment or another, sometimes in a single work. One of Velemir Khlebnikov's poems, for instance, published in a collection in 1916, described a pagan love ritual, while a second praised modern technology.[32] Three years earlier, the artists Mikhail Larionov and Natalya Goncharova issued a manifesto that proclaimed "the whole brilliant style of modern times—our trousers, jackets, shoes, trolleys, cars, airplanes, railways, grandiose steamships—is fascinating, is a great epoch, one that has known no equal in the entire history of the world." Thus briefed, readers might not have expected the following cry a few sentences later. "Long live the beautiful East! We are joining forces with the contemporary Eastern artists to work together. . . . We are against the West, which is vulgarizing our forms and Eastern forms, and which is bringing down the level of everything."[33] In addition to these differences, the Soviet setting of the 1920s raised the question of ideology but did not require a specific response. The regime naturally preferred that futurists trumpet socialism, and some did. But others mused introspectively or shocked the public with mischievous displays—while a few disclosed misgivings about the new Soviet milieu.

That said, most futurists shared certain views, with distaste for cultural tradition the closest thing to a common denominator. Their artistic techniques favored removing objects from customary contexts and rearranging them in unexpected groups or sequences to create startling impressions. Often their subjects concerned the urban machine age. Though the Soviet environment did not impose conformity, it was much more encouraging to those futurists excited by machines, and their voices rang louder than the apprehensions of colleagues with darker visions of mechanized society. Prerevolutionary futurist passion for cars, planes, and the bustle of urban rhythms thrived in the new Soviet climate. Shortly before World War I Vasily Kamensky had spoken on "Airplanes and Futurist Poetry" with an airplane painted on his forehead, and numerous pronouncements of the 1920s equaled Kamensky's zeal. In 1922 four young futurists published a manifesto, *Eccentricity*, that demanded "study of locomotives, cars, steamers, engines, mechanisms." "Let us learn to love the machine!" they urged, and this could be the caption for a good deal of futurist work through the decade. Two years later, the prominent architect Moisei Ginzburg championed a style "born of clamorous life, steeped in the odors of the street, its maddening tempo, its practicality and everyday concerns." A fellow architect, Aleksander Vesnin, went even farther. "The contemporary engineer has created objects of genius:

the bridge, the steam locomotive, the airplane, the crane. . . . The contemporary artist must create objects that are equal to these in force, tension, and potential with respect to their psychological and physiological effect on human consciousness."[34] Otherwise, the new age would have no use for artists.

Indeed, declared the artist and designer Aleksei Gan in 1922, "Art is finished! It has no place in the human labor apparatus. Labor, technology, organization!"[35] He meant that traditional art forms and subjects were obsolete and must be replaced by new techniques linked to industry. Although this argument had circulated among Russian modernists before 1917, its champions won more attention in the avant-garde after the Revolution. What better setting could there be for the culture that Gan anticipated than the young Soviet state, with leaders bent on creating an industrialized society? In any case, futurists agreed that rapid mechanization of life in the twentieth century required new ways of portraying the world, and many accepted the machine as inspiration for cultural innovations. They included Alexander Rodchenko in 1921—"all new approaches to art arise from technology and engineering"—and, ten years later, the architect Yakov Chernikhov: "In former times machinery was considered something profoundly inartistic, and mechanical forms were excluded from the province of beauty as such." Now, he asserted, "for the first time in the history of man," we have been "able to unite the principles of mechanical production and the stimuli of artistic creation."[36]

Probably no aspect of the "cultural front" excited futurists more than works created and transmitted to mass audiences using technologies that helped distinguish the twentieth century from its predecessors. Enormous mass-produced billboards, radio, and especially film all celebrated the marriage of art and technology, heralding a new epoch. Art could even resemble the industrial process itself—symphonies that incorporated the sounds of generators and factory whistles, for instance, sculptures of riveted metal, and prose crafted to mimic the staccato rhythm or dizzying pace of a machine. In 1927 a Soviet theatrical group toured Latvia and Germany with a repertoire that offered a routine titled "Labor Productivity (Fordism)." The eight actors sought to create "the illusion of the production process" through "absolute synchronization of precise rhythmic movements," explained a Soviet author. This suggested a "free, emancipated human being, subordinating himself to technology, openly admitting its expediency and power."[37] It is not difficult to imagine Aleksei Gastev leading the applause at such a performance.

No one did more to link acting and machine culture than the renowned director Vsevolod Meyerhold, whose theatrical career began several years before the Revolution and continued into the 1930s (before his arrest in 1939 and execution the following year). Along with staging plays in settings that resembled machinery, he pioneered a method of training actors that drew on the work of Frederick Taylor. Biomechanics, the new method was called, and one of Meyerhold's associates explained that according to its first principle, "the body is a machine, the actor is the machinist." In line with Taylor's emphasis on precise and economical motion, actors practiced gestures stripped of all superfluous movements. Findings by Ivan Pavlov and others on psychological reflexes convinced Meyerhold that certain actions would trigger a desired emotion in audiences and in the actors themselves. By distilling these movements into a set of exercises, Meyerhold devised a training program that appeared scientific and lent itself to the instruction of any novice, including "mass actors" of humble background.[38]

Part of Taylorism's appeal resided in its applicability to throngs of unskilled laborers—a claim that had attracted Aleksei Gastev as he contemplated the creation of an industrial workforce from a nation of peasants. Gastev appears to have influenced Meyerhold's development of Biomechanics, and his name surfaced among the directors of Meyerhold's workshops in 1921, though it remains unclear what, if anything, Gastev actually did there. Be that as it may, the two friends left no doubt regarding the influence of Taylor on their work. While Meyerhold's Biomechanics was not identical to Taylor's (or Gastev's) training—an efficient pounding motion adopted by a worker with a hammer, for instance, would not be the best way for an actor to convey the impression of hammering to an audience hundreds of feet away—the exacting study of bodily motions in Biomechanics became "Taylorism on the Stage." This was the title chosen by one of Meyerhold's students in 1921 for an article describing "theatrical Taylorism," whose "goal is the struggle against *superfluous* and *unnecessary* 'gestures for the sake of gestures' on the stage. That theory is *Biomechanics*. The Taylor of the theatre is Vsevolod Meyerhold."[39]

Meyerhold may have been the most famous "Taylor of the theatre," but he was far from the only Soviet artist to apply Taylorist principles to stage and screen in the 1920s. The film director Lev Kuleshov instructed aspiring actors to analyze movements as a set of discrete stages rather than as a single, extended process, and he employed stopwatches and metronomes to help focus his students on the essential aspects of a routine. Kuleshov also devised charts with X and Y axes on which to portray bodily motions best calculated to produce specific responses from an audience. Actors might then consult the charts to assemble a series of movements appropriate for the scene in question.[40]

Meanwhile, in open competition with Meyerhold, the poet Ippolit Sokolov published an article titled "Industrialization of the Gesture" in order to promote his own system of Taylorist training for the theater:

> The actor on the stage must first of all become an automaton, a mechanism, a machine. . . . [H]enceforth painters, doctors, artists, engineers must study the human body, not from the point of view of anatomy or physiology, but *from the point of view of the study of machines*. The new Taylorised man has his own new physiology. Classical man, with his Hellenic gait and gesticulation, is a beast and savage in comparison with the new Taylorised man.[41]

The important point here is that America intrigued futurists who thought in these terms, for they imagined the United States as home to much of the energetic technocultural future they desired for the Soviet Union. Holly-wood movies, for example, brimmed with a vitality that often enticed intellectuals along with the rest of the Soviet public. Lev Kuleshov felt a con-nection between the dynamism of American films and the creation of a new society (though he had found reason to recant these views by 1935): "In our time [the 1920s], we were convinced that American montage [editing tech-niques] invariably inculcated boldness and energy, indispensable to revolu-tionary struggle, to revolution." A year before the revolution, Vadim Sher-shenevich extolled "urbanism with its dynamism, its beauty of speed, its intrinsic Americanism," while seven years later the "new type of worker" foreseen by Sergei Tretyakov required an "'Americanization' of the personal-ity" to loathe "all things unorganized, inert, chaotic, sedentary, and provin-cially backward."[42]

Not just futurists but virtually all Soviet travelers to the United States marveled at American technology in the 1920s, whatever else they con-cluded about the host country. For some, the scale of projects and the preva-lence of new equipment proved transfixing. Endless rivers of automobiles surged past the feet of skyscrapers, the likes of which Europe could scarcely imagine. Of course, noted the poet Sergei Esenin after a tour of America in 1922–23, oppression of the native Indian population accompanied America's rise. "But all the same, when you look at that merciless might of reinforced concrete, at the Brooklyn Bridge hanging between two cities at the height of twenty-story buildings, all the same no one will regret that wild Hiawatha no longer hunts deer here."[43]

Whether they stayed at home or crossed the Atlantic, Soviet observers of-ten identified cars as a symbol of American life. In 1923 a *Pravda* article ac-knowledged that "in America practically every family may own a car, which are more widespread there than are bicycles or even horses (in cities) in our country."[44] According to a Soviet engineer sent to the United States for training in 1930, "if you walk along the streets of Detroit on a Sunday or a holiday, you will have an absurd sensation. The sidewalks will be completely deserted, but the streets will be filled with a continuous current of automobiles, from old 15-dollar Fords to vehicles costing 10,000 dollars. Everyone is driving." He added that Americans thought nothing of driving around after work, simply for pleasure, and then concluded: "A person without 'wheels' is not a person. He doesn't know what to do with himself. Here the automobile is not simply a means of transportation; it is God, love, and a sense of existence."[45] The countless vehicles set the nation apart, as did the extensive system of highways and service stations. Yakov Dorfman, an engineer who visited the United States in 1925–26, marveled at the traffic lights on Chicago's street corners:

> It is remarkable how the Americans have worked out a type of signal light that is so bright it can be successfully used even in the daytime. . . . All the street signals are automatically engaged from a central station and their flashing rhythm controls the traffic of all of Chicago. One has to delve deeper into this manifestation to appreciate it in all its harmoniousness and beauty.[46]

And so it went, not just with automobiles but with many other forms of technology that characterized American society. Ingenious uses of electricity abounded, as did exotic gadgets ranging from those in self-service restaurants to the hot-air hand driers in washrooms. One need not be a futurist to notice this aspect of American life, and it became a routine feature of Soviet accounts in the 1920s. Much as it did for Bolsheviks, America served other educated Soviet citizens as a measuring stick. For Esenin, the brilliant lights of New York prompted comparison: "In Russia our streets are too dark for us to understand what the electric light of Broadway is. We are used to living by the light of the moon, to burning candles before icons but never before man." Dorfman illustrated the technological gap with comments on household utensils: "We have only found out that this type of steel [chromium] exists, while America has already produced millions of inexpensive products from it." Futurists' clamor swept beyond this engineer's advocacy of chromium kitchenware and linked their image of America to much of what they valued most. "TODAY—the technology of America," proclaimed the four young authors of *Eccentricity*. "Industry, production under the Stars and Stripes. Either Americanization or the undertaker."[47]

Theodore Dreiser encountered so much zeal for American ways during his trip through the Soviet Union in 1927 that he felt the nation's leaders "want

Russia to be like America—its cities like Chicago and Detroit, its leaders and geniuses like Ford and Rockefeller, Edison and Gary." He then added, "God! I pray not," expressing hope that the Soviet Union would avoid much of what he found objectionable in the United States.[48] But no Soviet official or intellectual wished to copy everything American; their praise did not eliminate criticism. If the lights on Broadway and the presence of radios in many apartments impressed Esenin—"When you see and hear all this, you can't help but be struck by the possibilities of man"—he also saw Americans as "a very primitive people when it comes to their own inner culture. . . . The American immerses himself entirely in business and has no interest in anything else."[49] Party officials, too, revealed ambivalence of one sort or another about the United States in the 1920s, especially when they sought to describe America itself, rather than focus on certain "American" features of use in the Soviet Union. Viktor Nogin, a Bolshevik since 1903, expressed amazement at the "colossal number of automobiles" in New York and the superb quality of food he encountered while traveling in the United States on official business in 1924. Even more remarkable, however, were the blatant manifestations of racism—separate train cars, public facilities, and even churches "for whites" and "for coloreds," to note a few of the examples that Nogin cataloged.[50]

Racism and the exploitation of workers figured prominently in Soviet criticism of America during the 1920s, especially in commentaries by party officials and journalists. Nogin's assessment was typical, as were portraits of robber barons and stories about poor people toiling as virtual slaves. Soviet discussions of Taylorism often included remarks on the abuse of the proletariat by such methods in the United States and other capitalist nations. Nor were these themes unusual in literary works. American tycoons and paupers, who had chilled some Russian descriptions of the United States long before 1917, required no alteration to fit in Soviet publications. So, too, with American racism, noticed by Russian travelers in the nineteenth century and ripe for Soviet commentary in the twentieth. Esenin may have regarded black Americans as primitive and unworthy of much sympathy, but other Soviet essays on American life in the 1920s raised the problem with indignation or at least concern.

Along with the cruelty in America cited frequently by Bolshevik leaders, early Soviet accounts included laments over American culture as well. Here lay terrain familiar to intellectuals, and they ventured forth with gusto. If some authors rhapsodized about American movies and brash techniques of advertising, others found Americans and their culture less seductive. Yes, American technology dazzled, and the nation did display a palpable vitality.

But Esenin was not alone in proclaiming Americans shallow and materialistic. Individual Americans might appear good-natured and even relentlessly cheerful, but their real concerns did not extend far beyond money. While traveling to America in 1924, the mathematician Vladimir Steklov met a retired colonel who owned a stockyard business in Kansas City. The colonel latched onto Steklov, offering "continual" practice in American English that "invariably ended with persistent invitations, almost demands, to visit him in Kansas City." This, Steklov concluded, was "a model of the natural American: somewhat rude, narrowly practical, entirely consumed by his business affairs (which he obviously considered the most important thing in the world), rather undereducated from the European point of view, narrowminded, and yet in his own way rather amiable and sincere."[51]

In similar fashion, Soviet fiction and cinema of the 1920s offered American characters whose vision did not transcend commercial endeavors. Ilya Ehrenburg's novel *Trust D.E.* includes a businessman rejected by his fiancée, Miss Kate, with the words: "Do you know anything about the stars, William? You know only about oil. . . . I would suffocate in your America." Ehrenburg could suppose that some Americans, Miss Kate at least, still possessed a healthy perspective—an assumption that a character in one of Esenin's stories might have disputed: "There is no place for dreams in America. Everybody, from Jew to Chinese, is only a businessman. If you begin to speak about souls, people will think that you are drunk or crazy."[52]

In a broader sense, beyond the character of businessmen in the United States, American culture struck a variety of Soviet commentators as mindless or excessive. They might disagree on matters of style—modernist or nineteenth-century traditional—but not on the proposition that American culture lacked refinement. The engineer Dorfman seized on advertising, a feature of the American landscape that jolted Soviet visitors much the way ubiquitous political proclamations affected Western travelers to the USSR. After Broadway, where "all the space available to human visibility is bestrewn with signs," Dorfman enjoyed a drive away from New York along the Hudson River. "The far shore is amazingly beautiful with its fantastic, unfettered crags. The human hand it seems, has touched it little." But, then, "O horrors: on a high, wild, poetic rock sharply jutting toward the river emerges as a sharp spot a sign: CASTOREA LAXATIVE." Alas, concluded Dorfman, "advertising chews up everything, shouts, has no shame and with its inappropriate tricks marks the successes of technical progress even here." If the placement of a billboard amid nature's beauty appeared crass to Dorfman, the fare at a movie theater in New York provided a similar contrast to Steklov. The orchestra played Rimsky-Korsakov's "Easter Night," by itself a pleasant

comments placed more emphasis than before on the need for Western expertise. This did not free the United States from charges of exploitation, racism, and imperialism, but it did suggest that Lenin had come to find America more useful as a technological guide than as an ideological target. Over the next seven decades, party leaders shifted this balance in one direction or the other as determined by domestic circumstances and the Kremlin's view of American policy abroad. Unflinching advice to learn from the United States disappeared for extended periods, but it surfaced late in the Soviet era and carried farther in the end than Lenin's call to study the methods of Taylor and Ford.

During the same prerevolutionary years in which Lenin pictured an America of contrasting hues, Mayakovsky developed a futurist outlook with its own discordant themes—though not applied so directly, at first, to the United States. In 1913, then only twenty years old, he championed "the poetry of the modern city" and explained to an audience in Kishinev that "the city has enriched our experiences by the new elements which the poets of the past did not know." Modern urban settings do indeed occupy Mayakovsky's work, but the view is sometimes dark. His tone ranges across the spectrum of futurist opinion, from a sense of despair and menace to unbounded enthusiasm. In the year of his Kishinev foray, he included these disturbing verses in his poem "Great Big Hell of a City":

> Windows split the city's great hell
> into tiny hellets—vamps with lamps.
> The cars, red devils, exploded their yells
> right in your ear, rearing on their rumps.
> . . . .
> In the gaps between skyscrapers, full of blazing ore,
> where the steel of trains came clattering by,
> an aeroplane fell with a final roar
> into the fluid oozing from the sun's hurt eye.[64]

On other occasions, notably public addresses, Mayakovsky described metropolises with delight worthy of Marinetti. At a recital in Moscow toward the end of 1913, and during his "futurist tour" of seventeen Russian cities that winter, he held forth in the following vein: "Great cities have arisen with proudly soaring skyscrapers, great forests of chimneys, . . . netted bridges that leap over rivers. . . . Like a graceful and light bird man has torn himself from the earth and hovers in the clouds in his aeroplane."[65] To an audience in the town of Nikolayev he declared that "the poetry of futurism is the poetry of the city, the modern city. . . . Telephones, airplanes, express trains, elevators, rotary presses, sidewalks, factory smokestacks, enormous stone buildings, soot and smoke—these are the elements of beauty in the new urban nature."[66] Automobiles, too, populated these urban visions, and Mayakovsky developed a personal enthusiasm for driving (and flying) that remained in harmony with his remarks on tour. Years later, in Paris, he purchased a six-horsepower Renault, "a gray-colored beauty" that filled him with pride: "The whole street / falls on its face / When my six beauties / neigh."[67] Giddy with the machine's power, Mayakovsky here displayed the ebullient side of futurism—the face most likely to revere America.

Almost at once, by the eve of World War I, Russian futurism acquired the label of *amerikanizm*, connoting to supporters and opponents alike a brash, iconoclastic, urban-technological animation. In this spirit Mayakovsky reportedly welcomed the epithet "demon in American boots" as suitable shorthand for disdain of established conventions in favor of a future symbolized by the audacious United States of his imagination. Thus he chose "Now to the Americas" as a title for a brief essay in defense of his artistic position. This orientation naturally dismayed poets of "wooden Russia," who found much to treasure in native traditions of the countryside. Chief among these "peasant poets" emerged Sergei Esenin, who once cried out to Mayakovsky: "Russia is mine, do you understand, mine, and you . . . you . . . are an American!"[68]

The Bolshevik Revolution brought little at first to smother Mayakovsky's praise of American technology, though the nation of the *ultimate* future now became socialist Russia. In the meantime, he could still place Thomas Edison in the same pantheon of genius as Lenin (and Einstein), as in his "Fifth Internationale" (1922): "I want to join / the ranks of Edisons, / the ranks of Lenins, / the ranks of Einsteins."[69] After 1917 Mayakovsky's literary ventures into the future often included a trip to America—by foot, steamship, underwater airplane, and even more exotic means—but this destination was not the promised land. Something more had to be added, and that would come from the new homeland of socialism.[70] In his long poem "150,000,000," Mayakovsky described an Armageddon between a giant Ivan (leading 150,000,000 Russians) and Woodrow Wilson, the bloated ruler of Chicago and the capitalist world. Mounted on a single screw, Chicago brims with technological miracles, "all electro-dynamo-mechanical." Electricity seems to power everything, and airports crown the tops of skyscrapers. Yet life is difficult in Chicago under the sway of the immense Wilson, whose defeat by Ivan's legions the poem celebrates. Only then, thanks to the revolutionary heroes, can inhabitants of Chicago and the world rejoice at the arrival of a better life.[71]

In 1925, following the path taken by characters in a number of his works, Mayakovsky decided to inspect this fabled America in person. When asked the reason for his journey he later replied: "Why did I travel to America? So that I, a poet promoting industrialization, could get to know the country in which industrialization has achieved the most. Early futurism championed the industrialization—'Americanization'—of Russia. So it was time to find out for myself about this Americanism." As it happened, Mayakovsky's rival, Esenin, had made the trip two years before and taken advantage of his observations to ridicule the images in "150,000,000."[72] This, too, may have encouraged Mayakovsky's departure, for he appeared keen to match Esenin's credentials as a commentator on the United States.

From Paris, Mayakovsky sailed to Mexico and then turned north across the border for a tour that lasted three months. During and immediately following this journey he wrote a series of poems and prose pieces that revealed his ambivalence about America in less cartoonish fashion than the images in "150,000,000." Much of the early futurist fascination with cities and technology remained, and Mayakovsky made no effort to disguise his awe at American accomplishments in this realm. "The convoluted nature of Mexico can amaze you with its vegetation and people," he observed, "but New York City, floating up out of the ocean with its massed buildings and technology, amazes you much more; it leaves you dumbfounded." He dismissed a *Pravda* article in which a "Comrade Pomorsky" had ridiculed railroad terminals in New York. "I don't know what personal accounts Comrade Pomorsky has to settle with New York train stations; I don't know their technical details, conveniences, and capacity; but externally, in appearance, judging from urbanistic sensations, New York train stations are one of the proudest sights in the world."[73] His poem "Broadway" marveled not only at the electrical power illuminating the night but also at the city's skyscrapers, breathtaking even by day:

> In between— / who on earth could have stretched them up so!—
> houses / a mile high each.
> Right up to the stars / some houses go,
> up to the moon / others reach.[74]

None of the city's technical wonders captivated Mayakovsky more than the Brooklyn Bridge, to which he devoted his best-known "American" poem. Like a pious believer bound for church, he confided, "I . . . step, with humble heart, on to Brooklyn Bridge." His visions came to life on "this steel-wrought mile," and he imagined a future archeologist studying remains of the bridge to deduce the technical achievements of the early twentieth century. Meanwhile:

> I stare like a savage / at an electric switch,
> eyes fixed / like a tick on a cat.
> Yeah, / Brooklyn Bridge—
> It's something, that![75]

Amid this splendid technology, however, Mayakovsky encountered an American population of victims and philistines. Upon entering Texas from Mexico he discovered segregated train stations and much else thereafter to indicate that "a person who calls himself American is a white who considers even a Jew black and does not shake hands with Negroes." He described poor neighborhoods in New York City as "even filthier than Minsk" and condemned the exploitation of workers at a Ford factory in Detroit. Although the assembly line spellbound him—"this process is already familiar from films, but you come out flabbergasted anyway"—the Taylorist routine's effect on the workers seemed disturbing: "At four o'clock at the Ford gates I watched the departing shift; people piled into streetcars and, exhausted, immediately fell asleep. Detroit has the greatest number of divorces. The Ford system makes workers impotent."[76]

Americans fortunate enough not to collapse on streetcars at the end of each day bent their efforts to sizing up others in terms of wealth. A person's income and possessions determined "everything: who your friends are, where you are received, where you'll go in the summer, and so forth. The way you acquired your millions is a matter of complete indifference in America. Everything is 'business'; work is anything that makes a dollar." No other nation "spouts so much moral, elevated, idealistic, hypocritical nonsense as does the United States," where business calculations always triumphed. "We can also call American sobriety—the dry law 'prohibition'—typical business and typical hypocrisy. Everybody sells whiskey."[77]

More fundamentally, Mayakovsky's tour of America reinforced his view that genuine progress required more than technological sophistication. In the United States, construction projects and other manifestations of technology seemed haphazard, even temporary, and certainly uninspired by any grand vision. Only considerations of utility and commercial profit shaped development. A true culture of the future could not interest an American society infused with, and even proud of, its confining bourgeois outlook. Like Gastev, Mayakovsky desired a technological culture that was as much an attitude as mere mechanical proficiency, and when he scrutinized the United

States he found petty-bourgeois narrow-mindedness. "I hate New York on Sunday," he declared:

> Around ten o'clock some clerk dressed only in a lilac undershirt raises his blinds across the street. Apparently without putting on his pants, he sits down by the window with the two-pound hundred-page edition of either the *World* or the *Times*. First he spends an hour reading the poetic and colorful section of department store advertisements (from which the average American world-view is formed); after the ads he looks through the sections on robberies and murders.[78]

Americans of higher station sought to copy their culture from Europe's past—even to the point of attaching gargoyles to modern skyscrapers—"with no concern for the fact that these statuettes and curlicues are good for six-story buildings but aren't even noticeable at any greater height. It is, however, impossible to place these stylish gewgaws any lower since there they would get in the way of advertisements, signs, and other useful things."[79] Like the United States itself, the ninety-story building in Mayakovsky's "A Sky-scraper Dissected" shone with promise from a distance. But a peek inside revealed inhabitants absorbed with commercial and amorous endeavors of the bourgeoisie—a bitter disappointment for the poet in quest of the future.

> I look / in a blend / of anger and boredom
> at the inmates / of the ninety-story shack.
> I'd meant / to go 7,000 miles forward
> but it looks, / I've been taken / seven years back.[80]

To a degree, Mayakovsky's criticism of the United States reflected a sensitivity to expectations of Soviet editors and radical audiences across America. In New York, for example, when he recited "Brooklyn Bridge" in public, someone with less enthusiasm for the edifice shouted from the balcony that unemployed men often jumped off the bridge in despair. Mayakovsky later added this theme to the poem.[81] Still, as Charles Rougle has argued persuasively, Mayakovsky's "American" writings do not amount to a propagandistic exercise at variance with the poet's convictions, and they do not signal a dramatic change in his stance.[82] Earlier in the 1920s, and in "150,000,000," Mayakovsky had contrasted American technical wizardry with the absence of a vision or culture required of a truly futurist society. His travels in the United States sharpened rather than inspired this image, which he continued to articulate on occasion during the five years that remained of his life.

Much of this overlapped Lenin's impressions, though the two men differed in their emphases and the evolution of their opinions, to say nothing of their appetites for the style of the avant-garde. (After receiving an autographed copy of "150,000,000," Lenin dismissed the work as "nonsense, stupid, double stupidity and pretentiousness" as well as "hooligan communism.")[83] Mayakovsky's early futurist embrace of America remained more abstract and fantastic than Lenin's assessment of the New World's modern industrial capacity. Nor did the "demon in American boots" rebuke the United States by name during the prewar years, as Lenin had. Garish urban landscapes in some of his early poems could be imagined in New York or Chicago, but they do not demonstrate a decision on Mayakovsky's part to target America.

By the 1920s the United States was clearly *the* other nation for Mayakovsky—and probably Lenin, too, before his incapacitation and death in 1923–24. Had Lenin survived to the end of the decade he would doubtless have emphasized more forcefully than ever, along with Mayakovsky, that America and the Soviet Union stood in the world's vanguard, one preparing to assume preeminence from the other. That said, Mayakovsky's disappointment with America grew more pronounced in the postrevolutionary period, while Lenin focused more on technology and skills he hoped could be obtained from the world's industrial leader. Lenin did not ignore America's faults, and Mayakovsky saluted the Brooklyn Bridge. But Lenin dwelled on the immediate, practical task of animating Russia's economy and regarded American experience as valuable in this regard. Mayakovsky's interest centered on a more distant transformation in which technology would be incorporated as an ingredient in a new culture worthy of a socialist vision unlike anything then in existence. For this goal, America seemed less useful.

Soon a new generation of party leaders turned to acquiring American technical expertise in support of an enormous industrialization drive—without the corresponding cultural transformation desired by Mayakovsky. Disappointment over the development of Soviet society seems to have played a part in his depression and suicide in 1930, but this final act did not discredit his writings on America in the view of Soviet officials.[84] Attacks on racism and exploitation remained acceptable, as did Mayakovsky's confidence that his homeland would one day outshine the United States. In 1929 he could imagine "Americans in Amazement" as they noticed the future under construction outside their own borders.

> From its far-distant coast, / as if staring at spooks,
> the USSR / with its eye / devouring,

rising on tiptoe, / America looks
through tortoise-shell specs, / unblinking, scowling.
What's that— / a new breed / of the species Man,
there, / on that far-off building-site piddling?
. . . .
Bourgeois, / stare at the Communist cohorts!
In trains, / in planes, / in work of all kind
your fleet-foot America, / famed for its know-how
we'll overtake / and leave way behind![85]

Poems of this sort, which did not reveal Mayakovsky's misgivings over the Soviet community forming around him, suited the tone of the decade that began with his death. He had something to offer, Stalin decided, and endorsed the bard posthumously as "the best and most talented poet of our Soviet epoch."[86] Thus began the assembly of Mayakovsky's official legacy. It included a bundle of "American themes"—at the core, criticisms of the United States along with confidence in Soviet superiority—that became a standard against which subsequent accounts of America would be judged in the Soviet Union for most of the remaining century.

Notes

1. E. M. Forster, *Two Cheers for Democracy* (London: Edward Arnold, 1951), 339.

2. I. V. Stalin, *Sochineniia*, vol. 13 (Moscow: Gosudarstvennoe izdatel'stvo politicheskoi literatury, 1952), 115; N. S. Rozenblit, *Fordizm* (Moscow: Izdatel'stvo ekonomicheskaia zhizn', 1925), 79; Kornelii Zelinskii, "Sotsialisticheskii biznes," in *Biznes: Sbornik literaturnogo tsentra konstruktivistov* (Moscow: Gosudarstvennoe izdatel'stvo, 1929), 54; V. Motylev, "Istochniki ekonomicheskogo prevoskhodstva Soedinennykh Shtatov," *Bol'shevik*, no. 12 (30 June 1928): 39–41.

3. A. I. Mikoian, "Dva mesiatsa v SShA," *SShA: ekonomika, politika, ideologiia*, no. 10 (October 1971): 74; Anna Larina, *This I Cannot Forget: The Memoirs of Nikolai Bukharin's Widow* (New York: Norton, 1993), 174.

4. "V bor'be za razvitie sovetskoi promyshlennosti. (Novye dokumenty F. E. Dzerzhinskogo)," *Voprosy istorii KPSS*, no. 9 (1977): 118; Maurice Hindus, "Henry Ford Conquers Russia," *Outlook*, 29 June 1927, 282; *New York Times*, 17 February 1928; "Russia Enters the Canning Business," *Food Industries* 4 (June 1932): 204; Records of the Department of State Relating to Internal Affairs of Russia and the Soviet Union, 1910–1929 (hereafter cited as State Department Records, 1910–29), 861.5017/79.

5. S. Shvedov, "Obraz Genri Forda v sovetskoi publitsistike 1920–1930-kh godov: vospriiatie i transformatsiia tsennostei chuzhoi kul'tury," in *Vzaimodeistvie kul'tur SSSR i SShA XVIII–XX vv.*, ed. O. E. Tuganova (Moscow: Nauka, 1987), 137; Jeffrey Brooks, "The Press and Its Message: Images of America in the 1920s and 1930s," in *Russia in the Era of NEP: Explorations in Soviet Society and Culture*, ed. Sheila Fitzpatrick, Alexander Rabinowitch, and Richard Stites (Bloomington: Indiana University Press, 1991), 240; Hindus, "Henry Ford," 282 (quoting *Izvestiia*).

6. Shvedov, "Obraz Genri Ford," 134, 136; N. S. Lavrov, preface to *Moia zhizn', moi dostizheniia*, by Henry Ford (1924; reprint, Moscow: Finansy i statistika, 1989), 7–11.

7. Timothy Green, *The New World of Gold: The Inside Story of the Mines, the Markets, the Politics, the Investors* (New York: Walker, 1984), 63–64.

8. Mark Hale Teeter, "The Early Soviet de Tocquevilles: Method, Voice and Social Commentary in the First Generation of Soviet Travel Publitsistika from America (1925–1936)" (Ph.D. diss., Georgetown University, 1987), 158. His real name was Valerian Obolenskii; he often published under the pseudonym of N. Osinskii.

9. *Pravda*, 31 October 1922, 3.

10. G. Rurskii, "Russkie amerikantsy," *Rabochaia gazeta*, 26 January 1923, 7.

11. Bertrand M. Patenaude, *Herbert Hoover's Brush with Bolshevism* (Washington, D.C.: Kennan Institute for Advanced Russian Studies, Woodrow Wilson International Center for Scholars, 1992), 13.

12. For a recent biography of Taylor, see Robert Kanigel, *The One Best Way: Frederick Winslow Taylor and the Enigma of Efficiency* (New York: Viking Penguin, 1997). The quotation is on page 333.

13. All quotations are from Kanigel, *One Best Way*, 19, 372, 472–73, 514, 522.

14. Kanigel, *One Best Way*, 10, 414–15, 416, 488, 493, 498.

15. Zenovia Sochor, "Soviet Taylorism Revisited," *Soviet Studies* 33, no. 2 (April 1981): 249, 257; Kendall E. Bailes, "The American Connection: Ideology and the Transfer of American Technology to the Soviet Union, 1917–1941," *Comparative Studies in Society and History* 23, no. 3 (July 1981): 438; Richard Stites, *Revolutionary Dreams: Utopian Vision and Experimental Life in the Russian Revolution* (Oxford: Oxford University Press, 1989), 145, 154, 161–62.

16. Sochor, "Soviet Taylorism," 250–51, 255; Stites, *Revolutionary Dreams*, 154.

17. Ford Motor Company, "Report of the Ford Delegation to Russia and the U.S.S.R." (1926), 64, Ford Motor Company Archives.

18. "K perepiske TsITa s Fordom," *Organizatsiia truda*, no. 2 (1928): 56; A. K. Gastev, *Kak nado rabotat'* (Moscow: Izdatel'stvo Ekonomika, 1966), 291; Aleksei Gastev, *Poeziia rabochego udara* (Moscow: Sovetskii pisatel', 1964), 273; *Pravda*, 27 November 1925, 3.

19. A. K. Gastev, *Trudovye ustanovki* (Moscow: Izdatel'stvo Ekonomika, 1973), 338; Stites, *Revolutionary Dreams*, illustrations between pages 164 and 165; Gastev, *Poeziia*, 244.

20. Roy A. Medvedev, *Nikolai Bukharin: The Last Years* (New York: Norton, 1980), 7; N. Bukharin, *Proletarskaia revoliutsiia i kul'tura* (Petrograd: Priboi, 1923), 16, 48–49.

21. Stalin, *Sochineniia*, 6:186–88.

22. *Izvestiia*, 5 August 1924, 4.

23. For examples of this formula expressed in other works, see Zelinskii, "Sotsialisticheskii biznes"; S. G. Ledenev, *Za stankom u Forda: Iz vpechatlenii uchastnika poezdki na traktornye zavody S.-A.S.Sh.* (Moscow-Leningrad: Gosudarstvennoe izdatel'stvo, 1927).

24. Boris Shumiatskii, *Kinematografiia millionov* (Moscow: Kinofotoizdat, 1935), 167.

25. *Za industrializatsiiu*, 14 August 1933, 1; V. M. Molotov, *The Success of the Five-Year Plan* (New York: International, 1931), 68.

26. *Pravda*, 2 July 1925, 1.

27. Ilya Ilf and Eugene Petrov, *Little Golden America* (New York: Farrar and Rinehart, 1937), 380.

28. Shvedov, "Obraz Genri Forda," 136.

29. *Pravda*, 19 May 1935, 2–3.

30. Halina Stephan, *"Lef" and the Left Front of the Arts* (Munich: Otto Sagner, 1981), 69.

31. For more on the Russian/Soviet futurists, see Victor Terras, *Vladimir Mayakovsky* (Boston: Twayne, 1983); Stephan, *"Lef"*; Vladimir Markov, *Russian Futurism: A History* (Berkeley: University of California Press, 1968); Vahan D. Barooshian, *Russian Cubo-Futurism, 1910–1930: A Study in Avant-Gardism* (Paris: Mouton, 1974); Edward J. Brown, *Mayakovsky: A Poet in the Revolution* (Princeton, N.J.: Princeton University Press, 1973).

32. Markov, *Russian Futurism*, 297.

33. John E. Bowlt, ed., *Russian Art of the Avant-Garde: Theory and Criticism, 1902–1934, with One Hundred and Five Illustrations*, rev. ed. (New York: Thames and Hudson, 1988), 89–90.

34. Markov, *Russian Futurism*, 134; Richard Taylor and Ian Christie, eds., *The Film Factory: Russian and Soviet Cinema in Documents 1896–1936*, trans. Richard Taylor (London: Routledge, 1994), 64; Moisei Ginzburg, *Style and Epoch* (Cambridge, Mass.: MIT Press, 1982), 102; *Art into Life: Russian Constructivism, 1914–32* (New York: Rizzoli, 1990), 68; Anna Lawton and Herbert Eagle, eds., *Russian Futurism through Its Manifestoes, 1912–1928* (Ithaca, N.Y.: Cornell University Press, 1988), 152, 156–57, 252.

35. *Art into Life*, 83.

36. Christina Lodder, *Russian Constructivism* (New Haven, Conn.: Yale University Press, 1983), 88; Bowlt, *Russian Art*, 260.

37. Elizaveta Dmitrievna Uvarova, *Estradnyi teatr: miniatiury, obozreniia, miuzik-kholly (1917–1945)* (Moscow: Izdatel'stvo Iskusstvo, 1983), 124–25.

38. Alma Law and Mel Gordon, *Meyerhold, Eisenstein and Biomechanics: Actor Training in Revolutionary Russia* (Jefferson, N.C.: McFarland, 1996), 34, 38–39, 103, 138; Edward Braun, *Meyerhold: A Revolution in Theatre* (Iowa City: University of Iowa Press, 1995), 172; David Elliott, *New Worlds: Russian Art and Society, 1900–1937* (New York: Rizzoli International, 1986), 18; Stites, *Revolutionary Dreams*, 160–61; Marjorie L. Hoover, *Meyerhold. The Art of Conscious Theater* (Amherst: University of Massachusetts Press, 1974), 314.

39. Law and Gordon, *Meyerhold*, 150–51. See also 36, 39–41; Stites, *Revolutionary Dreams*, 161.

40. Anna Lawton, ed., *The Red Screen: Politics, Society, Art in Soviet Cinema* (London: Routledge, 1992), 143–44.

41. Richard Taylor and Ian Christie, eds., *Inside the Film Factory: New Approaches to Russian and Soviet Cinema* (London: Routledge, 1991), 49.

42. Ronald Levaco, ed., *Kuleshov on Film: Writings by Lev Kuleshov* (Berkeley: University of California Press, 1974), 191; Lawton and Eagle, *Russian Futurism*, 149, 214.

43. Sergei Esenin, "An Iron Mirgorod," in *America through Russian Eyes: 1874–1926*, ed. and trans. Olga Peters Hasty and Susanne Fusso (New Haven, Conn.: Yale University Press, 1988), 151–52.

44. *Pravda*, 12 April 1923, 1.

45. *Andrei Konstantinovich Burov. Pis'ma. Dnevniki. Besedy s aspirantami. Suzhdeniia sovremennikov* (Moscow: Iskusstvo, 1980), 34.

46. Quoted in Teeter, "Soviet de Tocquevilles," 180–81.

47. Esenin, "Iron Mirgorod," 151; Teeter, "Soviet de Tocquevilles," 194; Taylor and Christie, eds., *Russian and Soviet Cinema in Documents*, 58.

48. Theodore Dreiser, *Dreiser Looks at Russia* (New York: Liveright, 1928), 76.

49. Esenin, "Iron Mirgorod," 153.

50. *Pravda*, 16 March 1924, 4.

51. Teeter, "Soviet de Tocquevilles," 83.

52. Valentin Kiparsky, *English and American Characters in Russian Fiction* (Wiesbaden, West Germany: Harrassowitz, 1964), 112, 166.

53. Teeter, "Soviet de Tocquevilles," 77–78, 195–96.

54. Regarding the *Babbitt* excerpts, see *LEF*, no. 2 (1923): 55–64.

55. See Anne E. Gorsuch, *Flappers and Foxtrotters: Soviet Youth in the "Roaring Twenties"* (Pittsburgh: University of Pittsburgh, Carl Beck Papers, 1994); Richard Stites, *Russian Popular Culture: Entertainment and Society since 1900* (Cambridge: Cambridge University Press, 1992), 49, 62; and S. Frederick Starr, *Red and Hot: The Fate of Jazz in the Soviet Union. With a New Chapter on the Final Years* (New York: Limelight, 1994), 56.

56. Denise J. Youngblood, *Soviet Cinema in the Silent Era, 1918–1935* (Ann Arbor, Mich.: UMI Research Press, 1985), 54–56; Denise J. Youngblood, *Movies for the Masses: Popular Cinema and Soviet Society in the 1920s* (Cambridge: Cambridge University Press, 1992), 61–62; Taylor and Christie, *Russia and Soviet Cinema in Documents*, 155.

57. V. I. Lenin, *Lenin on the United States: Selected Writings by V. I. Lenin* (New York: International, 1970), 51, 59–60, 97–98, 315.

58. Lenin, *Lenin on the United States*, 90–91, 115. For comparisons of Russia and America, see 62, 68–70, 72, 80–81.

59. For some critical comments about the United States made after the revolution, see Lenin, *Lenin on the United States*, 334, 349, 362.

60. V. I. Lenin, *Leninskii sbornik* (Moscow: Gosudarstvennoe izdatel'stvo politicheskoi literatury, 1959), 36:37–38.

61. Lenin, *Lenin on the United States*, 417, 447.

62. Dana G. Dalrymple, "The American Tractor Comes to Soviet Agriculture: The Transfer of a Technology," *Technology and Culture* 5, no. 2 (Spring 1964): 208; Lenin, *Lenin on the United States*, 589–92.

63. V. D. Banasiukevich, "V. I. Lenin i nauchnaia organizatsiia truda," *Istoriia SSSR*, no. 2 (March–April 1965); N. S. Il'enko and K. Sh. Shamsutdinov, eds., *Nauchnaia organizatsiia truda dvadtsatykh godov: Sbornik dokumentov i materialov* (Kazan': Kombinat pechati imeni Kamilia Iakuba, 1965), 37–38, 59–60; Stites, *Revolutionary Dreams*, 147; *New York Times*, 26 January 1924 (regarding Lenin's film of the Ford factory).

64. Victor Erlich, *Modernism and Revolution: Russian Literature in Transition* (Cambridge, Mass.: Harvard University Press, 1994), 37; Vladimir Mayakovsky, *Selected Works in Three Volumes* (Moscow: Raduga, 1985), 1:51; Barooshian, *Russian Cubo-Futurism*, 56.

65. Markov, *Russian Futurism*, 135; Brown, *Mayakovsky*, 88–89.

66. Arkady Yanishevsky, "The Urbanism of Vladimir Mayakovsky" (Ph.D. diss, Brown University, 1997), 141–42.

67. Terras, *Vladimir Mayakovsky*, 22; Brown, *Mayakovsky*, 342.

68. Vladimir Maiakovskii, "Teper' k Amerikan" (Now to the Americas), in *Polnoe sobranie sochinenii v trinadtsati tomakh* (Moscow: Gosudarstvennoe izdatel'stvo khudozhestvennoi literatury, 1955), 1:311–12; Charles Rougle, *Three Russians Consider America: America in the Works of Maxsim Gor'kij, Aleksandr Blok, and Vladimir Majakovskij* (Stockholm: Almqvist and Wiksell International, 1976), 63, 99–100, 146. The Esenin quotation is on page 99.

69. Maiakovskii, *Polnoe sobranie sochinenii*, 4:108.

70. Rougle, *Three Russians*, 105.

71. Maiakovskii, *Polnoe sobranie sochinenii*, 2:115–64. The quotation is from page 129.

72. Rougle, *Three Russians*, 113, 147.

73. Vladimir Mayakovsky, *My Discovery of America*, in Hasty and Fusso, *America through Russian Eyes*, 168–70.

74. Mayakovsky, *Selected Works*, 1:152.

75. Mayakovsky, *Selected Works*, 1:161–63.

76. Mayakovsky, *My Discovery of America*, 168, 174–75, 194, 203–205, 207.

77. Mayakovsky, *My Discovery of America*, 182, 184.

78. Mayakovsky, *My Discovery of America*, 177.

79. Mayakovsky, *My Discovery of America*, 195.

80. Mayakovsky, *Selected Works*, 1:156.

81. Brown, *Mayakovsky*, 281–82.

82. Rougle, *Three Russians*, 112–13, 131, 134–35, 139.

83. E. I. Naumov, "Lenin o Maiakovskom (novye materialy)," in *Literaturnoe nasledstvo. Novoe o Maiakovskom* (Moscow: Akademiia nauk SSSR, 1958), 210, 212.

84. Regarding Mayakovsky's suicide, see Yanishevsky, "Urbanism of Vladimir Mayakovsky," 165.

85. Mayakovsky, *Selected Works*, 1:247–48.

86. Robert C. Tucker, *Stalin in Power: The Revolution from Above, 1918–1941* (New York: Norton, 1990), 553.

CHAPTER TWO

~

Heavenly Miracles

The Russian people love us.

—Robert M. LaFollette

They say, citizens, that the public baths in America are excellent. There, for instance, a citizen goes to the bathhouse, takes off his clothes, puts them in a special box and goes happily off to wash. . . . This American will wash, then return to the dressing room and his clean underclothes are handed to him—all washed and ironed. His undershirt, believe me, is whiter than snow. His drawers are repaired and patched! What a life!

—Mikhail Zoshchenko

When Jesús Silva Herzog traveled to Moscow in 1929 to begin serving as Mexico's second ambassador to the Soviet Union, he anticipated a bond of sympathy between Mexican and Soviet citizens in light of the two countries' recent revolutionary origins. Thus he was not surprised by the warm welcome he received upon visiting a collective farm that summer—until he learned that the peasants thought Mexico was part of the United States. They took him to be the U.S. ambassador, and their welcome derived its warmth from the admiration for America common among them. Evidence of such feelings for the United States impressed numerous visitors to the USSR, including American engineers employed at Soviet construction projects and a German banker who noted that "among the Russian population as a whole, the United States enjoys a popularity difficult to describe."[1]

Maurice Hindus, who had grown up in a Belorussian village before emigrating to the United States in 1905, encountered similar sentiments on visits to the Russian countryside in the 1920s. At a wedding feast in a village near the Volga River he found himself peppered with questions about Henry Ford: "Was anyone in America as clever as he?" the peasants inquired. "Was it true that he was richer than any Russian Czar ever had been? Ah, if they could only just take one good look at him!" This open-mouthed fascination with Ford recurred elsewhere as Hindus traveled through the Soviet hinterland. Some villages held Fordson festivals, named after the popular tractor, and Hindus found people in remote areas who knew nothing of Stalin but had heard of the American who produced the "iron horses." In Moscow itself, a Soviet journalist surveying the throng that turned out to greet Douglas Fairbanks and Mary Pickford on their visit to the capital in 1926 felt no doubt about Ford's comparative standing with the Muscovite population. Fairbanks and Pickford were popular, but if Ford journeyed to the Soviet Union, predicted the reporter, "they would have to mobilize the entire Red army to keep the crowds in order."[2] Be that as it may, many Soviet citizens did regard Henry Ford with wonder—an emotion that differed from the respect shown him by the Soviet elite. Production methods lauded by Bolshevik leaders gave way in the popular mind to visions of Ford's wealth and inventive genius that reached fairytale proportions, with no qualifications about capitalist abuse of labor.

The contrast between these two "cults" of Ford—popular and official—suggests that ordinary citizens sustained an image of America different from the *Amerikanizm* of Bolsheviks and futurists featured in the previous chapter. Peasants and townsfolk had thought of America in their own terms well before World War I, and their notions survived the Revolution to intrigue foreign and domestic observers alike in the 1920s. "Never was one country technically or materially, or both, more overawed by another than is Russia to-day by the United States," concluded Theodore Dreiser after his journey through the Soviet Union in 1927.

> Indeed, I have stood in amazement at times at the childlike naïveté and wonder with which grown Russians (men and women who have been in China and all over Europe), to say nothing of the untraveled youth of the land, will listen to any exaggeration relative to the wealth or splendor or technical equipment of America. . . . "Everybody is well-dressed in America; no one is poor. Every one, including all workingmen, has a car, an apartment or a little house, a telephone, a radio, a victrola, electric lights, a gas stove, and time and means wherewith to travel." "Oh, yes, we know—it is perfect in America."[3]

To a degree, as Dreiser noted, the popular vision of America coincided with impressions prevalent among the intellectual and political elites, especially in the realm of technology. Mass-produced automobiles and radios suggested a land of unrivaled industrial development to all segments of Soviet society. For some imaginations, however, this was just the starting point.

Not only were Americans efficient and competent, they were thought capable of feats that could only be miracles elsewhere. Fabulous treasure, medicines, entertainments, and opportunities—anything one could dream of—abounded across the Atlantic. Stories circulating in Maurice Hindus's boyhood village told of a land in which not even beggars stooped to eat the coarse black bread familiar to Russian peasants. "Anybody could buy fat meat there, all he wanted and cheap," and even "the poorest man could afford cigarette paper, as fine and soft as the down of the feather of a fat goose." Why, Americans wore clothes of factory-made cloth and any color they desired, just like Russian nobles dressed up to go horseback riding. "Soap too was cheap, and the poorest people washed themselves with it not once a week or before holidays, but every day and several times a day." Even in the American army (for which nobody was drafted, peasants noted), a soldier "ate lots of meat and white bread and sugar, and he wore nice clothes and could save twenty and more roubles a month"—more than the haughtiest store clerks in the nearby Russian town. Mayakovsky, too, sensed an idealization of American prosperity among ordinary Russians. Our peasants, he told a New York audience in 1925, think of America and see "endless fields on which graze huge herds of plump cattle."[4]

Much of this appeal lay in the conviction that anyone in America who worked diligently could share the fortune. Such faith, complained an article in *Pravda*, gripped peasants most tightly during hard times. In the spring, with food reserves depleted and scarcely any strength left to work, "they talk about America." Stories circulated about "America's heavenly miracles," about the enormous yields surely enjoyed by every American farmer, who, moreover, "harvests his grain with his own machinery and drives home in his own car." The peasants were certain that Americans lived "on farms—though it's unknown exactly what a farm is—better than any *sovkhoz* [a state agricultural enterprise], and very easy to buy. You just work a couple years in a factory and save a little American money." Though he ridiculed these opinions, the author could not have expected his critique to reach the peasants, let alone change their minds.[5] Three years later, Soviet president Mikhail Kalinin regretted the belief "widespread among us that the United States is a heaven on earth not only for workers but for peasants. Perhaps, people say to me, it really is a heaven? I agree. Yes, it is a heaven—but for the rich, not for the workers."[6]

Kalinin himself, like many other Bolsheviks, probably applied an American standard to gauge industrial proficiency, but ordinary people judged whatever they pleased on the American scales. If the United States possessed something, it must be good, while something else that did not exist "over there" was probably obsolete or worthless. "Were there *kolkhozy* [collective farms] in America?" a peasant asked Hindus. "No? Ah, then perhaps they were not a good thing, because if they were, America would have had them, wouldn't she?"[7] Soviet journalists, including the author of the *Pravda* commentary on "America's heavenly miracles," frequently revealed their awareness of popular reverence for an imagined way of life in the United States. Ironic titles such as "Life in Rich America" and "In the Country of Freedom" signaled at a glance an author's desire to challenge widespread opinions by highlighting exploitation and discrimination in the "Land of Democracy."[8] The repetition of such articles year after year also betrayed official concern that the "American myth" had survived.

From the beginning, the party ruled a population in which favorable images of America ran deeper than interest in Marxist doctrine. To be sure, many Soviet citizens, perhaps millions, developed a rudimentary familiarity with Marxism and a faith in something they regarded as socialism. But they lived among tens of millions of people, mostly peasants, with no interest in Marxism or the party's ultimate goal. Try as the regime might, through books, movies, songs, and art, no socialist myth appeared compelling enough to erase the notions of America held by a substantial segment of the populace. These circumstances spawned a two-headed official line on the United States. Condemnation of America's flaws alternated with appeals to work like a Russian American and build a new Soviet America. In this spirit, throughout the 1920s, newspapers criticized the mistreatment of workers in the United States but at the same time often recommended products and procedures to readers by claiming that the innovation in question had been invented in America or was widely practiced there.[9]

No doubt Soviet efforts to popularize socialism and reveal America's shortcomings had some of the desired effect. The propaganda barrage, with few competing sources of information by the 1930s, nurtured pride in Soviet achievements while the West floundered in the Great Depression. Yet, twenty years after the Revolution, curiosity over America remained apparent and unquenched.[10] Soviet citizens continued to jump at increasingly rare opportunities to glimpse American life, and, given the choice, they responded more warmly to a sympathetic or entertaining portrait than to yet another official tour of capitalist hell. Signs of this popular interest in America persisted decade after decade like weeds in the socialist garden, surviving numerous efforts at eradication. In the end, they outlived the Soviet Union itself.

One may safely conclude that by the onset of the twentieth century, millions of ordinary Russians had developed a favorable impression of America, and they did so with no encouragement from the tsarist government. What, then, gave rise to their images of the United States? The absence of public opinion surveys and other individual testimony from most of the vast population bars mathematical precision, but a number of factors doubtless contributed. During the Romanov dynasty's last half-century, for instance, the spread of literacy helped disseminate glimpses and fantasies of American life. Rural primary schools multiplied from roughly 23,000 in the early 1880s to approximately 108,000 in 1914. Though most peasant children attended for no more than a year or two, and 60 percent of the population was illiterate on the eve of World War I, the schools reached far more of the young than ever before. Thus in 1913, two-thirds of the army's new recruits were literate, compared to only one-fifth in 1874. Among children twelve to sixteen years of age in European Russia, a census in 1920 found that 71 percent of the boys and 52 percent of the girls could read.[11]

As the reading public expanded in these decades, so did the volume of publications. Russian-language periodicals increased from 170 titles in 1860 to more than six hundred by the end of the century, while the array of newspapers and weeklies in all languages swelled by nearly 50 percent in the last seven years before World War I. Meanwhile, the 32,338 book titles (130 million copies) published in 1914 dwarfed the 7,366 titles and 24 million copies issued in 1887. Late in the same period, press runs of books for the "common reader"—detective stories, school texts, and children's fables, for instance— exceeded 54 million copies annually, nearly eight times more than the total printed for the previous generation.[12]

Amid this surge of Russian printing, a variety of sources encouraged a positive, if often fanciful, view of America. Translations of James Fenimore Cooper's stories about Indians, for example, fascinated Russian schoolchildren throughout the period, as did the tales of Mayne Reid and other authors of adventures in the New World. Chekhov described two boys who plotted an "escape" to America, where they expected to "get gold and ivory, kill their enemies, become sea pirates, drink gin, and end up by marrying beautiful ladies and owning big plantations." Though the lads' venture collapsed shortly after they left home, one of them continued to fantasize about America. So did other youths, including the future writer Leonid Andreyev.

"When I was a child I loved America," he confided in 1908. "Perhaps Cooper and Mayne Reid, my favorite authors in my childhood days, were responsible for this. I was always planning to run away to America." He never did, though at the time of his death in 1919 he was still contemplating the trip.[13]

Of course, Cooper's frontier America did little to nurture *modern* images of the United States. Aficionados of the Leatherstocking Tales might find much to sustain an impression of exotic settings and resourceful American individualism, but where did the Russian popular mind acquire its vision of American material comfort and technical wizardry? For those with more than rudimentary literacy, accounts by Russian visitors to the United States served this purpose. Despite the censure voiced by such figures as Fyodor Dostoevsky and Maxim Gorky, a larger number of favorable assessments of America reached the public from less-renowned pens. These articles, books, and stories, written to be widely accessible, have attracted the scholarly attention of Hans Rogger and helped him "explain the friendly fascination with America that was found among Russians of all classes" at this time. In a study of twelve Russian publications about America that were intended for the general reader around the turn of the century, Rogger encountered sweeping hostility to the United States in only two. The remaining works, while not oblivious to America's shortcomings, devoted more effort to portraying a land-of opportunity and wealth unattainable for most of the tsar's subjects.[14]

Augmenting Rogger's findings from the dozen texts in his sample, several additional narratives written late in the tsarist era offered similar conclusions from a diverse corps of observers that included Peter Demens, once an Imperial Guard officer.[15] Unlike other Russian authors, he settled in the United States and even pursued a number of business ventures there during the last quarter of the nineteenth century and the early years of the twentieth. Thus his descriptions of America, published in Russia as a book under the pen name Tverskoi in 1895, drew on firsthand experience beyond that acquired by other visitors. For some years thereafter Tverskoi continued to supply reports on America to a Russian periodical, and he may well have reached more readers than any other Russian commentator on the United States of his day.

He did not relish everything he saw. Pervasive advertising, speculative excesses, and powerful monopolies that seemed immune to legislatures and courts—these numbered among the tones in Tverskoi's American portrait. Yet no one could doubt that rosy hues predominated and matched many components of the ideal America taking root in Russian consciousness at the time. Over there, in the New World, technology made life better. "There is far less so-called unskilled work by day laborers in America than, for example, in Russia or in other European states," he affirmed. "Machines have replaced this hand labor to a significant degree." Wages rose, but prices of numerous basic goods did not, and banks proliferated to accommodate the savings of a prosperous society. While in Great Britain "one out of every 39 inhabitants was a beggar, in America there was only one out of every 857," and even the humblest born might make a fortune. Philip Armour, "who is now considered one of the richest people in America, began life fifty years ago as a village butcher in Wisconsin." He and his wealthy colleagues—Jay Gould, Andrew Carnegie, John D. Rockefeller, and others—"all began with pennies and now count their annual income in the tens of millions." Their treasure did not prevent them from mixing politely with ordinary Americans, portrayed by Tverskoi as literate, well-informed, and unconcerned with social distinctions to an extent inconceivable in Russia.[16]

Marginally literate readers, for whom Tverskoi was too difficult or too expensive, could turn instead to new mass-circulation newspapers and cheap serialized adventure stories. Here, scenes from American life, however improbable, often appeared in a positive light, as demonstrated in the serial detective tales of the early twentieth century. The escapades appeared as complete stories in fewer than fifty pages and cost less than ten kopecks. Well-known Western sleuths, especially Nick Carter and Nat Pinkerton (both American) and Sherlock Holmes, found themselves recruited in Russian adaptations to star in countless adventures, sometimes presented to the reader as fact: "Nick Carter is alive," proclaimed one issue. "He is an inspector of the New York secret police and there are daily descriptions of the feats of this man, the greatest American genius, in all American newspapers." Carter and Pinkerton dashed around the United States (and even the globe), availing themselves routinely of cars, airplanes, telegrams, and other modern technology. In the process, as they sped from Florida to New York and from Chicago to San Francisco, they left their Russian readers with images of a thoroughly modern America.[17]

The stories were wildly popular for several years before World War I, with millions of copies published in Russia—6.2 million Pinkertons, 3.1 million Carters (and 3.9 million Holmeses)—over a nine-year period beginning in 1907. As late as 1915, well past the peak of demand for the adventures, street sales in Petrograd (as the capital was renamed at the beginning of the war) totaled 288,225 Pinkertons and 72,380 Carters. Individual testimony corroborated the impression of working-class literary taste left by these numbers. "They read Nat Pinkerton and are satisfied with that," complained a trade unionist in 1910, while the literary critic Kornei Chukovskii added, "For a long time I could not believe my eyes when I saw the way the workers were gobbling up Nat Pinkerton." Even peasants encountered the tales on occasion at train stations or obtained them from workers and soldiers returning to their home villages.[18]

When Russian journalists and other authors described America for a mass readership around the turn of the century, they often produced a "moral fantasy" featuring successful outcomes scarcely possible under the tsars.[19] Comparable stories and travel accounts sold elsewhere in Europe had earlier created an impression powerful enough to help steer millions of emigrants to America from Ireland, Germany, and Scandinavia. Eventually, in the last two decades before World War I, such literature played a part in convincing thousands of Russians as well to embark for the New World in anticipation of rewards unattainable at home.[20] A much larger number stayed behind, of course, and they, not the immigrant communities in New York or Chicago, are the focus of this study. But people who never left the Old World often absorbed the same "information" about America as those who emigrated, and the fact that they had not set foot in the United States could aid them in clinging to the most outlandish assurances of opulence beyond the sea.

Throughout the period of peak European emigration, from roughly the middle of the nineteenth century to the eruption of World War I, glittering tales of America guided waves of people hoping for something better across the Atlantic. These images of bounty required no literacy for propagation—among peasants in particular, they commonly circulated by word of mouth, growing ever more remarkable in the process. According to a Swedish newspaper in 1846, a beggar girl roamed through villages spreading visions of America "in far more attractive colors than Joshua's returned spies portrayed the promised land to the children of Israel. 'In America,' the girl is reported to have said, 'the hogs eat their fill of raisins and dates that everywhere grow wild, and when they are thirsty, they drink from ditches flowing with wine.'" Naturally, continued the journalist, "gullible *bondfolk* [peasants] draw the conclusion from such stories that it is far better to be a hog in America than to be a human being in Sweden."[21] Half a century later, stunning claims about American wealth and opportunity reached Maurice Hindus's village in Russia. Here, too, the news spread from the mouths of visiting beggars, peddlers, and gypsies, people whose travels had previously exposed them to talk of the New World's affluence. Not long thereafter, "at the bazaar, one often stumbled on a crowd that listened eagerly to a man whose cousin or brother-in-law had written a letter from America."[22]

In such ways, word of America spread in numerous countries and tightened its hold. Among peasants in southern Italy, "along with the traditional and inevitable concept of America as the land with streets paved in gold," there developed such a strong "affection for America, this strange and distant land, that they seem tied to it by bonds stronger than the tenuous ones that link them with the capital of their own country, Rome."[23] A similar claim also applied to many among the persecuted or exploited portions of the Russian empire's population, including a Jewish family living in Lithuania in the 1880s. A brother's talk of going to America riveted the attention of his sister, who mused: "*America, the land where everyone was fabulously rich, the land where all sorts of exciting adventures took place. It was a golden land on the other side of the world.*"[24]

Immigration to America from the Russian empire (and from eastern and southern Europe generally) occurred quite late in Europe's exodus to the New World. For most of the nineteenth century the overwhelming majority of America's European immigrants—approximately 80 percent as late as the 1880s—came from northern and western Europe. But during the next decade the tide of people from southern and eastern Europe surged (to 54 percent of Europe's total) as sharply as it ebbed from countries to the west, and by the first decade of the twentieth century, such nations as Italy, Austria-Hungary, and Russia supplied three-quarters of Europe's immigrants to the United States.[25] From Russia alone, roughly 3.2 million passengers crowded ocean liners to America during the period 1880–1914, approximately 2.8 million of them in just fifteen years beginning in 1899.[26]

What finally loosed this torrent in the twilight of the Romanov dynasty? Certain pressures, including a population growing too large in some regions for traditional occupations, resembled developments in many countries during periods of mass emigration. Other considerations owed more to imperial policies, especially measures taken against non-Russian minorities. In 1882 the tsarist government announced new laws restricting Jews' opportunities to conduct business, worship, participate in local government, or enter a university. More ominous still, sporadic pogroms over the next twenty-five years terrified numerous Jewish communities beset by anti-Semitic mobs that were ignored, or even encouraged, by authorities. At the same time the government's Russification campaign attacked religious, administrative, and cultural practices of the Poles, Lithuanians, Finns, and other non-Russian subjects of the tsar. These measures alone go far in explaining why 44 percent of the immigrants to America from Russia in the years 1899–1910 were Jews, 27 percent Poles (from the portion of Poland absorbed by Russia in the eighteenth century), nearly 10 percent Lithuanians, and 8.5 percent Finns.[27]

The emigration process also reflected a spreading awareness of the United States and especially its image of abundance. Stories about America reached people in Russia's western provinces from Czechs, Germans, and other neighbors whose relatives or acquaintances had already ventured to the New World (as, later, Russians, Ukrainians, and Belorussians would hear about America from Jews or Poles). Thereafter the "news" spread rapidly through diverse conduits, including the peddlers and beggars previously mentioned. It seems scarcely coincidental that this dawning sense of a radiant America coincided with the deluge of voyagers arriving at Ellis Island from Russia by the turn of the century. Even if other factors, such as persecution, triggered a person's decision to emigrate, belief in "golden America" provided the destination. Immigration figures themselves suggest the rapid diffusion of this consciousness. During the 1870s, only 13 percent of the 367,000 emigrants from the Russian empire traveled to the United States. After soaring to 48 percent by the following decade, America's share of Russian emigration reached 61 percent in the 1890s and approached 90 percent only ten years into the twentieth century.[28]

Not only did mass emigration to the United States reveal the prevalence of an "American myth" in Russia's western borderland, developments associated with emigration spread the legend far and wide among people who never joined the traffic across the Atlantic. Certain businesses, for instance, profited from emigration and sought to encourage the flow by disseminating rosy advertisements of American life. In the half-century before the 1880s, these promotions occurred primarily in northern and western Europe and were often funded by American state governments (hoping to attract settlers or an industrial labor force) and railway companies (eager to sell parcels from their vast land holdings).[29] The Atchison, Topeka & Santa Fe Railway Company even dispatched an employee, Carl Schmidt, to persuade Russian Mennonites to settle on land owned by the railroad in 1875, a decade or more before recruiting agents were common in Russia. As Schmidt told it, he set out "preaching the gospel of emigration to Kansas from village to village, . . . earning among the Mennonites the title of their Moses."[30]

By the last ten or fifteen years of the century, American railroads and state governments felt less urgency about recruiting in Europe. But the same could not be said of the steamship companies, which depended heavily on a sustained current of transatlantic passengers. During the 1880s these firms— Hapag (based in Hamburg) and North German Lloyd (Bremen) being the two most important for eastern Europeans—became the principal solicitors of potential immigrants. In targeted regions the companies hired agents who fanned out and built up networks of subagents (mayors, innkeepers, clergymen, and other local notables) that could number hundreds of people. These agents earned a commission on the sale of steamship tickets, which moved them to glorify America without restraint. They put up posters in public locations, distributed translations of articles from the American press, and at times took more energetic measures, as in Italy, where some stood at church doors handing out cards printed with hymns and poems extolling the United States. When eastern and southern Europe emerged as fecund sources of immigrants in the 1880s, steamship agents turned an ever larger share of their efforts to people there, who previously had been less exposed to news of America.[31]

Russia's western provinces thus became familiar turf for these salesmen by the 1890s. A U.S. congressional commission concluded in 1911 that "the attempted promotion of emigration by steamship ticket agents is carried on to a greater extent in Austria, Hungary, Greece, and Russia than in other countries" and noted that Russia had not enjoyed much success in restricting the entrepreneurs. There were even reports, complained an official in Russia's Washington, D.C., embassy, "that in our western region, resources from German steamship companies operate cheap cinemas that show, in an attractive light, pictures of American life, rich fields of grain, fruit from California, and so forth."[32] While scholars have questioned whether these recruiters managed to sell tickets to many people whom poverty or persecution had not already inclined to emigrate, the agents did at least help spread the "American myth."[33] No one had a greater incentive to portray the United States in glowing hues, and their pictures helped shape the impressions of America formed by those who remained in Russia as well as those who departed.

An agent, of course, was a salesman, and his enthusiasm for America might arouse skepticism. More credible were emigrants already in the United States whose letters advertised the New World to relatives and friends in Europe—and represented another way in which rising literacy rates served to spread word of America. Between 1900 and 1906, more than five million letters traveled from America to Europe (with roughly three million mailed in the opposite direction), and while some lamented the authors' misfortunes abroad, sources agree on the generally enthusiastic tone of this testimony. According to the U.S. congressional commission studying emigration in 1911, these letters to friends back home "have been the immediate cause of by far the greater part of the remarkable movement from southern and eastern Europe to the United States during the past twenty-five years." A Russian official noted the letters' persuasive power with regret: "As the result of a natural desire to boast, the letters of emigrants always exaggerate considerably the attractive side of the life and the various wonders of America."[34]

Half a century earlier, letters from America to Sweden "were not only read and pondered by the simple and credulous individuals to whom they were addressed, and discussed in larger groups in homes and at markets and fairs and in crowds assembled at parish churches, but they were also broadcast through the newspapers, which, unwittingly or not, infected parish after parish with the 'American fever.'" A family in Russia learned of America when "some Jewish man or woman" would stop by to ask assistance in reading a letter from a relative now living in the United States. "What a ceremony would follow then—what excitement—a letter from America! Not even the Marco Polos with all their great wealth on their return from China, with all their treasured jewels, could cause the sensation that a 'letter from America' did."[35]

Such news agitated a village in one of Vladimir Korolenko's stories, when word arrived from a native son, Osip Lozinsky, who had gone to work in America. Everyone of any significance in Lozishtche read the letter before it reached the addressee, Lozinsky's wife, to whom he was sending a ticket for passage to the New World. What a country it was, Lozinsky reported— "workers live here much better than some masters" back home. "Lots of land, the cows yield a whole pailful of milk after every milking, and the horses are as strong as wild bulls." He even participated in the choice of the next president of the entire country, which impressed him and those in Lozishtche more than the fact that his vote went to a candidate who lost the election. Day after day, villagers filled the local tavern with animated discussion until dawn, and "had a stranger dropped in to hear some of their talk he would have thought that not a single young man would be left in Lozishtche within a week."[36]

Praise of America arose from more than a desire to boast. Immigrants able to find work in the United States might earn, and save, hundreds more dollars per year than they would in Europe.[37] When they sent some of this money to relatives back home, they enhanced the image of flourishing America. The sums involved clearly totaled tens of millions of dollars, though much escaped the attention of officials. In the form of money orders alone, 70 million dollars traveled from America to Austria–Hungary and Russia during the period 1902 to 1906—and it took very little of this to impress a peasant community. The congressional commission on emigration received reports from inspectors in Europe on the effect in a village of letters containing less than one hundred dollars. "The cottage of the recipient becomes at once the place to which the entire male population proceeds, and the letters are read and reread until the contents can be repeated word for word."[38]

Meanwhile, roughly a third of America's European immigrants in the first decade of the twentieth century later sailed back to the Old World. The figure proved to be smaller for people who reached the United States from Russia, owing to the prevalence among Russian immigrants of Jews, who remained in America at a much higher rate than did any other significant category of European newcomers. Of the 1.2 million people arriving from Russia between 1908 and 1913, approximately 93 percent of the Jewish contingent came to stay, compared to 74 percent of the Poles and only 59 percent of those identified as Russians (Great Russians, Ukrainians, and Belorussians taken together).[39] All told, 233,000 immigrants returned to Russia during this six-year period. Some, of course, did so in despair or bitterness over their experiences in the United States, but a larger number, it appears, had never intended to stay permanently. As ocean travel grew faster, safer, and less expensive during the second half of the nineteenth century, growing numbers of workers from southern and eastern Europe sought to take temporary advantage of the higher wages in America to accumulate savings sufficient to live more comfortably back home.[40] They might repeat this cycle and perhaps even collect their families in the end and move to the United States. Most important for our purposes, during their return visits in Europe, they served as live affirmation—even more convincing than letters—of America's affluence. Better dressed than their neighbors, with suitcases of gifts and pockets full of money to improve their households, they regaled friends and relatives with stories that gave substance to the "American myth."[41]

Images fostered by emigration traffic and by the popular press may have received substantiation from industrial products that entered Russia in larger numbers during the last prerevolutionary decades. Phonographs, telephones, elevators, cameras, and typewriters from the United States had all reached Moscow, St. Petersburg, and other large cities by this time and testified to American technological vitality.[42] Peasants—still three-quarters of the population—would rarely encounter these items, but they had a better chance of seeing or hearing about sewing machines from the Singer Manufacturing Company and agricultural equipment from International Harvester. Singer had made sales in Russia since the 1850s and won the Russian market from European rivals by the turn of the century. The company opened a factory near Moscow and employed 31,000 people throughout Russia by the summer of 1914, likely making Singer the country's largest commercial organization. Total annual sales peaked at close to 800,000 sewing machines.[43] International Harvester, founded in 1902 by Cyrus McCormick through a merger of the top four American makers of harvesting machines, towered along with

Singer over other American companies in Russia before the Revolution. Approximately 15–20 percent of the agricultural equipment exported from the United States went to Russia during the twentieth century's first decade, and the figure approached 32 percent by 1910, more than the share sold to any other nation. According to a publication of the Russian government in 1914, American-made harvesting and mowing machines amounted to 45 percent of the total to be found in the country, and an American traveler claimed that advertisements for International Harvester machinery "could be seen in every Siberian village."[44]

Of course, no one can specify how many people recognized American equipment or drew any conclusions from it about the United States. Although such opportunities certainly increased over the last few decades of the old regime, it seems unlikely that these products could have rivaled factors associated with the popular press and emigration in lauding America. As with other comments on Russian public opinion of the day, the current body of scholarship permits an estimate of plausibility but not statistical precision. We can, however, hypothesize confidently from this research that millions (probably tens of millions) of the tsar's subjects had developed notions of a shimmering America—before the collapse of the Romanov dynasty left most of them citizens of a new Soviet regime.

Revolutionary waves sweeping over Russia in 1917 bestowed a socialist government on the nation without washing away the attitude toward America that had crystallized earlier in much of the population. Moreover, new manifestations of the United States soon appeared on the Soviet landscape and reinforced common images of America despite the Kremlin's Marxist orientation. Scarcely had the Bolsheviks survived diverse threats during the civil war of 1918–20 than a famine in the Soviet heartland summoned more direct American involvement with the Russian people than at any time under the tsars.

By 1921, tens of millions of Soviet citizens faced starvation in a region centered among provinces along the Volga River. Dozens of relief campaigns in numerous countries collected food and other supplies for the victims, but one organization overshadowed them all. The American Relief Administration (ARA), established in 1919 to serve war-torn Europe, reached agreement with the Bolshevik government in 1921 and furnished over 90 percent of all famine assistance sent to the Soviet Union through 1923. At its peak, the ARA's staff numbered two hundred Americans who directed approximately eighty thousand Russians in operating thirty-five thousand aid stations that distributed nearly a million tons of food, seed, clothing, and medical supplies. More than seven million people received inoculations and vaccinations, and nearly eleven million were fed during the famine's most ominous period.[45]

While the scale of the ARA's work lends itself to statistical measure, such figures can do no more than suggest that the aid promoted a favorable image of the United States. However, certain points are clear. First, millions of people had direct contact with the ARA and received food, clothing, and medicine for themselves or their children. Second, American and Soviet officials *expected*, though they did not necessarily desire, that the ARA's assistance would indeed impress its recipients with the United States. The ARA's director, Herbert Hoover (then secretary of commerce), revealed a variety of motives for Russian relief work, ranging from humanitarian concern to preparation for subsequent American commercial activity in the region. But he also anticipated that the ARA's Soviet operation would highlight American efficiency, bounty, and generosity for the local population. "Friendliness" between Russia and the United States had existed before the Revolution, Hoover informed Secretary of State Charles Evans Hughes at the end of 1921, and he predicted that the ARA's mission would now help establish America's popularity in the Soviet Union: "The relief measures already initiated are greatly increasing the status and kindliness of relations and their continuation will build a situation which, combined with the other factors, will enable the Americans to undertake the leadership in the reconstruction of Russia when the proper moment arrives."[46] Hoover's well-known aversion to "Bolshevism" meant that the "proper moment" awaited the passage of Lenin's party from the scene.

Official Soviet expressions of gratitude usually acknowledged that the population had been disposed to look kindly on America as a result of the ARA's relief measures. "The peoples of the Union of Soviet Socialist Republics will never forget the aid extended to them by the American people through the ARA," proclaimed a government resolution in 1923, after crediting the ARA with saving millions from death.[47] Although these statements were prepared for American ears, Soviet officials occasionally affirmed the point in newspapers devoted to a domestic audience. Trotsky, for instance, labeled the ARA's aid "unforgettable" to "the hungry masses of Russia," while Leonid Krasin, a prominent diplomat, conjectured that this assistance would boost American "popularity" in the Soviet Union.[48] In any event, it stands to reason that individuals and families saved from starvation would esteem the United States and the ARA, as demonstrated in the scores of thank-you letters received by the agency from towns and villages across the famine region.[49] To be sure, the Soviet press as a whole remained ambivalent toward the ARA, with some authors describing the scale of relief in neutral or friendly terms and others portraying American participants in a callous or sinister light.[50] But even the negative tone suggested at times that the articles' hostility issued in part from concern that the ARA, through the example of its work, might diminish the Soviet government's standing in the eyes of the population.

Separate from the question of whether foreign aid discredited the Bolsheviks, there seems no reason to doubt that the ARA strengthened some aspects of the popular image of the United States. Like the money or gifts that a relative brought back from America, though now on a larger scale, the ARA's relief operation implied a thriving America and, perhaps, an efficient and generous one as well. Sixty years later, American visitors to the Soviet Union found survivors of the Volga famine who retained grateful memories of this assistance.[51] For millions like them, the ARA's famine relief must have conjured visions of the United States far removed from the themes of exploitation and oppression aired by Bolsheviks.

Well before the ARA completed its Russian labors in 1923, Soviet peasants could discover Americans and American equipment through other channels, such as agricultural communes established by volunteers from the United States. Many participants, including hundreds who had emigrated to America from tsarist Russia in the decades before 1920, were active in left-wing politics and jumped at the opportunity to help build a Soviet society free of the abuses they deplored in the United States. Some opted to form communes in Russia after being deported or otherwise harassed during the American red scare of the day. Back in their homeland, they were viewed as Americans, even if the U.S. government did not regard them as citizens. Perhaps as many as twenty groups from the United States attempted to make a new life in the Soviet countryside, and some collapsed in short order, undone by inferior buildings, equipment lost in transit, internal problems, and long delays in obtaining land. Still, many survived at least a few years and made their way into a government report that listed twenty-one foreign communes (fourteen American) functioning in 1925. Nearly all had been founded in 1922 or 1923, usually by one hundred to two hundred members.[52]

A commune's tractors (if it had any) fascinated neighboring peasants more than the members' radicalism. Lenin, too, appears to have valued the newcomers most for the lessons they could offer in "American" diligence and machinery. By means of an appeal circulated among émigrés living in America and Canada, he explained in 1921 that "the establishment by you of model farms with modern equipment and sophisticated techniques would serve as an outstanding example to our backward brothers, the peasants."

The next year he asked the Presidium of the All-Russian Central Executive Committee to provide every possible assistance to these ventures, adding the hope that participants for approximately two hundred communes would arrive soon from America along with eight hundred to one thousand tractors needed for a demonstration of American technology in every district.[53] Throughout the 1920s, Bolshevik authorities valued the communes primarily as showcases of advanced agricultural techniques. The members might experiment with communal lifestyles if they wished, but officials emphasized tractor demonstrations for nearby peasants.[54]

One of the first Americans to parade tractors through Russian villages was Harold Ware, an agriculture expert and member of the American Communist Party. In 1922 he and his wife, Clarissa, together with eight American farmers, took twenty Chase tractors to operate among peasants living in the foothills of the Ural mountains, near Perm. At summer's end the Americans visited Moscow, where Trotsky invited them for a talk. (The farmers had dressed up in their old army uniforms, "putting them to good use for once anyway," Trotsky noted with a smile, in reference to American intervention in the Russian civil war.) Hearing that most of the Americans, other than Ware, were only one generation removed from Scandinavia, Trotsky detected a parallel of significance for the Soviet Union. If the United States could "make Scandinavian peasants into American farmers and American tractor experts" so quickly, he explained, "well, we can make Russian peasants over like that too. We are going to. Go back to your tractors, and you will see."[55]

Back on their tractors, Ware's group toured villages near their headquarters on a state farm. The key point regarding popular visions of America is that the tractors—whether those of Ware's group or those of the agricultural communes—often captivated the peasants and must have contributed to (or spawned) images of American abundance and technological prowess. "Never have I seen more intense interest and enthusiasm than welcomed us as we drove two of the tractors to the market place," Clarissa Ware reported:

> Peasants came from miles around to see the tractors at work. We arranged to have demonstrations every Sunday afternoon and to follow them with moving pictures of the inside workings of the tractors. These pictures were the greatest success. The villagers would sit till midnight watching the workings of a steering gear or crank shaft, and the water cooling system was a thing of delight to them. The portable victrola was another machine that never ceased to interest them. It was amusing to watch their faces when for the first time they heard a Russian record. That an American machine could talk Russian was to them beyond comprehension.[56]

Delegations soon arrived from neighboring villages, asking the Americans to come plow their fields with the wonderful new machines.[57]

Apart from communes, the Soviet government provided a few large farms to groups of Americans for use in displaying machinery and training peasants who might then journey to other districts to share their knowledge. Harold Ware and approximately twenty Americans managed such a farm in southern Russia, near Rostov-on-the-Don, beginning in 1924.[58] If the generally left-wing views of Ware's community suggested an agricultural commune, some Americans at other sites possessed little zeal for socialism and were hired by the Soviet government solely for their agricultural expertise. Two farms in southern Russia—Verbliud (110,000 acres) and Gigant (500,000 acres)—featured modern techniques and housed a few dozen Americans during the last years of the decade. M. L. Wilson, a graduate of Iowa State College and later under secretary of agriculture, worked as an adviser at Verbliud in 1929; E. J. Stirniman, a former member of the agricultural engineering staff at the University of California, succeeded him for a two-year stint. The farms also attracted hands from other colonies, including Harold Ware, who left the estate near Rostov after a disagreement with officials and transferred his services to Verbliud. Meanwhile, the Caterpillar Company developed sufficient interest in the Soviet market to conduct demonstrations and other promotions of its equipment in the countryside. Assisted by twenty Americans at Verbliud, for example, Caterpillar ran a tractor school for roughly two hundred Russians in the winter of 1929–30.[59]

Even when peasants encountered tractors through purely Soviet agencies, with no foreigners in sight, the machines themselves likely came from the United States. Indeed, American companies manufactured virtually all the tractors at work in the Soviet Union during the 1920s, with the Ford Motor Company's Fordson alone accounting for 85 percent of the total in 1927.[60] The tractors' foreign provenance was stamped on them in bold letters, as evident in Sergei Eisenstein's film *The General Line*, in which members of a village cooperative struggle to acquire their own tractor. When the machine finally arrives, and eventually amazes the peasants with a display of power, it bears the name "FORDSON" for all to see. Though one may question other aspects of *The General Line*, numerous accounts corroborate the awe inspired by tractors in a community previously dependent on human and animal muscle.

The metallic prodigies really were creatures from another world, and that world was America. After Maurice Hindus left the rural wedding with which this chapter began, he visited a semiannual fair in another village. Thousands of peasants who had gathered for the trading opportunities and festive atmosphere suddenly noticed an approaching roar. Several Fordson tractors soon rumbled into the marketplace, prompting the bargainers to drop their transactions and flock around the machines, poking them as they might inspect cattle and bombarding the drivers with questions. These Soviet *traktoristy*, who later told Hindus that they frequently conducted such "excursions of enlightenment," addressed the peasants, "extolling the American tractor and pointing to it . . . as a symbol of a new day and a new life."[61]

Tractors also reached the Soviet countryside through the efforts of American Jewish organizations, notably the Joint Distribution Committee, which purchased eighty-six John Deere models in the fall of 1922 for export to the Soviet Union. A group of Americans, ready to serve as traveling instructors, accompanied the machinery on its voyage to southern Russia. Hundreds more tractors soon followed, and in 1924 the Joint Distribution Committee formed a corporation (Agro-Joint) to work with the Soviet government in establishing Crimean and Ukrainian agricultural colonies for Soviet Jews. Prominent American Jews contributed millions of dollars to these efforts, which after ten years had yielded 215 Agro-Joint colonies housing twenty thousand families. More to the point, the colonies received one thousand American tractors, seven hundred tractor plows, and thirty-six combine harvesters. This equipment clearly caught the eye of the surrounding population, for Agro-Joint used its resources to assist nearby communities, including fifteen thousand non-Jewish peasants. Some of the Jewish ventures even made it a primary goal to exhibit American machinery throughout their regions.[62]

The fact remains, of course, that tens of thousands of American tractors in the Soviet Union during the 1920s were spread thin among tens of millions of peasants. Perhaps a majority heard little or nothing about them. But the evidence at hand suggests, first, that at least many thousands of people—and probably far more—did see or otherwise learn of the machines. Second, peasants who witnessed one of Henry Ford's "iron horses" were likely amazed by the spectacle, and this could confirm in their minds a portion of the "American myth." The sources depict a peasantry more inclined, on the whole, to admire tractors than to see in them the devil's handiwork or dismiss them if they broke down. When the allure of tractors is combined with the potency of other factors, including profiles of the United States in the prerevolutionary popular press, praise for America stemming from immigration to the New World, and life-saving assistance from the ARA, no doubt remains that many people encountered stimuli to form favorable images of America. We cannot know exactly *how* many, but if all these influences are considered together, they clearly yield millions of Soviet citizens who remained, to one degree or another, intrigued and even dazzled by the United States of their imaginations.

Of all the factors that nudged the general population toward radiant impressions of America, those associated with emigration and popular publications appear to have affected the largest number of people. They did so mainly before 1917, creating visions of the United States that endured to flourish in the postrevolutionary scene at the center of our attention. During the first Soviet decade, famine relief from the ARA and demonstrations of American tractors did nurture inklings of American prowess, but only among a part of the population. Although the ARA assisted millions of Soviet citizens, the beneficiaries were concentrated mainly in the famine-stricken provinces, while people who witnessed or heard glowing stories about American tractors were probably fewer in number and mostly peasants. Inhabitants of Moscow, Minsk, or Petrograd had little opportunity for such contact in the 1920s. However, another mechanism emerged after the Revolution to advertise America as vividly as anything had done before 1917, and it enthralled millions of Soviet citizens largely untouched by the ARA or Fordson tractors.

American movies swept around the world in the decade after World War I and soon dominated the global market that French and other foreign distributors had controlled just a few years before. Once the Bolshevik government began importing foreign films in quantity by the mid-1920s, America's offerings drew enthusiastic audiences as readily in the Soviet Union as in other lands. The following chapter will explore Hollywood's prominent position in Soviet popular culture, but one aspect of these movies deserves attention here—their role in promoting certain images of the United States.

For a brief period following Russia's Revolution, the American Committee on Public Information (usually called the Creel Committee after its director, George Creel) showed films in regions not yet controlled by the Bolsheviks, and it did so with the intent of commending American life to the local population. Creel had been appointed in 1917 by Woodrow Wilson to conduct a propaganda campaign in the United States in support of the war, and before long the committee established a foreign section that sang America's praises abroad. To this end, motion-picture programs were assembled that included industrial footage (supplied by the Ford Motor Company, International Harvester, and other companies), as well as clips on American cities, farms, national parks, recreation, and anything else the compilers deemed impressive. Eventually, Hollywood comedies and dramas were added to the packages as their popularity with viewers became clear.

After the fall of the tsar early in 1917 the Creel Committee sought to present its films in Russia's principal cities until the Bolshevik Revolution later in the year drove the enterprise to distant zones controlled by the Bolsheviks' opponents—Archangel in the north and Vladivostok in the Far East. There, Creel's representatives screened their films for local inhabitants using existing theaters or resources supplied by the Red Cross, the Young Men's Christian Association (YMCA), and military organizations. For a time committee officials circulated as many as 1,500 reels of film across large tracts of Siberia and the Far East from their base in Vladivostok. Even after Creel's film division ceased operations early in 1919, the YMCA's portable projection units disseminated these movies from Vladivostok for several more months.[63]

One film favored by the State Department depicted "Ivan's visit to the United States at the personal invitation of Uncle Sam." "Ivan" assumed the form of a Russian immigrant who tours America, gazing in amazement at skyscrapers, factories, electric power plants, mines, and farms. According to a State Department official in the summer of 1917, the result was "ideal propaganda for Russia. . . . It is inspiring and has been carefully framed so as to reach the Russian public. I have no hesitancy in saying that fifty copies of this film should be bought at once and set up in fifty different centers in Russia." At least one copy fell into Bolshevik hands at some point, for it numbered among the three movies (together with an American presentation on Ford's automobile factory and a Soviet film on the Revolution) beside a projector in Lenin's office at the end of his life—a celluloid combination of American *tekhnika* and Russian revolutionary spirit.[64]

No statistics exist to suggest the number of people who viewed cinematic gospels of America during the civil war. The total must have been well into the thousands, given the amount of film traveling around the country, but nothing more than guesswork is possible. So, too, with the central question regarding the audiences' response. The films were assembled to promote features of the "American myth"—a smiling, sunny land of prosperity and technological marvels—and it seems prudent to suppose that they had some such effect on many viewers. Film crews did not, apparently, have difficulty attracting crowds to watch their programs, and one source indicated that people were especially taken by footage of agricultural methods in the United States. An American working to maintain railroads in the Russian Far East, not yet under Bolshevik control in 1921, wrote to the U.S. secretary of state that Russian railway employees had asked if American industrial films could be screened for them. With assistance from the YMCA, a projector was rigged in a railway car, and roughly one hundred Russian employees and their children squeezed in for a show featuring scenes of coal mining and the operation of several electric railway terminals in principal American cities. "The audience was a most appreciative one," reported the American, "and I have heard much talk among the Russians about it today. They want to know why they do not have such things. I have never seen an audience follow anything more closely than they did."[65]

This testimony should not obscure the fact that the entire Creel episode in Russia passed mainly in remote provinces and soon expired even there, for the Bolsheviks naturally put an end to it as they extended their sway through outlying regions. Thereafter, overt American propaganda films disappeared, though American companies still publicized their products occasionally on the flickering screen. According to a Ford delegation that toured the Soviet Union in 1926, "motion pictures constitute the best medium of advertising Ford products in Soviet Russia. . . . Should any new pictures be gotten out in the future (we have shown all the old ones and they are still being shown in the USSR), it is suggested that copies thereof with Russian titles be sent to the two largest distributing organizations for proper showing." The delegation set up its projector in "theatres, workers' clubs, in the streets, and in fact everywhere any large number of people collected." They even provided shows—detailing the assembly of a Fordson tractor, for example—while traveling on a boat up the Volga River. Much as Clarissa Ware discovered a few years before, audiences followed these industrial films avidly. "We cannot too highly recommend the use of up-to-date films illustrative of any or all phases of Ford industry . . . for future sales propaganda work in the Soviet Union," concluded the delegation.[66]

Attentive as viewers may have been to Ford's promotional footage, their number paled before the throngs drawn by hundreds of Hollywood features that played in Soviet cities and towns during the 1920s. Most important, the American comedies, adventures, and melodramas enjoyed by millions of Soviet citizens often included scenes that appeared to corroborate assumptions about thriving, fast-paced America. According to one film historian, Hollywood's offerings of that period (to say nothing of decades to come) teemed with characters who had "lovely homes and lovely clothes and lovely cars and lovely lives," while another account noted, "silk stockings, silk underwear, furs, automobiles, phonographs, elaborate furniture, servants, apartment houses, electrically equipped kitchens, hotels, night clubs, country clubs, resorts, sports, colleges—these were paraded across the screen in exaggerated splendor." Even when audiences watched a villain or buffoon from high society, they also saw the opulence of the characters' surroundings. As reported in *Pravda*, a study of several hundred Soviet juveniles (88 percent of whom attended the cinema at least three or four times a month) found that "almost all" of them ranked foreign films above Soviet alternatives because, among other things, "another life is shown there [abroad]," where "rich people live it up," while "what they show in our land is boring and *poor.*" Movies whose heroes employed skill and daring to climb the social ladder served to advertise not only American bounty but also the opportunities thought to exist there for one and all.[67]

Brewster's Millions (1921, starring Roscoe "Fatty" Arbuckle) represented a farcical extreme as it toured the Soviet Union during the second half of the decade. Riches galore cascade into the lap of Monte Brewster, more rapidly than his binges deplete them. Early in the story, he inherits two million dollars from one grandfather, prompting his other grandfather to offer him five times that amount if he can exhaust the original inheritance in one year while avoiding marriage. Try as he might to consume the two million dollars, Monte grows ever more wealthy until a yachting voyage to Peru turns calamitous and appears to bankrupt him. But all ends well when the salvaged yacht brings new funds, supplemented by the shrewd investments of his girlfriend (eventually his wife), who has secretly been making wiser use of Brewster's millions.[68]

This sort of tale prompted an article in a Soviet film journal to ask, "from our communist point of view," what benefit could come from foreign movies highlighting "the bourgeoisie living in palaces, dining in fashionable restaurants with orchestras and dancing, engaging in romance, and getting married (after all, every foreign film has a happy ending with a wedding)?" Even though Soviet authorities added subtitles to some foreign films in order to emphasize, for example, that "the exploiter-vampires spend their 'working day' in restaurants," the article's author doubted the effectiveness of this commentary. Officials "think they are compromising them [the bourgeoisie] with the extra titles, while the action in the film shows them in a good light, which sometimes pleases and infects the viewer."[69]

Observers in many countries had no doubt that Hollywood films heralded the United States. Will Hays, the powerful president of the Motion Picture Producers and Distributors of America, wrote in 1924 that "steps have been taken to make certain that every picture which is made here shall correctly portray American life, opportunities and aspirations to the world." When Hays concluded that "we are going to sell America to the world with American pictures," it sounded like a global public service. Foreigners, who recognized the marketing clout of American films, often found it difficult to share Hays's enthusiasm. "The fact is," complained a member of the British House of Lords in 1925, "the Americans realised almost instantaneously that the cinema was a heaven-sent method for advertising themselves, their country, their methods, their wares, their ideas, and even their language, and they have seized upon it as a method of persuading the whole world, civilised and uncivilised, into the belief that America is really the only country which counts." Four years later Horace Villard, a senior officer in the U.S. State Department, produced a memorandum grounded in the assumption that American movies influenced opinions formed about the United States. Alas, he argued, Hollywood's pictures featured crime and "scenes of wealth, fast living or immorality." Under this influence, more foreigners would soon regard America as "the land where everyone achieves financial or industrial success"—and seek to emigrate with unrealistic expectations that Villard predicted would result in "disillusion and resentment."[70]

American movies certainly entranced audiences in the Soviet Union during the 1920s, and many of these films portrayed a luxurious, mesmerizing life in which the fruits of modern technology figured as routine accessories. More difficult to confirm is the plausible assumption that Hollywood's fare helped shape Russian images of the United States. Nothing from this period enables the statistical exercises performed in surveys of American television's international impact, but the findings of these recent studies lend support by analogy to hypotheses regarding an earlier generation of Soviet movie audiences. However far-fetched the plots of some U.S. television programs, for instance, they are often assumed by foreign viewers to be taking place against a largely accurate background of American life. Most respondents in a Thai study declared American shows a reliable window on life in the United States and cited the program *Dallas* frequently in this regard, as did viewers in Taiwan and Mexico.[71] The power of television on their imaginations suggests a parallel role played by Hollywood movies during the Soviet Union's initial decade.

While the impact of American television varies from country to country, the programs have conveyed some of the same impressions as movies sixty years before. Asked to describe people living in the United States, respondents in the television studies supplied clusters of adjectives that included laudatory terms with which many Russians could have agreed in the 1920s. Although an audience often encounters self-centered and violent characters, even they cavort frequently in sumptuous settings that mislead foreign viewers about American prosperity. Little wonder, then, that a study in Israel reported American television contributing to exaggerated opinions of the wealth possessed by most citizens of the United States. Indeed, the heavier an Israeli's diet of American programs, a researcher concluded, the greater the overestimation of American abundance.[72]

These studies also noted that television's influence increased among people who had scant contact with Americans and that the programming's most pronounced effect was to reinforce opinions of the United States that viewers had already conceived from other sources of information.[73] Much the same might be said of American movies in the Soviet Union during the 1920s. Few among the millions of viewers could have relied on personal experience for impressions of America, while the substitute they received from Hollywood corresponded well with popular images of the United States widespread for decades. Testimony from the likes of Peter Tverskoi, the tales of Nat Pinkerton, letters from countrymen in the New World, American tractors, and famine relief all pointed to an affluent nation and sometimes encouraged visions of a people living like kings amid technology that bordered on the magical. Theodore Dreiser discovered Russians convinced of this with a certainty that owed much to Hollywood: "And, oh, if each could only get to America, melt (as each is sure he would) into all the joys and glories he sees depicted in the American movies! Oh! Oh! Oh!"[74] Dreiser may have been exaggerating, but he drew on fact rather than fiction.

Thus the "American myth" continued to receive nourishment from a variety of sources after the Bolshevik Revolution. Even works published by the party's own press sometimes included lines that seemed to encourage notions of the United States as a land of riches and astonishing technology. When *Pravda* mentioned that "wages in America for all segments of the population are higher than in Europe," or when a Soviet worker recently returned from training at a Ford factory could explain in print "how far domestic communications and the blistering pace of business in America surpass business activity in the most developed of the industrialized countries of Europe," the "golden America" in Russian imaginations faced no danger of extinction from criticism published by the same presses. How could *Pravda* discredit "American dreams" when the paper also carried an article by a prominent Bolshevik who noted that "each American farmer has his own car, . . . and a large number of workers have Fords"? Indeed, the article continued, "two years ago in America we saw migrant agricultural laborers (that is, the poorest peasants) traveling in their own Fords. Even Negro sharecroppers, the most deprived segment of the semi-proletariat, acquired these vehicles."[75] A remarkable amount of this positive comment reached the public for several years through channels maintained by the government itself. Similar doors would open for American popular culture when it arrived in force by the mid-1920s, despite the fact that it vexed many party members as much as it delighted the population they hoped to mobilize.

Notes

1. William Richardson, *"To the World of the Future"*: *Mexican Visitors to the USSR, 1920–1940* (Pittsburgh: University of Pittsburgh, Carl Beck Papers, 1993), 18, 23; Records of the Department of State Relating to Internal Affairs of Russia and the Soviet Union,1930–1939 (hereafter cited as State Department Records, 1930–39), 861.5017/79 and 861.5017/425.

2. Maurice Hindus, "Henry Ford Conquers Russia," *Outlook*, 29 June 1927, 280, 283; Kendall E. Bailes, "The American Connection: Ideology and the Transfer of American Technology to the Soviet Union, 1917–1941," *Comparative Studies in Society and History* 23, no. 3 (July 1981): 436.

3. Theodore Dreiser, *Dreiser Looks at Russia* (New York: Horace Liveright, 1928), 52–53.

4. Maurice Hindus, *Green Worlds: An Informal Chronicle* (New York: Doubleday, Doran, 1938), 74–75; Charles Rougle, *Three Russians Consider America: America in the Works of Maxsim Gor'kij, Aleksandr Blok, and Vladimir Majakovskij* (Stockholm: Almqvist and Wiksell International, 1976), 111.

5. *Pravda*, 3 April 1926, 1.

6. *Izvestiia*, 1 June 1929, 2.

7. Maurice Hindus, *Red Bread: Collectivization in a Russian Village* (Bloomington: Indiana University Press, 1988), 22.

8. Jeffrey Brooks, "The Press and Its Message: Images of America in the 1920s and 1930s," in *Russia in the Era of NEP: Explorations in Soviet Society and Culture*, ed. Sheila Fitzpatrick, Alexander Rabinowitch, and Richard Stites (Bloomington: Indiana University Press, 1991), 238.

9. Hans Rogger, "America in the Russian Mind—or Russian Discoveries of America," *Pacific Historical Review* 47, no. 1 (February 1978): 47–48; Brooks, "Press," 239.

10. Hans Rogger, "How the Soviets See Us," in *Shared Destiny: Fifty Years of Soviet-American Relations*, ed. Mark Garrison and Abbott Gleason (Boston: Beacon, 1985), 125.

11. Jeffrey Brooks, *When Russia Learned to Read: Literacy and Popular Literature, 1861–1917* (Princeton, N.J.: Princeton University Press, 1985), xv, 4, 38. The figure of roughly twenty-three thousand rural primary schools in the early 1880s covers only European Russia, though this is where the overwhelming majority of rural primary schools were located.

12. Brooks, *When Russia Learned to Read*, 61, 112. See also Louise McReynolds, *The News under Russia's Old Regime: The Development of a Mass-Circulation Press* (Princeton, N.J.: Princeton University Press, 1991), for more on increasing newspaper circulation.

13. Ernest R. May, *Imperial Democracy: The Emergence of America as a Great Power* (New York: Harcourt Brace, 1961; Chicago: Imprint, 1991), 190; Valentin Kiparsky, *English and American Characters in Russian Fiction* (Wiesbaden, West Germany: Otto Harrassowitz, 1964), 155–56; Anton Chekhov, *Boys* (Moscow: Progress, 1979), 15; Richard Ruland, *America in Modern European Literature: From Image to Metaphor* (New York: New York University Press, 1976), 71.

14. Rogger, "How the Soviets See Us," 115; Hans Rogger, "America Enters the Twentieth Century: The View from Russia," in *Felder und Vorfelder russischer Geschichte*, ed. Inge Auerbach et al. (Freiburg, West Germany: Rombach, 1985), 169.

15. For summaries of several such works, see Hans Rogger, "*Amerikanizm* and the Economic Development of Russia," *Comparative Studies in Society and History* 23, no. 3 (July 1981): 382–420. Regarding articles about the United States published earlier in the nineteenth century, see Ia. A. Ivanchenko, "Pozitsiia redaktsionnogo kruzhka 'Moskovskogo telegrafa' v otnoshenii Soedinennykh Shtatov," in *Amerikanskii ezhegodnik, 1980* (Moscow: Nauka, 1981), 216–35.

16. P. A. Tverskoi, *Ocherki Severo-Amerikanskikh Soedinennykh Shtatov* (St. Petersburg: Tipografiia I. N. Skorokhodova, 1895), 37, 142–43, 152.

17. Brooks, *When Russia Learned to Read*, 142–44, 147–48.

18. Brooks, *When Russia Learned to Read*, 142, 151–53.

19. Brooks, "Press," 236.

20. Regarding Germany, see Ruland, *America*, 25–26. Regarding Russia, see Rogger, "America Enters," 168–69; Rogger, "How the Soviets See Us," 115.

21. George M. Stephenson, "When America Was the Land of Canaan," *Minnesota History* 10, no. 3 (September, 1929): 238–39.

22. Hindus, *Green Worlds*, 72–73.

23. Ruland, *America*, 31.

24. Goldie Stone, *My Caravan of Years: An Autobiography* (New York: Bloch, 1945), 55. See also Mary Antin, *The Promised Land* (Boston: Houghton Mifflin, 1912), 162; Wasyl Halich, *Ukrainians in the United States* (Chicago: University of Chicago Press, 1937), 13; Merle Curti and Kendall Birr, "The Immigrant and the American Image in Europe, 1860–1914," *Mississippi Valley Historical Review* 37 (September 1950): 203–230; and Irving Howe, *World of Our Fathers* (New York: Harcourt Brace Jovanovich, 1976), 24, 35.

25. Figures derived from data in Maurice R. Davie, *World Immigration: With Special Reference to the United States* (New York: Macmillan, 1936), 53.

26. L. A. Bagramov, *Immigranty v SShA* (Moscow: Izdatel'stvo IMO, 1957), 31; A. N. Shlepakov, *Immigratsiia i amerikanskii rabochii klass v epokhu imperializma* (Moscow: Izdatel'stvo Mysl', 1966), 36; Dirk Hoerder and Diethelm Knauf, eds., *Fame, Fortune, and Sweet Liberty: The Great European Emigration* (Bremen: Edition Temmen, 1992), 55.

27. Davie, *World Immigration*, 135, 138, 142, 152; W. F. Willcox, ed., *International Migrations*, vol. 2 (New York: National Bureau of Economic Research, 1931), 529, 542–43; Shlepakov, *Immigratsiia*, 37; Bagramov, *Immigranty*, 32; V. M. Kabuzan, *Emigratsiia i reemigratsiia v Rossii v XVIII–nachale XX veka* (Moscow: Nauka, 1998), 143.

28. Willcox, *International Migrations*, 528.

29. Curti and Birr, "Immigrant," 206; Philip Taylor, *The Distant Magnet: European Emigration to the U.S.A.* (London: Eyre & Spottiswoode, 1971), 74. See also Adolf Gerd Korman, "A Social History of Industrial Growth and Immigrants: A Study with Particular Reference to Milwaukee 1880–1920" (Ph.D. diss., University of Wisconsin at Madison, 1959).

30. Carl B. Schmidt, "Reminiscences of Foreign Immigration Work for Kansas," *Transactions of the Kansas State Historical Society, 1905–1906* 9 (1905–1906): 493. Nearly 2000 Mennonites traveled to Kansas from Russia that year and purchased 60,000 acres of land.

31. Hoerder and Knauf, *Fame, Fortune, and Sweet Liberty*, 82, 94–95; *Emigration Conditions in Europe*, 61st Cong., 3d sess., 1911. S. Doc. 748, 61–62; Taylor, *Distant Magnet*, 79–81; Dirk Hoerder and Leslie Page Moch, eds., *European Migrants: Global and Local Perspectives* (Boston: Northeastern University Press, 1996), 184; Curti and Birr, "Immigrant," 211.

32. "Emigration Conditions in Europe," 62–63; I. K. Okuntsov, *Russkaia emigratsiia v Severnoi i Iuzhnoi Amerike* (Buenos Aires: Izdatel'stvo Seiatel', 1967), 219; "Konsul'skiia doneseniia. Russkaia emigratsiia v Soedinennye Shtaty. Sovetnika Posol'stva v Vashingtone st. sov. Shcherbatskogo," in *Izvestiia ministerstva inostrannykh del 1914 g.*, kniga VI (Petrograd: Tipografiia V. O. Kirshbauma, 1914), 126.

33. Shlepakov, *Immigratsiia*, 41; Sune Åkerman, "Towards an Understanding of Emigrational Processes," in *Human Migration: Patterns and Policies*, ed. William H. McNeill and Ruth S. Adams (Bloomington: Indiana University Press, 1978), 295; Taylor, *Distant Magnet*, 84–85.

34. *Emigration Conditions in Europe*, 57; "Konsul'skiia doneseniia," 128.

35. Stephenson, "When America Was the Land of Canaan," 238; Stone, *My Caravan*, 56. See also Jerome Dwight Davis, *The Russian Immigrant* (New York: Macmillan, 1922), 8; Konstantin Grigor'evich Voblyi, *Zaatlanticheskaia emigratsiia, ee prichiny i sledstviia* (Warsaw: Tipografiia Varshavskago Uchebnago Okruga, 1904), 94; Curti and Birr, "Immigrant," 216, 218; Taylor, *Distant Magnet*, 87; Korman, "Social History," 79.

36. Vladimir G. Korolenko, *In a Strange Land* (New York: Richards, 1925), 6–9.

37. Halich, *Ukrainians*, 15–16; Hoerder and Moch, *European Migrants*, 188; Curti and Birr, "Immigrant," 216.

38. Hoerder and Moch, *European Migrants*, 193; Okuntsov, *Russkaia emigratsiia*, 226; *Emigration Conditions in Europe*, 57; Hindus, *Green Worlds*, 76.

39. Willcox, *International Migrations*, 524, 530; Bagramov, *Immigranty*, 32; Davie, *World Immigration*, 165–66. See also Kabuzan, *Emigratsiia*, 187, 189, 192–94.

40. J. D. Gould, "European Inter-Continental Emigration. The Road Home: Return Migration from the U.S.A.," *Journal of European Economic History* 9, no. 1 (Spring 1980): 51–52, 65–68.

41. Halich, *Ukrainians*, 16–17; Taylor, *Distant Magnet*, 90; "Emigration Conditions in Europe," 52, 58; Janja Zitnik, "Louis Adamic's Image of America as It Has Been Presented to the Slovene Reading Public," *Slovene Studies* 13, no. 1 (1991): 115–16; Mark Wyman, *Round-Trip to America: The Immigrants Return to Europe, 1880–1930* (Ithaca, N.Y.: Cornell University Press, 1993), 201–202, 206.

42. Rogger, "How the Soviets See Us," 119.

43. For similar but not identical sets of figures, see *Making Things Work: Russian-American Economic Relations, 1900–1930* (Stanford, Calif.: Hoover Institution Press, 1992), 47, 51; Frederick V. Carstensen, "American Multinational Corporations in Imperial Russia" (Ph.D. diss., Yale University, 1976), 64.

44. Carstensen, "American Multinational Corporations," 301; Robert V. Allen, *Russia Looks at America: The View to 1917* (Washington, D.C.: Library of Congress; U.S. Government Printing Office, 1988), 179; *Making Things Work*, 13.

45. American Relief Administration. Russian Unit. A Register of its Records in the Hoover Institution Archives, ii, Hoover Institution Archives. Another source indicates that a total of roughly four hundred Americans worked for the ARA in Soviet Russia for varying periods during these years. Bertrand M. Patenaude, *Herbert Hoover's Brush with Bolshevism* (Washington, D.C.: Kennan Institute for Advanced Russian Studies, Woodrow Wilson International Center for Scholars, 1992), 2.

46. Walter A. McDougall, *Promised Land, Crusader State: The American Encounter with the World since 1776* (New York: Houghton Mifflin, 1997), 176. "The Secretary of Commerce (Hoover) to the Secretary of State," in *Papers Relating to the Foreign Relations of the United States. 1921*, vol. II (Washington, D.C.: Government Printing Office, 1936), 787–88. Regarding relief efforts in other European countries, Hoover wrote in 1925 that "at no time were we of any other mind than that the European relief in 1919 was the greatest battle ever made against Bolshevism." Patenaude, *Herbert Hoover's Brush with Bolshevism*, 3.

47. *Rossiia i SShA: torgovo-ekonomicheskie otnosheniia 1900–1930. Sbornik dokumentov*, ed. G. Sevost'ianov (Moscow: Nauka, 1996), 261–62. For a similar statement sent by Foreign Minister George Chicherin to the *Chicago Tribune*, see Tarun Chandra Bose, *American Soviet Relations 1921–1933* (Calcutta: Mukhopadhyay, 1967), 41.

48. Brooks, "Press," 245.

49. For the letters themselves, see American Relief Administration, Russian Operations, box 6, folder no. 2, Hoover Institution Archives.

50. Brooks, "Press," 244–45; Benjamin M. Weissman, "The Aftereffects of the American Relief Mission to Soviet Russia," *Russian Review* 29, no. 4 (October 1970): 414.

51. Anatole Shub, *What Russians Know and Think about America: A Survey in Summer 1995* (Washington, D.C.: Office of Research and Media Reaction, USIA, 1995), 2. See also David C. Engerman, "America, Russia, and the Romance of Economic Development" (Ph.D. diss., University of California at Berkeley, 1998), 288.

52. M. I. Rybinskii and G. Ia. Tarle, "O pomoshchi trudiashchikhsia zarubezhnikh stran sovetskomu sel'skomu khoziaistvu (1921–1925 gg.)," *Istoricheskii arkhiv*, no. 4 (1961): 74–75; *Pravda*, 16

November 1923, 1; Richard Stites, *Revolutionary Dreams: Utopian Vision and Experimental Life in the Russian Revolution* (Oxford: Oxford University Press, 1989), 211.

53. *Rossiia i SShA: torgovo-ekonomicheskie otnosheniia*, 318, 330; G. E. Reikhberg and B. S. Shapik, "Ob uchastii Amerikanskikh rabochikh v vosstanovlenii narodnogo khoziaistva sovetskoi respubliki," *Istoriia SSSR*, no. 1 (1961): 150–52; E. I. Popova, "1920–1922: Amerikantsy i Sovetskaia Rossiia," *SShA: Ekonomika, politika, ideologiia*, no. 11 (November 1970): 57–58.

54. Rybinskii and Tarle, "O pomoshchi trudiashchikhsia," 63, 72; *Pravda*, 5 December 1923, 4.

55. Dana G. Dalrymple, "The American Tractor Comes to Soviet Agriculture: The Transfer of a Technology," *Technology and Culture* 5, no. 2 (Spring 1964): 193, 202–203, 208–209.

56. Clarissa S. Ware, "In Russia with Western Pioneers," *Survey* 19, no. 3 (1 November 1922): 163–64.

57. *Rossiia i SShA: torgovo-ekonomicheskie otnosheniia*, 323; Bruce Bliven, "Mr. Ware and the Peasants," *New Republic*, 22 July 1925, 233; Ware, "In Russia," 164–65.

58. Dalrymple, "American Tractor," 203; Marian Tyler, "The American God in Russia," *Nation*, 12 January 1927, 37–38; Ford Motor Company, "Report of the Ford Delegation to Russia and the U.S.S.R." (1926) 14–46, Ford Motor Company Archives.

59. Dana G. Dalrymple, "American Technology and Soviet Agricultural Development, 1924–1933," *Agricultural History* 40 (1966): 197–98; Dalrymple, "American Tractor," 204–205.

60. Floyd J. Fithian, "Soviet-American Economic Relations, 1918–1933: American Business in Russia during the Period of Non-recognition" (Ph.D. diss., University of Nebraska, 1964), 307.

61. Hindus, "Henry Ford," 283.

62. Merle Curti, *American Philanthropy Abroad: A History* (New Brunswick, N.J.: Rutgers University Press, 1963), 365–69; Dalrymple, "American Tractor," 193, 203; *Pravda*, 26 July 1923, 3.

63. George Creel, *How We Advertised America* (New York: Harper & Brothers, 1920; reprint, New York: Arno, 1972), 274–75, 278–79; Kristin Thompson, *Exporting Entertainment: America in the World Film Market, 1907–1934* (London: BFI, 1985), 98; James R. Mock and Cedric Larson, *Words That Won the War* (Princeton, N.J.: Princeton University Press, 1939), 312.

64. State Department Records, 1910–29, 861.4061/12; *New York Times*, 26 January 1924.

65. Thompson, *Exporting Entertainment*, 98; State Department Records, 1910–29, 861.4061/14. See also 861.4061/13.

66. "Report of the Ford Delegation," 201, 264–65.

67. Garth Jowett, *Film: The Democratic Art* (Boston: Little, Brown, 1976), 186; Lewis Jacobs, *The Rise of the American Film: A Critical History* (New York: Teachers College, Columbia University, 1968), 276, 407; *Pravda*, 6 January 1928, 4. Regarding similar influence of Hollywood elsewhere in Europe after World War I, see Thomas J. Saunders, *Hollywood in Berlin: American Cinema and Weimar Germany* (Berkeley: University of California Press, 1994), 11, 14–15; Ralph Willett, *The Americanization of Germany, 1945–1949* (London: Routledge, 1989), 28; Doeko Bosscher, Marja Roholl, and Mel van Elteren, eds., *American Culture in the Netherlands* (Amsterdam: VU University Press, 1996), 14, 22.

68. In the Soviet Union the film was retitled *Fatty the Millionaire (Fatti-Millioner)*. For a list of American silent films distributed in the Soviet Union, see E. Kartseva, "Amerikanskie nemye fil'my v sovetskom prokate," in *Kino i vremia. Biulleten'*, no. 1 (Moscow: Vsesoiuznyi gosudarstvennyi fond kinofil'mov ministerstva kul'tury SSSR, 1960), 193–325. For plot summaries of American films from this era, see *The American Film Institute Catalog of Motion Pictures Produced in the United States: Feature Films 1921–1930*, ed. Kenneth W. Munden (New York: Bowker, 1971).

69. D. Liianov, "Ob upriamoi deistvitel'nosti i bol'nykh nervakh," *Sovetskoe kino*, nos. 2–3 (1925): 21.

70. All quotations are from Ian Jarvie, *Hollywood's Overseas Campaign: The North Atlantic Movie Trade, 1920–1950* (Cambridge: Cambridge University Press, 1992), 111, 305, 326.

71. Gabriel Weiman, "Images of Life in America: The Impact of American T.V. in Israel," *International Journal of Intercultural Relations* 8, no. 2 (1984): 185; Alexis S. Tan and Kultida Suarchavarat, "American TV and Social Stereotypes of Americans in Thailand," *Journalism Quarterly* 65 (Fall 1988): 650–51; Alexis S. Tan, Sarrina Li, and Charles Simpson, "American TV and Social Stereotypes of Americans in Taiwan and Mexico," *Journalism Quarterly* 63 (Winter 1986): 812. The Mexican sample ranked *Dynasty* and *Dallas* close together at the top of the list of programs thought to depict American life most accurately. For studies of American television and movies in diverse countries, and a discussion of the degree to which this entertainment contributes to the formation of images of the United States, see Yahya R. Kamalipour, ed., *Images of the U.S. around the World: A Multicultural Perspective* (Albany, N.Y.: State University of New York Press, 1999).

72. Tan and Suarchavarat, "American TV in Thailand," 651; Tan et al., "American TV in Taiwan and Mexico," 812–13; Weiman, "Images of Life," 188, 190; Reinhold Wagnleitner and Elaine Tyler May, eds., *"Here, There and Everywhere": The Foreign Politics of American Popular Culture* (Hanover, N.H.: University Press of New England, 2000), 141.

73. Tan and Suarchavarat, "American TV in Thailand," 654; Tan et al., "American TV in Taiwan and Mexico," 809; Weiman, "Images of Life," 195.

74. Dreiser, *Dreiser Looks at Russia*, 53.

75. *Pravda*, 21 July 1927, 3; S. G. Ledenev, *Za stankom u Forda: Iz vpechatlenii uchastnika poezdki na traktornye zavody S.-A. S. Sh.* (Moscow-Leningrad: Gosudarstvennoe izdatel'stvo, 1927), 119.

CHAPTER THREE

~

Happy Endings and Jolly Guys

The cinema is a club. People come together here to undergo a moral experience, to travel to America, to learn about tobacco farming and the stupidity of policemen, to sigh over the *midinette* who has to sell her body.

—Andrei Belyi

At the hotel I found a jazz dance in full swing—and an American jazz tune—A Night of Love. And Russian men in evening dress—and Russian girls, the smartest of course, in short skirts, and bobbed hair dancing the latest steps.

—Theodore Dreiser

"You know," Nikita Khrushchev told Dwight Eisenhower while visiting the United States in 1959, "when Stalin was alive, we used to watch Westerns all the time. When the movie ended, Stalin always denounced it for its ideological content. But the very next day we'd be back in the [Kremlin's] movie theater watching another Western. I too have a weakness for this sort of film."[1] Even during the most xenophobic period of Stalin's rule, when his own officials excoriated American culture, Stalin continued to enjoy Hollywood's sagas in private. Nor were Stalin and Khrushchev the only ones smitten. During the twentieth century American popular culture seduced millions around the world, regardless of their governments' dismay. Never had human beings witnessed such rapid transmission of mass entertainment—a feature of the new age, modernists proclaimed, and a phenomenon that bedeviled Soviet leaders throughout the twentieth century.

By 1928, when an author titled his essay on film "The Great American Art," few people doubted America's claim to preeminence in the motion picture industry.[2] If many would have argued the point two decades earlier, when Europe produced more than half the world's films, they could not have held such an opinion for many years thereafter. Halfway through the 1920s, American exports accounted for three-quarters of all the movies shown worldwide—95 percent of the market in Great Britain, Australia, New Zealand, and Canada, 90 percent in Argentina, 85 percent in Scandinavia, 75 percent in Brazil, and 70 percent in France.[3] As the Hollywood juggernaut obliterated foreign film industries in the 1920s, even the House of Lords stirred to ponder the virtual demise of British movie production. Viscount Peel echoed concerns of officials elsewhere, including the Soviet Union, when he observed, "If you talk to the exhibitors, they will tell you that, for some reason or other, these American films, whether owing to their good qualities or their bad qualities . . . for the moment seem to attract audiences far more magnetically than British films."[4]

Someone pursuing the topic that perplexed Viscount Peel would likely begin with World War I to explain Hollywood's success. While French companies ruled the world's trade in movies before 1914, the Great War soon undermined film industries throughout Europe. Wartime shortages of resources, and especially the disruption of the belligerents' customary international trade, left many parts of the world starved for movies. Hollywood not only benefited from the sudden absence of foreign competition in the United States, it plunged into the international market that its weakened rivals could no longer control. Here was another American industry invigorated by warfare that sapped its European counterparts. Within a few years of the armistice, American films crowded screens in Europe itself, to say nothing of other far-flung lands. Meanwhile, American distributors ceased to rely on British and other foreign agents to handle sales abroad. They opened their own offices around the world, establishing integrated systems that tied theaters and distributors together through standing film orders and other devices that had evolved in the United States during the war.

While European conflict and direct American involvement in foreign sales contributed to Hollywood's triumph, so did the films themselves. By the 1920s, even with the war now lifted from the neck of the European film industry, audiences craved American movies. Owners of foreign theaters agreed to American marketing terms as the surest way to sell tickets, for Hollywood's films had acquired a unique identity and appeal. Prior to the 1920s, and especially before 1914, American movies often carried a moralizing tone and attempted serious social commentary. But as the industry groped toward a mass audience, lighter fare appeared more frequently, and Hollywood soon mastered such categories as the western, slapstick comedies, melodramas, and costume adventures. All were silent films, of course, which speakers of any language could follow.

By perfecting these genres, American producers distinguished their films from foreign competition. They did so as well by developing a star system that promoted actors and actresses as heavily as the films themselves. People filled theaters not just to view a car chase or a cowboy but to see Mary Pickford, Douglas Fairbanks, and Charlie Chaplin. Audiences expected their idols to remain "in character" from one film to the next, and Hollywood learned not to disappoint them. Charlie Chaplin could not be Zorro, and Douglas Fairbanks could not be a bumbling tramp. American companies spent lavishly to promote their stars, who far exceeded in number and collective drawing power the most popular actors abroad. Hollywood also allocated more money to production, discovering that films with expensive technical features could still turn a profit, especially against shabbier foreign competition. In fact, by the mid-1920s, major American studios were spending so much to produce movies that they could not count on a profit from the domestic market alone. Hence their tenacious pursuit of foreign customers, whom they won by delivering a reliable supply of a popular product at a competitive price and with consummate publicity.[5]

Before World War I, European companies made most of the films shown in Russia. The French firm Pathé Frères began producing movies in earnest at the turn of the century and soon dispatched agents around the globe to sell films and projection equipment. Between 1904 and 1907 Pathé opened offices in Moscow, St. Petersburg, Rostov-on-the-Don, Kiev, and Warsaw, to say nothing of other sites from New York to Singapore. French and Italian producers provided most of the movies shown in Russia's 1,200 theaters in 1911, and this western European advantage survived for three more years. Business thrived, with paid admissions exceeding 100 million in 1910, more than the number of Russians who attended "legitimate theater," music halls, and variety theater combined. "On Sundays and holidays," reported the American consul general in Moscow, "crowds are so great that additional police officers are often required to keep the immense number of people moving and to prevent possible accidents." A year later, the symbolist author Andrei Belyi maintained that "absolutely everyone" went to the movies: "aristocrats and democrats, soldiers, students, workers, schoolgirls, poets and prostitutes."[6]

The war complicated trade with Russia, leaving the country's theaters ever more dependent on movies made by the isolated domestic industry. This trickle, supplemented by surviving copies of old foreign films, accounted for nearly the entire selection available to Soviet audiences during the years of civil war and economic collapse following the Revolution. As late as 1921, only three feature films entered the Soviet market from Europe and America. But over the next few years, when the German and Soviet economies stabilized and the two governments took measures to encourage trade in films, new foreign titles traveled east. Now they began arriving from the United States, shipped to Moscow through Berlin. In 1922 only seven American feature films appeared in the Soviet Union, compared to forty-one selections from Germany and fifteen from France. The next year, Hollywood's contribution jumped to 101 features (35 percent of the Soviet market) and then soared in 1924 to 231 titles (57 percent of the market). In every remaining year of the decade, American movies reached Soviet screens in quantities greater than all other foreign films combined and larger than the number of Soviet films produced until 1928.[7] At the same time "cinema installations," which included clubs and mobile projection units as well as theaters, multiplied to 7,331 by 1928. If this seemed modest compared to the roughly 21,000 projectors in the United States or the 27,578 in the Soviet Union five years later, it marked a significant increase over Russia's 1,412 cinemas in 1914. Projectors remained rare in the countryside, but most provincial cities had two or three theaters by 1927, and Moscow boasted fifty.[8]

Lenin hailed film as a device to educate and inspire the population to build socialism, a goal remote from the concerns of Hollywood studios. Thus the Soviet purge of American films from the nation's theaters in the early 1930s may seem less surprising than the fact that over the preceding decade the government imported nearly one thousand of Hollywood's offerings. Yet the very importance attached to cinema by Soviet officials helps explain their purchase of Western films with no redeeming revolutionary content. Just as Bolsheviks held their noses and legalized private trade in the 1920s in order to revive the economy and thereby lay a foundation for socialism, they hoped that profits made from foreign films would invigorate their own film industry. People willing to buy expensive tickets to see Douglas Fairbanks and Charlie Chaplin would be helping to purchase equipment that Soviet filmmakers sorely needed. Once these directors received adequate supplies, they could produce films in harmony with the party's agenda.[9]

Meanwhile, along with generating funds, foreign films would serve to keep Soviet theaters open until sufficient home-grown attractions were produced for their screens. American movies often debuted at the grandest cinemas in Moscow and other cities, where high ticket prices and large crowds yielded receipts far beyond those garnered from Soviet productions distributed to "cinema installations" in workers' clubs and the countryside. "If we import nothing from abroad," explained the commissar of enlightenment, Anatoly Lunacharsky, "then we will either have to hold our own pictures indefinitely in deserted theaters or produce at least twice as many films," requiring resources not yet at hand. Lenin acknowledged that viewers might not come at all to "educational" Soviet pictures without "useless" (that is, entertaining, often foreign) movies to entice them. As an antidote to the ideological contamination threatened by "bourgeois" imports, the government required that they be shown as part of a program that included a short Soviet film or even a lecture with a more suitable message.[10]

For nearly a decade, then, Soviet movie audiences possessed an array of options broader than any they would face thereafter. Straightforward political fare on the evils of capitalism and the virtues of socialism competed for attention with various films by modernist directors and also with escapist amusements from the West—along with combinations of these choices, such as avant-garde presentations of revolutionary themes or rousing adventures with a sprinkling of ideological comment. Among these possibilities, the government encouraged the first choice, political scripts, while Western intellectuals eventually applauded the second, namely works by such visionary directors as Sergei Eisenstein and Vsevolod Pudovkin. But the Soviet public clearly favored its third alternative: films designed to entertain. This brought crowds to Hollywood's domain, which they could enter freely, if not inexpensively, for the better part of the 1920s.

Shortly after the Revolution the young Soviet director Lev Kuleshov listed his conclusions regarding the preferences of Russian film audiences:

1. Foreign releases give more pleasure than Russian ones. 2. The most popular foreign films are all American-made detective pictures. The audience is especially receptive to American films. A successful move by the hero, a desperate chase, a daring fight causes whistles of delight, howls and whoops, and intensely interested figures jump up from their seats so that they can see the interesting action better.[11]

If Kuleshov's assessment appeared disputable when drafted in 1920 amid few American movies, or even when published in much the same form two years later, the influx of Hollywood films in 1923–24 erased any doubt about their popularity. Lunacharsky, whose Commissariat of Enlightenment oversaw the film industry, recognized the appeal of American imports. In an essay published at the end of 1926 he wondered how a movie could make a strong social or political statement and still attract an audience. After all, he explained, the public "wants to relax, wants to be entertained, wants to forget." When confronted with propaganda "it begins to get bored, it begins to feel that it is attending a lecture." It also rushes off to see Douglas Fairbanks in "such rubbish" as *The Thief of Bagdad*, which drubbed Soviet agitational films at the box office. If "propagandist cinema" lacked excitement, Lunacharsky emphasized, it would, "like a dry spoon, irritate the monk." Most politically minded films did not moisten the monk's spoon in the 1920s, prompting another commentator to observe more circumspectly that "our viewers often waver in their certainty that Soviet films will be entertaining."[12]

Lunacharsky understood the need to combine an appropriate political lesson with the spellbinding drama provided by Hollywood, and in 1926 a promising candidate reached Soviet cinemas. The *Battleship Potemkin*, Sergei Eisenstein's film about a mutiny of ill-treated sailors on a tsarist warship during the Revolution of 1905, seemed just the work Lunacharsky had in mind. Officials promoted the film heavily, even decorating as a battleship the Moscow theater in which *Potemkin* would open. Nothing, however, could lure much of the audience away from Douglas Fairbanks in *Robin Hood*. Later, following the success of *Potemkin* in Berlin, Soviet authorities tried again to establish the film as a popular triumph in Moscow. Larger crowds turned out to see what had caused a stir in the West—Douglas Fairbanks and Mary Pickford had been moved by the film in Berlin, *Pravda* reported—but the domestic response scarcely eclipsed Hollywood's appeal. "We have a whole series of examples of Soviet films that did not pay for themselves and failed," Lunacharsky declared in 1928. "True, many of them did not deserve success, but we also have examples of a different sort. It is rarely acknowledged that *Battleship Potemkin* did not have any success in our country."[13]

Kuleshov's essay located the attraction of American adventure films in "the build-up of the action and the entertainment value of the plot." The Americans emphasized movement, noted Kuleshov, and strove "to get as much plot as possible into a minute of footage." Hollywood had developed a formula for delivering excitement routinely at a level and pace that few Soviet features could match. Indeed, *The Thief of Bagdad* so captivated two Soviet critics that they found their own country's movies boring in comparison, as did many of their fellow citizens.[14] Fantasy worlds and gripping tales, not class struggle or grueling reality, sold tickets, and American films, especially comedies, also won favor with their cheerful tone. The brooding or fatalistic vision cultivated by much of the Russian artistic elite could not compete with the Hollywood *kheppi end* for the pocketbooks of the Soviet public. A film periodical noted that it had received numerous letters to the editor praising the upbeat conclusions of American movies: "You already know in advance what will happen in our [Soviet] movies," explained one viewer—"death, death without end. Soviet film is a story, sweetened by a hero and heroine, ending inevitably with death. Give us relaxation; it is for relaxation that people go to the movies."[15]

Film critics also pointed to the main characters in Hollywood pictures, calling them more believable or charismatic than their Soviet counterparts. Americans "know how to get the viewer to love the hero," observed a Soviet cinema publication. "We have not learned how to craft our heroes properly." And, of course, Hollywood's elite were *stars*, more famous than Soviet actors, even in Moscow or Leningrad. The Soviet film press itself promoted such foreign stars as Douglas Fairbanks, Mary Pickford, Charlie Chaplin, Buster Keaton, Lillian Gish, Harold Lloyd, and (the German) Harry Piel, who also appeared frequently in readers' letters to fan magazines. The Soviet publishing house for theater and film issued nearly two million copies of inexpensive biographies of foreign film idols over the period 1922–29, roughly one and a half million in 1926–27 alone (compared to only 260,000 copies of biographies of Soviet personalities). Revenue from these sales helped support the publishing house, just as ticket proceeds from foreign movies bolstered the Soviet film industry. Five reprintings of the Fairbanks and Pickford biographies totaled nearly a quarter of a million copies in just two years, while the biography of the most popular Soviet actor, the comic Igor Ilinsky, reached only sixty thousand copies.[16]

The money that foreign stars could generate for state agencies inspired diverse promotions. In Moscow, a neon display celebrated Fairbanks on a building in the Arbat district, while in a remote provincial town, the following advertisement invited locals to Pickford's film *The Love Light*, retitled *Light in the Darkness* in the Soviet Union:

> Light in the Darkness
> The international artist
> Mary Pickford
> In a new, never-before-seen role
> Hurry to see her!
> The Empress of the screen
> In Soviet Mikhailov
> Cinema "Armored Car"
> Only with us, almost monopolistically![17]

Soviet officials often retitled American films in order to feature the stars' names, as with twenty-two of the forty Charlie Chaplin movies they showed in the 1920s. Thus the *Champ* became *Charlie the Boxer* and *His Historic Past* (a caveman story) reached Soviet audiences as *Charlie Tarzan*, cashing in on both Chaplin and the popular Tarzan films of the day: *Romance of Tarzan*, *Return of Tarzan*, *Revenge of Tarzan*, and *Daughter of Tarzan*. While no one changed the titles of Fairbanks's films, his name appeared with them routinely in advertisements—"Douglas Fairbanks's *Robin Hood*," for instance, or "Douglas Fairbanks's *Mark of Zorro*"—something that was not done for Igor Ilinsky and other prominent Soviet actors. Fairbanks's *Thief of Bagdad* received unusually heavy promotion (even in the leading party and government newspapers) that included colorful leaflets scattered in the streets of Leningrad and a telephone campaign in which a hushed voice greeted residents with only the words "thief of Bagdad" before hanging up.[18]

Numerous people expressed admiration for Fairbanks in letters to editors or opinion surveys, and when he and Mary Pickford visited Moscow in the summer of 1926, they encountered the same enthusiastic crowds as elsewhere in Europe. A commemorative pamphlet titled "They Are Here" appeared in forty-five thousand copies, and cameramen filmed their every step.[19] In fact, enough film was shot of "Doug and Mary" to permit the director Sergei Komarov to combine footage of the two celebrities with his own material to produce a comedy the next year titled *The Kiss of Mary Pickford*. The plot features Igor Ilinsky as a minor cashier at a cinema box office. His love for a girl founders on her condition that he become famous before she will reciprocate his affection. One day, while he is serving as an extra in a stunt scene at a film studio, the crew dashes out to see Fairbanks and Pickford, who are visiting the facility. Left suspended in midair, he falls asleep until Pickford comes by. She gives him a kiss on the cheek, thereby guaranteeing his fame and the love of his girlfriend—at least until the lipstick wears off.[20] If Komarov was satirizing the cult of Fairbanks and Pickford, his film also recognized the existence of this adulation, without which *The Kiss of Mary Pickford* could not have been successful or even produced.

The prominence of American films surpassed their large share (over 40 percent) of new films released in the Soviet Union during the 1920s because Hollywood's pictures tended to run for periods of at least a few months in a city's biggest theaters. Soviet films, in contrast, often traveled directly to the libraries of unions and clubs without ever appearing in principal cinemas. If they did receive opportunities in prime facilities, the exposure generally did not exceed two weeks, while *The Thief of Bagdad* played Moscow's largest theater for three and a half months and remained in the capital for more than a year. Though few movies could rival the simultaneous appearance of Fairbanks's *Robin Hood* in fourteen of Moscow's fifty theaters, foreign films often graced more than one first-run screen at a time.[21] In the process they took in far more rubles per film than did Soviet movies, because the foreign pictures played before larger audiences and at premium ticket prices. Even as late as 1928, the state cinema agency received approximately 85 percent of its gross revenues from foreign (mainly American) films, though they represented only 33 percent of the titles shown that year. Viewed another way, the state reportedly collected a 100 percent profit on foreign films at this time, while suffering a 12 percent loss on the average Soviet movie. *The Thief of Bagdad*, which played for years in the Soviet Union after drawing over 1.7 million viewers in the first six months, may have been the decade's financial champion. Hollywood's box-office clout even persuaded authorities to advertise a Soviet film, *The Sold Appetite*, as a foreign production in order to enhance its appeal—much as a Soviet actress took the name Nina Lee for its American ring.[22]

Ignoring such evidence, a Soviet cinema official asserted in 1925 that "foreign films are unconditionally rejected by the worker audience almost without exception." Nothing could have been further from the truth, with the possible exception of his claim that the "Soviet scientific film *Abortion* had broken all the [box office] records set by foreign 'hits.'" This accomplishment allegedly occurred in Moscow's best theaters, demonstrating that "the workers' demand for really useful films is so great that they are not put off even by the high prices of the first-class cinemas." Compare this with the more accurate observation ventured a few months later by Grigory Boltiansky, head of Soviet newsreel production, that workers' film circles in clubs and factories displayed "a fascination for the superficial dynamism and composition of the American film." Officials, including Boltiansky, may have regretted the workers' preferences, but they had to show entertaining films in workers' clubs or watch their audiences dwindle.[23]

Not all Soviet films failed at the box office, and some won viewers with humor or drama that remains engaging today. They did so, however, by appropriating the style, if not the message, of the foreign competition. The more original a director's work—that is, the further he veered from Hollywood formulas—the smaller his chances of attracting a large audience. Komarov's *The Kiss of Mary Pickford* serves as an example of a popular Soviet film in the Hollywood style, and it was preceded by several others, including Lev Kuleshov's *The Extraordinary Adventures of Mr. West in the Land of the Bolsheviks* (1924). Mr. West, an American who arrives in Moscow with an anti-Soviet outlook and a cowboy bodyguard, suffers at the hands of various colorful scoundrels. Apart from borrowing American techniques, both films included American characters, as did a variety of other Soviet movies struggling to compete with imported hits. The amusing *Cigarette Girl from Mosselprom*, made the same year as *Mr. West*, presents a heroine whose suitors include a wealthy American entrepreneur and Igor Ilinsky (as a hapless accountant). Some Soviet movies tried to tap Hollywood's magnetism directly by spoofing the most popular American pictures and leaving no doubt about it with such titles as *The Mark of Zorro in the Village*, *A Thief but Not from Bagdad*, and even *The Thief of Bagdad*, which sought to parody the Fairbanks film of the same name while simultaneously advertising products for a state trade agency.[24]

Films shown during the 1920s were silent, and many Soviet theaters followed the common practice of supplying musical accompaniment. Pianists and ensembles often made some effort to match their performances to the films, including those from America, which helped introduce the public to ragtime and jazz during the second half of the decade. Wherever people first heard the music—at the cinema, in nightclubs, or from recordings—jazz and the dances it inspired soon won fans in Soviet cities. Just as the Bolsheviks tolerated American movies despite the pictures' "bourgeois" content, they raised no more objection to jazz, for a time, than did government officials in Europe or America. With this opportunity, the music attracted partisans in the Soviet Union, eclipsing the number who favored a new "proletarian" culture and yielding little even to the popularity of Hollywood's movies.

While the early history of film includes important developments in several countries and did not acquire a predominantly American hue until the 1920s, jazz sprang upon the world almost exclusively from America—especially black America. With roots in such genres as ragtime and spirituals, jazz assumed its own identity during the first two decades of the twentieth century through the innovations of numerous musicians, often with ties to New Orleans.[25] At the same time, technological advancements provided a means for the new music to burst across America beyond the black community and soon reach a much larger audience abroad than would have been possible twenty-five years earlier. Ragtime had depended on sheet music and player-piano rolls for transmission; jazz sped on the wings of radio and records. Annual production of phonographs in the United States, which was 500,000 at the start of World War I, surpassed 2.25 million by decade's end, while the nation's output of records doubled to reach 100 million in 1921. After radios appeared on the market as a household product in 1920, sales climbed to the point where six million sets were in use across the country by 1927. Not only did records and radios disseminate jazz quickly, they also did so more accurately than sheet music, by reproducing the rhythms and vocal patterns of a music that was often improvised. The new technologies even countered American racism to the extent of conveying black music into chambers of a white world closed to black musicians themselves.[26]

By the 1920s jazz had won a following across much of western and central Europe. Historians of jazz maintain that Europeans applied the term to everything from ragtime and Tin Pan Alley tunes to the blues, but such particulars mattered less to the enthusiastic audiences. As early as 1918 Igor Stravinsky composed a piece called "Ragtime," demonstrating "the passion I felt at that time for jazz, which burst into my life so suddenly when the war ended. At my request, a whole pile of this music was sent to me, enchanting me by its popular appeal, its freshness and the novel rhythm which so distinctively recalled its Negro origin." Records helped spread jazz rapidly in Europe, as did the comparative infrequency of racist objections to black performers. These musicians and dancers may have seemed wild or exotic to many Europeans, but that aura appears to have heightened early fascination with jazz as a music pulsating with primal vigor, alien to obsolete respectability. The Josephine Baker craze began in Paris with "*la danse de sauvage*," which a French reporter described as "barbaric . . . naughty . . . a return to the customs of the dark ages." Baker herself preserved "the untamed wildness of her forebears who were transplanted from the Congo basin to the Mississippi," concluded a German critic when the show reached Berlin.[27] For most fans, the fresh vitality of jazz and associated dances sufficed to explain the entertainment's appeal, without resort to theories on elemental potency or anything else. Modernists might welcome jazz either as a primitivist assault on prevailing mores or as a *new* music arising from the mechanized, urban life whose essence it allegedly captured. In all cases, though, and whether people enjoyed or loathed jazz, they regarded it as American—or, as one traveler put it in 1922, "American classical music."[28]

This may have been true in western Europe shortly after World War I, but in the Soviet Union jazz was scarcely known in 1922 and would not become truly popular for a few more years. The delay arose from many factors, especially the country's turmoil during the civil war and the government's control of foreign commerce thereafter—the same obstacles that postponed Hollywood's invasion of the nation's cinemas. Gradually, though, the new music and dances seeped across the border. Some Americans employed by the ARA to deliver famine relief in the early 1920s reportedly also found opportunities to demonstrate the foxtrot to better-nourished Russians in Moscow and Petrograd, while a handful of Soviet travelers brought back a zest for the dance steps they had witnessed in the West. Before long, state censors began to approve the publication of sheet music for the new recreations.[29]

Even earlier, in the summer of 1921, a Russian futurist poet who had been living in western Europe witnessed a performance by Louis Mitchell's Jazz Kings in Paris. Exhilarated by the music and especially the dancing, the young man attended shows by other American groups in Berlin later the same year and concluded that jazz and its dances expressed the essence of contemporary life, just as waltzes had in the previous century. This was Valentin Parnakh, whose futurist inclinations convinced him that jazz sounded "like an alternating current of electricity" as it captured the "eccentric" motion of modern times. After returning to the Soviet Union in 1922 he organized "The First Eccentric Orchestra of the Russian Soviet Federated Socialist Republic—Valentin Parnakh's Jazz Band"—which performed two concerts in Moscow later that year. Parnakh launched each session with a report on "eccentric art" and readings of his "jazz poetry," followed by exhibitions of American dance steps. His orchestra then offered a short program that consisted mainly of American songs and heavy, syncopated rhythms.[30]

Although little testimony has survived regarding these early concerts, two things are clear. First, American influence pervaded Parnakh's entire enterprise, from Mitchell's Jazz Kings in Paris to the American dances and songs performed in the Moscow concerts. Second, Parnakh's band—initially a piano, banjo, drums, xylophone, and two violins—produced nothing resembling American jazz. Within a few years, however, Soviet audiences heard the real thing from American groups: Sam Wooding's Chocolate Kiddies and Benny Peyton's Jazz Kings, both of whom reached Moscow early in 1926. Wooding's troupe included singers and dancers as well as musicians, and their two-act revue commenced with dancing followed by a jazz concert. Peyton's company consisted solely of seven musicians. The bands differed in their approaches to jazz, offering audiences a choice between Wooding's smooth, disciplined, "symphonic" jazz and Peyton's hotter, improvisational, New Orleans–style energy. Once in the Soviet Union, Wooding toured for three months, while the Jazz Kings prolonged their stay several months beyond that. "Much to our amazement," reported Wooding, "our Russian engagements were the best in all Europe. . . . There were no disturbances, and everywhere our music seemed to please immensely." Together, the American groups had an "enormous" impact, concludes the historian of Soviet jazz, Frederick Starr. They helped create a mass market for jazz in Soviet cities and inspired Soviet bands to affect the style of American musicians. Even the state publisher of music in Moscow hastened to issue an "American Blues" melody on the heels of the bands' Soviet tours.[31]

The government did more than publish American jazz. In 1926 the Commissariat of Enlightenment dispatched a young pianist, Leopold Teplitsky, to study jazz in America and procure the resources necessary to equip a jazz ensemble back in Leningrad. Along with these instructions, the commissariat apparently supplied Teplitsky with ample funds, for he purchased a car upon arriving in Philadelphia. He also joined a five-piece group that held forth in a bar, and soon began collecting music from the prominent band leader Paul Whiteman. On his return to Leningrad early in 1927, his baggage included more than twenty Whiteman arrangements, nearly four dozen musical instruments, and enough records to fill several trunks. With these assets he formed the First Concert Jazz Band, a fourteen-piece group that gave its initial concert in April. Along with jazzed-up classical numbers dear to Whiteman, the program included works by George Gershwin and Irving Berlin, James P. Johnson's "Charleston," and "Yes, Sir, That's My Baby." After playing Moscow, Teplitsky took his band through the provinces, where posters promised "the latest American music" and a demonstration of "American dances." Teplitsky even presented *himself* as an American now and then.[32]

In the wake of Peyton and Wooding, Soviet jazz bands multiplied sufficiently to shed the guise of curiosities. The question remains, though: did enough people listen or dance to warrant labeling the era the Soviet Jazz Age or Roaring Twenties? The absence of statistics does not cripple certain generalizations, including a judgment that the countryside, with its peasant majority, remained outside the realm of jazz. Peasants may have seen an occasional movie shown by one of the government's mobile projection units, but Bolshevik leaders could discern no benefit in providing similar backing for the Charleston in the countryside. Lunacharsky's support of Teplitsky's venture in Philadelphia was unusual and, moreover, aimed at creating a jazz band for Leningrad. When it toured, it played for urban audiences, not peasants. Even more than movies, then, jazz remained entertainment for the cities, an amusement that visitors to nightclubs, cinemas, restaurants, and casinos could expect with growing confidence by the second half of the decade. As one concerned socialist put it regarding Leningrad, "you could take the lift to the roof of the Hotel Europa, and there find another bar, like any in Paris or Berlin, full of lights, dancing and jazz, and even more depressing than the one on the ground floor."[33]

While jazz flourished at nightspots for the well-heeled, it also captivated a larger share of the urban population, especially young people and educated citizens not satisfied with nineteenth-century classical music, folk dances, or new "proletarian" culture. Bolshevik activists complained throughout the decade about youths who neglected ideology in favor of Western fashions and dances—a problem that troubled the party long thereafter. Ideology and entertainment were not easily blended, and much of the population clearly preferred the latter, as they demonstrated by lining up to see American movies. So, too, with jazz, even when exhibited as a symbol of decadence in the West. The director Vsevolod Meyerhold (noted previously in connection with Taylorism and Biomechanics) enjoyed jazz himself and may well have anticipated its enthusiastic reception by the audience at his new play, Trust D. E., when it debuted in the summer of 1924. The production adapted material from a number of sources, primarily Ilya Ehrenburg's novel of the same title, and developed a plot of acceptable political tone. A rogue named Jens Boot, in alliance with a trio of America's wealthiest capitalists, forms the D. E. ("give us Europe") Trust and proceeds to ravage the western portion of the Old World. Many workers from these lands find refuge in the Soviet Union, where Moscow's international organization of communists helps them construct a secret undersea tunnel between Leningrad and New York. Meanwhile, the D. E. Trust fails to overcome the Soviet Union and resigns itself to recognition of the world's socialist homeland. Too late! A proletarian rebellion erupts in the United States, its triumph ensured by assistance from the International Red Army arriving through the tunnel.[34]

Before the deluge, however, the bourgeoisie seemed to be having an awfully good time. Marching routines of the proletarian heroes, their biomechanical exercises, and other chaste exertions paled in comparison. Meyerhold engaged Valentin Parnakh's jazz band and a corps of risqué dancing girls to represent the West, and they strove to unmask the bourgeoisie's debauchery through eight energetic numbers. Several months earlier, on the sixth anniversary of the Bolshevik Revolution, Meyerhold had also accompanied bourgeois characters with American popular music in his production of Lake Lyul. But the brazen display in Trust D. E. broke new ground, and spectators flocked to discover the depths to which bourgeois society could sink. Trust D. E. sold out every performance for several years.[35]

Meyerhold's taste for jazz did not isolate him among the artistic avant-garde. Sergei Eisenstein, after hearing Parnakh's second concert in 1922, persuaded Parnakh to teach him the foxtrot. Dziga Vertov, another director well known to film historians, included a long excerpt from the Chocolate Kiddies' revue in his film A Sixth of the World, and the young composer Dmitry Shostakovich arranged "Tea for Two" as a symphonic foxtrot titled "Tahiti Trot."[36] Beyond the artistic vanguard, much of the larger urban clientele for jazz shared this interest in the foxtrot and other dances inspired by jazz. "So far the only place where they don't dance the fox-trot is on streetcars and in cemeteries," fretted a Soviet publicist in Leningrad, while a foreigner chose

similarly sweeping terms to describe the dance craze in Moscow: "From ballet dancers to former princesses, former manufacturers' daughters to former
janitors' daughters, every girl in Moscow has one great social ambition—to
learn the foxtrot. From former grand dukes' sons to shop workers, every
sprightly young man in Moscow wants to learn to foxtrot." While not every
inhabitant of Moscow trotted the night away, enough did to support robust
sales of sheet music by state and private publishers of such numbers as "Aero-
Foxtrot," "Miss Evelyn Foxtrot," and the foxtrot "Harry and Barry." Evidence
accumulated by Frederick Starr suggests that jazz "had gained general popularity among the educated public of Russia's cities" by the end of the
decade.[37]

Even a portion of the industrial workforce showed an interest. The frag-
mentary documentation cannot demonstrate widespread proletarian enthusiasm for jazz, but some desire for the entertainment is visible. In 1927
Leopold Teplitsky's First Concert Jazz Band played to a warm reception at the
Red Putilov steel works in Leningrad, while two years later workers at the
Dnieprostroy construction project chose to allocate all of their cultural fund
to provide themselves with jazz and other popular music. Some factory clubs
sponsored dances and advertised them with posters of the following sort:

> DIAMOND EVENING BALL
> Extraordinary concert
> Foxtrot 'til morning
> Amazing program with wine
> and
> Dancing between the tables.[38]

Evidence has also survived that certain officials themselves enjoyed jazz,
though no means exist to determine the extent of this interest among others
in the party. General Kliment Voroshilov, people's commissar of defense and
a member of the Politburo, surprised foreign diplomats already amazed by the
appearance of a jazz band at a Kremlin reception in 1934 when he and his wife
began foxtrotting to the music. A more formidable member of the Politburo,
Lazar Kaganovich, joined forces with the most popular Soviet band leader of
the day, Leonid Utesov, to produce in 1939 a brochure advising railway workers "How to Organize Ensembles of Song and Dance and Jazz Orchestras." To
be sure, Voroshilov and Kaganovich favored wholesome, bouncy rhythms, not
wild or ribald compositions, but even at this level their interest is revealing of
the music's popularity in the Soviet Union.[39] Some party members, of course,
remained thoroughly hostile to jazz, while others doubtless shared the ambivalence of Valerian Osinsky, an official who apparently took in a number of

performances during his visit to America in 1925. Along with its "vulgar" qualities, reported Osinsky, "this music is lively and dynamic. . . . During my stay in America, observing the pace and scope of life there, I came to sense clearly that all our esteemed, prewar classical music was an unbelievable waste of time." However, Osinsky emphasized, American jazz should not be imported wholesale. The Soviet Union had to produce a new music of its own, preserving jazz's desirable qualities but not its vices. Otherwise, he warned, "the American jazz band, in its naked and unadorned form and accompanied by the arch-vulgar fox-trot will begin to infiltrate us. And then [the Americans] will win over to their side our mass musical audience."[40]

By the end of the decade, voices echoing Osinsky's warning had largely drowned out those that shared his interest in some aspects of jazz or foreign culture in general. Activists who had long deplored jazz and Hollywood must have been heartened by an essay titled "On the Music of the Gross," which *Pravda* ran in the spring of 1928. Written by Maxim Gorky from his villa in southern Italy, it launched a ferocious attack on jazz that Soviet officials would cite for decades to come. First, though, Gorky invites the reader to savor an idyllic setting, a serene countryside resting in the evening darkness. This "perfection of tranquillity and beauty" soon has him rhapsodizing over "the stillness of the night," which "seems to whisper to the heart . . . a wonderful song of a new history—a song begun so boldly by the working people of my country."

Then, suddenly, from a radio in a nearby hotel, jazz shatters the reverie like "a bit of mud in the clearest translucent water." Racing through the air comes "a wild screaming, whistling, thundering, wailing, roaring, crashing . . . suggesting the grunting of a metal pig, the brays of donkeys, the amorous croaking of a huge frog," as if produced by "a mad orchestra in a state of sexual mania, directed by some sort of man-stallion brandishing an enormous phallus." More calmly, for a moment, Gorky identifies this noise as "a new foxtrot played by an orchestra of Negroes." It is, he continues, "music for the gross," to which degenerate dancers "simulate the impregnation of a woman by a man." Love, which over the centuries has inspired streams of beautiful poetry, now sinks to the act of an animal. "It is evolution from the beauty of a minuet and the lively verve of a waltz to the cynicism of a foxtrot with the spasms of the Charleston." For this, Gorky does not blame the black musicians. They are "probably laughing secretly" as "their white masters" embrace jazz and "evolve toward a barbarian condition that American Negroes have left and are putting ever farther behind them." At last the music subsides, no longer distracting Gorky's thoughts from his correspondence on the numerous benefits brought to Russian peasants by the Soviet regime. Jazz and "socialist construction" occupy no common ground and lead human beings to incompatible goals.[41]

Back in the Soviet Union, those who shared Gorky's views, if not his taste for sexual metaphors, weighed in with attacks on jazz and the foxtrot. A report delivered at an institute of the Communist Academy in 1930 (and later published in the journal *Literature and Art*) captured the tone of these charges by describing the foxtrot as an expression of the "consciousness of the slaves of capital, slaves of machines, completely reduced by capitalist society, having lost all ability not only to protest, but to think at all." This "American dance" reached the Soviet Union "through the bourgeois sector of our artists, through the bourgeois sector of our theater, and has unfortunately received wide distribution, because we have not yet completely torn out the roots of capitalism, because there still remains among us bourgeois artists, critics, and theoreticians of the arts, some of whom have taken up this art." Lest anyone dismiss the ominous implications of his remarks, the speaker emphasized that "defense of the foxtrot represents a striving to transplant to our soil the reactionary ideology of the contemporary bourgeoisie. It is always bound up in perversion, an anti-Leninist conception of our system, our Revolution and economy."[42]

Along with attacks on "bourgeois" music, the press rang with calls for a new "proletarian" culture—including a suggestion that music halls exchange their shallow, entertainment-minded fare for scientific and technical demonstrations accompanied by reports on politics and the international situation.[43] Even Anatoly Lunacharsky, who a few years before had sponsored Leopold Teplitsky's study of jazz in America, felt blown by the new winds to denounce the music in an address to the First All-Russian Conference on Music (a portion of which was circulated in the journal *Proletarian Musician* in 1929). He assailed the "opportunist tendency" to claim that the Soviet people's splendid accomplishments had provided them good reason to happily dance the foxtrot. "Why," Lunacharsky asked, "if they are to dance, is it only the foxtrot? I have not seen any reason for this, and I welcome an attempt to create our own proletarian dance." The foxtrot, with its "extreme mechanization of rhythm," made no secret of its roots in capitalist society. "A bourgeois and his slave are accustomed to machines, to machine technology, to machine rhythm in which there is nothing alive, in which the main thing is an extreme metronomic precision and also a sort of lifeless originality." Here lay the essence of the foxtrot, a relentless, mechanical pounding of sounds that "will all certainly lead to the direct antithesis of music, an anti-human sound, and with this, music will be finished." But not in the Soviet

Union, where Lunacharsky was confident that a proletarian alternative would sound forth to "accompany our labor, constantly ringing out and surrounding us with an atmosphere of liveliness, a joy of life, a readiness for challenges, a confidence in victory. It must burn like a flame, like a torch, and fill our heroic days."[44]

F. Scott Fitzgerald once remarked that the Jazz Age "had no interest in politics," and most Soviet foxtrotters doubtless carried on simply for the entertainment, with no thought of making a political statement. But if they had no interest in politics, "politics" developed an interest in them, as attacks on jazz mounted. The campaign against foreign popular music was, in turn, only a small part of feverish activity along multiple fronts that continued for roughly three years after 1928. Known as the Cultural Revolution, this ideological commotion featured proletarian militancy in diverse forms. People of non–working-class origins, for instance, feared dismissal from universities and government institutes, while "bourgeois specialists," such as professors and engineers, experienced harassment and even arrest. The Cultural Revolution expanded as a counterpart to the immense effort to force peasants into collective farms and build factories at blistering speed. Given Stalin's declaration that the successes in collectivization and industrialization had brought the nation to the verge of socialism, diverse visionaries and ideologues asserted that the time had arrived to replace all traces of bourgeois culture with alternatives suitable for a new socialist community.[45]

In this spirit, for example, jurists explained that bourgeois law codes stemmed from the institution of private property as wealthy owners sought to regulate exchanges characteristic of private enterprise. With the demise of these transactions at the onset of socialism, law would lose its traditional purpose and soon "wither away." Meanwhile, architects advanced plans anticipating the end of living space designed for the requirements of individual families. Bourgeois family units would go the way of bourgeois private property, with future living arrangements reflecting collectivist principles of one sort or another. These planners also hoped to break with current practice by spreading the population more evenly across the nation in order to eliminate the isolation of peasant villages and the impersonal congestion of cities. In many other fields as well, the atmosphere of the Cultural Revolution emboldened radicals to suppose that their outlook had finally prevailed.[46]

When they turned to prove bourgeois culture unfit for a socialist nation, partisans of the Cultural Revolution could find no better evidence than jazz, as we have seen, and also Western movies. Vindication arrived at last for those who had fumed for years over Hollywood's invasion of Soviet theaters. In March 1928 a Party Conference on Cinema instructed the film industry to strengthen itself ideologically in order to take part in class warfare and the Cultural Revolution. No trace of bourgeois influence could remain, because "cinema, like every art, cannot be apolitical," declared the conference's principal resolution. "In the hands of the bourgeoisie, bourgeois cinema is an instrument of class struggle, it inculcates the audience with the ideology that is necessary to strengthen the capitalist predominance and it diverts the masses from the revolutionary struggle." Soviet films had to steer the masses in the opposite direction, to socialism: "The whole ideological stance of Soviet cinema is different because the ideology of the proletariat must lie at the basis of the content of Soviet cinema."[47]

Two months later, a drive commenced to rid film libraries of foreign and Soviet pictures now deemed unsuitable. The purge focused on movies said to exalt bourgeois vices—and that included numerous American films attractive to Soviet viewers. In November a campaign to "cleanse the screen of trash" removed approximately three hundred foreign and twenty-six Soviet movies from distribution. Over the next few years, imports vanished. From sixty-eight new foreign films shown in the Soviet Union in 1929, the total fell to forty-three the next year and five in 1931, before reaching zero in 1932. Popular biographies of foreign movie stars, issued in millions of copies during the 1920s, ceased publication altogether by 1930.[48]

The attacks on "bourgeois" movies by partisans of the Cultural Revolution were so prominent that they obscured other reasons for the departure of Hollywood films. Whatever the nature of their content, foreign pictures bore substantial price tags at a time when the party desired to channel all available resources into industrialization. The new talkies in particular demanded costly projection equipment unavailable in Soviet theaters. Even films from Soviet studios, which did not require purchase with precious Western currency, could be produced only with labor and resources coveted by the insatiable industrial sector. As a result, Soviet releases dropped from 146 in 1930 to 35 in 1933.[49] A new "proletarian cinema," in other words, failed to emerge and fill the void left by the pruning of "bourgeois" titles—an indication that official priorities did not begin with cultural radicalism. Instead, other motives swayed Stalin and his associates, some of whom preserved comparatively private interests in American movies and jazz throughout the 1930s and beyond.

Stalin helped initiate the Cultural Revolution during his own struggle against opponents in the party who preferred to build socialism at a less frantic pace. His call for an immediate transition to socialism, combined with efforts to encourage a sense of menace from alleged enemies at home and abroad, served to undermine political rivals who favored the slower ascent to socialism chosen by the party earlier in the 1920s. The intolerance and impatience of the Cultural Revolution, striking hardest at targets who had been associated with the less-militant atmosphere of the mid-1920s, impugned Stalin's new political enemies. But this short-term political benefit did not generate passion in Stalin for the eruption of "leftist dreams" that inspired many of the Cultural Revolution's activists. Once they had served their political purpose by the early 1930s, the Cultural Revolution came to an end. Stalin certainly desired a cultural transformation and would implement something of the sort later in the 1930s. But it had nothing to do with—indeed, amounted to the antithesis of—much that cultural radicals proclaimed in 1929.

After the Cultural Revolution subsided, no more than ten new foreign films received public screenings during the remainder of the decade, compared to a total that exceeded 1,700 in the 1920s. If the ideological objections to "bourgeois contamination" lost some force with the waning of proletarian fervor, a revival of Russian nationalism undertaken by the government in the 1930s helped to thwart another mass importation of Hollywood movies. Now, in other words, the films' undoubted popularity with the Soviet public would not only retard socialism but would also pose as a national embarrassment. Were this not sufficient reason to turn away American movies, the nation's industrial priority continued to consume the money that would have been required to purchase and distribute them. Most foreign films were talkies by 1933, while the Soviet Union possessed only two hundred sound projectors (along with thirty-two thousand silent units) that year. Converting Soviet theaters to sound equipment was expensive, and it occurred at such a slow pace that Soviet studios produced silent versions of their own sound films until the end of the decade. Even if Hollywood's offerings had entered the country freely, in other words, many Soviet cinemas could not have shown them for much of the 1930s.[50]

Meanwhile, as foreign movies all but disappeared, the number of films produced in Soviet studios dropped by two-thirds (and would not return to the level of the 1920s until after Stalin's death in 1953).[51] This did not mean, however, that Stalin cared little for movies. On the contrary, he realized the public's thirst for films and sensed the opportunity afforded by the cinema to sway audiences. Hence the rapid multiplication of theaters during the 1930s. So strongly did Stalin feel about cinema's potential that he became, in effect, the head of the Soviet film industry. His Kremlin quarters contained a screening room where he previewed new Soviet works to judge their suitability for the public, while also enjoying other movies unlikely to gain release from his private domain. Among his favorites numbered American films, including screwball comedies and musicals along with the westerns that Khrushchev mentioned to Eisenhower.[52]

As Hollywood faded from public view, so did Soviet avant-garde styles of the previous decade. Futurist techniques puzzled audiences and had drawn fire on this point from the Russian Association of Proletarian Writers in 1929: "There can be no doubting the fact that some of these films are either almost inaccessible to the mass audience or include particular sequences which contain, at the expense of social content, experiments of a formal kind that are contrary to the film's fundamental purpose." The renown (and, occasionally, hard currency) earned abroad by the likes of Sergei Eisenstein, Vsevolod Pudovkin, and Dziga Vertov were welcome, but their films often failed the domestic test spelled out in 1928 by the Party Conference on Cinema: "The main criterion for evaluating the formal and artistic qualities of films is the requirement that cinema furnish a 'form that is intelligible to the millions' . . . without, of course, any accommodation on the part of these films to philistine petty bourgeois tastes."[53]

With foreign and modernist options now unacceptable in the 1930s, what did Soviet filmgoers see? The answer came to be known as *socialist realism,* a label applied to literature, art, sculpture, and other artistic endeavors as well as cinema. Not *all* movies of this sort were the clumsy displays of propaganda skewered in Western jokes about tractor-hugging peasants, but they did share certain basic traits important to Stalin and other officials of the day (and many days to come). Simple plots and uncomplicated editing, readily understood by a mass audience, became the norm. Most films also featured heroes struggling to overcome obstacles—in nature, perhaps, but more likely ideological foes or the protagonist's own lack of political awareness. Stalin himself became the supreme hero, as a valiant revolutionary and soldier of the civil war era or in his contemporary role as wise helmsmen guiding the nation to socialism. Many films also presented heroes from outside the leadership's ranks—workers, peasants, and other humble folk whose accomplishments set examples for the audience. Whatever the plot, its ending had to be positive to the extent of inspiring resolve and optimism about the emerging socialist society.

At first glance, little common ground appears between Hollywood and socialist realism, and one might dismiss talk of American influence on Soviet movies of the 1930s. Surely the time had passed when socialist art required anything from bourgeois practitioners. So thought partisans of the Cultural Revolution, and indeed the ideological themes in Soviet movies owed no debt to America. But in matters of structure—ranging from camera techniques to plot development and even lavish musical numbers—Soviet films continued to draw on lessons from Hollywood. In some cases, directors employed devices they had learned in the 1920s by watching American movies or editing them for distribution in the Soviet Union.[54] As Hollywood's releases grew more technically sophisticated by the end of the decade, occasional Soviet voices asserted (even in the middle of the Cultural Revolution) that "our films . . . can learn a lot from these brilliant models of film construction."

Thus argued Adrian Piotrovsky, artistic director of the Leningrad studios in 1929. If early American films now seemed silly and predictable, he explained, more recent imports from the United States—*Chicago* (1927), *Skyscraper* (1928), and *The Docks of New York* (1928)—forced an admission that "our view of American cinema will have to be reassessed." In particular, Piotrovsky continued, Hollywood had perfected techniques for conveying messages. "The philosophy of class reconciliation, the philosophy of success and fortune, the idea that 'a man can do anything as long as he wants to'" all figured in *Skyscraper*. Though no Soviet director could wish to promote such themes, "profoundly foreign to us," the American skill in doing so represented "a very clear, a very alluring formula, and we must make use of it" to advance the cause of socialism. "The ideological message [in new American films] lies philosophically well concealed beneath the plot. It emerges in the consciousness of the audience only as the final emotional sum." Similar deftness on behalf of socialism was essential in Soviet cinema, where currently "the entire plot is so frequently so completely immersed in the theme that an audience with the slightest degree of experience can predict it in advance."[55]

After the Cultural Revolution, a more authoritative figure in the person of Boris Shumyatsky, chief administrator of the Soviet film industry, offered much the same advice to the cinema community. Conceding the "enormous number of requirements that remain unsatisfied [in Soviet movies, including] . . . the requirements for the utmost laconicism in cinema language," Shumyatsky found it "particularly instructive to compare our films with Charlie Chaplin's latest film *Modern Times*," an example of the "complete mastery of film form."[56] Shumyatsky's clout allowed him to do more than write, and in 1935 he led a delegation to study the film industry in Western lands, especially the United States. His group visited New York, the Eastman Kodak plant in Rochester, and of course Hollywood, where Frank Capra welcomed them. They met Marlene Dietrich, Gary Cooper, Adolphe Menjou, Cecil B. DeMille, and Erich von Stroheim, among others, and observed Charles Laughton filming *Mutiny on the Bounty*. "After our trip," Shumyatsky informed a Soviet interviewer, "we sensed with special sharpness how far our cinema lags behind in the area of technical advances and the organization of film production." Noting that Hollywood turned out films more efficiently and in larger number than Soviet studios, the delegation's report called for construction of "a single cinema centre in the southern and sunniest part of the Soviet Union, near the sea and the mountains," a project soon dubbed "Soviet Hollywood" (*sovetskii Gollivud*). Shumyatsky had been impressed with the advantages offered to filmmakers by Hollywood's climate and location near Los Angeles, and he sought to duplicate these as far as possible by choosing a site in the Crimea for his new Hollywood. In the end, however, the project failed because of its expense and Shumyatsky's fall from Stalin's favor.[57]

Although he vanished mysteriously in the purges, the reasons for Shumyatsky's arrest must have included something other than his willingness to learn from the American film industry. Stalin himself went so far as to order that the Soviet adventure film *The Thirteen* (1937) be modeled directly on John Ford's *The Lost Patrol* (1934), and he arranged for some directors to view the latest Hollywood movies, ensuring that numerous Soviet films of the 1930s followed the structural conventions of their American counterparts.[58] He also supported enthusiastically a series of musical comedies—championed from the outset by Shumyatsky—that became the decade's most obvious examples of continued American influence on Soviet cinema.

Early in the 1930s, conversations with the jazz conductor Leonid Utesov had led Shumyatsky to contact Grigory Alexandrov, a filmmaker just returned from a lengthy stay in Hollywood. The movie *Jolly Guys* (sometimes translated *Happy Guys* or *Jolly Fellows*) was completed in 1934 and featured Utesov in the role of a shepherd whose devotion to music, especially jazz, carries him over various hurdles on a journey from the Black Sea to Moscow. In the process, he joins a jazz band whose name provides the film's title, and the group's antics culminate in a chaotically triumphant concert at the Bolshoi Theater itself. The film bulged with evidence of Alexandrov's sojourn in California. It was modeled after *The King of Jazz* (1931, starring Paul Whiteman), and its theme song (popular for years thereafter in the Soviet Union) came from a Mexican tune that Alexandrov heard in America, perhaps in Jack Conway's *Pancho Villa* (1931). Alexandrov also created opportunities in the plot to stage a Busby Berkeley spectacular, a New Orleans–style jazz funeral, and at the Bolshoi Theater, a rendition of the movie's theme song in a style borrowed from recordings by the Boswell Sisters. Scarcely a political film at all, this was the closest that Soviet studios would ever come in the 1930s to Hollywood entertainment. As such it could only reach the public after surviving a preview in Stalin's screening room—by no means a sure thing, it seemed to those responsible for the film. Imagine their relief, then, when Stalin remarked at the conclusion, "Good! I feel as if I'd been off on a month's holiday." Soviet audiences responded in similar fashion, and the movie became a hit upon its release at the end of 1934.[59]

Three more musicals followed at two-year intervals, all directed by Alexandrov and starring his wife Liubov Orlova, said to be Stalin's favorite actress. Socialist (and also nationalist) themes are now apparent, but so are traces of Hollywood's legacy. In *Circus* (1936), for instance, Orlova plays an American circus star, Marion Dixon, beset by white racists because she has given birth to a black son. After escaping a mob in Kansas, she embarks on a tour that lands her in Moscow. There her act, in which she is shot from a cannon, draws hearty applause, though she continues to suffer at the hands of her loathsome German costar and promoter. After Marion falls in love with a stalwart and patriotic Russian stuntman, the jealous German displays Marion's black baby to the audience, hoping to disgrace her. Instead, the multiethnic crowd dismisses the racist ploy and sings the baby a lullaby in several languages of the Soviet Union. Marion thus finds a new, enlightened homeland and marches happily through Red Square with her beaming boyfriend in the film's finale. Throughout the story, side by side with the politics (and a dose of nationalism in the film's anthem, "Song of the Motherland"), Alexandrov preserved Hollywood's narrative conventions down to the staging of an elaborate dance number worthy of any American musical of the period.[60]

The Cultural Revolution's activists sought to eliminate "bourgeois" aspects of Soviet cinema but not to eradicate movies altogether. Many of the same people, however, would have been delighted to witness the complete extinction of jazz, which offered scant promise as a means to advance socialism. Its foreign pedigree was more explicit, and all too often it seemed the stubborn champion of self-indulgence spilling over into depravity. Yet the music survived. In May 1933, more than a year before *Jolly Guys* appeared, the *New York Times* ran an article under the title "Jazz Gains in Popularity as Soviets Lift Ban." Jazz bands formed again and began to test the waters in hotels, restaurants, and amusement parks—a "remarkable comeback," noted the paper's correspondent, "after years of virtual prohibition."[61] The new atmosphere also encouraged formation of a Leningrad City Jazz Commission in 1933 to improve the quality of local bands. Its members included the composer Dmitry Shostakovich, who himself had incorporated jazz in his score for *Hamlet* the year before. In Moscow the Bolshoi Theater Orchestra played Milton Eidger's "King Jazz," and the Nemirovich-Danchenko Theater formed a vocal jazz ensemble. "The unprecedented explosion in the popularity of jazz," observed Frederick Starr, even extended to "many" factories, which began offering free foxtrot lessons to workers after their shifts.[62]

Half a decade of fervor and sacrifice associated with the government's industrialization campaign, combined with the Cultural Revolution's failure to produce a new music (or cinema or anything else) with mass appeal, explains the popular thirst for more entertaining, less militant forms of culture. This preference was not new. What changed in the early 1930s was official policy. During the period 1932–36, from the end of the Cultural Revolution to the onset of the major purge trials, the government took steps to improve the nation's standard of living and brighten the prevailing mood of austerity. Stalin had numerous motives for favoring the respite, among them, perhaps, a craving for genuine popularity. He may also have desired a period of calm in which to consolidate economic gains and prepare for the next phase of his domestic offensive. Among other things, a more relaxed climate could diminish the anxiety of future purge victims and encourage their cooperation in governmental activities until the Great Terror swept them away. In any case, the release of Jolly Guys and the return of jazz to prominence in Soviet cities were dramatic signs of the Cultural Revolution's demise and reason enough to hope that life really had become, in Stalin's famous words, "more joyous."[63]

To be sure, Soviet popular culture of the mid-1930s had changed, with American components less manifest than in the previous decade. Just as Hollywood films all but deserted Soviet screens, the revival of jazz after the Cultural Revolution brought no new tours by American bands. In the absence of these musicians, however, American influence on Soviet jazz lingered, as did the popular identification of jazz with the United States. Some of the more prominent Soviet ensembles even recruited black American expatriates to sing or dance with the bands and thereby enhance the groups' credibility and appeal. The handful of European jazz bands that toured the Soviet Union in the 1930s naturally featured American music and sometimes went further to demonstrate a link with the United States. In the spring of 1935, for instance, a group advertised as an "American jazz ensemble" completed a successful fifty-day engagement and returned in the fall for a year-long tour. The band, Weintraub's Syncopators, was in fact composed of musicians from a Berlin cabaret orchestra of the 1920s.[64]

With genuine American jazzmen nowhere in sight, Soviet musicians learned what they could from recordings. More effectively than the occasional performance by a touring European band, records transmitted reasonably current musical developments, and they could be replayed countless times in practice sessions as musicians labored to master new styles. The

problem (similar to that faced a few decades later by Soviet rock 'n' roll enthusiasts) was that the government issued scarcely any recordings of foreign
bands in the 1930s and permitted few citizens to travel abroad. As a result,
American jazz records reached Soviet fans only through "informal" channels.
The coveted discs could arrive in the hands of merchant seamen, angling for
a quick profit in the black markets of Soviet ports, or they might enter the
country in the luggage of Soviet delegations returning from business in other
countries. This flow tended to favor the record collections of the privileged,
as would be the case again with rock 'n' roll recordings during the Cold War.

Following the Cultural Revolution, then, jazz preserved a measure of its
American image in the Soviet Union, though the connection with the
United States was more sporadic than it had been in the mid-1920s. It was
also more dangerous, as xenophobia figured in the purge of jazz musicians
that shook the profession at roughly the same time as the dramatic public trials of illustrious Bolsheviks in 1936–38. Not all bandleaders perished, but
most of those who were arrested seem to have been tarred by travel in the
West or extensive contact with foreigners living in the Soviet Union. At the
beginning of this dark period, late in 1936, the newspaper Izvestiia attacked
the performances of three jazz bands in Moscow and identified their leaders
by name. One show presented the musicians clad in American marine uniforms playing such tunes as "Naval Rhumba" and "The Storm Blues," with
dancers helping to communicate the songs' spirit in a manner the article
termed indecent. Vexed that anything of the sort could still take place in
Moscow, the correspondent sampled music at a second establishment with no
better luck. "Can it really be that in all of Moscow's theaters they sing such
trash?" he wondered, while setting out to inspect a third venue. There the
band treated its audience to "American Rhumba" and Duke Ellington's
"Daybreak Express," among other temptations, leaving the author to shake
his finger at officials who presided over this entertainment. The three bandleaders were not arrested, but American songs disappeared quickly from their
repertoires. Groups that continued to perform American tunes often provided them now with Russian lyrics.[65]

The Kremlin did not desire jazz's extinction, and Pravda, the party's newspaper, even defended the music against some of the charges leveled by Izvestiia
in 1936–37. But neither Pravda nor such eminent supporters of jazz as
Kaganovich and Voroshilov wished to champion Duke Ellington and other
innovators of the 1930s. Instead, by the end of the decade, Soviet jazz became
"official" or "nationalized" music, played by large orchestras of disciplined musicians without spontaneity or spice. Even Utesov came under attack in the
press at the end of 1936. After an article dubbed him "the personification of

the ideological level of popular music" of the Soviet Roaring Twenties, he smoothed out his repertoire to the point where it scarcely resembled jazz at all. "It is clear to anyone," he wrote in 1939, "that our Soviet songs are fine material for jazz. It is only necessary to deal skillfully with this material, not to try to 'Americanize' it, but to find its own orchestral-jazz form."[66] A truly Soviet muse could no longer owe much to America.

In exploring American influence on the Soviet Union, we have charted a course through areas in which this theme was most pronounced. Fields with little evidence of an American element remain largely outside the book's covers. While such an approach preserves the narrative's focus and permits conclusions of the sort drawn in later chapters, it risks implying that the United States shaped all aspects of Soviet state and society. This was not the case, of course, as American prominence in certain sectors does not imply similar importance everywhere. In the realm of popular culture, recent publications describe some genres—amusements with peasant origins especially, but much else as well—in which contributions from the United States were trivial or absent altogether.[67] Nor does the theme of American influence saturate scholarly study of Bolshevik leaders and early Soviet intellectuals, as anyone can discover in the vast literature readily at hand.

Nevertheless, the fact remains that (1) no other foreign country approached America's influence on Soviet popular culture and (2) this influence was substantial, especially in such modern genres as movies and jazz. Millions of Soviet citizens enjoyed these diversions, which were copied by domestic practitioners. While it is important to note that the peasant majority saw little or nothing of Douglas Fairbanks, Charlie Chaplin, or the foxtrot during the 1920s, it is just as vital to recognize the mesmerizing power of these American commodities on urban Russians of all stations—despite the state's desire to win them over to alternatives deemed appropriate for "socialist construction." When officials complained about the seductiveness of "bourgeois" amusements from abroad, they were referring to entertainment that owed more to America than to any other nation and possibly to all other countries combined.

In the 1920s, these complaints drew answers from other commentators who explained that American films would reveal cinematic techniques useful for conveying a different, socialist message. "We evaluate the creative work of the American actor from the point of view of utilizing it in Soviet cinema," explained a book on Hollywood film artists in 1927, "and cannot but admire the colossal treasure house of riches accumulated over the years." A more combative article could still allow that "regarding ideology, we must learn from Western cinema as one learns from an enemy: master his methods but direct them to opposite ends."[68] Products of the Roaring Twenties, it seemed, might serve a socialist cause in spite of themselves.

By the following decade, with few American films in circulation, publications spoke less frequently of "studying Western technique" or "borrowing from the West in order to surpass the West." Although Stalin continued to enjoy American movies in private and advised Soviet directors to consult an American recipe on occasion—as Shumyatsky did in print—the nearly complete absence of American films in Soviet theaters eliminated most public discussion of mastering Hollywood's technical accomplishments. But this did not discourage appeals to apply American expertise to other endeavors. As the Soviet Union entered the 1930s and Hollywood receded from view, the Kremlin regarded America more insistently than ever as a vital source of skills necessary to outstrip the capitalist world in a different arena, more important to Stalin than any other.

Notes

1. Nikita S. Khrushchev, *Khrushchev Remembers: The Last Testament* (Boston: Little, Brown, 1974), 407.

2. Thomas Craven, "The Great American Art," *Dial* 81 (December 1926): 483–92.

3. D. Liianov, "Amerika i Evropa," *Sovetskoe kino*, nos. 4–5 (1925): 68; Garth Jowett, *Film: The Democratic Art* (Boston: Little, Brown, 1976), 203; Ian Jarvie, *Hollywood's Overseas Campaign: The North Atlantic Movie Trade, 1920–1950* (Cambridge: Cambridge University Press, 1992), 315; Ann Douglas, *Terrible Honesty: Mongrel Manhattan in the 1920s* (New York: Farrar, Straus & Giroux, 1995), 190–91.

4. Jarvie, *Hollywood's Overseas Campaign*, 112.

5. Regarding the various reasons for Hollywood's international success in the 1920s, see Jarvie, *Hollywood's Overseas Campaign*, 47–48, 109, 129–30, 275–76, 278–79; Jowett, *Film*, 54–57, 67–69, 186–89; Emily S. Rosenberg, *Spreading the American Dream: American Economic and Cultural Expansion, 1890–1945* (New York: Hill and Wang, 1982), 100–101; Victoria de Grazia, "Mass Culture and Sovereignty: The American Challenge to European Cinemas, 1920–1960," *Journal of Modern History* 61, no. 1 (March 1989): 57–61; Doeko Bosscher, Marja Roholl, and Mel van Elteren, eds., *American Culture in the Netherlands* (Amsterdam: VU University Press, 1996), 13–14.

6. Kristin Thompson, *Exporting Entertainment: America in the World Film Market, 1907–1934* (London: BFI, 1985), 4–5, 40; Richard Taylor, "Ideology and Popular Culture in Soviet Cinema: The Kiss of Mary Pickford," in *The Red Screen: Politics, Society, Art in Soviet Cinema*, ed. Anna Lawton (London: Routledge, 1992), 46; Robert V. Allen, *Russia Looks at America: The View to 1917* (Washington, D.C.: Library of Congress; Government Printing Office, 1988), 108; Andrei Belyi, quoted in Yuri Tsivian, *Early Cinema in Russia and Its Cultural Reception* (London: Routledge, 1994), 35.

7. Thompson, *Exporting Entertainment*, 90–91, 132–33; Denise J. Youngblood, *Movies for the Masses: Popular Cinema and Soviet Society in the 1920s* (Cambridge: Cambridge University Press, 1992), 14, 20. The figures cited here are from Thompson. Youngblood's data differ somewhat. Discrepancies in film statistics can occur for a variety of reasons, as when "shorts" are counted along with full-length films or when only new films are included in a year's total.

8. Richard Taylor and Ian Christie, eds., *The Film Factory: Russian and Soviet Cinema in Documents 1896–1936*, trans. Richard Taylor (London: Routledge, 1994), 423; Youngblood, *Movies for the Masses*, 7, 21. The figure of 7,331 "cinema installations" in 1928 includes 1,492 mobile units.

9. D. Liianov, "Ob upriamoi deistvitel'nosti i bol'nykh nervakh," *Sovetskoe kino*, nos. 2–3 (1925): 20–21; Vance Kepley Jr. and Betty Kepley, "Foreign Films on Soviet Screens, 1922–1931," *Quarterly Review of Film Studies* 4, no. 4 (Fall 1979): 431–33.

10. Kepley and Kepley, "Foreign Films," 435–36, 438–39; Richard Taylor and Ian Christie, eds., *Inside the Film Factory: New Approaches to Russian and Soviet Cinema* (London: Routledge, 1991), 72; A. V. Lunacharskii, *Kino na zapade i u nas* (Moscow: Teakinopechat', 1928), 70.

11. Taylor, "Ideology and Popular Culture," 48.

12. Taylor and Christie, *Russian and Soviet Cinema in Documents*, 155; Liianov, "Ob upriamoi deistvitel'nosti," 19.

13. Lunacharskii, *Kino na zapade*, 70–71; *Pravda*, 9 May 1926, 7.

14. Taylor, "Ideology and Popular Culture," 49; Youngblood, *Movies for the Masses*, 51.

15. Liianov, "Amerika i Evropa," 69; I. Urazov, "Vtoroi konets palki," *Sovetskii ekran*, no. 11 (1927): 3.

16. V. Muskin, "Podvodia kontsy," *Sovetskii ekran*, no. 15 (1927): 4; Youngblood, *Movies for the Masses*, 24–25, 53–56; Denise J. Youngblood, "'Americanitis': The *Amerikanshchina* in Soviet Cinema," *Journal of Popular Film & Television* 19, no. 4 (Winter 1992): 150; Richard Stites, *Russian Popular Culture: Entertainment and Society since 1900* (Cambridge: Cambridge University Press, 1992), 59–60; Taylor, "Ideology and Popular Culture," 56.

17. Kepley and Kepley, "Foreign Films on Soviet Screens," 437; Youngblood, *Movies for the Masses*, 52–53.

18. Kepley and Kepley, "Foreign Films on Soviet Screens," 437; Youngblood, *Movies for the Masses*, 52–53.

19. Jeffrey Brooks, "The Press and Its Message: Images of America in the 1920s and 1930s," in *Russia in the Era of NEP: Explorations in Soviet Society and Culture*, ed. Sheila Fitzpatrick, Alexander Rabinowitch, and Richard Stites (Bloomington: Indiana University Press, 1991), 237; Youngblood, *Movies for the Masses*, 53–54; Victor Ripp, *Pizza in Pushkin Square: What Russians Think about Americans and the American Way of Life* (New York: Simon & Schuster, 1990), 172; Richard Taylor and Derek Spring, eds., *Stalinism and Soviet Cinema* (London: Routledge, 1993), 76.

20. Taylor, "Ideology and Popular Culture," 56.

21. Youngblood, "Americanitis," 149–50; Youngblood, *Movies for the Masses*, 51–52.

22. Youngblood, *Movies for the Masses*, 5, 20, 29, 51, 59; Denise J. Youngblood, *Soviet Cinema in the Silent Era, 1918–1935* (Ann Arbor, Mich.: UMI Research Press, 1985), 57, 131; Taylor and Spring, *Stalinism and Soviet Cinema*, 76.

23. Taylor and Christie, *Russian and Soviet Cinema in Documents*, 124–25, 134; Stites, *Russian Popular Culture*, 56.

24. John David Rimberg, *The Motion Picture in the Soviet Union: 1918–1952: A Sociological Analysis* (New York: Arno, 1973), 146–47; Taylor, "Ideology and Popular Culture," 49; Youngblood, *Movies for the Masses*, 58, 60; Youngblood, "Americanitis," 150–51; *Sovetskie khudozhestvennye fil'my. Annotirovannyi katalog.* Vol. 1: *Nemye fil'my (1918–1935)* (Moscow: Iskusstvo, 1961), 82.

25. Marshall W. Stearns, *The Story of Jazz* (New York: Oxford University Press, 1956); Burton W. Peretti, *Jazz in American Culture* (Chicago: Ivan R. Dee, 1997); James Lincoln Collier, *The Making of Jazz: A Comprehensive History* (Boston: Houghton Mifflin, 1978).

26. Douglas, *Terrible Honesty*, 419–21; S. Frederick Starr, *Red and Hot: The Fate of Jazz in the Soviet Union. With a New Chapter on the Final Years* (New York: Limelight, 1994), 13–15.

27. Igor Stravinsky, quoted in Chris Goddard, *Jazz Away from Home* (New York: Paddington, 1979), 121; Jean-Claude Baker and Chris Chase, *Josephine: The Hungry Heart* (New York: Random House, 1993), 5–6, 126–27.

28. Douglas, *Terrible Honesty*, 352.

29. Edwin Ware Hullinger, *The Reforging of Russia* (New York: Dutton, 1925), 319–20; Starr, *Red and Hot*, 48, 59–60.

30. Starr, *Red and Hot*, 43–47.

31. Starr, *Red and Hot*, chapter 4; Samuel Wooding, "Eight Years Abroad with a Jazz Band," *Etude Music Magazine* (April 1939): 234.

32 Starr, *Red and Hot*, 66–69.

33 Victor Serge, *Memoirs of a Revolutionary 1901–1941* (Oxford: Oxford University Press, 1967), 199. See also Theodore Dreiser, *Dreiser's Russian Diary*, ed. Thomas P. Riggio and James L. West III (Philadelphia: University of Pennsylvania Press, 1996), 87, 92, 143.

34. Edward Braun, *Meyerhold: A Revolution in Theatre* (Iowa City: University of Iowa Press, 1995), 196–99; James M. Symons, *Meyerhold's Theatre of the Grotesque: The Post-Revolutionary Productions, 1920–1932* (Coral Gables, Fla.: University of Miami Press, 1971), 121, 158; A. Ia. Trabskii, ed., *Russkii sovetskii teatr 1921–1926* (Leningrad: Iskusstvo, 1975), 217–18.

35. Symons, *Meyerhold's Theatre*, 108, 121, 123, 132; Starr, *Red and Hot*, 50–52. Symons and Starr differ on the degree to which Meyerhold premeditated the appeal of the jazz in *Trust D. E.*

36. Starr, *Red and Hot*, 50, 56, 59, 64; Taylor, "Ideology and Popular Culture," 52.

37. Anne E. Gorsuch, *Flappers and Foxtrotters: Soviet Youth in the "Roaring Twenties"* (Pittsburgh: University of Pittsburgh, Carl Beck Papers, 1994), 7; Starr, *Red and Hot*, 59, 79; Stites, *Russian Popular Culture*, 49.

38. Starr, *Red and Hot*, 69, 111; Gorsuch, *Flappers and Foxtrotters*, 13.

39. Starr, *Red and Hot*, 17, 125–28.

40. Mark Hale Teeter, "The Early Soviet de Tocquevilles: Method, Voice and Social Commentary in the First Generation of Soviet Travel Publitsistika from America (1925–1936)" (Ph.D. diss., Georgetown University, 1987), 152–54.

41. *Pravda*, 18 April 1928, 2.

42. L. Lebedinskii, "Nash massovyi muzykal'nyi byt," *Literatura i iskusstvo*, no. 1 (1931): 75–79.

43. Elizaveta Dmitrievna Uvarova, *Estradnyi teatr: miniatiury, obozreniia, miuzik-kholly (1917–1945)* (Moscow: Izdatel'stvo Iskusstvo, 1983), 196–97.

44. A. V. Lunacharskii, "Sotsial'nye istoki muzykal'nogo iskusstva," *Proletarskii muzykant*, no. 4 (1929): 18–20.

45. Robert C. Tucker, *Stalin in Power: The Revolution from Above, 1918–1941* (New York: Norton, 1990), 101–106, 551–53.

46. Sheila Fitzpatrick, ed., *Cultural Revolution in Russia, 1928–1931* (Bloomington: Indiana University Press, 1978).

47. Taylor and Christie, *Russian and Soviet Cinema in Documents*, 208–209.

48. Youngblood, *Movies for the Masses*, 20, 30–32; Youngblood, *Soviet Cinema*, 162.

49. Kepley and Kepley, "Foreign Films on Soviet Screens," 439–40; Youngblood, *Movies for the Masses*, 20, 31, 64.

50. Youngblood, "Americanitis," 151; Taylor and Spring, *Stalinism and Soviet Cinema*, 49; Youngblood, *Movies for the Masses*, 66–67, 171–72; Youngblood, *Soviet Cinema*, 222.

51. Taylor and Spring, *Stalinism and Soviet Cinema*, 42; Youngblood, "Americanitis," 151.

52. Tucker, *Stalin in Power*, 556; Youngblood, "Americanitis," 151.

53. Taylor and Christie, *Russian and Soviet Cinema in Documents*, 212, 277–78. See also Peter Kenez, "The Cultural Revolution in Cinema," *Slavic Review* 47, no. 3 (Fall 1988): 414–33.

54. Youngblood, *Movies for the Masses*, 51, 67.

55. Taylor and Christie, *Russian and Soviet Cinema in Documents*, 267, 269–70.

56. Taylor and Christie, *Russian and Soviet Cinema in Documents*, 374, 376.

57. B. Z. Shumiatskii, "Tri mesiatsa v Amerike i Evrope," *Sovetskoe iskusstvo*, 23 August 1935, 3; Taylor and Christie, *New Approaches*, 213–15.

58. Youngblood, "Americanitis," 151; Taylor and Spring, *Stalinism and Soviet Cinema*, 47, 237.

59. Josef Stalin, quoted in Tucker, *Stalin in Power*, 556; Starr, *Red and Hot*, 153–55.

60. Stites, *Russian Popular Culture*, 89–90; Youngblood, "Americanitis," 152.

61. Starr, *Red and Hot*, 107. See pp. 110–11 for a lengthy quotation from the *New York Times* article.

62. Starr, *Red and Hot*, 108–109, 111, 126, 162.

63. Tucker, *Stalin in Power*, 283–84. For the original, presloganized version of the "more joyous" comment, see I. V. Stalin, *Sochineniia*, vol. 1 (Stanford, Calif.: Hoover Institution, 1967), 106. This is a continuation of the first 13 volumes, published in Moscow.

64. Starr, *Red and Hot*, 110–11, 114–15, 122–24.

65. *Izvestiia*, 11 December 1936, 4; Starr, *Red and Hot*, 167–69, 171; Tucker, *Stalin in Power*, 504; Stites, *Russian Popular Culture*, 75–76.

66. Leonid Utesov, *Zapiski aktera* (Moscow: Iskusstvo, 1939), 122; Starr, *Red and Hot*, 150–52, 164, 179.

67. See, for example, Stites, *Russian Popular Culture*.

68. I. Trauberg, *Akter amerikanskogo kino* (Leningrad: Academia, 1927), 132–33; I. P., "Nashe i za-padnoe kino," *Sovetskii ekran*, no. 19 (1929): 7.

CHAPTER FOUR

~

Arch-Bourgeois Machines

We watch developments in the USA, for that country ranks high in science and technology. We would like scientific and technical people in America to be our teachers in the sphere of technique, and we their pupils.

—Joseph Stalin

"I hear," [Henry Ford] said, "that you have agreed to build factories for the Russian Government. I am very glad of it. I have been thinking that these people should be helped."

—Albert Kahn

When Sergo Ordzhonikidze addressed a meeting of students in 1928, three weeks before *Pravda* ran Gorky's assault on jazz, he did not advise caution over contact with the United States. Soviet specialists had been "wracking their brains to solve certain problems," he informed the audience, while in America these challenges "had been solved long ago and were not a mystery to anyone." As an advocate of unbounded industrialization, Ordzhonikidze was climbing quickly to the top ranks of the Stalinist government—a vantage point from which the United States appeared essential to the party's bold plans. The Soviet Union must open its doors to foreign expertise as never before, he told the students, for "there is no place to boast here of our communism. If we compare an American 'arch-bourgeois' machine with our 'socialist' one, the first will be better. There is no doubt about this." In the end, of course, the homeland of socialism would surpass the United States, he believed, but it could not do so in isolation. "We must invite foreign technical experts, conclude technical-assistance agreements with them, and first and foremost, send hundreds and thousands of our young engineers to America so that they can learn for themselves what to do and how to work."[1]

Thus the heavy fire directed at American movies and music resounded alongside calls to expand economic contact with the United States—both developments stemming from the decision by Stalin and his supporters to accelerate the drive to socialism. Just as this goal required haste in removing all traces of "bourgeois" culture, it also demanded construction of an industrial economy as the backbone of the new society. Without a substantial industrial base there could be no significant proletariat, no means of producing enough goods to satisfy the population's needs, and no hope of defending the socialist outpost from foreign menace. No industry meant no socialism, while rapid progress to socialism through industrialization depended on extensive aid from the "capitalist" West.

It was not supposed to happen this way. According to classical Marxism, the fall of the tsar in March 1917 should have inaugurated a lengthy period of capitalism during which the Russian bourgeoisie would run the country and modernize it along the lines already followed in England, France, and Germany. During this era, vigorous capitalists and their government would transform the backward peasant country into an urban industrial state capable of producing far more than anyone could have imagined in previous centuries. Then, generations after the last tsar, with the productive power for socialism now at hand but inaccessible to a population exploited by the capitalist ruling class, proletarian revolutionaries would seize the sophisticated industrial creation of the bourgeoisie and transfer it to a new socialist government prepared to direct these ample resources in the interests of the workers. Industrialization was to occur during capitalism, in other words, as a precondition for socialism.

Well before 1917, Lenin and Trotsky grew impatient with this standard Marxist scenario. Timid and small the Russian bourgeoisie seemed to them, scarcely the class to overthrow Tsar Nicholas II. Even if the nation's liberals exceeded these expectations and pushed the tsar off his throne, a long bourgeois epoch thereafter would eliminate any hope that current revolutionaries could participate in the transition from capitalist exploitation to socialist equality. Their grandchildren might, but they would not, and ambitious revolutionaries found this unpalatable. Thus, both Lenin and Trotsky developed their own variants of Marxism for Russia that condensed the capitalist stage so severely that it all but disappeared and left Russia theoretically free to move quickly from the fall of the tsar to socialism. Trotsky, for example, argued that peasant Russia would not have to attempt a leap to socialism on its own because a revolution in Russia would spark revolutions in western Europe. Once the industrially advanced European nations acquired socialist governments, they would not hesitate to assist their comrades in Russia with the task of industrialization, thereby eliminating the need for capitalists to manage the process.

By the time the Bolsheviks seized power in 1917, Lenin had embraced this view (often called the theory of permanent revolution), which two years later appeared in *The ABC of Communism*, a guide to the party's program. This text noted many obstacles to socialism in a "backward" country but remained confident that these "would all be overcome if Russia were to form part of an international, or even merely a European, soviet republic, and thus to be associated with more advanced lands."[2] As time passed, and revolution did not engulf Europe, this "theory" grew more awkward because the absence of socialist regimes in western Europe seemed to block socialism in Russia. By the mid-1920s, with Lenin dead and a power struggle well under way among other party leaders, the faction that included Stalin endorsed an alternative dubbed "socialism in one country." Dismissing the "pessimism" of Trotsky, Stalin argued that the Soviet Union possessed sufficient resources to construct socialism on its own, in a single country. It need not wait until world revolution, some day, spread socialism abroad.

Action followed words at the end of the 1920s, when the Soviet Union launched an industrialization drive under the terms of the First Five-Year Plan (1928–32). Prodigious campaigns gathered speed to build factories, mines, and other projects across the country. As the new enterprises took shape around them, Bolsheviks demonstrated that industrialization required no wave of prior revolutions in the West. On this point they mocked Trotsky with abandon. When they did so, however, they rarely touched the related issue of Western technical assistance—safer left for discussion in other contexts. Champions of "permanent revolution" had regarded such aid as essential and assumed that it would be provided on favorable terms, if not gratis, because of the socialist bond between the governments involved. Under the banner of the First Five-Year Plan, Western advice and equipment remained indispensable but had to be sought now from unrepentant capitalists, many of whom lived in the United States.

In 1930 an engineer from a prominent family of children's authors published a book titled *Story of the Great Plan*. Designed to acquaint youths with the nation's industrialization effort, the narrative, with its simplicity and optimism, won many readers not only in the Soviet Union but also in the West, where it became a best-seller. Though the book differed from most other Soviet volumes on the topic by its appeal to children, it joined the other accounts in identifying certain major projects as flagships for the entire industrialization enterprise. These included a dam across the Dnieper River, a tractor factory in Stalingrad, an automobile plant at Nizhnii-Novgorod, and a steel mill at Magnitogorsk.[3] The public soon became familiar with these undertakings, for they and a handful of others represented an industrial pantheon to which Soviet accounts returned time and again to honor the vision and accomplishments of the period. Less often did the commentaries acknowledge the involvement of American engineers and equipment in any of the endeavors, when in fact American companies played a central role in them all.

Work began first on the huge dam to harness the Dnieper River, an edifice 51 meters high and 720 meters across, larger than any other in the world at the time. Its construction ranked as one of the First Five-Year Plan's greatest triumphs, and Dnieprostroy, as it was known in Russian, quickly became a showpiece of Soviet industrial accomplishment. "Here a structure has been created, never before seen in history," declared the project's deputy chief engineer at the ceremony to celebrate completion of the dam in 1932. "Only the October Revolution made possible the construction of such a giant." A banner headline in *Pravda* heralded Dnieprostroy as "THE GREATEST HYDROELECTRIC STATION IN THE WORLD, THE BEAUTY AND PRIDE OF THE FIRST FIVE-YEAR PLAN," while, in the same issue, Maxim Gorky applauded the dam as proof that "not a single one of the capitalist states is able to undertake anything like that which the proletariat— the master of the Soviet Union—is accomplishing." Amid countless newspaper articles in this vein, the *Story of the Great Plan* did not exaggerate much in claiming that "there is not a person in the Soviet Union who has not heard of Dnieprostroy."[4]

In 1926 the Soviet government signed an agreement with the American firm of Colonel Hugh Cooper to serve as a consultant to Soviet engineers on the construction of the dam. Cooper, famous for his work on numerous dams in the United States, led a team of engineers to study the proposed site. Soviet authorities also retained a German firm as a consultant, and disagreement arose between the Germans and Americans over the most suitable construction methods. Thus in 1927 work began on the dam using Cooper's techniques on one side of the river and the German preference on the other. Before the end of the year, top Soviet engineers on the project judged the American approach superior, and Cooper's firm soon became the only foreign consultant guiding the primary work.[5] This meant not only that most of the major construction techniques were American but also that most of the electrical equipment—roughly 70 percent, according to an estimate in 1929—came from the United States. The General Electric Company (GE) had as many as sixty technicians and engineers at work on Dnieprostroy and supplied such crucial components as the nine generators for the power plant. Five of these generators, the biggest in the world, were built at General Electric's plant in Schenectady, while the remaining four were assembled in Leningrad from GE parts and with the assistance of GE engineers.[6]

By 1932 Dnieprostroy was ready to produce electrical power. Hugh Cooper described the enterprise (on which thirty thousand workers toiled in 1930) as one of the greatest engineering challenges anywhere in the world. The project's success so pleased Soviet leaders that they granted high state honors to Cooper and six other Americans—two each from Cooper's firm, the General Electric Company, and the Newport News Shipbuilding & Drydock Company (which had built and installed the power plant's hydraulic turbines). Even Vyacheslav Molotov, by then chairman of the Council of People's Commissars, praised American work on Dnieprostroy in his book *The Success of the Five-Year Plan*. Though scarcely effusive, Molotov's acknowledgment is striking in a volume generally critical of the West. He is able to credit Cooper with improving construction of Dnieprostroy and explains that "the cause of our success lies in the adoption of American mechanisation of the building work and in our own Bolshevik energy." A year later *Izvestiia* printed remarks by Cooper lauding the Soviet-American partnership at Dnieprostroy: "The practical experience obtained by the people of the USSR in applying American methods is a lever which will raise the standard of living in the USSR."[7]

For party leaders, Dnieprostroy was only the beginning. On 7 November 1929, *Pravda* celebrated the twelfth anniversary of the Bolshevik Revolution with an article by Stalin titled "The Year of the Great Turn." Full of enthusiasm for the revolutionary transformation then under way in the country, Stalin boasted that "we are moving full steam ahead down the path of industrialization—to socialism, leaving behind our age-old 'Russian' backwardness. . . . And when we put the USSR in an automobile and the peasant on a tractor—then let the esteemed capitalists, who boast so much about their 'civilization,' try to overtake us."[8] If success for the party's economic offensive required a Soviet population at the controls of automobiles and tractors, little wonder that massive factories soon arose to produce them both. In the case of tractors, the government hoped to eliminate its dependence on vehicles imported from America—nearly ten thousand of which entered the country in 1926, compared to about nine hundred machines manufactured domestically (a majority of which were copies of the Fordson model). As late as 1930, when domestic production approached thirteen thousand (still mostly Fordson copies), tractors purchased from the United States topped twenty-three thousand.[9]

The leap to self-sufficiency began with a new tractor factory in the city named for Stalin himself. Although officials and engineers had selected a site and discussed preliminary plans as early as 1926, serious work did not commence until 1929, after a Soviet delegation reached agreement with the American industrial architecture firm of Albert Kahn. According to the Soviet newspaper *For Industrialization*, "the shortage of our own qualified workers and technical personnel, and the delay in preparing cadre, now force the Stalingrad Tractor Factory to increase as much as possible the invitation of American technical specialists for work at the Stalingrad plant." No other major project of the First Five-Year Plan was more thoroughly American in its design, construction, and equipment. As the Soviet Supreme Economic Council put it simply in 1929, "the plan for the Stalingrad Tractor Factory was made by America." Albert Kahn's firm, which had designed the Ford plant at River Rouge in Michigan and was apparently recommended to Soviet officials by Ford, provided the general plans; the Frank D. Chase Company designed the foundry; and R. Smith, Incorporated, saw to the forge shop. On and on went the list of American participants. Technicians and machinery from the International Harvester Company figured prominently, for the factory was designed to produce a copy of the International Harvester 15/30 tractor. Structural steel came from the McClintic Marshall Company, and a group of American engineers supervised by John Calder oversaw the day-to-day construction work.[10]

Ultimately, about 90 percent of the factory's basic equipment was purchased in the United States from more than one hundred American firms, some of which also trained groups of Soviet engineers in their own factories. Along with American planning, equipment, and engineers, Soviet agencies responsible for the Stalingrad factory also desired American foremen and other skilled workers, not just for construction duties but to help guide and train a labor force once the plant began production. Thus a Soviet recruiting office opened in Detroit, and Soviet advertisements appeared in American newspapers. By 1931 some 380 American workers had congregated in Stalingrad, forming the largest colony from the United States at any Soviet industrial site.[11]

The plant opened in June 1930, several months ahead of schedule, to great fanfare around the country. Stalin himself sent a message of congratulations that surpassed the combative tone of his *Pravda* article the year before. "The 50,000 tractors that you will give the country each year are 50,000 shells blowing up the old bourgeois world and cutting a road to a new socialist order in the countryside." He then expressed a desire "to extend thanks to our technical advisers, the American specialists, who aided in the construction of the factory."[12] As it happened, the factory managed to assemble only one thousand tractors that year, for the plant had been opened prematurely and production remained disorganized for months. Not until 1933 did output reach the planned capacity of forty thousand tractors, to say nothing of Stalin's vision of fifty thousand machines.[13] Nevertheless, the difficulties at Stalingrad provided lessons that eased the completion of the next tractor factory, at Kharkov, the second of three giants built in the 1930s with substantial American assistance.

The Kharkov plant was designed as a copy of the Stalingrad facility, with some improvements added. Soviet administrators had apparently hoped to do much of the construction themselves, benefiting from the experience at Stalingrad, but American engineers were soon brought into the project. Leon Swajian, a construction engineer at Ford's River Rouge factory, had served for a time as chief engineer for construction in Stalingrad, before assuming the same position at Kharkov in 1931. His work there prompted the Soviet government to award him the prestigious Order of Lenin. As late as the middle of 1933, by which time the facility had been operating for more than a year and a half, at least twenty-five Americans were still on duty, including the foundry maintenance superintendent and the assistant maintenance superintendent. Soviet agencies also hired hundreds of American (and other foreign) workers and foremen who possessed skills needed at the factory. Most of the equipment in the Kharkov plant was foreign as well, "either of American origin or of German make, patterned after American designs," according to information received by the State Department from an American engineer employed by Soviet authorities. The factory, like its counterpart in Stalingrad, produced a copy of the International Harvester 15/30 tractor.[14]

Although the American role appears less overwhelming at Kharkov than at Stalingrad, it was clearly of major importance to the success of the Kharkov facility. So, too, with the decade's third behemoth, opened in 1933 at Cheliabinsk, just east of the Ural Mountains. A team of American and Soviet engineers in Detroit designed the Cheliabinsk plant, and dozens of Soviet technicians from the Cheliabinsk project studied in the United States, as did their counterparts from Kharkov and Stalingrad. A group of American engineers led once again by John Calder supervised construction of the factory, and Edward Terry served as chief consulting engineer from 1931 to 1933. When the plant commenced production, it rolled out copies of the

Caterpillar-60 tractor—10,100 in 1934, more than 20,000 the next year, and 29,000 in 1936. Thus, by the mid-1930s the Soviet Union produced over 100,000 tractors annually, a major accomplishment in light of the minuscule output just a few years before. Nearly all were copies of American machines, assembled in three new factories of American design, whose construction had been supervised by American engineers.[15]

Stalin's *Pravda* article in 1929 called not only for tractors but also for a national leap into the automobile age. To Soviet officials, the subject of cars and trucks brought to mind the United States, for America possessed advanced manufacturing technology capable of producing automobiles in the colossal quantities envisioned by the Five-Year Plan. According to the Soviet journal *Planned Economy*, America turned out 5,358,000 cars and trucks in 1929, compared to only 248,000 in France, 80,500 in Germany, and fewer than 2,000 in the USSR. The same year, another Soviet economics journal began an article on "automobilizing" the nation by explaining that "automobile transport is a powerful factor in the industrialization of a country. We see in the example of America the enormous role that the automobile played in the development of the nation's productive forces." More bluntly, a commentary in *Pravda* declared two years earlier that "nothing would better break the notorious 'idiocy of rural life' than when the Russian, Ukrainian, Belorussian, and Tatar peasantry replaces the antediluvian Russian cart with the American automobile."[16]

When Soviet leaders scrutinized the automotive industry in the United States, their gaze focused on the Ford Motor Company. Ford's Model A cars and Model AA trucks accounted for approximately a third of the small automobile fleet already in the Soviet Union, and the vehicles had generally performed well. They were also comparatively inexpensive and ideal for mass production. These considerations, bolstered by the mystique of Henry Ford's industrial methods, inclined Soviet authorities to Ford. They recognized that without some means of transferring technology from the United States, the Soviet Union could not possibly erect a modern automotive factory as demanded by the First Five-Year Plan. Consequently, in 1928, a Soviet delegation journeyed to America and began prolonged negotiations with the Ford Motor Company that yielded a contract in May 1929.[17]

The terms required Ford to furnish technical assistance in the construction of an automobile factory just outside the city of Nizhnii Novgorod, a few hundred miles east of Moscow on the Volga River. Along with providing advice on the layout of equipment in the plant and the organization of the manufacturing process, Ford agreed to place its patents at the disposal of the new facility and to train Soviet engineers in America. In exchange, the Soviet negotiators promised to purchase seventy-two thousand Ford cars and trucks in the form of partially assembled vehicles and individual parts. During the first two years of the contract, all of the Ford automobiles produced in the Soviet Union (a total of twenty-four thousand Model As and AAs) would come from these American parts shipped to facilities in Moscow and Nizhnii Novgorod. Over the next two years, as the main factory in Nizhnii Novgorod took shape and began to supply some of the necessary parts itself, Soviet authorities planned to manufacture a growing number of automobiles from domestically produced components, while continuing to assemble some vehicles from imported Ford parts as well. By 1933 production was scheduled to reach a target of 100,000 cars and trucks per year—twenty-four thousand from American-made parts and the rest from copies of these parts crafted at Nizhnii Novgorod and other Soviet factories. Thereafter, Soviet administrators hoped to be self-sufficient, with no further need or obligation to purchase imported Ford components in order to manufacture 100,000 vehicles annually. As a result, the last five years of the nine-year contract anticipated less interaction between the Soviet and American signatories. Ford was still expected in this final period to share its innovations with the factory at Gorky (as Nizhnii Novgorod was renamed in 1932), but directors there rarely displayed an interest in major changes.[18]

First and foremost, Soviet officials desired to produce a large number of vehicles (mostly trucks, not cars) as rapidly as possible. These were vital to the economy and too expensive to import in large quantities indefinitely. Hence the purchase of advanced manufacturing technology abroad and the concentration on mass production of the same standardized vehicles over the long term. Periodic retooling for new models was costly, which helped prompt Soviet authorities to decline their option to incorporate the V-8 engine developed by Ford in the 1930s. Instead they continued to manufacture a copy of the Model AA truck throughout the decade, with only minor and infrequent modifications.[19]

During the construction of the Nizhnii Novgorod plant, Ford engineers supervised the interior layout and the selection of most of the machinery, but they did not design or construct the building itself. That responsibility fell to the W. J. Austin Company of Cleveland, which had built automobile factories for Ford and other American businesses. For roughly a year and a half in 1929–30, a group of Soviet engineers worked in Cleveland with Austin experts to prepare a construction plan for the factory and much of the necessary infrastructure—roads, railroads, water systems, a power station, and so forth—as well as for a surrounding residential district sufficient to accommodate fifty thousand workers and their families. Once these plans had been drafted in the United States, Austin agreed to advise Soviet administrators and engineers during the construction phase at Nizhnii Novgorod. Other American and European companies also provided equipment for the project, and many former Ford employees worked there under contracts signed individually with the state automobile construction agency, rather than as part of the arrangement with Ford.[20] But the agreements with Ford and Austin stood alone as the two most important steps in supplying the Soviet Union with machinery and expertise necessary to build the factory.

This is not to suggest that Ford and Austin enjoyed a constantly harmonious relationship with their Soviet associates. For a time in 1931–32 Soviet officials complained about overcharges and thus withheld payments to Ford, while the company alleged that the Soviet Union had not purchased all of the automobile parts specified in their agreement. Along with disputes over contractual terms, Soviet administrators sometimes exercised their right to modify plans received from Ford and Austin. They might purchase certain equipment from a source other than that recommended in the plan, for example, or forego the machinery in favor of a more labor-intensive arrangement. In the end, the plant that emerged did not stand as an exact copy of Ford's River Rouge facility. Still, it was close enough to appear more an American factory than the product of any other country, even with the Soviet modifications. An enterprise of this urgency and scope could not have succeeded without the designs, equipment, supervision, and training provided by the American companies, especially Ford.[21] As at Dnieprostroy, Stalingrad, and other major projects, Soviet labor and materials were certainly essential, but they were not sufficient to complete the projects in such modern form and in such a short period of time.

The more emphasis party leaders placed on automobiles and tractors, the more vital became steel mills, without which the state could never satisfy its thirst for large machinery. "Metal draws all industry along with it, all spheres of human life, beginning with the production of turbines, tractors, harvester combines, textiles, food, and ending with books. Metal is the basis of modern civilization," declared a Soviet author in 1932. The *Story of the Great Plan* put it more succinctly: "Iron is bread to us." Valery Mezhlauk, assistant director of the Supreme Economic Council, compared iron to oxygen and warned in 1931 that "the country is suffocating from the lack of metal." Stalin's own name, Man of Steel, came to imply not only his personal toughness but also the party's resolve to boost steel production, and no other industrial sector received more emphasis during the First Five-Year Plan. "In those years," recalled a Soviet journalist, "the names of the leaders of metallurgical factories were known not simply to a narrow circle of economic officials, but to broad sections of the Soviet public. The country followed their work and their successes as in the days of war it had followed the successes of the most visible military leaders." News from this "iron front" soon featured reports from a sparsely inhabited region just east of the Ural Mountains, home to the largest single venture of the period. There rose the new factory and city of Magnitogorsk, which gained as much renown as any undertaking of the "Great Plan"—"living proof," a Soviet journal proclaimed, "of what Bolsheviks are able to achieve."[22]

In 1928 a delegation traveled from the Soviet Union to Cleveland for discussions with representatives of the Arthur G. McKee Company regarding the design of a mammoth steel works at Magnitogorsk. The talks produced agreement on a general plan based on the United States Steel plant in Gary, Indiana, and over four hundred American engineers then prepared a set of drawings for the project. So detailed and complex were these designs that they required approximately twenty months to complete and resulted in a bill to the Soviet Union of two million gold rubles. In March 1930 Soviet authorities hired the McKee Company to advise them during the construction of the Magnitogorsk factory—"according to the latest achievements of American *tekhnika*," a Soviet official had specified in the negotiations—and roughly two months later the first eleven men from McKee arrived at the site. By the time construction activity reached its peak at the end of 1931, some 250 Americans (and hundreds of other foreign technicians and laborers) worked at the complex, including twenty-seven American engineers devoted to blast-furnace construction alone. Among the American companies involved with Magnitogorsk, the Koppers Corporation of Pittsburgh played a role of importance second only to McKee. Koppers secured a contract for installing coke ovens and sent a team of engineers from the United States and Koppers's German subsidiary in 1930.[23]

Many other German engineers and pieces of German equipment could be found at Magnitogorsk. Some technicians and officials in the Soviet steel industry had favored German methods, which involved less mechanization and smaller blast furnaces than those in the United States. But by the close of the 1920s, Soviet advocates of an American approach gained the upper hand in debates over the most suitable Western technology for Soviet steel mills. The triumph of these "Americanists"—including the prominent engineer Ivan Bardin, who had worked earlier at the steel plant in Gary—also ensured the victory of the McKee Company in its competition with Siemens of Germany for the primary Magnitogorsk contract.[24] Thus, although Soviet authorities at Magnitogorsk rejected some American recommendations and turned on occasion to Germany and elsewhere for advice and equipment, the American contribution to the steel mill sur-passed that of other foreign countries.

American economic influence did not confine itself to a handful of showcase projects like Magnitogorsk and Dnieprostroy. At nearly the same moment that Ford agreed to help erect the automobile factory at Nizhnii Novgorod, Soviet officials hired the A. J. Brandt Company of Detroit to reorganize and expand the prerevolutionary AMO truck factory in Moscow. The two-year modernization project—designed to produce twenty-five thousand copies annually of an American Autocar 2½-ton truck—resulted in a facility that one observer described as "by far the largest and best-equipped plant in the world devoted solely to the manufacture of trucks and buses. Basically, the equipment is the last word in American practice."[25]

In the case of the steel industry, the celebrated factory at Magnitogorsk was conceived as one end of a tandem called the Ural-Kuznetsk Combinat. More than a thousand miles east of the Urals and Magnitogorsk lay the Kuznetsk coal deposits in Siberia. Soviet officials planned to link the two sites by building a second steel mill at Kuznetsk. Trains could then carry iron ore from the Urals to Kuznetsk and, on their return, bring Kuznetsk coal to Magnitogorsk, never traveling empty between the two locations, each rich in a resource needed by the other. The Freyn Engineering Company of Chicago designed the Kuznetsk plant and oversaw most of its construction. From 1929 through 1932 a Freyn employee, with several dozen American engineers working under him, supervised the building and operation of the initial sec-tion of the Kuznetsk complex, second in size only to Magnitogorsk. A report prepared for other Soviet officials by the Commissariat of Heavy Industry re-ferred to thirty Freyn engineers still at the site early in 1933 and confirmed that "the experience of the firm and its engineers was used heavily in the planning, construction, and startup of the Kuznetsk plant."[26]

Freyn's association with the Soviet Union began in 1927 through an agreement that required the company to provide technical assistance in modernizing antiquated metallurgical plants and in designing the new Kuznetsk facility. This contract did not obligate Freyn personnel to live and work inside the Soviet Union, but a new agreement the following year called on the company to establish a permanent group of roughly a dozen engineers attached to the Leningrad headquarters of Gipromez, the state institute for designing metallurgical factories. Freyn accepted the task of planning the re-construction of forty existing mills while building eighteen new iron and steel plants crucial to the objectives of the Five-Year Plan. Henry J. Freyn, president of the company, described the broader goal of the 1928 agreement as "making available to Soviet executives, engineers, and operators the American training, knowledge and practical experience of our organization, to the end that the reconstruction and enlargement of the existing plants and the planning and construction of new iron and steel works be predominantly of American design and standards." Gipromez continued to hire foreign consultants until they reached roughly four hundred in number by 1930, most of them American. Their influence expanded substantially, as described by W. S. Orr, who worked at Gipromez from 1929 to 1933:

> When we first joined Gipromez we were only asked questions—the Russians made the layouts, reports and decisions. In about six months we were asked in on the layouts and decisions, in about nine months we were made Chief Engineers of steel plant projects and at the end of the first year some of our men were heads of departments. Last year one was the Assistant Chief Engineer of the entire bureau.[27]

Soviet experts formed similar views of Freyn's role, as did the report from the Commissariat of Heavy Industry: "Freyn engineers have played an important part in all the large projects of Gipromez over the last 4–5 years. This has enabled Gipromez to adopt the latest achievements of American metallurgical practice." Ivan Bardin, the steel engineer, wrote in 1936 that Freyn personnel had participated "in all questions of project-making and reconstruction for our iron and steel industry." Indeed, he continued:

> The arrival of Americans was a great event. Until then Gipromez was lame in all four legs. It was a puny establishment, highly liable to empty talk and unprincipled chatter, incapable of elaborating technical ideas either in writing or in drawing. . . . The Americans left behind them a serious trace. Our young people learned a lot from the Americans; they had borrowed from them both technical knowledge and—the main thing—a way of working.[28]

Avraam Zaveniagin, director of Gipromez in 1930, later recalled this "opportunity to work with the well-known group of American engineers of the Freyn Engineering Company and to supervise the designing of nearly all of our new giant steel plants. I must say frankly that we were very much impressed with the work of the American group of specialists." This experience benefited Soviet engineers, he explained, for "they successfully went through an American school and with the knowledge acquired, they are carrying out in our metallurgy the last word in American technique which has been derived from many years of experience."[29] Some types of American equipment—including blast furnaces designed by Freyn and coke ovens by Koppers—became standards, copied in the Soviet iron and steel industry for years.

Meanwhile, in the manufacture of agricultural machinery and supplies, Americans worked in diverse locations outside the tractor factories at Stalingrad, Kharkov, and Cheliabinsk. Engineers from the Ford Motor Company supervised the remodeling and expansion in 1929–31 of the old Putilovets tractor plant in Leningrad, which emerged with new German and American equipment, organized along American lines, and with Americans managing several of the factory's departments. Production, which had not exceeded seven hundred tractors annually until 1928, soared to eleven thousand in 1930 and peaked near nineteen thousand in 1931. It is less clear whether Americans designed Soviet factories that produced other types of farm machinery, though American equipment certainly appeared in many of these plants, including the enormous Selmashstroy complex at Rostov. During this period the Du Pont Company and especially the Nitrogen Engineering Corporation of New York assisted in the construction of new nitrogen fertilizer factories, while in 1929 Soviet importers began a three-year buying spree of American combines, plows, and other agricultural implements that cost over $17 million—in addition to tractors worth $83 million.[30]

Americans served as advisers and instructors in numerous branches of production related to agriculture, including the flax/linen sector, hog raising, and the operation and repair of tractors. To boost cotton output and shrink imports, Soviet agencies also hired several eminent American experts who journeyed to Central Asia and Transcaucasia to assume posts as consulting engineers on extensive irrigation projects. Bound in the opposite direction, a delegation of officials and technicians from the Soviet meat industry arrived in Chicago to study American meat-packing plants. In line with the practice of other groups, they opened an office in the United States for planning Soviet factories and hired Americans to supervise design work in Chicago and construction in the Soviet Union. The previous year, 1929, a delegation from the Soviet canning industry had come to the United States to launch plans for several enterprises, including a large vegetable cannery in the Northern Caucasus. Designed by Gerlach Brothers of Minnesota, which also oversaw construction, the cannery received half a million dollars of American equipment. Despite this assistance, the plant initially operated at only a fraction of its planned capacity, in part because Soviet engineers had sought to copy much of the machinery by taking it apart for study, after which they failed to reassemble it properly.[31]

In the electrical industry, Hugh Cooper and the Dnieper dam were only part of a major American presence led by the General Electric Company. Although GE's initial involvement in the Soviet Union had been circuitous, conducted through its European affiliates, the company signed two contracts at the end of the decade that brought it directly into the Soviet Union's industrial tempest. The first agreement, in 1928, called for GE to sell between $21 million and $26 million worth of equipment to the USSR over a six-year period, while the next year the two parties signed a sweeping technical-assistance contract intended to cover a full decade. The technical-assistance agreement of 1929 included an exchange of patents, training of Soviet technicians in the United States, and the dispatch of GE engineers to assist the Soviet Union in developing most phases of its electrical industry. The second contract did not cover certain important electrical devices, such as communications gear and apparatus for the generation of weak current, but only because this equipment figured in a technical-assistance agreement signed earlier by the Soviet Union and the Radio Corporation of America.[32]

During the 1930s General Electric's equipment, and often its engineers, turned up at nearly all the Soviet Union's important industrial enterprises. One agreement secured GE's assistance in organizing a design bureau—headed by GE engineers—to plan the installation of electrical systems at the Magnitogorsk and Kuznetsk metallurgical complexes. The company's engineers also worked on numerous projects to generate electricity, including power stations at Nizhnii Novgorod and Stalingrad as well as Dnieprostroy. When Soviet officials decided to build a turbine factory at Kharkov, they relied on GE for the architectural plans and engineering designs. After the plans were prepared in Schenectady, GE engineers traveled to Kharkov to supervise the construction of the plant and the installation of German equipment. Upon completion in 1935, the factory produced turbines of a GE type in quantities that dwarfed the output of any other facility in the world. According to the Commissariat of Heavy Industry, "technical assistance from the firm [GE] reached all the major factories of VEO" (a state organization in charge of large electrical enterprises). Apart from the work of GE personnel on major projects, thousands of the company's motors and other mundane equipment appeared in Soviet factories around the country. If these items are considered together with copies of GE devices manufactured in the Soviet Union and the electricity generated by GE equipment in Soviet power stations, it would be safe to conclude that no significant branch of Soviet industry developed in the 1930s without some assistance from the General Electric Company.[33]

American guidance and machinery reached beyond automobiles, electricity, farm equipment, and steel to such important endeavors as mining. Regarding coal, for instance, Soviet officials appeared at first to prefer German mining techniques, but in 1926–27 they undertook a comparison of the methods used in several countries, including the United States. Administrators of the Soviet coal industry even staged a competition in which foreign firms were each allotted two mines to operate as best they could, with the results to help determine which companies would win technical-assistance contracts. American techniques prevailed, and by the end of the decade most large new Soviet mines were designed by Americans, notably experts from the firm of Stuart, James & Cooke of New York. The company had sent a group of engineers to the Soviet Union as early as 1926, and officials later negotiated a new agreement with the firm to modernize production in the Donets Basin when the First Five-Year Plan demanded much more coal from Soviet mines than ever before. Two other American companies, Allen & Garcia of Chicago and Roberts & Schaefer of New York, also signed contracts to design new mines and provide technical assistance in the Donets Basin and in newer areas like Kuznetsk, but Stuart, James & Cooke remained the preeminent foreign adviser to Soviet agencies concerned with coal production.

In 1930 the Soviet government requested a comprehensive report from Charles Stuart (senior member of the firm) on the status of the nation's coal industry. Stuart's report, which bluntly described many inefficiencies in Soviet coal production, was welcomed by top officials, who had it translated into seventy-five languages of the USSR and then distributed thousands of copies to administrators around the country. Although industry leaders in Moscow did not accept all the suggestions in the document, it served as the basis for reforms demanded by the party and the highest economic councils. As Stuart himself put it, "we have introduced innovations from every branch of American practice, and many of these innovations have been adopted and have been incorporated in other projects besides our own." Between 1928 and 1933 foreign assistance helped increase the output of Soviet coal by more than 100 percent. In 1932, when the government ended its technical-assistance contracts with foreign coal-mining firms, the Commissariat of Heavy Industry sent a letter to Stuart, James & Cooke, thanking the company for the "removal of many difficulties in the development of the coal industry and . . . [for] the speeding up of coal production which in turn had a favorable effect on the steel industry."[34]

At roughly the same time that Charles Stuart supplied advice on coal mines, American experts arrived to extract other resources from Soviet soil. In 1930 the entire nonferrous metals industry (including gold, silver, copper, aluminum, zinc, and lead) employed only 346 Soviet engineers and 458 Soviet technicians—three-quarters of whom possessed less than one year of experience. This small, unseasoned contingent could not possibly manage the surge in output dictated by the First Five-Year Plan, and Soviet officials quickly looked to the West, most importantly the United States, for assistance. Americans designed some Soviet zinc and lead plants and played prominent roles as consulting engineers in the brass/copper and aluminum industries. John Littlepage, who worked as a mining engineer in the Soviet Union for nearly a decade and eventually became deputy chief engineer of the entire Gold Trust, was honored with the Order of the Red Banner of Labor for his services. He reported that many of the mines employed American engineers and equipment—four or five American engineers at every large copper mine in the Urals, for instance—while an article published in 1930 referred to seventy-eight engineers from the United States working in various branches of the Soviet nonferrous metals industry. Antony Sutton's research in this area led him to conclude that between 1929 and 1933 the Soviet nonferrous industry as a whole depended heavily on American engineers, before newly trained Soviet counterparts replaced them over the next few years.[35]

American corporations and individual engineers on personal contracts assisted in other sectors of the Soviet economy, including the railroads, petroleum refining, chemical production, and machine building. Their participation resembled in form and significance the American aid described in preceding pages and may pass here without elaboration. But one firm, barely mentioned so far, deserves a concluding moment of attention, because it designed hundreds of factories across the Soviet industrial spectrum. In 1929 the Albert Kahn Company of Detroit commenced a remarkable period of collaboration with Soviet leaders when it began drafting blueprints for the Stalingrad Tractor Factory. Publications of the day acknowledged the Soviet Union's shortage of experts capable of planning large factories, and Albert Kahn, whose company had designed most of the major American automobile plants, among other projects, seemed an ideal candidate for such work. Soviet officials proposed to hire Kahn to conceive numerous industrial facilities, and by 1930 a team of some two dozen American engineers, architects, and draftsmen, led by Albert Kahn's brother Moritz, had organized a design bureau in Moscow. The bureau also housed several hundred Soviet employees, many of whom had been sent there to receive training from the Americans. Before long the group became the primary Soviet industrial planning body, responsible for designing factories in many branches of production—in contrast to the focus on metallurgy of the Freyn Engineering staff at Gipromez. One of Kahn's engineers headed the organization, which also guided the work of branch offices in other important cities. Soviet officials indicated the general nature of diverse factories they desired, and Kahn's unit produced the plans.[36]

In 1930 *Izvestiia* announced the agreement with Kahn and expressed hope that the arrangement would "instill in our planning the latest methods and achievements of American *tekhnika*." Two years later, much had been accomplished along these lines according to the same report from the Commissariat of Heavy Industry that praised Freyn Engineering: "[Kahn's staff in the Soviet Union] took part in planning all major projects undertaken by these [industrial design] organizations. As a result, our personnel received the opportunity to study and become familiar with American methods of construction planning."[37]

This opportunity did not last as long as either Kahn or Soviet officials expected. By 1932 the government could no longer acquire a sufficient amount of Western currency to continue paying all of the foreign companies and individual experts at work on industrial projects—a problem due largely to the depression. Soviet industrialization strategy required export of grain, timber, and other raw materials in order to amass the dollars, pounds, marks, and so forth to purchase Western equipment and the services of foreign engineers. As the depression wore on, the prices of commodities exported by the Soviet Union dropped faster than the cost of the machinery the government imported. More and more grain was sold abroad in a frantic but futile effort to keep pace with mounting debts until finally, in 1931, the Kremlin concluded that imports and technical-assistance agreements would have to be curtailed sharply.[38]

During the previous year Soviet imports of "machinery and equipment" had increased by 87 percent and then jumped another 20 percent in 1931. But thereafter, in a reversal of the original plan, these imports plummeted along with the government's ability to pay for them. By 1932 the value of imported "machinery and equipment" had dropped 34 percent, followed by consecutive declines of 62 and 61 percent over the next two years.[39] Soviet officials also applied themselves to technical-assistance contracts, canceling some and seeking to renegotiate others in ways that would eliminate payment in Western currencies.[40] "It is only natural that they should try to drive sharp bargains," observed Albert Kahn. "They, like us, are upset by the Depression. My firm, of course, would prefer to be paid in dollars." But dollars disappeared from subsequent proposals to Kahn, and by the spring of 1932 his employees (and many other Americans) had returned to the United States. Over the previous few years, though, they had left a vivid mark on the Soviet industrial landscape, now dotted with more than five hundred enterprises designed by the team. According to a partial list published by Kahn in

1936, these factories spanned the gamut of industrial activity. Aircraft parts, automobiles, forge shops, machinery and machine tools, roller bearings, foundries, power plants, metallurgy, and tractors do not complete the roster of Kahn's industrial projects in the Soviet Union. Moreover, when Kahn's experts departed in 1932, they were obliged to leave behind all of their blueprints and other materials, thus enabling Soviet architects to duplicate their designs for years to come.[41] A reckoning of the buildings that were largely copies of earlier facilities designed by Kahn's group would help place the Albert Kahn Company atop the list of American corporations that influenced Soviet industrialization in the 1930s.

Kahn's reputation in the Soviet Union survived the parting of ways in 1932. Years passed, and Soviet technical volumes continued to cite works from the Kahn firm that a more recent Soviet source described as "handbooks for the first generations of Soviet industrial architects." Looking back in 1938, an article in the Soviet periodical Architecture USSR reminded readers that before 1930 the nation had possessed little experience in designing large industrial enterprises. Therefore, "in 1930–31, technical leadership in the [industrial design and planning] trust was in fact carried out through consultation with a group of architects and engineers from the firm of Albert Kahn." A decade later, in the autumn of 1942, it seemed to an American journalist reporting from Stalingrad that "the names of Henry Ford and Albert Kahn are known to every child" in the city. When Kahn died that winter, Soviet officials sent a telegram to his widow expressing condolences from "Soviet engineers, builders, and architects" over the "death of your husband, Mr. Albert Kahn, who rendered us great service in designing a number of large plants and helped us to assimilate the American experience in the sphere of building industry."[42]

All of these instances of technology transfer clustered in a period of little more than five years beginning late in the 1920s. Previously, a handful of American companies had provided economic assistance to Soviet organizations— developing oil fields, for example—but the impact of this work could not compare with that to come at decade's end. Once Stalin and his allies spurred industrialization with the First Five-Year Plan, they poured money into scores of technical-assistance contracts with European and, especially, American businesses. Western expertise would accelerate the nation's industrial growth, party leaders hoped, and with this aim they purchased far more American guidance than tsarist Russia or the Soviet Union had ever experienced before.

Soviet officials had made some effort earlier in the 1920s to attract Western capital by offering "concession" agreements whereby a foreign partner would operate an industrial facility for a fixed number of years, after which the state took possession of the enterprise. During the period of the contract, the Western participant agreed to expand or modernize the business in return for profits expected from sale of the output. These arrangements attracted few important American companies, primarily because of the risks associated with investing in the Soviet Union. Shortly after seizing power in 1917 the Bolsheviks had confiscated the Russian assets of several American businesses, including International Harvester, General Electric, and the Singer Manufacturing Company. Such recent memories left "capitalists" wary of extended commitments whose payoffs were both distant and uncertain. American firms willing to test Soviet waters preferred the sale of equipment—for cash or short-term credit.

By the end of the decade, equipment transfers often formed part of broader technical-assistance agreements that eclipsed concessions. In exchange for specified payments, the contracts secured Soviet authorities some combination of the services described in this chapter: access to technological innovations, training in American factories, design work, advice on mechanization, supervision of construction, and so forth. Soviet officials could concentrate Western assistance precisely in areas of top priority, while foreign companies avoided much of the risk associated with concessions and usually received prompt payment in their own currencies. As a result, when the Soviet demand for Western technology soared at the outset of the First Five-Year Plan, so did the number of technical-assistance agreements. Compared to only seven such contracts concluded in the fiscal year 1925/26, one source reported seventeen new agreements in 1927/28, followed by thirty-three in 1928/29 and thirty-nine more over the next eight months. German and American businesses accounted for 80 percent of the total, with a majority of the contracts going to American firms during the last two years of the period.[43]

This surge of technical-assistance agreements initiated a flood of foreign engineers to the Soviet Union. From approximately two dozen in 1924, their number increased to nine thousand in 1932, with Americans totaling between two thousand and three thousand and Germans roughly twice that. Sources differ on precise figures, partly because reports did not always distinguish clearly between engineers and the less-schooled foreign workers who entered the Soviet Union in even larger numbers.[44] As Western engineers and laborers ventured east, they passed Soviet counterparts propelled in the opposite direction by the same flurry of technical-assistance contracts. In 1930 the State Department counted nine hundred Soviet citizens arriving for business purposes under the auspices of the Soviet trade mission in the United States—compared to totals of only 86 in 1926 and 163 in 1927. These delegations changed not only in size but also in primary purpose. In the mid-1920s, before the advent of many technical-assistance agreements, most Soviet visitors to America came to purchase machinery and raw materials such as cotton. Five years later, more than three-fourths of the (much larger) Soviet contingent arrived to consult or train at industrial enterprises.[45]

Desire for American expertise also fostered a thirst for technical journals published in the United States. Soviet subscriptions to U.S. periodicals multiplied from only a few hundred in 1926 to roughly eight thousand in 1927/28 and twelve thousand the following year, according to Amtorg, a Soviet trade agency based in the United States. Amtorg also distributed its own journal (in Russian), titled *American Technology and Industry*, which contained articles on current American equipment and practices. In 1931 the editors celebrated eight years of publication and emphasized their mission "to satisfy the ever-growing need of wide engineering circles in the USSR for familiarity with the achievements of advanced American *tekhnika*." Hence their gratification that twenty-five thousand copies of the journal now reached the Soviet Union, many times more than its initial circulation.[46]

In similar fashion, imports of American industrial products by 1930 dwarfed the acquisitions of a few years before. According to a study by the State Department, Soviet purchases of American "industrial and power plant equipment" quadrupled from 1927/28 to 1929/30—a jump nearly as extraordinary as the 344 percent increase in the value of Soviet imports of American agricultural machinery and supplies over the same period. In 1930 the United States accounted for a quarter of *all* foreign commodities sold to Stalin's government, moving it ahead of Germany as the leading exporter to the Soviet Union.[47]

As noted earlier, the peak of American technical assistance coincided with sustained attacks on jazz and Hollywood movies. In 1928, the same year that witnessed Gorky's article "On the Music of the Gross" and a campaign to "cleanse the screen of trash," Soviet delegations commenced negotiations with Ford over the factory at Nizhnii Novgorod and traveled to Cleveland to discuss the design of a steel works at Magnitogorsk. This pattern has appeared in various guises for centuries in Russian history, as aversion for Western culture or politics frequently accompanied quests for Western technical innovations. In these instances, tsarist and Soviet governments felt compelled to acquire Western expertise in order to repulse or surpass foreign rivals while at the same time blocking Western religious, cultural, or ideological contamination. Technically advanced the West might be, but it appeared to lack other virtues that distinguished Russia. "We must admit, we always considered ourselves superior to the Americans because of our socialist, communist ideals," mused a Soviet journalist in 1988. "And in our consciousness we tried to combine, somehow, the fact of our economic backwardness with a superiority of ideals."[48]

In this spirit the party denounced "bourgeois" culture, while craving Western technology—and America stood out on both fronts. By the 1920s any offensive against foreign popular culture in the Soviet Union had to target amusements from the United States, for no other country exported recreation as enthralling to millions as American jazz and movies. The Cultural Revolution and subsequent government restrictions drove these bourgeois temptations from general view and soon replaced them with "socialist realist" alternatives. For the next half-century, American popular culture assumed a lower profile in the Soviet Union, though its appeal persisted and developed a new significance over the decades to come. Meanwhile, in contrast to foreign movies and music (to say nothing of Western political and economic systems in vogue for a time during the 1990s), technical assistance from the United States topped the shopping list of party leaders. Here the challenge lay not in reducing contact but in securing Western aid on an unprecedented scale and then maximizing its contribution to the First Five-Year Plan.

By this time America had become *the* economic standard of comparison, a nation that represented not just a source of assistance but a challenge. No socialist state could be seen as less proficient in technology than a country still in its capitalist stage of development, and yet there loomed the United States, a formidable presence in reality and imagination alike. The Bolsheviks soon proclaimed the goal of surpassing America and set out to do so at almost any cost. As fortune would have it, the West sank ever deeper into the Great Depression, adding luster to the industrial boom under way in socialism's showcase. Victory appeared close at hand. The fact endured, though, that American technical assistance contributed a good deal to this achievement, especially to projects celebrated most by the party. It remained to be seen how much of the "capitalist" role could be acknowledged publicly, without tarnishing the Kremlin's triumph.

Notes

1. G. K. Ordzhonikidze, *Stat'i i rechi v dvukh tomakh*, vol. 2 (Moscow: Gosudarstvennoe izdatel'stvo politicheskoi literatury, 1957), 121.

2. N. Bukharin and E. Preobrazhensky, *The ABC of Communism* (Ann Arbor: University of Michigan Press, 1966), 159.

3. The book, by M. Ilin (Ilya Marshak), was published in 1931 in the United States by Houghton Mifflin under the title *New Russia's Primer*.

4. Floyd J. Fithian, "Soviet-American Economic Relations, 1918–1933: American Business in Russia during the Period of Non-recognition" (Ph.D. diss., University of Nebraska, 1964), 264; Antony C. Sutton, *Western Technology and Soviet Economic Development*, 3 vols. (Stanford, Calif.: Hoover Institution, 1968–1973), 1:203; Anne D. Rassweiler, *The Generation of Power: The History of Dneprostroi* (Oxford: Oxford University Press, 1988), 3; *Pravda*, 10 October 1932, 1; Ilin, *New Russia's Primer*, 36.

5. N. Anov, "Dneprostroi," *Nashi dostizheniia*, no. 3 (1930): 32; Kendall E. Bailes, "The American Connection: Ideology and the Transfer of American Technology to the Soviet Union, 1917–1941," *Comparative Studies in Society and History* 23, no. 3 (July 1981): 439–40; Rassweiler, *Generation of Power*, 70.

6. Barbara M. Kugel, "The Export of American Technology to the Soviet Union, 1918–1933, including the Ford Motor Company-Soviet Government Relationship, 1918–1933" (M.A. thesis, Wayne State University, 1956), 28; Fithian, "Soviet-American Economic Relations," 298–99; Wladimir Naleszkiewicz, "Technical Assistance of the American Enterprises to the Growth of the Soviet Union, 1929–1933," *Russian Review* 25, no. 1 (January 1966): 67.

7. Fithian, "Soviet-American Economic Relations," 272–73; Pitirim A. Sorokin, *Russia and the United States* (New York: Dutton, 1944), 166; V. M. Molotov, *The Success of the Five-Year Plan* (New York: International, 1931), 67–68; *Izvestiia*, 6 September 1932, 2.

8. *Pravda*, 7 November 1929, 2.

9. Dana G. Dalrymple, "The American Tractor Comes to Soviet Agriculture: The Transfer of a Technology," *Technology and Culture* 5, no. 2 (Spring 1964): 194, 197; Norton T. Dodge, *The Tractor Industry of the U.S.S.R.* (Washington, D.C.: Council for Economic and Industry Research, 1955), 117. Virtually all tractors imported by the Soviet Union from 1924 through 1931 came from the United States. Dana G. Dalrymple, "American Technology and Soviet Agricultural Development, 1924–1933," *Agricultural History* 40 (1966): 193; Dodge, *Tractor Industry*, 68.

10. Rossiiskii Gosudarstvennyi Arkhiv Ekonomiki (hereafter cited as RGAE), fond 7620, opis' 1, ed. khr. 712, ll. 25–28; *Za industrializatsiiu*, 5 July 1930, 5; "The Utilization of Foreign Technical Assistance with Particular Reference to American Technical Assistance in the Carrying Out of the Bolshevik Economic Program," June 15, 1931, National Archives, U.S. Department of State, Record Group 59, Office of Eastern European Affairs, Staff Studies and Memoranda, 1917–1941, Entry 555-24A (hereafter cited as "Utilization of Foreign Technical Assistance"), 26–27; *Industrializatsiia SSSR, 1929–1932 gg. Dokumenty i materialy* (Moscow: Nauka, 1970), 112; Dalrymple, "American Tractor," 198–99; Sutton, *Western Technology*, 2:185–86, 283; Fithian, "Soviet-American Economic Relations," 235; *Those Who Built Stalingrad as Told by Themselves* (Moscow-Leningrad: Cooperative Publishing Society of Foreign Workers in the USSR, 1934), 48.

11. "Utilization of Foreign Technical Assistance," 27; Dalrymple, "American Tractor," 199; Dalrymple, "American Technology," 195–96; Fithian, "Soviet-American Economic Relations," 228.

12. *New York Times*, 19 June 1930.

13. Dodge, *Tractor Industry*, 4, 97.

14. Dodge, *Tractor Industry*, 52; Dalrymple, "American Tractor," 200; Dalrymple, "American Technology," 195–96; State Department Records, 1930–39, 861.5017—Living Conditions/677.

15. Dodge, *Tractor Industry*, 5, 52, 97; Sutton, *Western Technology*, 2:188–90; Dalrymple, "American Tractor," 200–201; Dalrymple, "American Technology," 195–96.

16. "'GAZ' i 'Ford,'" *Planovoe khoziaistvo*, nos. 6–7 (1932): 242; M. Sorokin, "Ob avtomobilizatsii Soiuza," *Ekonomicheskoe obozrenie*, no. 7 (July 1929): 93; *Pravda*, 22 July 1927, 2.

17. George D. Holliday, *Technology Transfer to the USSR, 1928–1937 and 1966–1975: The Role of Western Technology in Soviet Economic Development* (Boulder, Colo.: Westview, 1979), 118–21; Ford Motor Company, "Report of the Ford Delegation to Russia and the U.S.S.R." (1926), 234, Ford Motor Company Archives.

18. Holliday, *Technology Transfer*, 116–17, 121–22; Fithian, "Soviet-American Economic Relations," 327, 329.

19. Holliday, *Technology Transfer*, 131–32.

20. "Utilization of Foreign Technical Assistance," 27; Fithian, "Soviet-American Economic Relations," 259, 330, 332; Holliday, *Technology Transfer*, 122–23; Sutton, *Western Technology*, 1:248–49.

21. Fithian, "Soviet-American Economic Relations," 262, 331, 335–45; Holliday, *Technology Transfer*, 121–23, 128–29.

22. Ilin, *New Russia's Primer*, 80; Stephen Kotkin, *Magnetic Mountain: Stalinism as a Civilization* (Berkeley, Calif.: University of California Press, 1995), 37, 51, 55, 70–71.

23. Loren R. Graham, *Science in Russia and the Soviet Union: A Short History* (Cambridge: Cambridge University Press, 1993), 255; Naleszkiewicz, "Technical Assistance," 58; *Iz istorii magnitogorskogo metallurgicheskogo kombinata i goroda Magnitogorska, 1929–1941 gg. Sbornik dokumentov i materialov* (Cheliabinsk: Iuzhno-Ural'skoe knizhnoe izdatel'stvo, 1965), 60; Sutton, *Western Technology*, 2:62, 75, 116.

24. Bailes, "American Connection," 438–39; Sutton, *Western Technology*, 2:75–76; Fithian, "Soviet-American Economic Relations," 246.

25. "Utilization of Foreign Technical Assistance," 28; W. H. Chamberlin, "Missionaries of American Techniques in Russia," *Asia* (July–August 1932): 425; Sutton, *Western Technology*, 1:248; 2:177–78.

26. H. J. Freyn, "The Life and Work of American Engineers in Soviet Russia," *Engineers and Engineering* 48, no. 6 (June 1931): 142–43; RGAE, fond 7297, opis' 38, delo 67, l. 135.

27. A. Kolomenskii, *Kak my ispol'zuem zagranichnuiu tekhniku* (Moscow: Gosizdat, 1930), 24, 30; Fithian, "Soviet-American Economic Relations," 245–46; Bailes, "American Connection," 439; Henry J. Freyn, quoted in Sutton, *Western Technology*, 2:61, 63; W. S. Orr, quoted in Sutton, *Western Technology*, 2:74–75.

28. RGAE, fond 7297, opis' 38, delo 67, l. 135; R. W. Davies, *The Industrialization of Soviet Russia*, vol. 3, *The Soviet Economy in Turmoil, 1929–1930* (London: Macmillan, 1989), 217.

29. A. Zaviniagin [Zaveniagin], "U.S.S.R. Favors American Engineers & Equipment," *Freyn Design* (March 1934): 19.

30. Dalrymple, "American Technology," 192, 196, 199; Sutton, *Western Technology*, 2:191, 193; Dodge, *Tractor Industry*, 97.

31. Dalrymple, "American Technology," 194, 198–201, 205; Sutton, *Western Technology*, 2:32, 34, 38, 42–43; Anastas I. Mikoian, "Dva mesiatsa v SShA," *SShA: ekonomika, politika, ideologiia*, no. 10 (October 1971): 74.

32. Fithian, "Soviet-American Economic Relations," 282, 285, 287, 292–94; Tarun Chandra Bose, *American Soviet Relations 1921–1933* (Calcutta: Mukhopadhyay, 1967), 58, 64–65; Sutton, *Western Technology*, 1:252.

33. Sutton, *Western Technology*, 2:153–54, 163–65; Kugel, "Export of American Technology," 34–35; Chamberlin, "Missionaries," 425; Naleszkiewicz, "Technical Assistance," 68; RGAE, fond 7297, opis' 38, delo 67, l. 138; Fithian, "Soviet-American Economic Relations," 262, 296–97, 299–300.

34. Sutton, *Western Technology*, 1:51; Bailes, "American Connection," 439; Bose, *American Soviet Relations*, 63–64; "Report of Stuart, James & Cooke, Inc. to V.S.N.Kh.," Hoover Institution Archives, Charles Stuart Collection, Box 1, Folder 1-R, chapter 1: 5; Fithian, "Soviet-American Economic Relations," 252–55 (the quotation of the letter from the Commissariat of Heavy Industry is on 254).

35. Sutton, *Western Technology*, 1:81; 2:44–47, 55, 57, 60; Bose, *American Soviet Relations*, 67; Naleszkiewicz, "Technical Assistance," 72; John D. Littlepage and Demaree Bess, *In Search of Soviet Gold* (New York: Harcourt, Brace, 1938), 87–88, 120, 207.

36. William C. Brumfield, ed., *Reshaping Russian Architecture: Western Technology, Utopian Dreams* (Cambridge: Cambridge University Press, 1990), 155–57, 203; I. Kas'ianenko, "Ispol'zovanie amerikanskogo opyta v period stanovleniia sovetskogo promyshlennogo zodchestva (sotrudnichestvo s firmoi Al'berta Kana)," in *Vzaimodeistvie kul'tur SSSR i SShA XVIII–XX vv.*, ed. O. E. Tuganova (Moscow: Nauka, 1987), 112, 118; Sutton, *Western Technology*, 2:249–52, 343.

37. *Izvestiia*, 5 February 1930, 4; RGAE, fond 7297, opis' 38, delo 67, l. 142. See also *Ekonomicheskaia zhizn'*, 31 July 1929, 1; *Torgovo-promyshlennaia gazeta*, 16 May 1929, 1.

38. RGAE, fond 7297, opis' 38, delo 67, ll. 20, 147.

39. Calculations made from figures in Holliday, *Technology Transfer*, 45.

40. RGAE, fond 7297, opis' 38, delo 19, ll. 103, 105.

41. Brumfield, *Reshaping Russian Architecture*, 157, 173 (note 32), 201, 206–207 (the Kahn quotation is on 206); Kas'ianenko, "Ispol'zovanie," 114.

42. Kas'ianenko, "Ispol'zovanie," 116; E. Popov, "Iz praktiki promyshlennoi arkhitektury," *Arkhitektura SSSR*, no. 6 (June 1938): 42; Brumfield, *Reshaping Russian Architecture*, 201–202, 208.

43. "Utilization of Foreign Technical Assistance," 11.

44. R. W. Davies, *The Industrialization of Soviet Russia*, vol. 4, *Crisis and Progress in the Soviet Economy, 1931–1933* (London: Macmillan, 1996), 493; Bailes, "American Connection," 433; Sylvia R. Margulies, *The Pilgrimage to Russia: The Soviet Union and the Treatment of Foreigners, 1924–1937* (Madison: University of Wisconsin Press, 1968), 227–28; Andrea Graziosi, "Foreign Workers in Soviet Russia, 1920–40: Their Experience and Their Legacy," *International Labor and Working-Class History*, no. 33 (Spring 1988): 40. For documents on the hiring of American specialists to work in the Commissariat of Transportation, see RGAE, fond 1884, opis' 60, ed. khr. 877, ll. 63–64; RGAE, fond 1884, opis' 60, ed. khr. 976, ll. 24–26. On the rapid increase in the number of foreign experts employed by the Commissariat of Heavy Industry between 1927 and 1932, see RGAE, fond 7297, opis' 38, delo 19, l. 102.

45. RGAE, fond 1884, opis' 60, ed. khr. 591, ll. 32, 34; "Utilization of Foreign Technical Assistance," 21; Kolomenskii, *Kak my ispol'zuem*, 11; Sutton, *Western Technology*, 2:275–76.

46. RGAE, fond 1884, opis' 60, ed. khr. 872, l. 67; *Economic Review of the Soviet Union* 3, no. 22/23 (1 December 1928): 382; *Amerikanskaia tekhnika i promyshlennost'* 8, no. 10 (October 1931): 618.

47. "Utilization of Foreign Technical Assistance," 25; Jon Kenton Walker, "Soviet-American Trade and the Amtorg Trading Corporation during the Period of Nonrecognition" (M.A. thesis, University of Tulsa, 1981), 80, 82.

48. *Moskovskie novosti*, 2 October 1988, 6.

CHAPTER FIVE

~

Catch and Surpass

A red light is going to be raised to the tower on the left side of the Volga. Do you know what that means? As soon as the red light appears there, it will be a signal to us that we have surpassed the American *tempo*. Watch the left tower, comrades.

—*Tempo* (by Nikolai Pogodin)

Beginning with the first spare parts used to reconstruct our factories in the 1920s, from the construction in Magnitostroy, Dneprostroy, the automobile and tractor factories built during the first five-year plans, on into the postwar years and to this day, what they [Soviet leaders] need from you [Americans] is economically absolutely indispensable.

—Alexander Solzhenitsyn

"The Americans helped us a great deal," Stalin remarked to an interviewer from the United States in 1933. "This must be acknowledged. They helped us better and more boldly than did others. We thank them for it."[1] He had already commended American technical advisers in the message read at ceremonies inaugurating the Stalingrad Tractor Factory, and later, during World War II, he informed the visiting president of the U.S. Chamber of Commerce that two-thirds of the nation's large industrial establishments had been built with American assistance.[2] However, this trio of statements, spanning more than a decade, represents most of what the nation's leader cared to say on the subject. Though he realized that American experience and equipment figured importantly in Soviet industrialization, Stalin almost never gave voice to these thoughts in statements destined for the Soviet public—where he preferred to emphasize the role of the party and the proletariat. Soviet triumphs, not dependence or backwardness, were the keynotes during the First Five-Year Plan and long thereafter.

But they were not the only words heard from officials in the 1930s, before the purges and especially the Cold War made it difficult to admit Western contributions to icons of Soviet progress. For several years after the acceleration of the First Five-Year Plan, various authorities stressed without restraint the importance of assistance from abroad. In September 1929, for example, the assistant director of the Supreme Economic Council told the American Section of the Soviet Chamber of Commerce for the West that "the tempos of industrial development called for by the Five-Year Plan require the use of [foreign] technical assistance to an even greater degree than at present." Another member of the council presumed that "the great Five-Year program of industrialization of the U.S.S.R. can be realized within the time prescribed only on the condition that we master in the decisive spheres in the shortest time the latest attainments of American and European technical skill."[3] At the end of the plan's run, the Commissar of Heavy Industry received a report from subordinates who cited "the colossal and extremely valuable work done by foreigners in the automobile, tractor, machine-building, electrical, ferrous and nonferrous metallurgical, chemical, [and] construction [industries], some parts of fuel industry, and other branches of heavy industry." In 1931 the State Planning Agency notified the Council of Labor and Defense that without the participation of foreign workers and specialists, the new Soviet industrial enterprises "cannot be built and put into operation."[4]

Acknowledgments also singled out individual sectors of the economy, including the domain of the State Automobile Plant Trust in 1929. Its director wrote that "in our program of automobile manufacture we are orientating ourselves on the American automobile industry," adding elsewhere that "copying foreign automobile models will allow us to avoid numerous 'childhood diseases' and start up production less expensively."[5] The same year, a resolution from the party's Central Committee stated bluntly that "the proper tempo and rational development of the chemical industry depends directly on the receipt of foreign technical assistance."[6] As late as 1938, a book emphasizing recent economic advances in the Soviet Union could still remind readers that the Stalingrad Tractor Factory "was imported from abroad almost in its entirety." Such remarks were unequivocal. "It is completely clear," asserted an article in the journal *Party Construction* at the beginning of the decade, "that without the mastery of the latest achievements of capitalist *tekhnika,* we would not successfully develop our own gigantic building projects."[7]

Most of these comments reached officials or specialists, rather than the general public, and thus might be considered more forthright than articles in *Pravda, Izvestiia,* and other publications with a broader circulation. However, a book about the construction of the Stalingrad Tractor Factory, written for a mass audience in 1933, included this reminiscence from the factory's first director: "I openly put it to our engineers that they should learn from the Americans and imitate their methods." In 1929 *Pravda* reported a speech in which Aleksei Rykov, a Politburo member and chairman of the Council of People's Commissars for much of the 1920s, declared it "clear that American and western European *tekhnika* has made great progress and developed new means of solving technical problems that we must make use of as widely as possible in our own construction work."[8] Numerous mass-circulation newspapers ran occasional stories on this theme and also printed the names of Western experts who received the Order of Lenin, the Order of the Red Banner of Labor, and other honors for valuable work on prominent construction projects.

Some authors combined endorsement of foreign technical assistance with attacks on those who regarded Western aid as unnecessary. A book titled *How We Are Using Foreign Technical Know-how,* written in readily accessible language in 1930, noted substantial contributions by numerous Western participants—among them Hugh Cooper at Dnieprostroy; Stuart, James & Cooke in the coal industry; Albert Kahn and Freyn Engineering in factory design, along with General Electric and Ford—and reminded readers of the arguments in favor of this nonnative presence. "The use of foreign experience to assist the development and rationalization of our industry is necessary so that we do not waste effort and resources on reinventing . . . that which has already been invented," explained the introduction, thereby anticipating the book's concluding line: "we must utilize foreign technical assistance much more widely and vigorously than we have done up to now." Between these pages appear numerous variations on the same theme, including criticism of officials who asserted that foreigners, unfamiliar with Soviet conditions, could offer little of value. "It is necessary to struggle resolutely against such a short-sighted position," countered the author. "You won't get far with such cheap slogans as 'we can manage by ourselves' and 'we can cope just as well as the foreigners.'"[9]

Western expertise did not come exclusively from the United States, of course, and Germany in particular contributed much to the economic development of Stalin's realm. In the nineteenth century German industrialization had impressed Russian officials, many of whom envied or feared their formidable neighbor. Germany's reputation for technical proficiency survived the demise of the kaiser's empire in World War I, and Bolshevik leaders welcomed economic assistance from the Weimar Republic as they waited for revolution to erupt in Berlin. During the first two Soviet decades, German engineers, architects, and other experts formed a majority of the foreign specialists who worked for the Bolshevik state, and Germany ranked as the Soviet Union's principal trading partner over the period as a whole.

Clearly, if Western *tekhnika* did make a critical contribution to the achievements of the First Five-Year Plan, much of it arrived from Germany rather than America. Although the United States became the leading exporter to the Soviet Union in 1930, American manufacturers did not retain this position for long. Three years later, the volume of trade from America had not only shriveled, it did so even faster than the reduction of goods from Germany and elsewhere, leaving America with no more than 2 percent of the (much smaller) Soviet market in 1933. Over the same period Germany's share nearly doubled, from 24 to 47 percent, while the British portion climbed from 8 percent to 13 percent.[10]

America's tumble from the position of chief exporter to the Soviet Union owed much to the generous credits granted Moscow at this time by various European nations and to the fallout from restrictions placed by the U.S. government on some imports from the Soviet Union. As the depression forced down prices of the growing volume of grain and other commodities exported by the Soviet Union, cries arose from businessmen and politicians in the United States that the Kremlin had embarked on a "dumping" campaign—a supposed plot to destroy American farms and other enterprises by flooding markets with goods priced below cost or produced by inexpensive prison labor. Meanwhile the German government rejected French appeals to join an antidumping league and, most important, increased the amount of credit it would guarantee to finance Soviet purchases of German manufactured wares. The U.S. government still refused to guarantee (and thus encourage) credit extended by American companies to Soviet buyers, more desperate than ever for financing as the depression dried up their reserves of foreign currency. Little wonder, then, that by 1931 the Soviet government began shifting its dwindling list of orders from the United States to Germany and other European countries.[11]

Yet America stood out in the Soviet industrialization drive and swayed many prominent officials to affirm that the United States, much more than Germany, should serve as a guide. "It is completely clear," asserted Valery Mezhlauk, assistant director of the Supreme Economic Council, "that in order to overcome all difficulties in a short period we will have to acquire experience from the most advanced capitalist countries—mainly the experience of America. It is possible to learn something from Germany, but regarding agriculture and much machinery it is necessary to learn from America."[12] America was young; America was modern; America had developed the means to solve industrial challenges similar to those now facing the Soviet Union—and for which traditional European techniques seemed puny and outmoded.[13] Beyond statistical comparisons of technical-assistance agreements, engineers, and levels of foreign trade, other terms best capture the preeminence of America's influence. For instance, any reasonable effort to list the ten or fifteen industrial projects of greatest importance to Soviet leaders in the era of the First Five-Year Plan would yield a roster of endeavors whose principal foreign advisers for planning and construction were much more likely to be American than German. In these ventures American equipment and methods frequently became Soviet standards, adopted for years to come in countless other factories and mines. Even some of the equipment imported from Germany had been manufactured there according to American design.[14]

None of this pleased German entrepreneurs, including the secretary of the Association of German Manufacturers Doing Business with Russia. To Charles Stuart (the coal-mining expert), he expressed vexation at "the extent to which Russian business was being handed to America" despite "all that Germany had done in extending credits and otherwise assisting Russian rehabilitation."[15] When Germans complained about Soviet preferences for American alternatives, they could hope for nothing more than assurances that government agencies bought the most suitable technology wherever it could be found and did not confine purchases to a single country. On this point, compare two addresses given by Soviet officials to foreign businessmen in 1929 at Moscow's Chamber of Commerce for the West. Mezhlauk emphasized to the Chamber's American Section that Soviet industrialization "requires use of the experience of the advanced industrial countries and first and foremost the construction experience of America. . . . Such enormous construction as is currently underway in the Soviet Union can be found only in America. Therefore, American engineers and technicians are the most suitable choice to apply their experience and knowledge to the construction of factories and plants in the USSR." Though the government was not "closing the door to technical assistance from other countries," Mezhlauk added, "the leading role must belong to American engineers and technicians."[16]

German diplomats and entrepreneurs were not heartened to read these remarks in the newspaper and doubtless hoped for reassurance when they gathered two weeks later to hear a lower-ranking official from the Supreme Economic Council address the German Section of the Chamber of Commerce. "Recently," began the speaker, "'jealous notes' and dissatisfaction have appeared in the German press, claiming that the Soviet press has begun to devote serious attention to questions of American *tekhnika* and the use of American technical assistance. Certain German circles see in this a change in the orientation of Soviet economic policy." This would be a mistake, he continued, for "we do not confine ourselves to an English, German, or American orientation. Our orientation is Soviet." The nation's commissariats sought the best technology wherever it beckoned. "When we were faced with the task of developing the petroleum, automobile and tractor industries, we turned to the USA because we consider America to be the leading country in these branches of industry. In the case of the chemical industry, we turned for assistance to Germany, and it is not our fault if we also had to turn to other countries [especially America] for some technical assistance in this branch of industry."[17]

Perhaps the audience derived some reassurance from the talk up to that point. The United States still seemed the most important source of equipment, but not as overwhelmingly as in Mezhlauk's telling. However, the address then grew sterner, beginning with a warning to "people in Europe and especially Germany" that "we do not intend to debate the issue of industrialization in the USSR and the fulfillment of the Five-Year Plan." The speaker rejected German concerns that economic aid to the Soviet Union would ultimately reduce imports from Germany, and he dismissed German worries over acquisition of trade secrets by the Soviet Union. "I will not hide the fact that in recent years we have met a better response from America than from Germany in providing us with technical assistance. In America they are not so jealous about production secrets, and they have long understood that the best conveyor of goods is the assimilation by the importing country of the *tekhnika* of the exporting country."[18]

Two years later, the German author Emil Ludwig detected abundant enthusiasm for things American while visiting the Soviet Union. If this did not distinguish him from numerous foreign observers, his opportunity to raise the matter with Stalin certainly did. During an interview with the Soviet leader in December 1931, Ludwig described his impressions: "I see in the Soviet Union an exceptional respect for everything American, I would even say a worship of everything American, that is, of the country of the dollar, the most thoroughly capitalist country. These feelings exist in your working class, too, and they pertain not only to tractors and cars, but to Americans in general." When asked to explain the appeal of America, Stalin replied, "You exaggerate. We don't have any special respect for everything American. But we respect American efficiency in everything—in industry, in *tekhnika*, in literature, in life." While the United States was a capitalist country, Stalin explained at some length, it lacked the pernicious feudal traditions that still plagued Europe. He praised America's tradition of independence—"a country of 'free colonizers'"—and "democratic" simplicity of the sort that made it hard to detect, by external appearance, American engineers among American workers.[19]

Stalin's elaboration, as it drifted away from the original question, presented America in a positive light while criticizing Europe. Suddenly, as if seeking to end on a conciliatory note for Ludwig's readers, Stalin changed course. "But if we have strong sympathies for any particular nation, or, more correctly, for the majority of people in any particular nation, then, of course, one must speak of our liking for the Germans. One cannot compare these sympathies with our feelings for Americans." Ludwig must have found this judgment surprising and asked what there could be about the Germans that inspired warm feelings in the Soviet people. Stalin preferred to confine his explanation to a reminder that Germany "gave the world such people as Marx and Engels. It is enough to state the fact as such." Ludwig chose not to explore the popularity of this gift in Russia and turned the discussion to foreign policy.[20]

If Stalin sought to assuage German feelings with an offhand remark about Marx and Engels, other Soviet officials did not bother. "In our studies of both European and American railway systems," declared the assistant commissar for railways, "we have come to the conclusion that the achievements of the United States in railway transportation and in the field of industries serving transportation, especially locomotive and car building, are far above those that we have seen elsewhere."[21] The director of the State Trust of Automobile Plants penned an article that might well have produced "'jealous notes' and dissatisfaction" in the German press: "We do not close the road toward cooperation in this business with other countries. Still it is indisputable that conditions are currently more favorable for the use of American *tekhnika*, American engineers, and American equipment than for the use of those of other countries."[22] A few months earlier, in the spring of 1929, *Izvestiia* carried an article explaining why America offered the best guide to Soviet industry: "The United States has the most advanced technical development in the world. In the production of many machines that are of particular interest now to the Soviet Union (agricultural machinery, electrical products, heavy industrial equipment, and so forth), America currently stands above all competition."[23] No dissent issued from Vasily Ivanov, the first director of the Stalingrad Tractor Factory. The party line "demands that we do not pass through all the intermediate stages of technical development that capitalism went through; where it is possible to establish American methods of work there should be no question of delaying the process and going the European way. This is clear, I should think?"[24]

Germans themselves embraced Fordism and other American industrial innovations, as a variety of Soviet economists and officials noted. Among them numbered Semyon Lobov, head of the Supreme Economic Council of the Soviet Union's Russian Republic, who welcomed the signing of numerous technical-assistance contracts with American firms in 1929: "Formerly we were not successful in this, and many achievements of American technical skill came to us second-hand, as it were, through Germany. . . . In the electro-technical industry we were for a long time resorting to the aid of Germany, but it turned out that Germany itself is learning from America." The time had come, Lobov added, for Soviet administrators and engineers to stop "looking at Europe as their example," for "Europe is perceptibly lagging behind America."[25] Avraam Zaveniagin, a prominent administrator in the metallurgical industry (including a period as director of the Magnitogorsk project), celebrated just such a change in outlook. "Before meeting the Americans, our engineers were under the influence of European practice and were afraid to work on such a [large] scale. Following the lead of American metallurgical technique, we soon left the European plants far behind us."[26]

To be sure, Soviet officials proved adept at playing foreign nations and firms against each other to obtain technology on the best terms. Many countries besides America contributed to Soviet industrialization, especially in narrow branches of production in which they had established a reputation. European companies were also logical choices to replace equipment in older factories built according to designs pioneered and widely adopted within their borders. But in fundamental disputes between those Soviet authorities who favored European methods and others who advocated techniques associated with the United States, the champions of an American approach generally prevailed. The American option, which Soviet officials viewed as utilizing the latest technology to produce massive quantities of standardized products, seemed more appropriate for the demands of the Five-Year Plan than did the European pattern of smaller-scale, less capital-intensive enterprises.[27] So concluded an article in *Izvestiia* describing the growth of American industry "on the base of an enormous domestic market and colossal concentration of capital" and that employed "the methods of standardization and mass production" in "huge production units." As this was "closer than the industry of any other country to the form and type of Soviet industry" desired in 1929, "it is precisely American models that are most instructive for us now, and not the smaller and less-advanced models of the majority of European countries."[28]

In tune with the nation's administrators, socialist-realist culture of the period acknowledged Western experts routinely. Novels and plays, for instance, could be expected to incorporate American engineers into stories involving the new industrial projects that often filled their pages. Although the plots did not dwell on the magnitude of American involvement in the Five-Year Plan, the appearance of Americans as standard characters in the "construction novels" of the era must have caught readers' attention. Along with their ubiquity, these fictional experts possessed personal attributes that conformed to predictable patterns—and sometimes reflected assumptions about Americans widespread even before the Revolution.

For one thing, the role of villain did not fall to American specialists. Saboteurs abounded, but readers learned to suspect descendants of the pre-revolutionary elite and older Russian engineers already established in their careers before 1917. Novelists saw something of value in American experts and rarely presented them as overwhelmingly unpleasant. Mister Barker, a character in Bruno Jasienski's Man Changes His Skin, is a repulsive extreme and very much the exception. His thirst for alcohol does him no honor; nor does his incessant complaining and disdain for work. In a silk jacket and white English helmet, he supervises a project with palpable contempt for the Soviet laborers—who mock him in return. Loathed by other foreigners and Soviet personnel alike, Barker soon abandons the project and returns to the United States, leaving the stage to a more sympathetic American colleague.[29]

Despite his myriad flaws, Barker appeared reasonably competent within his narrow field, and most American engineers in these stories left no doubt regarding their technical qualifications. They worked hard, knew their specialties, and often commanded respect from positive Soviet characters. Nikolai Pogodin's Tempo, a play set amid the construction of the Stalingrad Tractor Factory, introduces engineer Carter, a near duplicate of John Calder, the chief construction engineer at both the Stalingrad and Cheliabinsk tractor plants and a troubleshooter dispatched by Soviet authorities to numerous industrial projects around the country. When a homegrown technician remarks that Carter works like a machine, the Soviet superintendent replies, "That's good practice for you fellows, you need this sort of experience."[30] Carter's roll-up-the-sleeves dynamism epitomizes both the practicality and proficiency displayed by other American engineers in these novels, including

Valentin Kataev's panorama of Magnitogorsk, *Time, Forward!* There, an American asserts with unwavering confidence that "technically, everything is possible. Where there's a will, there's a way."[31] Even in stories with Soviet specialists who devise better methods than those proposed by Americans, or workers who finish a job more rapidly than the Americans thought possible, neither the authors nor the Soviet heroes regard the Americans as useless. Only ignorant or treacherous characters find these foreign experts of no value to the grand endeavors of the First Five-Year Plan.

Sooner or later, of course, a construction novel would demonstrate the superiority of the Soviet system, a task aided immeasurably by the depression in the West. What better way to contrast Soviet vitality with the devastation of fabled America than to let American engineers themselves confront the two alternatives and reach suitable conclusions? In *Time, Forward!* Kataev offers Thomas George Bixby, a veteran of work on such projects as Dnieprostroy and the Stalingrad Tractor Factory. Bixby has learned Russian mannerisms and the language itself, prompting Soviet colleagues to address him as Foma Yegorovich, rather than Mister Bixby. His affability and professional acumen are never questioned, nor is his sympathy with the efforts of the principal Soviet engineer in the story. But he is not motivated by socialism. Bixby receives a salary in dollars and saves as much as possible to spend on his return to the United States. Nothing at Magnitogorsk compares with the pleasure he experiences when ogling advertisements in American magazines for cars, refrigerators, gas stoves, furniture, and much else: "Slowly, pleasantly, he sank, page by page, into the luxurious world of ideal things, materials, and products. Here was everything that was necessary for full and complete satisfaction of man's needs, wishes, and passions." A cornucopia of American merchandise greets the reader as Bixby leafs through the magazine, seeming to confirm earlier Russian impressions of American abundance. Then, like an avenging angel, the depression topples a large Chicago bank and eliminates Bixby's savings with a single blow. Reduced to drunken rage by the news, he smashes everything at hand in his quarters ("with mechanical thoroughness") and cannot stir to save himself as flames engulf the room.[32]

To a less destructive end, the depression touched an American engineer in Iakov Ilin's *Great Conveyor,* a novel centered on the Stalingrad Tractor Factory. Mister Stevenson is skilled, if not as congenial or Russified as Bixby, and he shares Bixby's apolitical willingness to work in any country to which his profession leads him. If the "Russians want to industrialize without capitalists," he thought, "that is their right. But production always remained production—it had its own laws." Until Soviet administrators grasped this and learned to look to American experts for guidance, proclaimed Stevenson more than once, the factory would not operate properly. "One had to know how to organize production, and Americans had shown the whole world that there were no better organizers of production than they." Stevenson is didactic, but not mean-spirited, and Ilin appears to accept a bit of his criticism of Soviet economic practice. The American cannot have the last word, however, and here again the depression intervenes. On a vacation visit to the United States, Stevenson witnesses the suffering that he earlier believed had been exaggerated in Soviet press reports. Thereafter, his doubts about American superiority increase in step with his favorable comments on Soviet achievements: "A poor, backward, peasant country is building factories, roads, and cities; the richest country in the world is curtailing production and cannot provide an energetic and able-bodied population with a standard of living made possible by modern technology."[33]

In *Man Changes His Skin*, America's economic crisis comes into play at the outset, encouraging Jim Clark to accept work as an engineer on an irrigation project in Soviet Central Asia. Uninterested in socialism at first, Clark gradually changes his views over the novel's nine hundred pages and travels much farther than Stevenson in this respect. By the middle of the book he is prepared to jump into the spot of a laborer felled by malaria and work an extra shift. Thereafter, members of the party's youth organization "greeted him not simply as an acquaintance but as one of themselves," and he finally marries his interpreter, an activist of unswerving dedication to socialism. Clark's marriage suffers at first from his "petty-bourgeois" instincts, which steer him to oppose his wife's departure for a few months on a new assignment, but the two eventually reconcile with the understanding that he was at fault. On her return she notices with gratification that he has been reading Stalin's *Problems of Leninism,* and Clark demonstrates his mettle at the novel's close by alerting the secret police to a "counterrevolutionary" attack.[34]

Taken as a group, these construction novels (and movies with similar plots) make clear that American engineers worked on the era's famous projects and thereby contributed something to Soviet industrialization. The extent of this assistance is generally obscure, though a few stories indicate the earlier presence of numerous foreign experts as well as the commitment of Soviet officials to send workers to the United States for training. More often, America figures as a measuring stick to illustrate Soviet progress. So argued a "class-conscious metal worker" in *Tempo:* "We are considered backward, they sneer at us and try to convince us that we cannot surpass the leading capitalist countries. You lie, you snakes! We were given ninety-five days, but we did it in eighty! . . . Such tempos are unknown even in America." Engineer Carter himself, on the final page of the play, congratulates workers with the remark that "such a record is outside the reach of any country with a different political organization from yours here." In the *Great Conveyor*, the Stalingrad plant's director travels to America for an inspection tour. At each city on his itinerary he attends a banquet sponsored by American manufacturers who sell equipment to the Soviet Union. When asked to address the gatherings, he declares: "You, sirs, are our teachers in *tekhnika*. But I give you my word, sirs, I give you my word—we will soon overtake you."[35]

Soviet leaders had vowed for years to "catch and surpass" the West, and by the end of the 1920s the goal became one of the Five-Year Plan's relentless themes. "The slogan at present which one sees exhibited in many public places is, 'To Catch Up to and Surpass America,'" reported an American on the scene. "Frequently, when we would improve our system in the plant, some worker would come up to me and say: 'Look how we are catching up to and surpassing America.'"[36] An article in *Planned Economy* on the automotive plants at Gorky and Detroit linked foreign assistance to "the realization of the slogan 'to catch up and surpass' in the area of automobile construction," while the introduction to *How We Are Using Foreign Technical Know-how* explained that the Five-Year Plan required the nation to "move to a higher technical level, catch up to capitalist countries with highly developed *tekhnika*, and then surpass them."[37]

If Soviet authorities hesitated to claim parity with America early in the Five-Year Plan, they also did not expect to wait long, especially as the depression weighed down on the West. Mezhlauk assured the nation's Central Executive Committee at the end of 1929 that "we are now able to move forward with such large strides that we will be able to catch and surpass the United States in this area [production of agricultural machinery] in a comparatively short period."[38] The pace of Bolshevik labors eclipsed American tempos, it appeared, and soon the results would dwarf achievements in the United States. Much as Mayakovsky predicted, Americans would be astonished. Indeed they were already, boasted a Soviet publication on the Stalingrad Tractor Factory that invoked no less a figure than Albert Kahn. Accustomed though he was "to the dizzy speed records of America," Kahn could only marvel at the miracle that arose in a single year at Stalingrad. "He wrote from America: 'I have just received a report from Kandler [Calder, evidently], chief construction engineer in Stalingrad. If his report is true (and we have no reason to doubt his word), the workers and technical staff of Stalingrad are accomplishing results that are out of the question in our country.'"[39]

As the following decade progressed, this sense of attainment spiced commentary on the United States. No longer did America seem so distant technologically—or even geographically, once Soviet aviators completed record-breaking flights between the two countries. Much like the nation's successes in space exploration two decades later, Soviet aerial exploits received extensive publicity that invited comparison with the United States. As early as 1929, when a Soviet plane named *Land of the Soviets* reached New York from Moscow, the editors of a technical journal struck a tone to be heard in years to come: "The flight, for the first time, demonstrated visibly to America the significant accomplishments of Soviet aviation technology, the first-class skill of our pilots, and especially our ability not only to learn the lessons of things accomplished by foreigners but also our own ability to cope with major aeronautical challenges." Among those congratulating the pilots, observed the editors, stood Charles Lindbergh himself.[40]

Themes of backwardness grew rarer. In 1933, five years after he had insisted that thousands of Soviet trainees should cross the ocean to study "arch-bourgeois" machinery, Sergo Ordzhonikidze no longer shrank from praising his own nation's technical expertise. "The time has gone forever," he told a meeting of party members, "when we, having packed our bags, set out for Europe or America to undertake the design of our tractor and automobile factories."[41] If "'foreign' was always a synonym for the best" in Russia, editorialized the *Moscow Daily News* in 1935, "the situation has changed radically now. The Soviet Union has a powerful industry, which is able to produce any machine, any metal or any chemical." Three years later, a book on foreign trade conceded that "technical backwardness" had necessitated the importation of unprecedented numbers of machines during the First Five-Year Plan—which had yielded such splendid results that "not a trace of the former dependence on imports remained during the Second Five-Year Plan." Stalin himself reported to the Eighteenth Party Congress in 1939 that in some statistical categories, such as the adoption of modern industrial *tekhnika*, "we have already caught and surpassed the principal capitalist countries."[42]

A few months after Stalin spoke in Moscow, the Soviet Union welcomed crowds to its towering pavilion at the New York World's Fair. American organizers had chosen the slogan "Building the World of Tomorrow" as the official theme of the exposition, and President Franklin Roosevelt predicted at the opening ceremony that visitors would "find that the eyes of the United States are fixed on the future." General Motors distributed buttons labeled "I Have Seen the Future," intended especially for those who toured the company's depiction of life as it might be in the second half of the century. By the time of the fair, however, Soviet officials regarded their own country as sufficiently developed to offer a better glimpse of a better tomorrow. To this end, the Soviet pavilion contrasted scenes of dark, impoverished prerevolutionary

Russia with huge exhibits of the nation's recent achievements. These included a model of Magnitogorsk, scenes of tractors, trucks, and combines on a collective farm, and a model of the hydroelectric station built at Dnieprostroy. Another hall, heralding the advantages of planned cities, boasted a full-scale replica of a station on the new Moscow metro, more sumptuous than the New York subway that delivered many people to the fair.[43] If American eyes were indeed "fixed on the future," *Pravda* explained, they would have to be gazing at the Soviet exhibits: "The [American and foreign] press, which highly values the Soviet pavilion and unanimously considers it an adornment of the exposition, cannot but note that only here is there really displayed a corner of the world of the future, a world built on new social foundations, with *tekhnika* devoted to service and the welfare of the people."[44] Years of dependence on foreign technical assistance now seemed remote.

The Cold War climate following World War II encouraged Soviet scholars not only to laud recent feats but to devalue Western involvement in the projects of the original Five-Year Plan. Vasily Kasyanenko, the most prolific author on the subject, devoted an entire chapter to "exposing the groundlessness of falsifiers' assertions about the allegedly substantial significance of foreign technology and technical assistance in the industrial development of the Soviet Union." Many capitalist firms sent poorly trained specialists, Kasyanenko complained, and they often failed to live up to their agreements. Moreover, the foreigners attempted to transfer their experience to the Soviet Union without regard for local conditions, thereby requiring Soviet specialists to modify imported machinery and plans. "Soon after the engagement of foreign firms to plan industrial enterprises," he argued, "the ineffectiveness of this assistance became evident."[45] According to a volume on Soviet-American relations by Viktor Furaev, technical-assistance agreements during the First Five-Year Plan "rigidly delimited the role of American specialists."

> The final word in planning and in construction belonged to Soviet organizations, specialists, engineers, technicians, and workers. They not only introduced significant changes in the plans presented by American specialists, but often replaced them with their own plans, significantly reducing the cost of construction and surpassing the Americans' plans in their creative boldness and their tempo of execution.[46]

As for Soviet experts sent to study in the United States, Furaev added, "many of these engineers surpassed their American teachers, and they became important leaders of socialist production." The Soviet government did bestow honors on a handful of foreign specialists, acknowledged Kasyanenko, and Western assistance did "accelerate somewhat" the tempo of industrialization. But "Soviet engineers, builders, and architects, with rare exceptions, could have handled independently many of the problems that foreigners played a part in resolving."[47]

Not until the second half of the 1980s and the emergence of Mikhail Gorbachev as party leader did there evolve a more favorable assessment of American work on the projects of the First Five-Year Plan. As early as 1987 a volume on Soviet-American interaction included comments whose tone would soon grow more common: "In the period of the reconstruction of the national economy and the first five-year plans there took place not only a creative assimilation of the achievements of American architecture, but direct borrowing of design-construction decisions, especially in the realm of industrial construction."[48] Gorbachev's policies—which aimed to revive a stagnant economy by, among other things, looking abroad for useful equipment and techniques—encouraged recognition of Western assistance, which now appeared attractive again.

When the early (1924) Russian edition of Henry Ford's *My Life and Work* was reprinted in 1989, it contained a new introduction by E. A. Kocherin, an economist and editor of a projected series of books on proper methods of work. Ford's volume would be the first in this series, Kocherin announced, while explaining that the book had "engrossed millions of readers around the world. Generations of businessmen and theoreticians of management have been raised on it. The ideas of Henry Ford are still fundamental to contemporary management worldwide." But not, alas, in the Soviet Union. "For long decades we have been cut off from the experience accumulated in the developed capitalist countries," and Soviet managers have found it difficult to learn how to run their enterprises effectively. "In our opinion, this problem may be solved by consulting the classic works of management." According to a brief description of the book printed next to its table of contents, Ford's views carried more than historical interest. "In many respects they remained relevant" to those seeking "the basic restructuring of all links of our economic system."[49]

More than half a century earlier, in June 1930, Henry Ford himself explained in the pages of *Nation's Business* "why I am helping Russian industry":

> I believe it is our duty to help any people who want to go to work and become self-supporting. I have long been convinced that we shall never be able to build a balanced economic order in the world until every people has become

as self-supporting as possible. . . . Only stupid greed—but more stupidity than greed—could think of the world continuously dependent on us or think of our people as the perpetual factory hands of the nations.

"By taking advantage of American methods now the Russians get the benefit of a half century of experience," Ford explained. "They start abreast of the times, industrially. Experiments that took years in this country will be unnecessary."[50]

The following month, at a congressional hearing on communism in the United States, Father Charles Coughlin—who acquired a large following in the 1930s as a right-wing "radio priest"—deplored Ford's technology transfer to the Soviet Union and charged him with contributing to the spread of international communism. In a radio sermon that year titled "The Red Serpent," Coughlin belabored "so-called patriotic American manufacturers caressing these agents of Sovietism—selling them automobiles, buying their stolen oil, loaning them money, helping them indirectly, at least, to carry on their propaganda of destroying America from within and of raising the red flag of Communism atop our Capitol." These industrialists would do anything for money, Coughlin explained, and then asked: "Shall we say that the spirit of Benedict Arnold is creeping into the hearts of certain manufacturers, the names of whom have been published by the Soviet Government, or shall we pass it by, attributing it to ignorance of facts?"[51]

Both Ford and Coughlin, while disagreeing over the wisdom of technical assistance to Stalin's government, regarded this aid as exceedingly beneficial to the Soviet Union. So did American diplomats. According to the head of the State Department's Office of Eastern European Affairs in 1931, "the Bolshevik leaders are utilizing on a very extensive scale the experience and technical achievements of the United States in carrying out their program of economic development contained in the Five-year Plan." Many American engineers also considered their labors in the Soviet Union to be of substantial value and even expressed confidence on occasion that the resulting progress had largely freed the nation from dependence on technical assistance in the future.[52]

As Western scholarship on the Soviet Union emerged in later decades, an occasional pen highlighted American involvement in the major projects of the early Stalinist era. These works generally described America's part as "very important" or "crucially important" to the success of the enterprise under consideration and raised implicitly the question of whether the Soviet Union could have industrialized at all without Western, primarily American, assistance.[53] A handful of accounts dismissed all doubt, none more bluntly than Werner Keller's *East Minus West = Zero: Russia's Debt to the Western World, 862–1962*. Soviet industrialization in the 1930s "was impossible without the active help of Western industry with its unlimited supplies and its expert technical knowledge," insisted Keller, and "even at this moment [the Khrushchev era], Russia can only keep up by the continuous theft and exploitation of every new development in the free world." Indeed, Keller concluded, any industrial success trumpeted by Soviet leaders is actually "a triumph for international capitalism, which supplied the credit, the machinery, the designs, the patents, the engineers and the technicians. . . . And it is still being supplied."[54]

Several other scholars, while noting important services from Western experts, have been more inclined to credit Soviet contributions as well.[55] Some differentiate the heavy industrial sector (where Western assistance on major projects was often crucial) from segments of the economy where equipment and advice were seldom imported.[56] More often they portray Soviet engineers as keen to modify foreign designs to suit local conditions, rather than stand aside passively as Western technology entered the country.[57] Much of the rest of Soviet society, above and below the engineers, likewise played vital roles in the industrialization drive. Virtually all of the labor came from the muscles of Soviet citizens, while the government supplied the iron will to force drastic sacrifices on the population so that the nation's resources could be channeled into factories or exported to acquire the foreign currency necessary to purchase Western expertise. Along with ruthless determination, the government displayed skill in identifying the most qualified foreign companies and in negotiating contracts with them.[58] It also trained tens of thousands of technical specialists, an accomplishment impossible in a truly backward nation. Far from becoming a colony of the West, the Kremlin maintained control over the transfer of technology and emerged with expanded industrial might. If the methods employed to reach this goal seemed brutal or counterproductive to Western observers, that underscored the extent to which Soviet authorities, and not foreign experts, conducted the nation's industrialization.[59]

Assessments of Western aid must also consider factors that *reduced* the influence of foreign equipment and advice. Most of the evidence presented so far has accentuated the significance of technical assistance from the United States, but American practices also encountered impediments that diminished their impact. No country, including Soviet Russia at the end of the 1920s, could import foreign techniques en masse and adopt them without complications.[60] Even the Stalingrad Tractor Factory, designed and equipped almost entirely by American firms, produced only a trickle of vehicles long after its official completion. One setback after another for more than a year prevented the plant from operating at anywhere near its planned capacity, while the tractors that did emerge from the factory ordinarily malfunctioned in short order. The title of Molotov's *The Success of the Five Year Plan* (1931) could not hide its author's vexation: "For some months now the [Stalingrad] works have not been fulfilling their production programme. It has been shown that we are better able to build new great works than to organise their production afterwards."[61]

Difficulties caught the eye at every turn: raw materials of poor quality, management unprepared to administer mass production, and workers (often peasants) unfamiliar with machinery or even electric lights. Assembly-line apparatuses failed repeatedly in the hands of a workforce that sometimes chose crowbar and sledgehammer to assemble or repair complex equipment. Records for 1931 show 2,788 breakdowns of machine tools in just four months.[62] As Nikita Khrushchev commented during his American tour nearly three decades later, "when you helped us build our first tractor plant, it took us two years to get it going properly, because we had no experience."[63] Similar adversity plagued the automobile plant at Gorky after its official opening in January 1932. Extensive American participation in planning and construction could not overcome the obstacles that led to such meager output in 1932 that Moscow dispatched investigators from the Politburo and reprimanded labor and management alike.[64]

At most facilities designed and built with American assistance, the government trimmed Western involvement toward the end of construction rather than hire dozens of foreigners to remain in management capacities until Soviet personnel could be trained to run the enterprise. By setting out on their own, officials saved precious foreign currency that would otherwise have gone to advisers, and they decreased the possibility of ideological contamination from "capitalist" experts working for years among Soviet citizens. Their confidence in the nation's ability to master new technology and soon surpass the West, combined with a sense that "socialism" had little use for principles of American management (as opposed to equipment), encouraged a decision to operate the new plants with far less foreign counsel than had been enlisted to build them.

Had the will and the funds been available to retain hundreds more Western experts to instruct Soviet managers, it is far from certain that foreign techniques would have produced spectacular results simply through their bestowal on Soviet administrators. American management practices represented a harder sell than U.S. design and construction methods, and even the latter did not experience clear sailing. In 1929, for instance, *Pravda* complained that the work of Western experts "meets with hostility from some jingoists and bureaucrats" who objected to recommendations from abroad. The newspaper illustrated its displeasure by describing the efforts of local administrators to thwart an American expert at a copper mine in the Ural region. After he proposed a new method of work, the American found his phone service cut and his mail blocked, while his proposal faced stubborn resistance. If unenthusiastic managers rarely demonstrated this level of hostility, they might at least pigeonhole suggestions from foreign specialists.[65] Not all provincial authorities, in other words, shared the sense among party leaders that economic development required Western experts. Much as the legalization of private trade and manufacturing in 1921 had alarmed many in the party who expected the Revolution to end domestic "capitalism," some also viewed advice from foreign "capitalists" with aversion. Officials of this persuasion felt no more need of foreign assistance to complete the Revolution in 1929 than they did to commence it in 1917.[66] Even if ideological misgivings waned, the arrival of Western experts would not cheer administrators who feared erosion of their control over a project more than they desired its efficient execution.

Soviet engineers, too, displayed less than unanimous excitement upon their introduction to Western counterparts. As the author of *How We Are Using Foreign Technical Know-how* complained, "normal relations do not always exist between our specialists and foreign specialists. Some of our engineers behave jealously, negatively, toward the 'enemy.'"[67] Tensions arose from disagreement over suitable procedures on the job and from rancor bred by subordination to outsiders. American engineers tended to be practical-minded, while their Soviet colleagues often preferred a more theoretical approach to solving problems. This applied especially to the older generation of engineers, trained in Russia before the Revolution, who also inclined toward European methods that American specialists sometimes dismissed as outdated. At the Stalingrad Tractor Factory, Vasily Ivanov rebuked Soviet experts "harnessed to Russian technique, trailing along in the leading strings of Europe." From this laggard vantage point, "many of them . . . got angry and started heckling us, taking a skeptical attitude to the plan for going full speed ahead along the line of American technique."[68]

Occasionally the tension burst into full view, as when John Calder took a position at Magnitogorsk and encountered opposition from the chief Soviet engineer, who was then dismissed for failing to follow Calder's lead—as was another Soviet engineer not long thereafter.[69] If Calder and other Americans wrung their hands over Soviet specialists who turned a deaf ear to foreign advice once they formed a general idea of how to proceed, Soviet "students" resented Westerners who exuded a sense of superiority. "Even to-day," objected an article in the Soviet journal *Construction Industry* in 1928, "the foreigners treat us as residents of the western part of Asia, rather than the eastern part of Europe."[70] Similar complaints would resound again from both sides in the 1990s.

By no means all Soviet administrators and engineers frowned at Western specialists, but discord was common enough to surface frequently in the sources and hinder the transfer of technology to the Soviet Union. In the absence of such animosity, Soviet management practices and a shortage of qualified interpreters could still obstruct the application of foreign expertise. Frequent turnover of administrators, endless discussions without resolution, and frantic sprints to finish projects in time for a political holiday all frustrated Western engineers.[71] In some cases, foreign equipment and the foreign specialists themselves languished, unutilized, for extended periods. So it was at the Stalingrad Tractor Factory with a group of American instructors, ignored for a month by Soviet administrators, party members, and everyone else except the city's prostitutes.[72] Whether the delays reflected routine confusion or disapproval of Western assistance, they slowed the spread of modern techniques to Soviet industry.

Foreign engineers might also stir bitterness among ordinary workers, some of whom associated these advisers with the hardships brought by industrialization—at a time when Western specialists lived in relative splendor, as required to attract them to work in the Soviet Union.[73] Experts from the United States appear to have received better terms on the whole than their German peers, in part because more of the Germans were politically sympathetic with the USSR and thus needed less inducement. In any case, American experts collected much higher pay than the Soviet workforce, and their housing seemed palatial compared to the ramshackle barracks and tents surrounding most industrial projects. They also shopped in special stores, stocked with goods unknown to all but the Soviet elite, and enjoyed travel prerogatives denied to the general population. American laborers with less-impressive qualifications accepted lower pay (likely in rubles rather than dollars) and fewer privileges, though many still lived in better conditions than their Soviet counterparts.[74]

Even without their privileged living conditions, foreign engineers would have faced hostility from portions of the Soviet proletariat. The broad social gap between workers and Russian engineers had long encouraged resentment from below, especially after the Bolshevik Revolution cast engineers as "bourgeois specialists" of dubious loyalty in a land where the proletariat enjoyed billing as the ruling class. In 1928, when the party began staging widely publicized trials of technical experts charged with sabotaging the economy (including a few German defendants but no Americans), engineers experienced more insubordination, contempt, and suspicion from workers and local officials who viewed the public trials as a green light. Russian specialists suffered more than their foreign counterparts, but the latter did not enjoy complete immunity. If workers regarded Western experts as proponents of reforms that accelerated the pace of tiring labor, resentment would be all the more natural. Whatever the cause of the ire, complained a publication of the Communist Youth Organization in 1931, it retarded the transfer of American skills. "The anti-American feelings [at the Stalingrad Tractor Factory] with which at first a significant part of the workers, foremen and sometimes our engineers at the plant were infected" produced a "lack of desire to learn from the Americans, to see in them representatives of a higher technical culture." As a result, some Soviet workers refused to carry out instructions from American foremen.[75]

It was a complicated phenomenon, this American presence, and certainly one whose influence defies quantification. As public-opinion surveys would demonstrate more clearly in the 1990s, a positive impression of life in the United States itself might coexist with misgivings over advice from an American "expert" close at hand. That said, and with allowance for the qualifications above, there seems no reason to dispute those who portray Western assistance as essential to Stalin's industrialization campaign. None of the major projects of the First Five-Year Plan could have been realized in anything resembling their actual form without Western contributions in design, construction, and equipment. The core (foreign) technology generally represented a small percentage of a venture's total expenses for roads, secondary structures, building materials, and wages, but the enterprise could not function without it. If Soviet authorities had been able to undertake these projects on their own, they would have done so. Indeed they tried on occasion, only to fail and then hire experts from abroad. Nor did foreign guidance and machinery confine themselves to a handful of industrial sectors. They appeared across the manufacturing spectrum, most spectacularly in endeavors of top priority to Soviet leaders, but also in secondary spheres of production and in hundreds of plants smaller than Magnitogorsk or Dnieprostroy. From the beginning, then, Western technology served as the primary standard in factories of the new "socialist" era. It was often copied with only minor modifications and thereby accounted, in Kendall Bailes's estimation, for "the vast proportion of Soviet technology prior to World War II."[76]

Still, Western aid is by no means sufficient to explain the industrial feats celebrated by Soviet leaders in the 1930s. Social and political characteristics of any country help shape the results yielded by the importation of sophisticated technology and go far in determining whether the new skills take root at all. If certain aspects of the Soviet landscape impeded application of Western technology, the Soviet system also displayed qualities that facilitated widespread transplanting of this expertise and its adaptation to the Soviet environment. Charles Stuart, the mining expert, acknowledged as much: "The surface projects of Stuart, James & Cooke, Inc., have invariably been made along the lines of American practice. The underground work has been partially in accordance with American practice, but has largely been modified by Russian practice and by the peculiar conditions existing in different mines. This is as it should be."[77]

Moreover, the factories described in these pages would not have arisen in the span of half a decade without the single-minded determination of the Bolshevik leadership. It was Soviet, not Western, resolve that fashioned the First Five-Year Plan, including its industrial emphasis and breakneck pace. Soviet officials took the lead in deciding which foreign companies would work in the USSR and did not lose control of the contractual process. After making the decision to channel most of the nation's meager resources into industrialization, even at the price of what Alec Nove has described as "the most precipitous peacetime decline in living standards known in recorded history," Stalin and his associates devised means to inspire as well as coerce a largely unskilled workforce to accomplish many of the regime's goals.[78] For better or worse, few governments have been able to make such dramatic use of foreign technical assistance.

Western criticism of the Soviet Union during the second half of the twentieth century has often included claims that wiser leaders could have industrialized the nation sufficiently to meet the coming challenge of Nazi Germany while requiring less draconian sacrifices and avoiding famine and mass purges altogether. Perhaps so, but the issue at hand is not a question of alternatives to the First Five-Year Plan or better ways to use foreign skills. Our concern remains the importance of American assistance to the industrialization drive as implemented by Stalin and his supporters. Their general approach did not *require* American prominence, for Europe also had technology to sell. The results would have featured fewer enormous enterprises and less-advanced machinery overall, but industrialization with aid from the West excluding the United States would still have been conspicuous if pushed by a Stalinist government. However, party leaders desired more, not less, American assistance, and they made technology from across the Atlantic the centerpiece of foreign contributions to the modernization of Soviet industry. This by itself was not an absurd or disgraceful decision. Why not seek out the most sophisticated technology from abroad—as various Western powers had done themselves when industrializing in the nineteenth century—rather than rely mainly on domestic innovations? The strategy appeared sensible at the time, and most contemporary observers, whether in fear or hope, supposed that the more foreign technology the Soviet government imported, the sooner it would catch up to the United States. That moment seemed to be approaching as the Soviet Union surged to complete the Five-Year Plan with apparent immunity to the economic afflictions of capitalist society in the Great Depression.

Later in the 1930s, technical-assistance agreements and industrial imports fell to a small fraction of their levels in 1928–32. Some American companies continued to provide expertise under contracts signed deep into the 1930s (now with much less publicity in Moscow), and by 1937–38 the United States again led all nations in the value of its exports to the Soviet Union.[79] But neither the trade nor the assistance rivaled the scale of activity that prevailed during the First Five-Year Plan. After the early 1930s, Stalin and his officials continued to pursue Western technology, but they did so more than ever by copying equipment without the involvement of foreign experts. Even in the 1920s, of course, the Soviet government had regarded technical assistance as a means to mass produce copies of reliable Western products, including Model A automobiles, International Harvester tractors, and General Electric motors. Nothing shrouded this activity from Western view, and nothing inhibited the Soviet trade organization in the United States from noting in 1931 that "much of the American equipment purchased in past years is used by the Soviets as models for the construction of similar machinery in their own plants."[80] Thereafter, as the number of technical-assistance agreements and the volume of foreign trade plunged, Soviet officials devoted more attention to copying foreign equipment on their own, without licensing agreements or other contracts. Efforts to pirate Western machinery—by ordering a few prototypes and studying their components, for example, and also by scrutinizing foreign technical journals—had dotted the 1920s but became central to the transfer of Western technology after 1932. The practice required much less hard currency than the sums spent in 1928–32 to hire experts from abroad, and it could draw on the nation's new factories and growing corps of technical specialists.

Frequent Soviet efforts to copy Western equipment raise the question of whether one should be struck more by the need to copy or the ability to make a serious attempt. Western observers commonly described Soviet copying with amusement or disdain, viewing the practice as testimony to woeful

backwardness. Had they been aware of the extent to which their own countries relied on copying and other foreign assistance during earlier periods of
industrialization, they might have been slower to ridicule Soviet practice. To
this day, all of the world's economic powers copy technology from one another. Only a society with considerable technical sophistication can identify
and master foreign progress quickly, adapt it to local needs, and then produce
new advances on the basis of the original breakthrough. The Soviet Union
was not so backward that its experts failed to comprehend achievements
abroad and adopt them to reduce the technical gap with the West. Theirs became a significant accomplishment, a vital step toward economic preeminence beyond the capacity of many less-developed countries. To Soviet officials, it heralded the dawn of a new era.

When Thomas Edison died in 1931, an obituary in *Pravda* announced that
"a whole epoch of the technical development of capitalism has gone to the
grave. . . . Dispirited by the world crisis, the bourgeoisie throws a stone on
the grave of Edison. Only in our proletarian state, which has written on its
banner—Soviet power plus electrification of the whole country—are the inventions of Edison finding complete and bright incandescence."[81] After as-
similating the skills of capitalist industry, ran the official line, Soviet society
would apply its superior creativity and dynamism to generate innovations
that would astound the international community. As it turned out, this rarely
occurred beyond early triumphs in space flight. Instead, with the ascension
of Mikhail Gorbachev in 1985, the Soviet Union acquired a leader who
would soon speak of Soviet "stagnation" and the need to combat it with measures that once again included assistance from the West.

Here lay a critical difference with other powers that had also utilized substantial foreign contributions to industrialize. Countries such as Germany,
Japan, and the United States reached a point from which they sustained a
level of productivity that kept them among the world's elite. The Soviet effort to join this group recalls similar attempts under the tsars. A binge of
technical acquisitions, which sometimes strengthened military sectors of the
economy sufficiently to help defeat formidable foes, would subside while the
West advanced at a pace that sooner or later persuaded another leader to initiate reforms designed to borrow from the West with renewed urgency.

Now, in the aftermath of the Soviet period, Russia's new republic finds itself far below the social and economic indicators of many nations. Even the
Kremlin's imposing nuclear arsenal seldom prompts the term "superpower" to
issue in the same breath as "Russia," unless to specify something the country
is no longer. Rarely in the past millennium has Russia fallen behind its rivals
so precipitously. Meanwhile, no country has emerged to match the global

profile of the United States, salient since the first decade of Bolshevik rule. The nation of Boris Yeltsin and Vladimir Putin differs dramatically in some respects from that of Lenin and Stalin, but not in the fact that both states came into being with American vitality a fact of life across much of the globe. Whatever the contrast between the goals of Lenin and Putin, the mere presence of the United States has helped establish certain standards of development central to each man's notion of success. As a result, the twenty-first century continues to spawn (quieter) pronouncements in Moscow of "catch and surpass," along with warnings of peril in the event of failure. To what degree, then, will the Russian Republic repeat experiences of the young Soviet Union in absorbing and resisting American practices ranging from popular culture to reforms desired by officials? If much has changed in Russia and the United States over the past century, these issues of influence and image have not faded at all.

Notes

1. I. V. Stalin, *Sochineniia*, vol. 13 (Moscow: Gosudarstvennoe izdatel'stvo politicheskoi literatury, 1952), 266.

2. Antony C. Sutton, *Western Technology and Soviet Economic Development*, 3 vols. (Stanford, Calif.: Hoover Institution, 1968–1973), 2:3.

3. *Ekonomicheskaia zhizn'*, 14 September 1929, 2; "Utilization of Foreign Technical Assistance," 1–2.

4. Rossiiskii Gosudarstvennyi Arkhiv Ekonomiki (hereafter cited as RGAE), fond 7297, opis' 38, delo 19, l. 107; *Industrializatsiia SSSR, 1929–32 gg. Dokumenty i materialy* (Moscow: "Nauka," 1970), 405.

5. "Utilization of Foreign Technical Assistance," 19; M. L. Sorokin, *Za avtomobilizatsiiu SSSR* (Moscow, Leningrad: Moskovskii rabochii, 1928), 85.

6. *Kommunisticheskaia partiia Sovetskogo Soiuza v rezoliutsiiakh i resheniiakh s"ezdov, konferentsii i plenumov TsK*, 8th ed., vol. 4 (Moscow: Izdatel'stvo politicheskoi literatury, 1970), 303.

7. Dmitrii D. Mishustin, *Vneshniaia torgovlia i industrializatsiia SSSR* (Moscow: Mezhdunarodnaia kniga, 1938), 168; G. Voiloshnikov and Ch. Sommers, "O partiino-massovoi rabote s inostrannymi rabochimi," *Partiinoe stroitel'stvo*, no. 3–4 (February 1931): 42.

8. *Those Who Built Stalingrad as Told by Themselves* (Moscow-Leningrad: Cooperative Publishing Society of Foreign Workers in the USSR, 1934), 42 (the Russian edition appeared the previous year); *Pravda*, 28 September 1929, 3.

9. For the quotations, see A. Kolomenskii, *Kak my ispol'zuem zagranichnuiu tekhniku* (Moscow: Gosizdat, 1930), 6, 19, 64. Regarding the American participants listed above, see 30, 35, 37, 42–43, 45. For criticism of such remarks as "we can manage without foreigners" at the Kharkov Tractor Factory, see I. I. Kolomiichenko, "Sozdanie traktornoi promyshlennosti v SSSR," *Istoriia SSSR*, no. 1 (1957): 96.

10. Jon Kenton Walker, "Soviet-American Trade and the Amtorg Trading Corporation during the Period of Nonrecognition" (M.A. thesis, University of Tulsa, 1981), 122–23. Regarding the predominant German share of technical-assistance agreements surviving in 1933 in the area of heavy industry (where American companies had formerly been more in evidence), see RGAE, fond 7297, opis' 38, delo 67, ll. 9–13.

11. *Stalin i Kaganovich. Perepiska, 1931–1936 gg.*, comp. O. V. Khlevniuk et al. (Moscow: ROSSPEN, 2001), 64–65; "Dokumenty. Iz istorii sovetsko-amerikanskikh kul'turnykh i ekonomicheskikh sviazei (1931–1937 gg.)," *Istoricheskii arkhiv*, no. 1 (1961): 13; "Russia Enters the Canning Business," *Food Industries* 4 (June 1932): 203; Peter G. Filene, *Americans and the Soviet Experiment, 1917–1933* (Cambridge, Mass.: Harvard University Press, 1967), 230–35; Harvey L. Dyck, *Weimar Germany and Soviet Russia 1926–1933* (New York: Columbia University Press, 1966), 214–25; R. W. Davies, *The Industrialization of Soviet Russia*, vol. 4, *Crisis and Progress in the Soviet Economy, 1931–1933* (London: Macmillan, 1996), 314–15.

12. *Torgovo-promyshlennaia gazeta*, 10 December 1929, 3.

13. In addition to sources already cited, see A. K. Gastev, *Kak nado rabotat'* (Moscow: Izdatel'stvo Ekonomika, 1966), 364; Adolf Carl Noé, *Golden Days of Soviet Russia* (Chicago: Rockwell, 1931), 26; Records of the Department of State Relating to Internal Affairs of Russia and the Soviet Union, 1930–1939, 861.5017—Living Conditions/616.

14. Sutton, *Western Technology*, 2:79, 163–64, 194, 343; Kendall E. Bailes, "The American Connection: Ideology and the Transfer of American Technology to the Soviet Union, 1917–1941," *Comparative Studies in Society and History* 23, no. 3 (July 1981): 432–33.

15. Charles Stuart, "Industrial Conditions in Russia," Hoover Institution Archives, Charles Stuart Collection, Box 2, Folder 12-R, 9.

16. *Ekonomicheskaia zhizn'*, 14 September 1929, 2.

17. *Ekonomicheskaia zhizn'*, 29 September 1929, 3.

18. *Ekonomicheskaia zhizn'*, 29 September 1929, 3.

19. Stalin, *Sochineniia*, 13:114–15.

20. Stalin, *Sochineniia*, 13:115.

21. "Utilization of Foreign Technical Assistance," 18.

22. *Ekonomicheskaia zhizn'*, 17 July 1929, 4.

23. *Izvestiia*, 12 April 1929, 3.

24. *Those Who Built Stalingrad*, 37.

25. Semyon Lobov, quoted in "Utilization of Foreign Technical Assistance," 13–14; Bailes, "American Connection," 430.

26. A. Zaviniagin [Zaveniagin], "U.S.S.R. Favors American Engineers & Equipment," *Freyn Design* (March 1934): 19.

27. George D. Holliday, *Technology Transfer to the USSR, 1928–1937 and 1966–1975: The Role of Western Technology in Soviet Economic Development* (Boulder, Colo.: Westview, 1979), 52–53; Bailes, "American Connection," 429, 438–39; Sutton, *Western Technology*, 1:295; 2:143.

28. *Izvestiia*, 12 April 1929, 3.

29. Bruno Jasienski, *Man Changes His Skin* (Moscow-Leningrad: Cooperative Publishing Society of Foreign Workers in the USSR, 1935). Regarding Barker, see, for example, 18, 171, 193–95.

30. Nikolai Pogodin, "Tempo," in *Six Soviet Plays* (London: Victor Gollancz, 1935), 246.

31. Valentin Kataev, *Time, Forward!* (Bloomington: Indiana University Press, 1961), 126.

32. Kataev, *Time, Forward!*, 279, 326.

33. Iakov Il'in, *Bol'shoi konveier* (Moscow: Sovetskii pisatel', 1960), 348–49, 354.

34. Jasienski, *Man Changes His Skin*, 411.

35. Pogodin, "Tempo," 270, 296; Il'in, *Bol'shoi konveier*, 104.

36. "American Engineers in Russia," Hoover Institution Archives, Russian Subject Collection, Box 20, Folder 52 (hereafter cited as "American Engineers in Russia"), 21–22; Lement Harris, "An American Workman in Russia," *Outlook and Independent*, 25 February 1931, 316–17.

37. "'GAZ' i 'Ford,'" *Planovoe khoziaistvo*, nos. 6–7 (1932): 243; Kolomenskii, *Kak my ispol'zuem*, 4.

38. *Torgovo-promyshlennaia gazeta*, 10 December 1929, 3. See also *The Dzerzhinsky Tractor Plant at Stalingrad: A Sketch of Its Construction* (Moscow: Co-operative Publishing Society of Foreign Work-

ers in the USSR, 1932), 4; A. I. Gurevich, *Za 10 millionov tonn chuguna. Zadachi chernoi metallurgii v 1932* (Moscow: Partiinoe izdatel'stvo, 1932), 3.

39. *The Dzerzhinsky Tractor Plant at Stalingrad*, 35. See also L. Ostrover, *Sare-Su: Ocherk o stroitel'stve Stalingradskogo traktornogo zavoda* (Moscow: Molodaia gvardiia, 1931), 9; *Za industrializatsiiu*, 14 August 1933, 1.

40. *Amerikanskaia tekhnika i promyshlennost'*, (February 1930): 3 (from the Aviation Supplement).

41. G. K. Ordzhonikidze, *Stat'i i rechi v dvukh tomakh* (Moscow: Gosudarstvennoe izdatel'stvo politicheskoi literatury, 1957), 2:434.

42. *Moscow Daily News*, no. 127 (4 June 1935): 2; Dmitrii D. Mishustin, *Vneshniaia torgovlia i industrializatsiia SSSR* (Moscow: Mezhdunarodnaia kniga, 1938), 39, 76; *XVIII s"ezd vsesoiuznoi kommunisticheskoi partii(b) 10–21 marta 1939 g. Stenograficheskii otchet* (Moscow: Gosudarstvennoe izdatel'stvo politicheskoi literatury, 1939), 17. For an example of an article, less common than a decade earlier, on an American enterprise (railroad-engine maintenance facilities) clearly superior to Soviet counterparts, see *Pravda*, 9 February 1935, 4. Such articles, which did not vanish altogether, helped preserve America as the primary standard of comparison.

43. Larry Zim, Mel Lerner, and Herbert Rolfes, *The World of Tomorrow: The 1939 New York World's Fair* (New York: Harper and Row, 1988), 9; *Pravda*, 18 May 1939, 6. See also Joseph Philip Cusker, "The World of Tomorrow: The 1939 New York World's Fair" (Ph.D. diss., Rutgers, the State University of New Jersey, 1990).

44. *Pravda*, 9 June 1939, 5.

45. Vasilii I. Kas'ianenko, *Kak byla zavoevana tekhniko-ekonomicheskaia samostoiatel'nost' SSSR* (Moscow: Mysl', 1964), 16, 200–204. Archival, Western, and Soviet sources all indicate that Soviet officials were unsatisfied with the performance of the McKee Company at Magnitogorsk (though most of the work removed from McKee's hands seems to have been transferred to other Western companies). RGAE, fond 7297, opis' 38, delo 67, l. 136; Davies, *The Industrialization of Soviet Russia*, 4:492; *Iz istorii magnitogorskogo metallurgicheskogo kombinata i goroda Magnitogorska, 1929–1941 gg. Sbornik dokumentov i materialov* (Cheliabinsk: Iuzhno-Ural'skoe Knizhnoe Izdatel'stvo, 1965), 10–11, 73–74, 97, 100.

46. V. K. Furaev, *Sovetsko-amerikanskie otnosheniia 1917–1939* (Moscow: Mysl', 1964), 154.

47. Furaev, *Sovetsko-amerikanskie otnosheniia*, 155; Vasilii I. Kas'ianenko, *Zavoevanie ekonomicheskoi nezavisimosti SSSR (1917–1940 gg.)* (Moscow: Politizdat, 1972), 191.

48. V. Khait, "Rol' i mesto arkhitektury SShA v mirovom zodchestve XX v. i osvoenie ee opyta v sovetskoi arkhitekture," in *Vzaimodeistvie kul'tur SSSR i SShA XVIII–XX vv.*, ed. O. E. Tuganova (Moscow: "Nauka," 1987), 128.

49. Genri Ford, *Moia zhizn', moi dostizheniia* (Moscow: "Finansy i statistika," 1989), 5–6.

50. Henry Ford, "Why I Am Helping Russian Industry," interview by William A. McGarry, *Nation's Business* (June 1930): 20–23.

51. *New York Times*, 26 July 1930, 14; Charles E. Coughlin, *Sermon: The Red Serpent* (Detroit, Mich.: Radio League of the Little Flower, 1930), pages not numbered.

52. Andrew J. Steiger, *American Engineers in the Soviet Union* (New York: Russian Economic Institute, 1944), 8–9; Walker, "Soviet-American Trade," 85; State Department Records, 1930–39, 861.5017—Living Conditions/616.

53. Floyd J. Fithian, "Soviet-American Economic Relations, 1918–1933: American Business in Russia during the Period of Non-recognition" (Ph.D. diss., University of Nebraska, 1964), 355; Holliday, *Technology Transfer*, 172. See also Bruce B. Parrott, "Technology and the Soviet Polity: The Problem of Industrial Innovation, 1928 to 1973" (Ph.D. diss., Columbia University, 1976), 142, where he writes: "In keeping with this strategy, the USSR's dependence on foreign technology during the First Five Year Plan was almost total."

54. Werner Keller, *East Minus West = Zero: Russia's Debt to the Western World, 1862–1962* (New York: Putnam, 1962), 207, 368, 370. Antony Sutton's three volumes on *Western Technology and Soviet*

Economic Development share much of the spirit of Keller's book, while resting on a more substantial body of research for the period at issue here. If the Revolution of 1917 produced little change in Keller's argument—both the tsars and the Bolsheviks "equaled zero" without the West—Sutton viewed tsarist Russia more favorably: "a relatively advanced industrial structure with definite signs of indigenous Russian development" (2:318). It was the triumph of Lenin's Communist Party in the October Revolution that doomed the nation to industrial stagnation, Sutton claimed, for most of Russia's skilled engineers either died or fled the country in the ensuing turmoil. The Bolsheviks' inability to revive production in the 1920s compelled them to engage foreign experts, whose work "was decisive in Soviet economic development during this period" (1:4). Once party leaders opted to accelerate the pace of industrialization at the end of the decade, Sutton continued, they embarked alone on a number of projects (such as Dnieprostroy and the Stalingrad Tractor Factory), only to find themselves unable to cope. Not until they signed scores of technical-assistance contracts with American and other Western firms could the Five-Year Plan's ventures come to life. In short, "without assistance from capitalist countries the Soviet Union would not have had the technical resources to make any economic progress during the 1930s and 1940s" (2:286). See also 1:177, 347; 2:2, 6, 284, 299, 339.

55. Disagreement also exists over the degree of Western responsibility for the Soviet industrial recovery earlier in the 1920s. See John P. McKay, "Foreign Enterprise in Russian and Soviet Industry: A Long Term Perspective," *Business History Review* 48, no. 3 (Autumn 1974): 351; Sutton, *Western Technology*, 1:9.

56. Holliday, *Technology Transfer*, 51, 57.

57. See Bruce Parrott, ed., *Trade, Technology, and Soviet-American Relations* (Bloomington: Indiana University Press, 1985), 178, 180; Bailes, "American Connection," 440; Holliday, *Technology Transfer*, 124, 128–29; Steiger, *American Engineers*, 13. Even Sutton occasionally acknowledges Soviet innovation (in military industries, for example) and competence (converting U.S. and British equipment to the metric system). Sutton, *Western Technology*, 2:248, 329.

58. Fithian, "Soviet-American Economic Relations," 300; McKay, "Foreign Enterprise," 354; Parrott, "Technology," 595–96.

59. McKay, "Foreign Enterprise," 356; Holliday, *Technology Transfer*, 86–87, 179. A number of arguments advanced by the authors cited in this paragraph also appeared in critical reviews of Sutton's volumes. See, for example, *Slavic Review* 31, no. 4 (December 1972): 904–5; *Journal of Economic History* 29, no. 4 (December 1969): 816–18; *Journal of Modern History* 44, no. 4 (December 1972): 647–48; *American Political Science Review* 67, no. 3 (September 1973): 1126–28.

60. Raymond P. Powell, "Industrial Production," in *Economic Trends in the Soviet Union*, ed. Abram Bergson and Simon Kuznets (Cambridge, Mass.: Harvard University Press, 1963), 173–74.

61. V. M. Molotov, *The Success of the Five-Year Plan* (New York: International, 1931), 66. On the breakdown of tractors, often hastened by misuse and poor maintenance in the field, see Dana G. Dalrymple, "The American Tractor Comes to Soviet Agriculture: The Transfer of a Technology," *Technology and Culture* 5, no. 2 (Spring 1964): 205–207.

62. Kolomiichenko, "Sozdanie traktornoi promyshlennosti," 97; Fithian, "Soviet-American Economic Relations," 238–43; Dalrymple, "American Tractor," 199; Norton T. Dodge and Dana G. Dalrymple, "The Stalingrad Tractor Plant in Early Soviet Planning," *Soviet Studies* 18, no. 2 (October 1966): 167; Samuel Lieberstein, "Technology, Work, and Sociology in the USSR: The NOT Movement," *Technology and Culture* 16, no. 1 (January 1975): 54.

63. N. S. Khrushchev, *Khrushchev in America* (New York: Crosscurrents, 1960), 107.

64. Khrushchev, *Khrushchev in America*, 107; Holliday, *Technology Transfer*, 125–29; Fithian, "Soviet-American Economic Relations," 334–35.

65. *Pravda*, 16 October 1929, 2; RGAE, fond 7297, opis' 38, delo 67, l. 150; John D. Littlepage and Demaree Bess, *In Search of Soviet Gold* (New York: Harcourt, Brace, 1938), 89, 97–98.

66. Fithian, "Soviet-American Economic Relations," 109, 238, 249; Sutton, *Western Technology*, 1:305, 308; Sylvia R. Margulies, *The Pilgrimage to Russia: The Soviet Union and the Treatment of Foreigners, 1924–1937* (Madison: University of Wisconsin Press, 1968), 195.

67. Kolomenskii, *Kak my ispol'zuem*, 20; State Department Records, 1930–39, 861.5017—Living Conditions/677.

68. Vasily Ivanov, quoted in *Those Who Built Stalingrad*, 37; "Report of Stuart, James & Cooke, Inc. to V.S.N.Kh.," Hoover Institution Archives, Charles Stuart Collection, Box 1, Folder 1-R (hereafter cited as "Report of Stuart, James & Cooke, Inc. to V.S.N.Kh."), chapter 4: 1–2; chapter 6: 2; "American Engineers in Russia," 10, 15, 17, 19–21, 23.

69. Maurice Hindus, "Pinch Hitter for the Soviets," *American Magazine* 113, no. 4 (April 1932): 134–35.

70. Fithian, "Soviet-American Economic Relations," 249; Sutton, *Western Technology*, 2:75; William C. Brumfield, ed., *Reshaping Russian Architecture: Western Technology, Utopian Dreams* (Cambridge: Cambridge University Press, 1990), 159.

71. "Report of Stuart, James & Cooke, Inc. to V.S.N.Kh.," chapter 4: 2–3; chapter 9: 2; "American Engineers in Russia," 100; Littlepage and Bess, *In Search of Soviet Gold*, 90; *Those Who Built Stalingrad*, 90–91.

72. *Za industrializatsiiu*, 18 August 1931, 2. See also RGAE, fond 1884, opis' 60, ed. khr. 877, ll. 63–64; RGAE, fond 7297, opis' 38, delo 67, ll. 155, 157; *Izvestiia*, 31 March 1928, 4; *Ekonomicheskaia zhizn'*, 7 March 1928, 2; *Ekonomicheskaia zhizn'*, 25 March 1928, 3; *Ekonomicheskaia zhizn'*, 7 April 1928, 3.

73. Andrea Graziosi, "Foreign Workers in Soviet Russia, 1920–40: Their Experience and Their Legacy," *International Labor and Working-Class History*, no. 33 (Spring 1988): 45; W. H. Chamberlin, "Missionaries of American Techniques in Russia," *Asia* (July–August 1932): 462.

74. "American Engineers in Russia," 18, 21; Margulies, *Pilgrimage*, 92–95; Fithian, "Soviet-American Economic Relations," 223.

75. Bailes, "American Connection," 441–42.

76. Bailes, "American Connection," 445. See also R. W. Davies, *The Industrialization of Soviet Russia*, vol. 3: *The Soviet Economy in Turmoil, 1929–1930* (London: Macmillan, 1989), 123, 216; 4:491.

77. "Report of Stuart, James & Cooke, Inc. to V.S.N.Kh.," chapter 5: 2.

78. Alec Nove, *An Economic History of the U.S.S.R.* (Harmondsworth, England: Penguin, 1982), 208.

79. Furaev, *Sovetsko-amerikanskie otnosheniia*, 283–84; Bailes, "American Connection," 443; Sutton, *Western Technology*, 2:13, 219–20, 345. For examples of Soviet shopping lists of American industrial equipment in 1939, see RGAE, fond 4372, opis' 37, ed. khr. 951, ll. 85, 88–89; RGAE, fond 4372, opis' 38, ed. khr. 1309, ll. 51–55.

80. Sutton, *Western Technology*, 2:164; "Russia Enters the Canning Business," 203–204; Parrott, "Technology," 152.

81. *Pravda*, 20 October 1931, 4.

PART TWO

THE CONTEMPORARY ERA

CHAPTER SIX

~

Holy Communion at McDonald's

Are we to grovel before every foreign thing?

—Andrei Zhdanov

The picture of America that our generation pieced together in its imagination was impossibly idealized and distorted, but it also had an amazing—astral, if you like—truth to it.

—Vasily Aksenov

In the twilight of the Soviet era, "everything that we used to watch stealthily was now awaiting us everywhere," observed the playwright and historian Edvard Radzinsky. "American movies in theaters and on TV; videos selling at the kiosks. . . . During the failed coup in August 1991, there were as many people in line for McDonald's as there were defending Yeltsin's White House." American fads and pastimes spread with abandon, often in forms that seemed to mock vital components of Soviet society. The Communist Party's newspaper, *Pravda*, which had published Maxim Gorky's assault on jazz in 1928 and denounced rock 'n' roll for decades after World War II, survived to the day when Russian rock fans arrayed in leather and chains scalped tickets openly outside the paper's editorial offices.[1] Even then, in 1987, who could have imagined that in ten more years Mikhail Gorbachev would be long out of office and filming a commercial for Pizza Hut, or that Moscow's Palace of Young Pioneers would become Gold's Gym, a health club catering to the nation's new rich? Gold's leased its name from an American enterprise and installed indoor tennis courts, exercise machines, and much else to attract the handful of Russians who could afford annual membership fees of $2,000.[2] These affluent customers had doubtless joined the Pioneers in Soviet times because the party's youth organization enrolled most children of primary-school age. If they had grown up in Moscow, they may well have attended Pioneer functions in the same building where they now came for American-style aerobics.

Perhaps this headlong spread of American recreations would not have seemed improbable from the vantage point of 1926, when Hollywood movies, jazz, and nightclubs for the new rich all flourished in Soviet cities. Soon, though, the climate of the 1930s stifled American cultural influence and discouraged public praise of the United States in other areas—an atmosphere that persisted with comparatively little change for decades after World War II. During the war itself, to be sure, the circumstances that made allies of the Soviet Union and America summoned more positive comments from each nation. In 1942, a booklet titled *America and Russian Society*, published in Moscow, explained that "the Soviet people rejoice to see among their allies the great transoceanic republic—the United States—a country to which we are linked by historic friendship." The next several pages reviewed interest in American freedoms shown by members of the Russian intelligentsia through the eighteenth and nineteenth centuries, while a section on the postrevolutionary era devoted more attention to mutual respect between Soviet and American luminaries than to, say, American intervention against the Bolsheviks during the civil war. Neither a threat nor a land of misery, the United States appeared nearly benevolent at times, as in the period of maximum technical assistance to Soviet industry during the First Five-Year Plan. The final page quoted Franklin Roosevelt to reemphasize that "the American people 'are linked to the Russian people by strong bonds of historical friendship'" that would help preserve freedom everywhere.[3]

Stalin's comments adorned the book, too, including excerpts from his interview with Emil Ludwig in which he praised a New World largely free of feudal remnants that littered Europe. The text did not find room to repeat his insistence on Russian fondness for Germans and moved on instead to remind readers of the long-distance records set by Soviet flights to the United States in the 1930s. These were more than displays of derring-do, for they symbolized the close connection now said to exist between the two countries: "If it is possible to fly from Moscow to the heart of America in 60 hours, then both great powers turn out to be not so far from one another." The aerial exploits had thus helped to develop bonds extolled by Stalin when he spoke of "the united front of peoples standing for freedom against subjugation and the threat of subjugation from the fascist armies of Hitler."[4]

During the war, much of the Soviet population encountered American imports on a larger scale than ever. Shipments from the Lend-Lease program not only helped sustain and transport the Red Army, they appeared behind the lines in numerous kitchens (Spam, for instance) and streets (Studebaker trucks).[5] In the cities, Soviet cinemas began showing Hollywood movies again, including *Sun Valley Serenade*, with Glenn Miller's orchestra playing such numbers as "Moonlight Serenade," "In the Mood," and "Chattanooga Choo-Choo."[6] Dozens of other popular American songs circulated freely, performed by Soviet bands at the German front, the Far East, and thousands of points in between. Once the wartime alliance with the United States opened doors to music banned just a few years before, Eddie Rosner, the Soviet Union's leading jazzman during the war, felt it safe to select "Anchors Aweigh!" as the theme song in many of his concerts.[7]

As relations between the two countries improved, American characters enjoyed more favorable treatment in Soviet artistic productions, just as Hollywood now presented Russians in a positive light.[8] Audiences even witnessed an American happy ending in the remake of Frank Capra's romantic comedy *It Happened One Night* (1933), adapted for the Soviet stage and reportedly popular during its run in Leningrad, Moscow, and elsewhere from 1943 to the last year of the war. An original Soviet work, *The Mission of Mister Perkins to the Land of the Bolsheviks* (1944), featured an American industrialist who visits the Soviet Union determined to ascertain if postwar commerce can flourish between the two countries. Despite the negative opinions of an American journalist along on the trip, Mister Perkins reaches an optimistic conclusion after conversations with earnest Soviet citizens. Among them numbers a Red Army sergeant who praises the wartime alliance and admires Franklin Roosevelt. After a series of performances during the second half of 1944, the play acquired some new lines criticizing British-American delay in opening a second front against Germany in the West. But the principal theme of fruitful association remained—and would soon appear unacceptable to both sides.[9]

With the announcement of victory over Nazi Germany on 9 May 1945, thousands of Muscovites poured into the streets to celebrate. Throngs arrived at the American embassy, where George Kennan watched them stop to demonstrate emotions "of almost delirious friendship" to any American in sight. Hour after hour the sea of well-wishers grew. "If any of us ventured out into the street," Kennan observed, "he was immediately seized, tossed enthusiastically into the air, and passed on friendly hands over the heads of the crowd, to be lost, eventually, in a confused orgy of good feeling somewhere on its outer fringes." Kennan also recognized the dismay felt by Soviet officials as cheering continued throughout the day, despite efforts to distract or disperse the celebrants.[10] Spontaneous demonstrations, especially of solidarity with Americans, could only have alarmed a government accustomed to controlling its subjects and suspicious of American intentions. Such a display would soon become as unthinkable as it had been in 1937, testimony more to the muscle of the state than to soured public opinion.

By the following year, with the wartime alliance in shambles and the Cold War's chill settling across much of the globe, Western influence came under ferocious attack from the Soviet government. More than at any point since 1917, party leaders sought to isolate the population from the outside world of imperialist bourgeois states purportedly bent on thwarting the ascent of socialism. In contrast to the prewar era, when Soviet officials generally focused their alarm on countries closer at hand, the United States now stepped forward as the chief menace. With its power swelled by a military buildup during the war and exclusive possession of the atomic bomb, America dominated the attention of the Kremlin's denizens. Here, they asserted, was the nation that led international opposition to peaceful Soviet initiatives and schemed to corrupt the resolve of Soviet citizens to improve their socialist community.

Even if relations with the United States had taken a smoother course, Stalin would probably have increased repression to some degree after the war. The challenges of digesting new or recaptured territories and harnessing the entire population to rebuild the shattered country were sufficient to fire his authoritarian impulses. But the growing tension with the world's first nuclear superpower further tightened the government's grip on Soviet citizens during the final years of the dictator's life. Officials portrayed the West as a source of contamination, and Stalin himself complained to a group of Soviet writers in 1947 that the nation's technical intelligentsia possessed "an unjustified admiration of foreign culture." Scientists, scholars, and artists all received orders to reject Western theories and methods in favor of Soviet approaches. "Is it fitting for us Soviet patriots, the representatives of advanced Soviet culture, to play the part of admirers or disciples of bourgeois culture?" asked Andrei Zhdanov, the nation's chief of ideological control in the late 1940s. It was not fitting, and the party's Central Committee made this clear to composers in 1949 with instructions to banish "vestiges of bourgeois ideology, nourished on influences from the decadent West," and "permeate themselves with the high demands of the musical creation of the Soviet people." The journal *Soviet Music* warned that "all attempts to engulf the world with the scanty products of the venal American muse are nothing but frontier ideological expansion of American imperialism, propaganda for reactionary-obscurantist misanthropic ideas."[11] As the party pulled up the drawbridge and manned the parapets, it fostered a paranoia that stifled many other areas of domestic endeavor. In this stark setting, more vigorously than ever before in Russian or Soviet history, authorities launched an offensive among their own people against the image and cultural influence of the United States.

Soon appeared a flurry of articles on Mayakovsky's American tour enlisting the poet's legacy in the new crusade. His observations bore fresh study, "especially now," emphasized the journal *Literature in School* in 1950, "when Soviet society struggles daily against kow-towing before the 'culture' of the capitalist West." American entertainments, skyscrapers, and bridges had not infatuated Mayakovsky during his travels in 1925, declared myriad authors who left no doubt that the country again required stalwart immunity to bourgeois temptations. The lesson seemed clear to Konstantin Simonov, a prominent literary figure who commented on Mayakovsky and America in 1949: "No marvels of American *tekhnika* or conveniences of American 'service,' no ostentatious side of American life and routine could to the slightest degree strip Mayakovsky—as a citizen of the Soviet Union, armed with progressive communist ideas—of the feeling of the magnificent superiority of the Soviet Union over that bourgeois country, the United States."[12]

While American protagonists had appeared in favorable roles on Soviet stage and screen during the war, and even in some "construction novels" of the 1930s, the next decade unmasked them as unscrupulous and belligerent. Soviet audiences still met individual Americans sympathetic to Moscow's socialist labors, but villainous representatives of the capitalist camp now dominated lists of foreign characters. Authors and directors who placed scenes in the United States did so to emphasize American greed, warmongering, racism, and other social injustices, while American characters taken abroad by the story line spared no effort to impede the development of Soviet socialism. Nikolai Pogodin, who in 1930 had used John Calder as a model for the competent and sympathetic engineer Carter in *Tempo*, relied two decades later on the machine politician Tom Pendergast of Kansas City to create Thomas Brown, a ruthless Democratic Party boss in Pogodin's play *The Missouri Waltz*. If Pogodin revealed no malice or even misgivings about the United States in *Tempo*, his *Missouri Waltz* unveiled a bleak land in which Big Tom's wealth and underworld cronies vanquish rivals and reformers at every turn. A young man who tries to expose Brown's crimes is branded an agent of Moscow, even by his own father, and fails to break the boss's grip on Kansas City.[13]

When American characters turned their attention to other countries, they sought domination with a confidence that could reach that of Senator Herbert D. Wheeler in Boris Lavrenyov's play *The Voice of America* (1949): "From now on nothing will happen anywhere in the whole world without our knowledge and approval. We have a right to this because our American way of life is the most reasonable in the world." With growing frequency, Soviet citizens heard warnings that praise of conditions in the United States simply camouflaged efforts to extend American sway. A reviewer in *Izvestiia*, speaking of a positive Soviet character in Simonov's play *The Alien Shadow* (1949), commended the hero for making clear that "servile deference to foreigners is not simply a matter of liking foreign refrigerators or trousers, but can be far more serious." The worst danger, explained the article, lies in overestimating the virtues of hostile Western societies by considering "their pretended freedom, their conscience, sold to capitalism, clear, and their brazen advertisement of their own achievements, talents and mental capacity" to be "a true mirror of their life."[14]

With the United States plying its siren song around the globe, nothing vexed Soviet authorities more than displays of American culture within their own borders. The Kremlin's watchdogs suspected the United States of trying to lure nations into its orbit by seducing foreigners with American amusements, and they cautioned Soviet citizens to be wary of *Music in the Service of Reaction* (to cite a work by Grigory Shneerson published in 1950). "Several times each evening," complained Shneerson two years earlier, "propagandists from the Voice of America present us with examples of American music, evidently with complete certainty that such musical seasoning added to the verbal propaganda of 'Americanism' will attract a larger number of listeners." Thus "the open propaganda of American and British imperialism" arrived in the company of the "sugary-sentimental, castrated eroticism of American popular songs and dances."[15]

In short order, Soviet officials gutted the repertoires of jazz bands, arrested some musicians, confiscated saxophones, and denounced jazz in terms borrowed from Gorky's "The Music of the Gross." Under these attacks, musicians either abandoned jazz altogether or made so many concessions to cultural guardians that their music did not resemble jazz played in the West. Soviet authorities hoped to replace American-style entertainment by promoting folk music and traditional dances together with wholesome movies of a proud fatherland and its inspiring future.[16] These alternatives doubtless satisfied some people who asked nothing more than stability and calm after fifteen years of upheaval. But to others, especially youths coming of age after the war, American temptations would soon demonstrate their resilient spell.

Meanwhile, Soviet publications, films, and television programs presented America as a nation of largely unpleasant features. The harshness varied, of

course, along with the opportunity for positive comments, as relations between the two countries improved or soured over the coming years. But the
basic themes did not vanish, even during the brief "thaw" commenced by
Nikita Khrushchev in the 1950s and the détente pursued by the Brezhnev
regime in the 1970s. Throughout, Soviet journalists preserved the image of
America as an imperialist power and, domestically, a land whose vaunted
ideals could not conceal unemployment, racism, crime, and unequal access
to such necessities as health care and education.[17] How could such a country exert any appeal, asked the Kremlin's ideologues, especially in contrast to
the Soviet Union, where people worked to build something better?

But there was an appeal, as the press itself acknowledged through persistent
censure of those "who blindly imitate foreign fashion and bow before 'the
American way of life.'"[18] The principal newspaper of the Communist Youth
Organization ridiculed adolescents who aped Western teenagers: "If he is
Boris," the paper noted in 1956, "he calls himself Bob; if Ivan—then John. . . .
He 'worships' everything foreign."[19] Twenty-eight years later a commentator at
the same paper presented a similar complaint, scolding young Russians who incorporated numerous English words into their colloquial discourse and lusted
after foreign products. "Cutting the ties uniting you with a people and society
that gave you everything possible is self-decapitation, self-destruction," the author fumed, after quoting with approval Fyodor Dostoyevsky's rebuke a century
before of Russians who preferred to speak French: "Crawling like slaves before
linguistic forms and the opinions of garçons, Russian Parisians naturally become
slaves to French thought as well."[20] Now the United States had replaced France
as the most beguiling of Western temptresses, enticing youths to abandon their
native culture.

In 1980 the newspaper decried the popularity of American clothing obtained from tourists. T-shirts with slogans at odds with Soviet ideals were bad
enough, but second-hand American military apparel amounted to an outrage:
"disgraceful, stupid, senseless," pronounced the critic, who wondered how Soviet citizens could wear "a conscious advertisement of a way of life that is alien
to us." He decided that "in the overwhelming majority of cases, it is blind im-
itation of ludicrous, inappropriate fashion—a craving for a 'Western brand-
name' item no matter what the cost and without thinking about what the item
is or means."[21] Variations on this theme recurred for decades after World War
II, as demonstrated by another publication for youth that lashed out in 1984
with indignation soon to be muted by the disintegration of the Soviet Union:

On the jackets and T-shirts of our young people one can sometimes see the
Stars and Stripes, pictures of rock-music "idols," slogans like "free love," and
so forth. Young people do not always stop to think that in pursuing the bright

and the unusual, in challenging generally accepted norms, they are blas-
pheming, trampling the dignity of their motherland. After all, khaki shirts
with "US Army" labels carry the blood of Vietnamese villagers of Song My,
patriots of Grenada, and Salvadoran guerrillas. The attitude toward clothing
that we choose ourselves is not only a matter of morals and aesthetics. It is
also a matter of ideology.[22]

No matter how harsh the denunciation of the United States and its culture,
signs of interest persisted. Citizens with determination or good connections
could taste the forbidden fruit even during the frostiest years of the Cold
War, and the government itself provided occasional opportunities. With Soviet film output plunging to record lows in the difficult postwar years—
twenty-three pictures in 1947, thirteen in 1950, and nine in 1951, compared
to annual totals of more than a hundred in the late 1920s—the authorities
kept starved theaters alive with a diet heavy on captured German movies
and American productions acquired through various channels during the
war. Officials retitled a number of these foreign films and sometimes accompanied them with introductory lectures to steer audiences toward suitable in-
terpretations of the events about to appear on screen. Thus Mr. Deeds Goes
to Town (1936, starring Gary Cooper) played the Soviet Union as The Dollar Rules, while Stagecoach (1940, starring John Wayne) appeared as The Journey Will Be Dangerous and was said to chronicle heroic Indian resistance
against white encroachment.[23] In his youth, the novelist Vasily Aksenov
viewed Stagecoach numerous times and visited the cinema even more often
to see another American film, The Roaring Twenties (retitled The Fate of a
Soldier in America—callous treatment of veterans). Judging from comments
by Western observers and complaints in the Soviet press, audiences included
many who appeared to enjoy the foreign films without taking to heart the in-
terpretations desired by party ideologists. In villages visited by mobile projection units as well as in Moscow and other cities, reports told of youths im-
itating the mannerisms of European and especially American stars, including
Jeannette MacDonald, Deanna Durbin, James Cagney, and Johnny Weismueller. The Tarzan films starring Weismueller—notably Tarzan's New York
Adventure (1942), which featured zoot suits and action in Manhattan—
spellbound audiences with an ease beyond the reach of any late-Stalinist celluloid hymn.[24]

American music, too, reached avid Soviet fans, even during the cultural
freeze of Stalin's last years, and not only through the soundtracks of Hollywood movies. Members of the Soviet elite who could travel abroad, and the
larger circle of people with whom they had contact, continued to acquire

recordings of American jazz. Nikolai Pogodin (who linked jazz with disquieting events in his *Missouri Waltz*) succeeded in keeping his own collection of Duke Ellington records up to date, while Stalin's daughter found opportunities to hear contemporary jazz at the home of an acquaintance. Fresh from the provincial city of Kazan in 1952, Aksenov used the connections of a friend to gain entry to a party at the Moscow residence of a prominent Soviet diplomat. The guests were mainly "golden youths," offspring of lofty officials accustomed to a lifestyle all but unknown to Aksenov.

It was the first time I had ever seen an American radiola, the kind that let you stack twelve records at a time. And what records! Back in Kazan we spent hours fiddling with the dials on our bulky wireless receivers for even a snatch of jazz and here it was in all its glory—with the musicians' pictures on the albums to boot. There they all were: Bing Crosby, Nat King Cole, Louis Armstrong, Peggy Lee, Woody Herman.

The anti-Western storms of the time did not trouble the revelers, evidently certain that the clout of their parents bestowed on them a license to enjoy activities condemned in the press. "Don't you just love the States?" the daughter of a high-ranking police official asked Aksenov, who learned during the course of the evening that some of the youths called themselves *shtatniki* (Stateniks).[25]

More boldly, a small number of young Russians even flaunted their fascination with American style on the streets of Moscow, especially a stretch of Gorky Street that they renamed Broadway. Dubbed "style hunters" (*stilyagi*) in 1949, they dressed in what they took to be American fashion—jackets with padded shoulders, ties with American motifs, narrow pants, turned-back cuffs, and large shoes, preferably yellow or light tan with thick crepe soles. Girls wore short, clinging skirts, heavy lipstick, and "Roman" sandals in the summer and often cropped their hair. As to the males' haircuts, a former *stilyaga* explained, "the model, of course, was Tarzan—long hair combed straight back and smeared generously with briolin, sort of like in the film 'Grease.' The back was turned up with a curling iron (I remember I constantly had burns on my neck), and definitely a straight parting." *Stilyagi* also made clear their passion for contemporary jazz and other fragments of life associated with America: cocktails, Lucky Strikes, and American slang. Some even adopted English nicknames.[26]

Most important to this study, Soviet culture had alienated or at least bored the *stilyagi*, prompting them to look to the West and especially America for alternatives. Orchestrated enthusiasm for socialist construction, heavy-handed patriotism, and the conformity of a collective society sparked their maverick urge for something more personal and entertaining. The scattered glimpses of American life that captured their imaginations provided a style in vivid contrast to their Soviet surroundings. They never amounted to more than a tiny percentage of their generation in the 1950s (after which the term *stilyagi* fell from use), but their disaffection with official Soviet standards and their appetite for American mass culture eventually spread to millions of their fellow citizens.

By 1954 signs of this change had reached the provincial city of Kuibyshev, where a lad named Fyodor enjoyed evening strolls. One night, complained the Communist Youth Organization's newspaper, Fyodor noticed a group in long jackets and tight pants gazing up at an apartment balcony from which a loudspeaker blared a tango. When the record ended, a disheveled fellow emerged with another disc and launched the "grating sounds of American jazz" to the crowd below.

> The young people began lurching around in an indecent dance called the "boogie-woogie." "What is this?" Fyodor thought. "Why are *stilyagi* dancing the boogie-woogie on the main street of a Soviet city? Who is playing that record?" He waited until the tousled youth appeared again on the balcony. "Well! It is one of our students—Oleg Potapov, from the second-year class."
>
> Fyodor did not oppose dances. But fox trots performed by American jazz bands disgusted him. When he turned the dial of the radio for relaxation, Fyodor passed over the stations taken by these bands.
>
> But Potapov, evidently, not only enjoyed listening to this music himself; he disseminated it. Why?[27]

A decade later, the hair, clothing, and lifestyle of Soviet hippies set them even farther from the mainstream of Soviet society than the *stilyagi* had been on "Broadway." While European contemporaries (including the antinuclear and Green movements) and the Soviet environment itself helped shape the hippie subculture that developed from the late 1960s to the early 1980s, American influence was essential to the advent of hippies in Soviet cities. "They looked and acted very much like the Americans whom they wanted desperately to imitate," observed a specialist on the Soviet counterculture, and they would not have appeared at all without the prior evolution of hippies in the United States. Even more than the *stilyagi*, they incorporated English words into their slang—*klous* (clothes), *dzhinsy* (jeans), and *gerla* (girl), for instance—and sported slogans in English that included "make hair everywhere," "long live butterflies," "love" and "rock explosion." A group in Moscow took such names as Ophelia, Shaman, Mango, Chicago, Limey,

Bumblebee, Dandelion, Jagger, Nixon, and Kennedy. Like the *stilyagi* before them, they demonstrated the magnetism of American popular culture, while remaining a small minority of their generation.[28]

Although few Soviet teenagers adopted the attire and lifestyle of hippies, many soon shared the counterculture's taste for certain American imports, especially rock 'n' roll. Shortly after the Voice of America began broadcasting rock 'n' roll to the Soviet Union in the 1950s, the music's energy captivated young listeners around the country. Recordings of Bill Haley and the Comets, Elvis Presley, and others—often "homemade" on used x-ray plates or smuggled into the country—spread from Moscow and Leningrad to the provinces by the end of the decade. Thereafter, as thousands of Westerners learned while visiting the Soviet Union over the next thirty years, Soviet black marketers thrived on the resale of rock 'n' roll recordings obtained from foreigners. The burgeoning demand for the music promised lavish profits to wheeler-dealers skillful enough to avoid policemen deployed to prevent these ubiquitous transactions.[29]

By the early 1960s the "twist" swept the country, spawning "a mass youth dance craze" according to a Russian account and catching the eye of Western journalists invited by the Soviet government to admire the nation's accomplishments in 1967, the fiftieth anniversary of the Revolution. A reporter for the *New York Times* noticed current American hits playing in "every restaurant and what passed for a nightclub" on the eve of the holiday. Thousands of homegrown bands tested the limits by operating outside the ranks of "official" musicians and playing at universities, high schools, institutes, restaurants, and even factories. Occasional visits by Western stars, such as B. B. King's 1979 tour, drew large crowds—two people in every seat at a concert in Tbilisi—with no advance publicity. An investigation of graffiti in Moscow a few years later discovered not only references to major Western bands but also the names of foreign groups obscure even in the West, thereby demonstrating the familiarity some Russians had developed with the international world of rock 'n' roll.[30]

Rock quickly eclipsed jazz in the Soviet Union and weathered official censure with the strength of a truly popular culture. Scathing attacks in the press, patrols of hangouts favored by teenagers, and jamming of foreign radio broadcasts all failed to dampen the popularity of American music.[31] When movies and plays employed rock numbers to stigmatize a location or character, they stood a good chance of reaching an audience pleased at the opportunity to hear the music—just as crowds relished the jazz played in Meyerhold's *Trust D. E.* during the 1920s. In 1960, for example, a state folk-dance troupe supplemented its program of ethnic dances with a satire of American rock 'n' roll in Moscow's Tchaikovsky Concert Hall. "When we are in foreign lands," explained an announcer, "we sometimes see how Western youth enjoy themselves. Some members of our company wished to comment on it. . . . We tentatively called this dance 'Back to the Monkeys.'" Discarding their peasant apparel, the performers burst into a raucous number wearing tight pants and sideburns in the style of Elvis Presley. Cheers resounded from the audience—the most enthusiastic of the evening.[32]

Viewed in broad perspective, officials retreated before the onslaught of rock 'n' roll. Sweeping condemnation failed to repulse the invasion and, as the decades passed, energetic prohibition yielded to grumpy acceptance within limits always under challenge by musicians and fans. In the 1970s the government made a deep bow to the music when it opened channels for what might be termed "official" rock. Bands that agreed to tone down their music and avoid themes with social or political sting received concert bookings and recording opportunities. After 1975 the Communist Youth Organization even began sponsoring discos. These ventures did attract audiences, but they scarcely dried up demand for Western recordings on the black market or for "unofficial" performers who displayed more daring in their stage antics or their lyrics. Whatever label one chooses for the postwar Soviet state—authoritarian, totalitarian, or the Evil Empire—its failure to eradicate or even control rock 'n' roll reveals something short of omnipotence.[33]

Official opposition to rock 'n' roll not only proved ineffective, it enhanced the music's appeal. In Western countries too, of course, rock challenged established conventions and won young listeners with its rebellious image. But in the Soviet Union, disparagement of the music often included *political* attacks stemming from the origins of rock 'n' roll in the nation's great adversary, the United States. Thus in 1984 the Communist Youth Organization's newspaper published an excerpt from a document attributed to NATO officials: "Special attention must be paid now to youth, not yet experienced in life and receptive to everything new, unusual, colorful, and gaudy in a material and technical sense. Our task is to enthrall the youth of the USSR with the ideals of the West." How was this to be accomplished? The Soviet author pointed to a recent article in the German magazine *Der Spiegel* that described American efforts to mesmerize Germans during World War II by broadcasting U.S. musical hits into the Third Reich. "And now," he warned, "when sharp American propaganda is directed against socialist countries, its methods have not changed," for the United States hoped to ensnare Soviet youth with rock 'n' roll delivered by radio. "This 'commodity,' immune to all customs inspections and duties, has become an outpost on the ideological front. Noticing that youths are captivated by rock music,

Western 'chefs' in the kitchen of ideas have concocted a dish of so-called rock culture."[34]

Characterizations of rock as a poisonous American conspiracy inclined those drawn to the music to accept the connection with the United States, but to do so with favor rather than alarm. If rock was exhilarating and born in America, and if ideologues insisted that it had nothing in common with true Soviet culture, then rock and America validated each other, while the label "Soviet" seemed ever more staid and monotonous. By the Brezhnev era, such a gap had developed between officials and much of the nation's youth that a film character meant to seem negative because of an association with rock 'n' roll could charm teenagers in the audience for the same reason.[35]

Indeed, virtually any product that trickled in from the West—including plastic shopping bags, used food containers, and other items that most Americans would discard, to say nothing of blue jeans, tennis shoes, cigarettes, and much else offered by foreign visitors—likely found a grateful Soviet recipient. Such commodities appealed to their new owners for diverse reasons: the status bestowed by an object that few could obtain or the convenience provided by something that worked better than a Soviet alternative, perhaps, but also the simple fact of the object's foreign origins. For some people, *Pravda* complained, Levi's jeans and other goods from abroad represented "a measure of success, a sign of social distinction. The possessor of such an item need not expend any intellectual or moral effort in order to be noticed—'esteemed.' You, on the other hand, are an ordinary person, insignificant 'like everyone else.'" To be sure, western European products mingled with those of America on the altar of Soviet consumers, just as Great Britain and other European countries joined the United States after the 1950s in supplying popular rock 'n' roll. "Bourgeois culture" from any Western nation could count on some favor in the Soviet population, but no other country matched America's clout in defining popular styles in music and clothing through the postwar period. This held true in western Europe itself. In the case of the Soviet Union, America as the distant land of beaches, movie stars, and material abundance withstood criticism focused by the Soviet media on the Western world's leading nation. For Soviet citizens dissatisfied with the goods or the restrictions produced by their own society, America's appeal grew at the expense of their own national image.[36]

Even the conventions of Soviet graffiti revealed this development. When practitioners resorted to English, they did so to convey approval—"ONLY HEAVY METAL," for instance, or "MAKE LOVE NOT WAR" and "TIME MACHINE FOREVER"—while negative comments about rival groups and genres of music appeared in Russian. English indicated something good, never bad. This linguistic "rule," concluded a scholar who surveyed Moscow's graffiti, demonstrated "the prestige associated with Western popular culture" and "the rejection of officially approved Soviet culture."[37] A similar practice spread in the argot of black marketers dealing in Western goods. The adjective American (*amerikanskii*) suggested excellence, whether or not the item in question had any connection to the United States. Praise for an "American supper" might refer to a meal of superb sturgeon, caviar, and vodka, all of Russian provenance. "Slavic" (*slavianskii*), by contrast, meant inferior (perhaps a box of rotten "Slavic" oranges), whatever the product's actual origins.[38]

During the forty years between the end of World War II and the promotion of Mikhail Gorbachev to leader of the Communist Party, diverse sources provided the Soviet population with bits and pieces of information about America. A good deal flowed from the pens of Soviet journalists, scholars, and literary figures, and it reached the public through government-controlled channels of publication. As previously noted, the large majority of these works presented an America in dark colors, even during the interval of détente in the 1970s. A sampling of Soviet articles and books about the United States from that decade exposed an America of vulgar materialism and cynical individualism, a country of random violence, unemployment, social stratification, and racism, with narcotics and pornography never far from hand.[39] Only a rare book about the United States, notably Viktor Nekrasov's *On Both Sides of the Ocean* (1962), emerged from the state presses to reveal an author more interested than hostile—and soon earned Nekrasov a tongue-lashing from Khrushchev and a demand that he revise the text.

Glimpses of the United States also arrived in the form of American literature (along with the films mentioned earlier) chosen by state agencies for distribution within the Soviet Union. The selection process favored radical authors such as Theodore Dreiser, Howard Fast, and Albert Maltz, though older novels by Mark Twain, Jack London, and James Fenimore Cooper, long popular in Russia, continued to appear as well. Most of the stories set in twentieth-century America dwelled on the same desolate themes that predominated in portraits of the United States penned by Soviet authors themselves.[40] These works, both Soviet and American, doubtless affected some people as officials desired, though leaden propaganda could also develop contrary sympathies.[41] Moreover, a film or play might contain scenes that nullified inadvertently much of the official rationale for the presentation. Poverty depicted in the American film *Grapes of Wrath*, for example, reportedly moved some Soviet audiences less than did the number of cars motoring

through the Oklahoma dust bowl. In the film version of Konstantin Simonov's play *The Russian Question*, an American journalist engaged to smear
the Soviet Union is offered a new house as a bribe. When the screen showed
the modern American kitchen in this dwelling, a Soviet audience responded
with admiration for the room rather than indignation at the bribe. *Pravda*
expressed similar concern over a production of Boris Lavrenyov's play *The
Voice of America*. "Unmasking the fascist clique of bankers and officials" in
the United States pleased the reviewer, but he worried that one of Moscow's
theaters had "embellished the world in which ordinary Americans live."
More specifically, the stage sets included "luxurious rooms and exotic ocean
views that clearly do not correspond to the lifestyle of the honest toiler Walter Kidd and give a false, distorted impression about the life of ordinary people in America."[42]

The fact remains, of course, that favorable images of America surfaced
rarely in movies and literature approved by Soviet authorities. Only sources
beyond the government's control promoted the United States without restraint. In 1947, for example, the Voice of America inaugurated its Russian
Service and soon developed broadcasts combining denunciation of Moscow's
policies with features on American life calculated to dazzle a Soviet audience. Problems of American society received occasional comment, but Russians learned much more about supermarkets, single-family homes, cars,
clothing, health care, and popular music—a "good life" linked to political
freedom and a capitalist economy. "Our broadcasts described the way people
lived" in the United States, recalled Victor Franzusoff, whose career at the
Voice of America took him from newswriter in 1947 to head of the Russian
Service in 1978. "It had to be clear to Soviet listeners that the lifestyle and
standard of living of most Americans was a hundred times higher than their
own." American officials also hoped that the picture magazine *Amerika* (distributed by the U.S. embassy in quantities limited by the Soviet government) would stir Soviet readers with images of living conditions in the
United States. According to George Kennan, a photograph of "an average
American school, a small town, or even an average American kitchen dram-
atizes to Soviet readers" that Americans possess, "contrary to everything they
are told by their propaganda, a superior standard of living and culture."[43]

No doubt some in the target audience reached this conclusion, though it
is impossible to determine the level of skepticism maintained by individual
listeners and readers. Testimony from traveling diplomats, refugees, and German prisoners of war released years after 1945 all suggested a large audience
at any rate, and the Kremlin certainly feared that foreign broadcasts and publications might beguile its subjects. The barrage of Soviet criticism directed

at the Voice of America, along with efforts to jam the incoming signals, may have discouraged some listeners, but not Vasily Aksenov: "Every night the Voice of America would beam a two-hour jazz program at the Soviet Union from Tangiers. The snatches of music and bits of information made for a kind of golden glow over the horizon when the sun went down, that is, in the West, the inaccessible but oh so desirable West." Though future research may yield a more precise reckoning of those who shared Aksenov's reverie in the 1950s, one can suppose for now that he was far from alone.[44]

A more tangible sense of popular interest materialized at the end of the decade, following agreement between the United States and the Soviet Union to broaden cultural exchanges. Months of negotiations opened the door for each country to advertise itself on the shores of its adversary, and in 1959 the United States Information Agency launched an American National Exhibition in Moscow's Sokolniki Park. American officials anticipated a subversive effect on Muscovite viewers and gave voice among themselves to the very strategy that agitated Soviet sentinels. The U.S. ambassador in Moscow, Llewellyn Thompson, sounded a common theme when he declared that the exhibition should "endeavor to make the Soviet people dissatisfied with the share of the Russian pie which they now receive and make them realize that the slight improvements projected in their standard of living are only a drop in the bucket to what they could and should have." At the pinnacle of Soviet power, officials ruminated on the response of their population to the displays in Sokolniki Park. A report to the party's Central Committee expressed worry over American efforts at the impending exhibition "to demonstrate various conveniences of everyday life so as to make the Soviet people believe in the allegedly high standard of living of the 'average' American and to distract the visitor's attention from the real vices of capitalism with its mass unemployment and impoverishment of the broad masses of the working people, race discrimination, etc." In the days before the exhibition, the party ordered a preemptive propaganda campaign to contrast the flaws of capitalist society with the accomplishments of the Soviet Union and to discourage crowds from attending the exhibition. Once the gates opened, authorities sought to hold down attendance by showing foreign films on television and scheduling more than the usual number of carnivals, art exhibitions, and other entertainments elsewhere in Moscow.[45]

Much to the amazement of anyone steeped in the tensions of the Cold War, the exhibition opened on schedule in June for a six-week run. It included a two-hundred-foot-wide dome that housed seven large screens on which were projected pictures of American supermarkets, highways, universities, and other structures selected to impress. The dome also sheltered various technical exhibits, including an IBM computer that provided answers in Russian to visitors' questions about American life. Beyond the dome stood a fifty-thousand-square-foot glass pavilion that featured all manner of American consumer goods. "It is almost like a great bazaar of the conveniences that the American family enjoys," beamed Harold McClellan, the exhibition's general manager. Elsewhere around the site Russians discovered a model American home, new cars and trucks, sport boats, playground equipment, and much else, including booths dispensing free samples of Pepsi-Cola. "You Americans think the Russian people will be astonished to see these things," remarked Nikita Khrushchev during a tour of the model home with Vice President Richard Nixon (the occasion of their famous kitchen debate). "The fact is, that all our new houses have this kind of equipment." Khrushchev must have known better, as did the many spectators who left positive comments in the "remarks book." Despite the fact that officials stocked the crowds with people instructed to badger the American guides, no one could mistake the atmosphere of fascination and the clamor to gain admittance to the grounds. The official total of 2.7 million visitors shared the exhibits with tens of thousands of gate crashers.[46]

In decades to come, as cultural and educational exchanges multiplied along with tourism, more Russians encountered Americans and their possessions face to face—both in the Soviet Union and, for members of the elite, during visits to the United States. Nothing else, concluded the political scientist Jerry Hough, did more to foster "the growing dissatisfaction of the upper and middle elite with the gray egalitarianism of Soviet society and the low level of privilege in their lives in comparison with their counterparts in the West." "The exchange programs of the West," he added, "were far more crucial in destroying communism than the [American] military buildup of the early 1980s." In any case, to focus on the point at hand, the expansion of exchange visits provided another source of information about the United States that contradicted images presented by the Soviet media.[47]

Scarcely had Mikhail Gorbachev succeeded Konstantin Chernenko as general secretary of the Communist Party in 1985, than he began casting about for some way to close the technological gap between the Soviet Union and the United States. Though Gorbachev proved willing to support a variety of reforms in the following years, he did not advocate "catching up" with the Western world by absorbing a level of American popular culture comparable to that visible in France or Germany. Yet his relaxation of domestic controls produced this result, and with greater "success" than any of the economic reforms that held his attention. The freedoms he bestowed on the population led to an ever more open embrace of American amusements and styles that astonished anyone old enough to recall the official ire that had greeted "bourgeois contamination" in the past. James Billington, the Librarian of Congress and historian of Russia, noticed a powerful "fascination with the spontaneity and directness of American mass culture, which has conquered Russia even more than it has many Western countries. The rock music, the slogans on T-shirts and buttons, the world of jeans, guitars, and jogging clothes—all have grown continuously in popularity" during the half decade before the collapse of Gorbachev's political career and the Soviet Union itself in 1991.[48] Thereafter, as the new Russian Republic opened its doors wider to the West than had any Soviet or tsarist government, nothing seemed likely to stem the American tide.

Hollywood movies set an example. Well-connected individuals had brought small numbers of videocassette recorders and tapes of foreign films into the Soviet Union before 1985, but once travel restrictions loosened in the second half of the decade, the equipment and the tapes entered in greater quantities. Private entrepreneurs opened "video salons" in their apartments and other discreet locations, where they showed American movies to paying customers. Much of this activity was illegal, but as the years passed and the laws changed (or ceased to be enforced), video parlors expanded. By the end of the 1980s, Hollywood's creations turned up routinely in Soviet movie theaters and before long they appeared on television. The popularity of these films made them profitable and thus secured their place in a Soviet film establishment that suffered from the same economic hardship as the rest of the country. In April of 1991, only 22 of the 313 movies in Moscow's theaters were Soviet made; most of the remaining 291 were American. The following year, a guide to movies playing on 22 October in Moscow indicated that no more than 10 percent were Russian.[49]

Seventy years after Lev Kuleshov tried to account for the popularity of American movies, an article in a Russian film journal wrestled with the same question. The author rejected claims that Hollywood's appeal lay in the technical superiority of its equipment, dismissing this as an excuse raised by Russian filmmakers. Soviet and now Russian productions—which often suffered from an "unhurried, outmoded manner" or "didacticism and messianism"—could not compete with American movies that exalted the "code of individualism" and the "possibility of the hero to come through in any circumstances." At a Hollywood movie, a person "finds himself in a country where his thoughts come true, where for two hours he can imagine himself a 'real' person." Indeed, the essay continued, these American pictures "are a part of utopia, a realization of dreams about a worthwhile life. We underestimated the impact on the Soviet viewer of the reconstruction on the screen of seductive material surroundings, interiors of homes and rooms, clothing, hairstyles, gestures, and the characters' manner of behavior."[50] At this time, early in the 1990s, similar comments dotted interviews with Russians who had begun to sample American television and movies. "It should be this way all the time," declared a thirty-three-year-old electrician. "The American films are better. They're more colorful and happier." A teacher of similar age favored American films "because even in the worst situation, there's always some hope. . . . Now all of a sudden we're free, and no one knows quite how to live. These films teach us that in America, if a person wants something, he can go out and get it."[51]

For these reasons and others, including the attraction of forbidden fruit now readily available, lines formed outside theaters showing American movies. In 1991, a half-century after its premier in the United States, Gone with the Wind reached the Russian public and drew large crowds for months. Many other Hollywood productions, especially action-adventure stories, also sold out cinemas on a daily basis, and not just in Moscow. A survey in 1995 of 1,822 people (weighted to represent the national adult population) in 108 cities, towns, and villages across Russia included the following question: "Can you remember the names of some actors or actresses in American films whom you liked?" Among the respondents, who were allowed to specify more than one performer, 27 percent named Sylvester Stallone, 25 percent Arnold Schwarzenegger, and 18 percent Jean-Claude van Damme—by far the three highest individual totals.[52] This list suggests that America's finest offerings did not lead the parade across Russian screens, where indeed viewers were likely to encounter The Beach Girls, Hot Target, Nine Deaths of the Ninja, and other B-movie debris from Hollywood's mill. In 1991 Izvestiia printed an essay that termed the recent box-office failure of foreign masterpieces a disgrace. "Not for the masterpieces [by Fellini, Bergman, Kurosawa, and others], of course; it's shameful for you and me. . . . It's sad but true that the Soviet moviegoer, confused by politics and worn out by daily life, chooses pure 'escapism,' preferably 'Made in the USA.'" Disgraceful or not, 64 percent of the sample in the 1995 national survey reported seeing at least one American movie per week during the previous year.[53]

At roughly the same time that Hollywood movies crowded into Russian cinemas, American television programs appeared in Russian homes. In January 1991, even before the Soviet Union's downfall, the Walt Disney Company began one-hour Sunday afternoon airings of cartoons, while two months later Tribune Entertainment licensed the talk show Geraldo for periodic broadcasts. During a week in July, state television filled its entire prime-time schedule with American programs, including *Dallas* (the most popular), *The Streets of San Francisco, Little House on the Prairie, The Love Boat, Beverly Hills 90210,* as well as cartoon shows such as *The Jetsons* and *The Flintstones.*[54] After 1991, American shows (and some from other countries, including popular Latin American soap operas) ran daily in the new Russian Republic's broadcasts. A report in 1995 from a village in what nationalists might term the heart of Russia included the following caption for a photograph: "Maria Petrovna and her granddaughter Lena prepare lunch. During an average workday, Mrs. Petrovna sits down only long enough to watch the much-beloved American soap opera 'Santa Barbara.'"[55]

While *Santa Barbara* became the most popular American program on Russian TV in the 1990s, many other U.S. shows gained avid followers. Evidence appeared in surprising places, including a Moscow police station where a visitor noticed two detectives with their feet propped up on desks—unusual and ill-mannered behavior in Russia. It turned out that the policemen had learned the practice from episodes of the television drama *Starsky and Hutch,* just as some Russian organized-crime bosses copied the mannerisms of Mafia dons in Hollywood movies. The two detectives were not the only ones emulating American TV programs, as various Russian shows also drew from American models. Through much of the 1990s the game show *Field of Miracles,* derived from *Wheel of Fortune,* remained one of the most popular Russian productions in any genre.[56]

American music, long broadcast by short-wave radio to the Soviet Union, followed the paths that opened for U.S. television programs and movies. Rock videos by Michael Jackson and others surfaced on Soviet television before 1991 and appeared with greater regularity in Russian TV programming thereafter. In the national survey of 1995, 36 percent of the sample had viewed American music videos (on TV or cassette) at least once a week over the previous year, with another 16 percent "about once a month." Piracy of Western recordings became commonplace—to the point where one could provide a blank tape to the proprietor of a kiosk on the street and select the music to be copied from a list of titles in stock.[57] Corresponding to the generation gap in other countries, Russians under thirty years of age listened most often to American popular music, and their interest continued to find expression in graffiti. "Even today," lamented the novelist Victor Pelevin in 1997, "Russian inscriptions are depressingly unoriginal." They consist either of "the words Holden Caulfield tried to erase from the wall at his sister's school" or "the words rap and techno and the names of U.S. rock bands. It is hard to drive through some neighborhoods without absorbing a scrawled update from American show business."[58]

This hunger for American popular culture, increasingly visible in the late 1980s, burst into full view during the first years of the following decade. Russians even formed small leagues to play American football, with exchange visits in the United States for coaching and competition.[59] American consumer goods—Coca-Cola, candy bars, gum, cigarettes, cosmetics, detergents, and cars—appeared everywhere, from the trays of street vendors to showrooms frequented by the new rich. Billboards and television advertisements hawked these commodities, as did trade fairs in which representatives of American firms demonstrated their products and offered free samples. Companies staged lavish spectacles, including a competition to choose the first native playmate for the centerfold of *Playboy*'s Russian edition and Cokefest 94, a sprawling party at Moscow's Radisson Slavyanskaya Hotel to celebrate the opening of the first Coca-Cola bottling plant in Russia. English-language promotional messages ceased to surprise foreigners or Russians. "If in an ad you need to portray something as attractive," complained the nationalist intellectual Igor Shafarevich, "they speak English," much as English had served to convey merit in Soviet graffiti. American clothing, long popular on the black market, now circulated without the precautions necessary during the Brezhnev era and reached young people even in remote areas.[60]

Moscow and some other cities also acquired American restaurants at this time, including Pizza Huts and a 1950s diner shipped in pieces from Florida and reassembled near Moscow's Tchaikovsky Concert Hall. In the same vicinity, and far more significant as an icon of American culture, stood the capital's first McDonald's. *Izvestiia* noted the symbolic punch carried by the restaurant and described it as a source of food "for a people on the go. It is democratic. It is a display of Americanism, American rationalism and pragmatism applied to food." Terms common in the 1920s—"American efficiency" and "American scale"—appeared in the article as praise for McDonald's methods, but there ended the similarity with the early Soviet period. By 1990 *Izvestiia* could no longer muster the confidence of Bolshevik founding fathers in a socialist (or any other) vision that, blended with American efficiency, would astound the world. The article recalled hopes advanced in previous decades "about knocking Coca-Cola from the world market with our Russian *kvass* [a lightly fermented drink]" and "convincing the planet of the delights of our Siberian *pelmeni*" (small, stuffed dumplings). But "all this has turned to sand."[61]

Alexander Rutskoi, an important ally of Boris Yeltsin in 1991 who became a leader of the parliamentary opposition to Yeltsin in 1993, understood and lamented the appeal exerted by McDonald's as a Western idol in Russia.

The long wait outside McDonald's is not in expectation of food but of holy communion. Yes, these people, young and old, stand silently in line for hours as though trying to commune for a moment with the Western way of life after being locked for decades in a totalitarian utopia. They, too, want to feel themselves a part of that most civilized world brimming with freedom, abundance, and prosperity. The brightly lit McDonald's wigwam [*vigvam*] in the very heart of the former superpower is a miniature copy of the "shining temple" on the mountain that Ronald Reagan pathetically described while praising America.[62]

Between 1990 and 1995 this McDonald's on Pushkin Square attracted eighty million customers, more than Lenin's Tomb and more than any other McDonald's in the world.[63]

No longer did Russia seem distant from the world of Western consumer societies. "Instead of the 'radiant future of Communism,'" explained Edvard Radzinsky, "suddenly we awaited the 'radiant future of capitalism.'" The national opinion poll of 1995 found that two-thirds of the respondents under thirty chose the adjective "appealing" to describe the American popular culture available at every turn.[64] Among those over fifty, to be sure, only 15 percent shared this view, and some Russians, whose voices resound in chapter eight, expressed dismay at Western contamination. For them the radiant future lay not in blue jeans, rock 'n' roll, Coke, or Hollywood. But even they believed, perhaps more than anyone else, that a cultural invasion from the United States had taken place.

The influx of American mass culture represented one channel through which images of life in the United States entered Russia in swelling volume after 1985. American movies, rock 'n' roll videos, television dramas, and talk shows presented the United States in pictures of sharp contrast. Sometimes they portrayed a blighted and violent America writhing before Russian viewers as if to confirm charges made for decades by Soviet ideologues. Yet reports told more often of audiences focusing on America the bountiful and glamorous. In some cases this was the message intended, as in advertising campaigns for American products. Billboards all over Russia exalted American cigarettes with pictures of majestic skyscrapers or sandy beaches accompanied by such slogans as "Total Freedom" or "Rendezvous with America." Even programs centering on American crime could leave viewers more taken by the material surroundings than the mayhem driving the plot. So it was in 1991, when a *Baltimore Sun* correspondent found himself talking with a small group of bankers and government officials in Vladikavkaz, the capital of North Ossetia in the Northern Caucasus. As one of the bankers ran through some American movies on his office videocassette recorder, the correspondent noticed from remarks made by the viewers that they "were looking beyond the violence, sleaze, and corruption of the plot at sleek cars, designer apartments, glittering high rises, and well-stocked stores. Whatever happened up front, the background was the promised land." Radzinsky, too, discovered audiences entranced by the luxurious world revealed in American movies: "'I don't follow the plot or the actors, I just look around them,' many people said."[65]

Apart from U.S. popular culture, other vehicles conveyed impressions of the United States to Russia late in the twentieth century. With the easing of travel restrictions, direct contacts multiplied as delegations, exchange students, entrepreneurs, and tourists ventured in growing numbers between the two countries. Even Russians without unusual connections could now make the trip. Meanwhile, the U.S. government maintained windows on America first opened in previous decades. Along with cultural and educational exchanges, these included short-wave broadcasts about American life and, most dramatic, traveling exhibitions in the Soviet Union itself. Khrushchev may have told Nixon during the kitchen debate in 1959 that the Soviet public possessed consumer goods on par with those of the West, but in the portion of his memoirs unpublished until 1990, he complained that people "hang around foreign delegations and tourists and con them out of these kinds of items or simply buy them outright. In our market we cannot hope to compete. It's too bad; it's shameful, but it is a fact that can't be denied."[66] Popular reaction to subsequent exhibitions steered other observers to similar conclusions about the gap between the two countries.

In 1988, the U.S. Information Agency launched its *Information USA* exhibit on a Soviet tour that included Magnitogorsk, home to the famous but outmoded steel works. "As the exhibit drew near, our curiosity reached personally dangerous levels," explained a local scientist:

> For us it all looked like science fiction. What kind of civilization could afford personal computers for school children! I'm a scientist, yet I'm without one. Telephones for the deaf. How could that be? Videodisks, facsimile machines, plastic money, bar codes controlling inventories—I have not the words to explain to you what all this looks like to us.

Approximately 245,000 people attended the spectacle in Magnitogorsk, more even than in Moscow. Many openly expressed awe, sometimes combined with shame over the Soviet system. "You should have heard their comments," remarked a steelworker, describing his children's response to the exhibition. "'Enough,' they said, 'we're going to America.' This is wrong, but I can't blame them."[67]

A year later, on the thirtieth anniversary of its exposition in Sokolniki Park, the U.S. Information Agency staged *Design USA* in Moscow. The exhibit, which ran for twenty-four days in the capital before traveling to other Soviet cities, sought to demonstrate "the role of design in American life" through displays of architectural models, a modern American kitchen (evidently regarded as a "can't miss" item by the USIA), toys, appliances, sports equipment, a bright red Chevrolet Corvette, and much else. Day after day, the Soviet media provided substantial and positive coverage, while no agitators materialized to harass the American guides or intimidate Soviet crowds, which they had done at U.S. shows as recently as 1987. The comment book and the exit poll at *Design USA* revealed the grounds for apprehension felt by Soviet officials over the years. Most visitors were impressed: "For us, this is, God willing, the 21st century," or "How beautifully the bourgeoisie is decaying!" Some even felt moved to write in the following vein: "Thanks, but it would have been better if I had not seen all this—I feel ashamed for my country."[68]

The Kremlin had distributed an overwhelmingly negative picture of the United States for decades, which made the favorable press coverage of *Design USA* remarkable. Nor was this an isolated instance, as would have been the case with a complimentary reference to America earlier in the postwar era. The Soviet media changed, in breathtaking fashion, the facets of America presented during Gorbachev's ascendancy. To be sure, champions of a bleak view did not vanish altogether after 1985, as films and publications decrying American militarism, cultural imperialism, and domestic sores continued to appear from time to time. But studies of Soviet newspaper and television reporting on America found hostile accounts rare by 1989, in contrast to the prevailing tone a few years before. Researchers at Emory University demonstrated that the principal TV news program devoted an ever-increasing share of its international coverage to the United States in this period, with a more positive slant on the reporting. "There is no question," they concluded, "that in terms of images and models, the United States is in a class by itself, and its importance to the Soviet Union cannot be overemphasized."[69] Some publications, quoted in the following chapter, even offered praise for the American political system and suggested that its study would disclose features of use to Soviet reformers.[70]

On a visit to America in 1989, Boris Yeltsin acknowledged the transformation that had occurred in his own thinking, and his remarks published in Soviet newspapers may have nudged some readers toward a similar appraisal.

This is my first time in the USA, and I must say—not because I am the guest and you are the hosts, but really sincerely—that the opinion dinned into us and me all our lives, including by means of [a book produced under Stalin, titled] the *Short History Course of the All-Union Communist Party (Bolsheviks)*, with regard to capitalism, America, Americans, and New York has been turned through 180 degrees during this day and a half. It turns out that capitalism is not decaying and, thus, will not soon rot, as we were told all the time, but is flourishing.[71]

Émigré opinions provided another indication of the change, as Soviet periodicals began to publish essays and interviews in which prominent expatriates described their new home with acclaim more often than frustration.[72] Some spoke in grandiose terms about a special American atmosphere, as did the painter Mikhail Shemiakin, who professed shock at the brightness of the sun when he arrived in America: "You know the light is really like in India, not like in Europe, and these handsome, laughing people are walking around, and you have the feeling of total lack of constraint, an extraordinary self-confidence and friendliness." Others recalled for Soviet readers the attractive images they had held of America while still in Moscow or Leningrad and saw no need to reject them after living in the United States. "We, my circle, we were more American than, perhaps, the Americans themselves," explained the poet Iosif Brodsky. "When I spoke about the ideal of individualism, that was what we were dreaming of. And for us the only place where it was embodied was the United States."[73]

Nothing in these new pictures of the United States more captivated the Soviet audience than displays of American affluence, visible to Boris Yeltsin at a supermarket in Houston. "When I saw those shelves crammed with hundreds, thousands of cans, cartons, and goods of every possible sort," he wrote in his autobiography, "for the first time I felt quite frankly sick with despair for the Soviet people."[74] At about the same time *Izvestiia* published a similar comment by a Soviet economist who had spent nearly a year studying agriculture in the United States. He pointed to supermarkets in order to reject claims that Soviet agriculture could compare with practices in America:

> The utter absurdity of such assertions can be demonstrated simply by considering the quantity and assortment of food. The selection in the United States, for example, is such that not all of our fellow citizens, finding themselves for the first time in any—I emphasize any—supermarket, will be able to regard calmly this staggering abundance.[75]

For those who did not cross the ocean to see for themselves, the Soviet media (including the publishers of Yeltsin's book) provided similar glimpses. A television feature on an American construction worker revealed a life bounteous by Soviet standards and concluded with the reporter's observation that "unquestionably this country has come a long way from barbarous capitalism as it was known in the classics to today's relative abundance and comfort—at least for the majority of those who live here." The declining level of consumption in the Soviet Union only sharpened the contrast with America. Even in 1988, with the worst years of economic disarray still to come, a Soviet article whose findings were cited widely in the nation's press indicated that personal consumption in the USSR probably hovered between 30 and 50 percent of that in America.[76] Some authors made the point with humor, as in a list of ten "travel tips" for Russian visitors to the United States. Number three advised, "If a friend offers you a busted answering machine or, still better, if you find an old VCR on the sidewalk (stop laughing—in America there are VCRs on the sidewalks!), stuff it in your suitcase," while number five added, "Ignore panhandlers. Virtually any American beggar is wealthier than you."[77]

No single image of America dispensed with all others during the years that spanned the passing of the Soviet Union and the birth of the Russian Republic. Contradictory assessments persisted then, just as they had in the 1920s. Alarm and revulsion over the United States, encouraged by the Soviet government for decades, maintained their hold on a minority of the population and will color an ensuing chapter. But these reactions could not eclipse notions of an America brimming with fabulous goods and technologies. The appeal of American consumer culture in even the most inhospitable intervals of Soviet history should prevent surprise over the results of opinion polls that showed widespread favor toward the United States after the party began to loosen its grip in the late 1980s. The national poll of 1995 found that 80–90 percent of its sample associated a high standard of living with America, and that at least 70 percent rated the United States positively in several other categories, including "promotion of science and culture" and "individual liberties" (but not "rights of ethnic and racial minorities"). When asked "which qualities or traits first come to mind when you think of Americans," the respondents volunteered desirable characteristics—efficiency, diligence, practicality, lack of inhibition, openness, kindness, confidence, among many others—far more often than vices or defects. A quarter of the responses mentioned American "efficiency" (praised by Bolshevik leaders sixty years earlier), while only 4 percent cited "arrogance or impudence," 3 percent "avarice or materialism," and no other flaw occurring to more than 2 percent of the sample.[78]

The Soviet Union's final years brought unprecedented liberties accompanied by hardship as the centralized economy and welfare state crumbled. The new freedoms improved the reliability of opinion polls, while the economic austerity prompted respondents to look with increasing favor toward the West at the expense of their own country. A series of surveys in the city of Tambov, conducted among secondary students from 1988 to 1991, found opinions ever more favorable regarding life in America, as they turned pessimistic about conditions in the Soviet Union. To these students, Americans seemed enterprising, peaceful, free, rich, and trustworthy rather than unpleasant or dangerous.[79] Another study, in 1990, compared impressions held by college students in Moscow and New Mexico and found that "the Russians appear to have a more negative view of themselves than they have of Americans or than Americans have of them, most likely because of the dramatic changes that Russia was undergoing at the time of the study." The students in Moscow saw fellow Russians as "patient, oppressed, and passive" but regarded Americans as "spontaneous, independent, and energetic." Here glimmered a contrast that Hilary Pilkington's research led her to describe as an "inferiority complex *vis à vis* the West, which is virtually a reflex reaction amongst young Russians."[80]

Numerous Russian observers agreed, including a researcher at the Academy of Sciences who noted that when the Iron Curtain came down, "most Russians were almost in shock at what they had discovered about their country, in which they had always taken such pride. Against the background of this growing inferiority complex, the West began to appear to many as a heaven-on-earth, populated by angels." Vasily Aksenov recalled that "in the early days of reforms everybody was nuts on the West and notably, America. The fascination with them so often as not bordered on absurdity." Thus it appeared to a *Pravda* commentator in 1990: "Sometimes we are gripped by a sort of 'tinseled euphoria' in perceiving that which is shown or said about the United States. And this is not surprising—ever more often on the screen and in the press there is portrayed a completely problem-free, 'shining' image of America and its culture." After the failed coup of August 1991, "one did not sense anti-Western, anti-American moods in Russia," recounted the prominent politician and former ambassador to America, Vladimir Lukin, and his coauthor, the history professor Anatoly Utkin. "On the contrary, one sensed a clear sympathy, seemingly unnatural after seventy years of ideological confrontation and single-minded propaganda." In short order, added the pair, "Russians willingly agreed to reverse the former scheme of things: now the West seemed the embodiment of good and Russia the embodiment of evil." America reigned as "the sun-country," gushed a young woman from Leningrad. "There is sunlight everywhere, a lot of fruit, lots of beautiful people. Lots of beautiful cars." In her hometown, less than two months after the attempted coup, on a large wall where people often posted announcements and personal opinions a "declaration to the Russian people" offered readers little solace by asserting that "it's better to be a farmer in Texas than president of this country."[81]

Russia now appeared a land of dimming prospects, quite different in this respect from Lenin's domain of the 1920s. Young Soviet Russia, still a peasant society and scarcely a superpower, was led by a party successfully extending its control throughout the land and animated by a sense of mission in the world. If the country was poor, that would surely change once socialism's advantages made themselves apparent over a United States struck in 1929 by economic disaster. Soon the Soviet Union's strength increased sufficiently to bring triumph in World War II and then parity with America's armed forces. By 1990 the Kremlin's realm had been recognized for years as a superpower, with a well-educated, predominately urban population that enjoyed a standard of living far higher than the norm in 1925. All to no avail. Officials now pointed to stagnation at home rather than in the West, as the Soviet Union lagged farther behind the United States with every year. No longer did the party exude the energy of its youth, and its morale shriveled along with its clout as Gorbachev's tenure drew to a close.

Meanwhile, throughout the century, American mass culture retained its magnetism. Neither Lenin nor Gorbachev desired such an attraction, yet each endured it in his day. Early Bolsheviks tolerated American entertainment under the assumption that this temporary eyesore would yield to the advanced outlook of a new socialist community. Until then, much as with other types of American expertise, various officials believed that study of American cultural techniques would reveal innovations that could be utilized to promote a socialist message. By the 1930s, and for decades thereafter, the government sharply restricted the importation of American popular culture, until Gorbachev accepted Western pastimes in larger volume than at any other moment in the Soviet era. He did so more in the hope that this (and other freedoms) would impress the population as treatment worthy of mature citizens and thus inspire them to work with enthusiasm and initiative. It no longer seemed a temporary concession, and Soviet commentators no longer filled the media with talk of creating a superior socialist alternative.

As for popular visions of the United States, much that was widespread in the 1920s—an aura of a bounteous land full of technical marvels and opportunities for success—remained at the end of the century. To be sure, new images emerged as well, especially America as a menacing military giant, a specter that did not trouble the Russian countryside in the 1920s. It may also be that the predominantly peasant population of the 1920s shared folkloric vistas of American bounty that grew less fanciful among succeeding generations educated in Soviet schools. But the collapse of the Russian economy in the 1990s left such a chasm between the two countries' standards of living that even an accurate picture of life in the United States supported conclusions of comparative American prosperity that differed little from those common among immigrants to the New World one hundred years earlier. No other nation had ever attracted such interest from ordinary Russians. If European practices did excite some tsarist administrators and intellectuals to a degree that matched America's subsequent influence on the Soviet elite, nothing from Europe in any period of the Romanov dynasty could compare with the spread of American images and popular culture among the broader population in the twentieth century.

Party officials labored for decades to counter the charm of their primary foreign rival, and the government's formidable resources doubtless swayed domestic opinion to some degree. Western publications themselves spoke of America's shortcomings, and these helped Soviet ideologists to enhance the sophistication and credibility of their attacks. At the same time though, the resilient popularity of American mass culture and the persistence of official reproaches suggest that authorities sensed the buoyant reputation of the land beyond the sea.[82] While other countries also absorbed much from the United States in the twentieth century, the Soviet Union stood out in this regard by virtue of the Kremlin's own global impact and ambitions. Here, in an imposing country leading an international movement bound for a society superior to that of its main "capitalist" adversary, American entertainment and example revealed an unsinkable appeal. Once the two governments confronted each other in the Cold War, popular culture became a battleground as never before: one side enlisting mass consumption and entertainment to help discredit its foe; the other combating this subversion desperately. Amid such tension, the robust esteem of jazz, Hollywood, rock 'n' roll, and English-language phrases on T-shirts carried much more electricity than anything generated by the same products elsewhere. The context of the struggle was momentous, and this lent an unprecedented gravity to the role thrust on mass culture and its images of America.

As a rule, those who had grown up in the Soviet Union during the Cold War harbored more misgivings about one aspect or another of the United States than did young adults coming of age as the Soviet Union collapsed. A national poll in the summer of 1992 found that 81 percent of the respondents between eighteen and twenty-nine had a "very favorable" or a "somewhat favorable" opinion of the United States, while among those over sixty, the figure dropped to 58 percent.[83] When another national survey inquired about Americans "as persons," a warmer response accumulated from Russians under thirty (83 percent positive and 3 percent negative) than from fellow citizens over fifty (56 percent positive and 14 percent negative).[84] Had a survey on impressions of America been conducted in the 1920s, it would probably not have revealed a similar division. Indeed, a gap in reverse might have registered, with older people in greater awe of America (along traditional peasant lines) than younger people, whose generation included more of those who combined respect for American technology with confidence in the ultimate superiority of a Soviet socialist future. Later, in any case, the experience of the Cold War helped persuade older Russians in the 1990s to view the United States more as a rival than a model, while their children or grandchildren detected less of the Soviet heritage worth preserving and more in the United States to value.

It seems plausible to suppose that Soviet opinions of America commonly mixed varying proportions of fear (the United States as militaristic) and aversion (domestic American crime, unemployment, and so forth) with respect for technology in the United States and affinity for American popular culture. Among intellectuals in particular, admiration could also encompass individual freedoms unavailable at home. For people who found the Soviet environment oppressive or at least shabby, the comfort in imagining a gilded alternative in America recalls the solace or hope sought by other human beings who, in trying times, have created mental images of promised lands. A reasonable conclusion might hold that a substantial portion of the Soviet population during the Khrushchev and Brezhnev eras felt a strong curiosity toward the United States that was by no means instinctively unfriendly. If they suffered concern regarding America's nuclear intentions and worried that the United States misunderstood the Soviet Union, this need not cancel their respect for American proficiency or their appetite for some form of American mass culture. Misgivings about the Pentagon and the White House, in other words, could coexist with positive inklings of American life, even after crediting some of the party's contentions about, say, American racism.[85] Once the official attacks diminished in the late 1980s, enthusiasm for things American burst into view with a force built up over decades under the party's lid. Many people clamored for helpings of American popular culture with no more restraint than in the 1920s, and before long some began looking to America for guidance of other sorts that no Bolshevik would have tolerated even as a temporary concession.

Notes

1. *New York Times Magazine*, 8 June 1997, 82; Timothy Ryback, *Rock around the Bloc: A History of Rock Music in Eastern Europe and the Soviet Union* (Oxford: Oxford University Press, 1990), 229.

2. *New York Times*, 4 February 1997.

3. A. V. Golubev, ed., *Rossiia i zapad. Formirovanie vneshnepoliticheskikh stereotipov v soznanii rossi-iskogo obshchestva pervoi poloviny XX veka* (Moscow: IRI RAN, 1998), 283–84; I. A. Startsev, *Amerika i russkoe obshchestvo* (Moscow: Izdatel'stvo akademii nauk SSSR, 1942), 1–2, 32.

4. Startsev, *Amerika i russkoe obshchestvo*, 1, 31. See also Kevin J. McKenna, *All the Views Fit to Print: Changing Images of the U.S. in* Pravda *Political Cartoons, 1917–1991* (New York: Peter Lang, 2001), 52.

5. Varlam Shalamov, *Kolyma Tales* (New York: Norton, 1980), 174; Nikita Khrushchev, *Khrushchev Remembers* (Boston: Little, Brown, 1970), 226; Vasily Aksyonov, *In Search of Melancholy Baby* (New York: Random House, 1987), 14; Nina Tumarkin, *The Living and the Dead: The Rise and Fall of the Cult of World War II in Russia* (New York: Basic, 1994), 87; Walter L. Hixson, *Witness to Disintegration: Provincial Life in the Last Year of the USSR* (Hanover, N.H.: University Press of New England, 1993), 107.

6. S. Frederick Starr, *Red and Hot: The Fate of Jazz in the Soviet Union. With a New Chapter on the Final Years* (New York: Limelight, 1994), 193.

7. Starr, *Red and Hot*, 190–95.

8. Regarding the more favorable portrayal of Russians in Hollywood films during the war, see Jeffrey William Peck, "Structural Film Analysis and the Pro-Soviet Dramatic Films of Wartime America, 1942–1945" (Ph.D. diss., University of Wisconsin at Madison, 1975).

9. Eric Rhode, *A History of the Cinema from Its Origins to 1970* (London: Allen Lane, 1976), 414; J. N. Washburn, *Soviet Theater: Its Distortion of America's Image, 1921–1973* (Chicago: American Bar Association, 1973), 43–45. See also Valentin Kiparsky, *English and American Characters in Russian Fiction* (Wiesbaden, West Germany: Otto Harrassowitz, 1964), 150–51.

10. George F. Kennan, *Memoirs (1925–1950)* (New York: Bantam, 1969), 253–55.

11. Konstantin Simonov, "Glazami cheloveka moego pokoleniia (Razmyshleniia o I. V. Staline)," *Znamia*, no. 3 (1988): 59; Thomas Riha, ed., *Readings in Russian Civilization* (Chicago: University of Chicago Press, 1964), 690; J. D. Parks, *Culture, Conflict and Coexistence: American-Soviet Cultural Relations, 1917–1958* (Jefferson, N.C.: McFarland, 1983), 119–20. See also Bruce B. Parrott, "Technology and the Soviet Polity: The Problem of Industrial Innovation, 1928 to 1973" (Ph.D. diss., Columbia University, 1976), 222.

12. V. D. Duvakin, "Stikhi Maiakovskogo ob Amerike," *Literatura v shkole*, no. 1 (January–February 1950): 29; N. Maslin, "Maiakovskii ob Amerike," *Bol'shevik*, no. 17 (1949): 75; Konstantin Simonov, "Maiakovskii ob Amerike," *Kul'tura i zhizn'*, 10 April 1949, 4.

13. For a description of *Missouri Waltz* and many other Soviet plays of this period, see William J. McBrearty, "The Characterization of Americans in Post-War Soviet Drama" (M.A. thesis, Columbia University, 1952).

14. McBrearty, "Characterization of Americans," 31, 155. Regarding Soviet films of this period, see Maya Turovskaya, "Soviet Films of the Cold War," in *Stalinism and Soviet Cinema*, ed. Richard Taylor and Derek Spring (London: Routledge, 1993), 131–41; Peter Kenez, *Cinema and Soviet Society, 1917–1953* (Cambridge: Cambridge University Press, 1992), chapters 10 and 11.

15. G. Shneerson, *Muzyka na sluzbe reaktsii* (Moscow: Muzgiz, 1950); G. Shneerson, "Vrednyi surrogat iskusstva," *Sovetskaia muzyka*, no. 7 (1948): 87–88.

16. Richard Stites, *Russian Popular Culture: Entertainment and Society since 1900* (Cambridge: Cambridge University Press, 1992), 117–19; Starr, *Red and Hot*, 218, 221, 233.

17. The party's magazine of humor and satire, *Krokodil*, illustrates these themes over the decades. For cartoons in *Pravda*, see McKenna, *All the Views Fit to Print*. Regarding more scholarly Soviet assessments of the United States in this period, see Richard M. Mills, *As Moscow Sees Us: American Politics and Society in the Soviet Mindset* (Oxford: Oxford University Press, 1990).

18. A. Rymashevskaia and N. Rubetskaia, "Nashi disputy," *Molodoi kommunist*, no. 1 (January 1959): 82.

19. *Komsomol'skaia pravda*, 11 August 1956, 2.

20. *Komsomol'skaia pravda*, 8 January 1984, 2.

21. *Komsomol'skaia pravda*, 13 August 1980, 2.

22. Evgenii Nozhin, "Ni slova ne voz'mut na veru," *Molodoi kommunist*, no. 8 (August 1984): 31–32.

23. Maya Turovskaya, "The Tastes of Soviet Moviegoers during the 1930s," in *Late Soviet Culture: From Perestroika to Novostroika*, ed. Thomas Lahusen and Gene Kuperman (Durham, N.C.: Duke University Press, 1993), 97; Stites, *Russian Popular Culture*, 125.

24. Arnold McMillin, "Western Life as Reflected in Aksenov's Work before and after Exile," in *Under Eastern Eyes: The West as Reflected in Recent Russian Emigre Writing*, ed. Arnold McMillin (New York: St. Martin's, 1992), 51; Stites, *Russian Popular Culture*, 125–26; John David Rimberg, *The Motion Picture in the Soviet Union: 1918–1952. A Sociological Analysis* (New York: Arno, 1973), 148–49, 197.

25. Starr, *Red and Hot*, 223–24; Aksyonov, *In Search of Melancholy Baby*, 12–13.

26. Hilary Pilkington, *Russia's Youth and Its Culture: A Nation's Constructors and Constructed* (London: Routledge, 1994), 244, 246; Ryback, *Rock around the Bloc*, 9, 56; Starr, *Red and Hot*, 238–43; *Komsomol'skaia pravda*, 26 September 1954, 3; Artemy Troitsky, *Back in the USSR: The True Story of Rock in the Soviet Union* (London: Omnibus, 1987), 3; Rodger P. Potocki Jr., "The Life and Times of Poland's 'Bikini Boys,'" *Polish Review* 39, no. 3 (1994): 260, 286 (note 118).

27. *Komsomol'skaia pravda*, 28 September 1954, 2. The article then proceeds to the challenge of how to rehabilitate Potapov.

28. John Bushnell, *Moscow Graffiti: Language and Subculture* (Boston: Unwin Hyman, 1990), 7, 114–18 (the quotation is on 116); *Newsweek*, 8 December 1975.

29. Stites, *Russian Popular Culture*, 132; Bushnell, *Moscow Graffiti*, 69–70, 75; Starr, *Red and Hot*, 241, 293, 304; Ryback, *Rock around the Bloc*, 109–110.

30. Troitsky, *Back in the USSR*, 17; Ryback, *Rock around the Bloc*, 102; Starr, *Red and Hot*, 294, 297, 301, 303; Bushnell, *Moscow Graffiti*, 67.

31. Pilkington, *Russia's Youth*, 68; Bushnell, *Moscow Graffiti*, 70. For much more on official criticism of rock 'n' roll, see Ryback, *Rock around the Bloc*.

32. Ekaterina Dobrotvorskaja, "Soviet Teens of the 1970s: Rock Generation, Rock Refusal, Rock Context," *Journal of Popular Culture* 26, no. 3 (Winter 1992): 150; *New York Times*, 7 March 1961.

33. Ryback, *Rock around the Bloc*, 233; Bushnell, *Moscow Graffiti*, 69, 72, 74; Starr, *Red and Hot*, 303–304, 337.

34. *Komsomol'skaia pravda*, 16 September 1984, 4. See also *Komsomol'skaia pravda*, 11 January 1984, 4.

35. Dobrotvorskaja, "Soviet Teens," 150.

36. Regarding the popularity of Western products in the Soviet Union by the 1970s, see Svetlana Boym, *Common Places: Mythologies of Everyday Life in Russia* (Cambridge, Mass.: Harvard University Press, 1994), 65. On the link between official Soviet criticism and unofficial popularity of Western culture, see Jerry F. Hough, *Russia and the West: Gorbachev and the Politics of Reform* (New York: Simon and Schuster, 1988), 28; Peter Klebnikov, "'Markeeting Imedge': American Popular Culture in the New Russia," *World & I* 7, no. 7 (July 1992): 636; Bushnell, *Moscow Graffiti*, 218–19. The quotation is in *Pravda*, 22 May 1984, 3. See also the chapter titled "O mode,

prestizhe i sile simvolov" in A. I. Bastrykin and E. B. Shiriaev, *Moda, kumiry i sobstvennoe "ia"* (Leningrad: Lenizdat, 1988).

37. Bushnell, *Moscow Graffiti*, 201.

38. Michael A. Korovkin, "An Account of Social Usages of Americanized Argot in Modern Russia," *Language in Society* 16, no. 4 (December 1987): 513–14.

39. Hans Rogger, "How the Soviets See Us," in *Shared Destiny: Fifty Years of Soviet-American Relations*, ed. Mark Garrison and Abbott Gleason (Boston: Beacon, 1985), 133–34.

40. Leonid Ignatieff, "American Literature in the Soviet Union," *Dalhousie Review* 35 (Spring 1956): 56–57, 61–62; Melville J. Ruggles, "American Books in Soviet Publishing," *Slavic Review* 20, no. 3 (October 1961): 426, 431–32, 435; Lana C. Fleishman, "The Empire Strikes Back: The Influence of the United States Motion Picture Industry on Russian Copyright Law," *Cornell International Law Journal* 26, no. 1 (Winter 1993): 218; Denise J. Youngblood, "'Americanitis': The *Amerikanshchina* in Soviet Cinema," *Journal of Popular Film & Television* 19, no. 4 (Winter 1992): 152.

41. McMillin, "Western Life," 52.

42. Fleishman, "The Empire Strikes Back," 218; Ruggles, "American Books," 429–30; *Pravda*, 16 May 1950, 5.

43. Walter L. Hixson, *Parting the Curtain: Propaganda, Culture and the Cold War, 1945–1961* (New York: St. Martin's, 1997), 43–45, 51; Donald W. White, *The American Century: The Rise and Decline of the United States as a World Power* (New Haven, Conn.: Yale University Press, 1996), 239.

44. Thomas Cushman, *Notes from Underground: Rock Music Counterculture in Russia* (Albany, N.Y.: SUNY Press, 1995), 71; White, *American Century*, 239; Philo C. Wasburn, *Broadcasting Propaganda: International Radio Broadcasting and the Construction of Political Reality* (Westport, Conn.: Praeger, 1992), 29–30; Hixson, *Parting the Curtain*, 33, 47; Parks, *Culture*, 87; Aksyonov, *In Search of Melancholy Baby*, 18.

45. Hixson, *Parting the Curtain*, 167, 186. For much more on the exhibition, see chapters 6 and 7.

46. Hixson, *Parting the Curtain*, 175, 179. See also Vladislav Zubok, "Zato my delaem rakety. Strasti vokrug amerikanskoi vystavki v Sokol'nikakh 1959 goda," *Rodina*, no. 8 (1998): 76–78.

47. Jerry F. Hough, *Democratization and Revolution in the USSR, 1985–1991* (Washington, D.C.: Brookings Institution Press, 1997), 497; James H. Billington, *Russia Transformed: Breakthrough to Hope* (New York: Free Press, 1992), 99; Sylvia R. Margulies, *The Pilgrimage to Russia: The Soviet Union and the Treatment of Foreigners, 1924–1937* (Madison: University of Wisconsin Press, 1968), 201; "Did Cultural Exchange Win the Cold War for the West?" (discussion of an unpublished paper by Yale Richmond, titled "Cultural Exchange and the Cold War: How the West Won"), from David Johnson's Russia List, #6075, 13 February 2002.

48. Billington, *Russia Transformed*, 104.

49. Youngblood, "'Americanitis,'" 153; Dmitry Shlapentokh and Vladimir Shlapentokh, *Soviet Cinematography 1918–1991: Ideological Conflict and Social Reality* (New York: de Gruyter, 1993), 241.

50. Igor' Lukshin, "Daesh' 'fabriku grez'!," *Iskusstvo kino*, no. 9 (September 1992): 46–49.

51. *Boston Globe*, 31 January 1992.

52. *New York Times*, 29 August 1994; Fleishman, "The Empire Strikes Back," 218 (note 183), 229 (note 231); Anatole Shub, *What Russians Know and Think about America: A Survey in Summer 1995* (Washington, D.C.: United States Information Agency, 1995), 12. Many other actors were also mentioned by smaller numbers of people in the 1995 survey.

53. *Izvestiia*, 6 May 1991, 3; Shub, *What Russians Know and Think about America*, 10.

54. "U.S. Shows Get Week on Soviet TV," *Hollywood Reporter*, 22 April 1991, 25; "Soviet Television Ropes in 'Dallas' for Three-year Run," *Hollywood Reporter*, 9 July 1991, 6; *Boston Globe*, 31 January 1992.

55. *New York Times*, 14 August 1995. Regarding other American programs on Russian TV, see *New York Times*, 12 January 1997; Fleishman, "The Empire Strikes Back," 229.

56. Klebnikov, "'Markeeting Imedge,'" 638–39; *Moscow News*, no. 6 (15–21 February 1996): 13; *New York Times*, 26 November 1995, 12 January 1997; Martin Walker, "Geraldoski," *New Republic* 205, nos. 8–9 (19–26 August 1991): 17.

57. Bushnell, *Moscow Graffiti*, 78; *Wall Street Journal*, 1 November 1990; Shub, *What Russians Know and Think about America*, 13; Christopher Boffey, "Avtorskoye Pravo [Author's Law]: The Reform of Russian Copyright Law toward an International Standard," *Maryland Journal of International Law and Trade* 18, no. 1 (Spring 1994): 83.

58. Shub, *What Russians Know and Think about America*, 12; *New York Times Magazine*, 8 June 1997, 65.

59. *New York Times*, 4 July 1996.

60. Shub, *What Russians Know and Think about America*, 16–18; *AmCham News*, July–August 1997 at www.amcham.ru/publicat.htm (accessed March 1998); Gary Burandt with Nancy Giges, *Moscow Meets Madison Avenue: The Adventures of the First American Adman in the U.S.S.R.* (New York: HarperBusiness, 1992), 120–25; Ludmilla Gricenko Wells, "The Role of Advertising in the Soviet Union" (Ph. D. diss., University of Tennessee, 1992), 71–72; Ryback, *Rock around the Bloc*, 7; *New York Times*, 17 February 1996, 5 June 1996, 3 October 1999; *New York Times Magazine*, 19 June 1994, 31, 52.

61. *Izvestiia*, 31 January 1990, 6.

62. *Izvestiia*, 31 January 1992, 3.

63. Richard Pells, *Not Like Us: How Europeans Have Loved, Hated, and Transformed American Culture since World War II* (New York: Basic, 1997), 303; *New York Times*, 28 January 1990; 1 February 1990; 2 January 1996; Hilary Pilkington, "Farewell to the *Tusovka*. Masculinities and Femininities on the Moscow Youth Scene," in *Gender, Generation and Identity in Contemporary Russia*, ed. Hilary Pilkington (London: Routledge, 1996), 239.

64. *New York Times Magazine*, 8 June 1997, 81–82; Shub, *What Russians Know and Think about America*, 10.

65. Hixson, *Witness to Disintegration*, x; Bushnell, *Moscow Graffiti*, 241; Scott Shane, *Dismantling Utopia: How Information Ended the Soviet Union* (Chicago: Ivan R. Dee, 1994), 207–208; *New York Times Magazine*, 8 June 1997, 81.

66. Nikita S. Khrushchev, *Khrushchev Remembers: The Glasnost Tapes* (Boston: Little, Brown, 1990), 137.

67. Stephen Kotkin, *Steeltown, USSR: Soviet Society in the Gorbachev Era* (Berkeley: University of California Press, 1991), 51–52.

68. *The "Design USA" Exhibit in Moscow (September 4–October 1, 1989)* (Washington, D.C.: United States Information Agency, 1989), 7–8, 13.

69. Victor Ripp, *Pizza in Pushkin Square: What Russians Think about Americans and the American Way of Life* (New York: Simon & Schuster, 1990), 126; *Boston Globe*, 31 May 1990; Everette E. Dennis, George Gerbner, and Yassen N. Zassoursky, eds., *Beyond the Cold War: Soviet and American Media Images* (Newbury Park, Calif.: Sage, 1991), 26, 109.

70. For examples, see Dennis et al., *Beyond the Cold War*, 96, 108–109; Jonathan A. Becker, *Soviet and Russian Press Coverage of the United States: Press, Politics and Identity in Transition* (New York: St. Martin's, 1999), 123–26.

71. *BBC Summary of World Broadcasts*, SU/0565, 19 September 1989, A1/1 (quoting from a Tass report printed in the newspaper *Sovetskaia Rossiia*, 13 September 1989).

72. For numerous examples, see Julian Graffy, "Émigré Experience of the West as Related to Soviet Journals," in *Under Eastern Eyes*, ed. McMillin.

73. Graffy, "Émigré Experience," 128, 129.

74. Boris Yeltsin, *Against the Grain: An Autobiography* (New York: Summit, 1990), 255.

75. *Izvestiia*, 23 March 1990, 6.

76. Shane, *Dismantling Utopia*, 167; A. S. Zaichenko, "SShA—SSSR: Lichnoe potreblenie (nekotorye sopostavleniia)," *SShA: ekonomika, politika, ideologiia*, no. 12 (1988): 12; Michael Ellman and Vladimir Kontorovich, eds., *The Disintegration of the Soviet Economic System* (London: Routledge, 1992), 29–30.

77. Viktor Viktorov, "Tips for the Russian Tourist," *Harper's* 284, no. 1703 (April 1992): 16.

78. Shub, *What Russians Know and Think about America*, 8, 20. See also Richard B. Dobson, *Exhibit Poll Explores Soviet Visitors' Opinions of the U.S.* (Washington, D.C.: United States Information Agency, 1989), 14–15 (the sample in this case was not a cross section of the Soviet population). In national polls conducted in the winter of 1991–92 and the summer of 1992, approximately three-fourths of the respondents had favorable opinions of western Europe and America. Hugh W. Olds, *Russians Favorable toward U.S. and President Bush* (Washington, D.C.: United States Information Agency, 1992), 5; Rachel Halpern, *Russians View U.S. and Other Western Democracies Favorably* (Washington, D.C.: United States Information Agency, 1992), 5–6. When asked in December 1991 which country they would visit first if they could travel wherever they pleased, more than twice as many respondents chose America than any other country. Olds, *Russians Favorable*, 7.

79. Steven A. Grant, *Changing Perceptions of Youth in European Russia, 1988–1991* (Washington, D.C.: United States Information Agency, 1992), 3–5. See also Shub, *What Russians Know and Think about America*, 21.

80. Walter G. Stephan et al., "Measuring Stereotypes: A Comparison of Methods Using Russian and American Samples," *Social Psychology Quarterly* 56, no. 1 (March 1993): 61–62; Pilkington, *Russia's Youth*, 199.

81. Tatyana Matsuk, "War or Peace? The Reasons for and Possible Consequences of Anti-Western Feeling in Russia," *Jamestown Foundation Prism*, 23 April 1999, from David Johnson's Russia List, #3257, 25 April 1999; Vasily Aksenov, "Nostalgia or Insanity?" *Moscow News*, no. 45 (20–26 November 1997): 4; *Pravda*, 25 June 1990, 6; V. P. Lukin and A. I. Utkin, *Rossiia i zapad: Obshchnost' ili otchuzhdenie?* (Moscow: SAMPO, 1995), 7–9; *Boston Globe*, 31 May 1990; Tim McDaniel, *The Agony of the Russian Idea* (Princeton, N.J.: Princeton University Press, 1996), 6. See also Klebnikov, "'Marketing Imedge,'" 635; Kotkin, *Steeltown, USSR*, 53; Aleksandr Zakharov and Natal'ia Kozlova, "Pis'ma iz nedalekogo proshlogo," *Svobodnaia mysl'*, no. 7 (1993): 81.

82. For a range of opinions, see Suzanne Massie, "To the Russian People, We're Ugly Americans," *Surviving Together* 12, no. 1 (Spring 1994): 6; Vladimir Shlapentokh, "The Changeable Soviet Image of America," *Annals of the American Academy of Political and Social Science* 497 (May 1988): 165–66; McBrearty, "Characterization of Americans," 28; Kiparsky, *English and American Characters*, 133.

83. Halpern, *Russians View U.S.*, 5.

84. Shub, *What Russians Know and Think about America*, 7.

85. For an assortment of views, see George F. Kennan, *The Nuclear Delusion: Soviet-American Relations in the Atomic Age* (New York: Pantheon, 1982), 45; Rogger, "How the Soviets See Us," 139; Hough, *Democratization and Revolution*, 51; Ryback, *Rock around the Bloc*, 10; Shlapentokh, "Changeable Soviet Image," 158, 163; Stites, *Russian Popular Culture*, 127; Klebnikov, "'Marketing Imedge,'" 636.

CHAPTER SEVEN

~

The American Model

The Statue of Liberty is not some sort of a witch, but a very attractive lady.

—Boris Yeltsin

Now, as before, we know what choices we want Russia to make and what kind of state we want it to be. . . . These, of course, are not just our aspirations for Russia—they are also the wishes of the great majority of the people of Russia.

—Strobe Talbott

In the ninth century, according to the ancient *Primary Chronicle*, discord rose among the East Slavs, prompting them to seek assistance from Vikings who lived nearby. "Our whole land is great and rich," the Slavs explained, "but there is no order in it. Come to rule and reign over us."[1] Suggesting as it does that the Slavs required foreign hands to set their affairs in order, this passage has long stirred controversy among commentators. Archeological and linguistic evidence places the Vikings at the scene, but the text of the chronicle deserves a skeptical reading. Vikings did not insist on invitations before their visits, and few people welcomed them. Conquerors they were, not benefactors whom the East Slavs would care to summon. Eventually, though, various tsars did extend invitations to Westerners able to provide guidance in fields ranging from the fine arts to the military, and later the Soviet regime relied on the capitalist world to help erect industrial projects during the First

Five-Year Plan. This influence was substantial, whether it arrived at the behest of Peter the Great or Stalin. But nothing since the sweeping task allegedly set before the Norsemen has matched the potential impact of foreign models and assistance in transforming both the economic and political systems of Russia at the end of the twentieth century and the beginning of the twenty-first.

Although Stalin and his lieutenants thought that the large dose of Western skills they digested in the 1930s would soon enable the Soviet Union to catch and surpass the American economy, such confidence faded gradually from one decade to the next after the 1950s. Before long, statements by Soviet leaders revealed occasionally an awareness that the country trailed advances in foreign technology. As early as 1965 Premier Alexei Kosygin acknowledged that "the pattern of production of machinery and equipment being turned out by many branches of Soviet industry does not conform to modern standards." Praise of domestic achievements still predominated at this time, but the words seemed hollow to a young party official from Stavropol after his first trips to western Europe in the 1970s. "The question haunted me," recalled Mikhail Gorbachev in his memoirs. "Why was the standard of living in our country lower than in other developed countries? It seemed that our aged leaders were not especially worried about our undeniably lower living standards, our unsatisfactory way of life, and our falling behind in the field of advanced technologies."[2]

When Gorbachev rose to power a few years later, he left no doubt over his concern for drooping Soviet productivity and technological innovation. An "acceleration of social and economic development" must commence, he asserted, if the Soviet Union wished to escape from the "period of stagnation" and remain a great power on the world stage. Time and again, prominent Soviet voices developed variations on this theme. In 1988 *Pravda* reported a warning from the party's ideology secretary that "since the end of the 1970s, negative tendencies have become ever more apparent in our development. Socialism has lost its advantage over capitalism regarding the tempo of economic development and has begun to lag behind in the new spheres of technology." *Izvestiia* chimed in with an economist who concluded that "if we preserve the existing economic model, we will scarcely be able to approach the existing capitalist countries regarding the basic parameters of efficiency of social production in the foreseeable future."[3]

With a frequency unequalled since the First Five-Year Plan, Soviet pronouncements recommended "capitalist" lands as a source of desirable expertise. "We want to attract advanced technology and managerial experience," explained the economist Abel Aganbegyan when the government began encouraging joint ventures with foreign businesses in 1987. Two years later, a deputy to the new Soviet legislature declared it "vital for us to take a close look at the experience of other countries, especially countries that are far ahead of us technologically. Not everyone understands that we lack not only new machines, but also, still more, new types of worker, factory hand, farmer, manager."[4] This, too, resembled an earlier day's appeal—the call in the 1920s for such "new types" of workers as the Taylorized products of Gastev's institute and the "Russian-Americans" touted in the press.

Through the remainder of the 1980s, however, Gorbachev's measures accelerated not the revitalization but the collapse of the economy, leaving a chasm beyond which the United States and other nations sped off toward the twenty-first century. Following the disintegration of the Soviet Union itself, government leaders spoke more openly than at any time since the 1920s of "our technological backwardness," to quote Foreign Minister Andrei Kozyrev in 1992.[5] Facing this plight, reformers looked to numerous countries for assistance, but no nation received more scrutiny than the United States. Just as it had in Lenin's day, America seemed the most advanced and most applicable guide to Russians in pursuit of modernization.

Many Americans themselves viewed their country as a global beacon, and these universalistic pretensions had long vexed Soviet leaders who portrayed their own society as an international inspiration. As late as 1985 two Russian authors could remain squarely in the official mainstream by publishing a book titled The "American Model," which was critical of American designs to shape the development of other nations. Picking through a rich field of quotations to illustrate the outlook they rejected, the pair chose Albert Beveridge, senator from Indiana, who advised his congressional colleagues in 1900: "He [God] has made us adepts in government that we may administer government among savage and senile peoples. . . . And of all our race He has marked the American people as His chosen nation to finally lead in the generation of the world."[6] American influence did expand after 1900, the authors granted, but the harmful nature of America's ways could not be obscured forever. The text explained that other countries balked at emulating a land bent on maintaining its standard of living by plundering the globe's natural resources while supporting "democracy" by means of alliances with dictators abroad. Eventually, Americans themselves "began to realize that the image of their country had lost much of its former attraction, and that the rest of the world by no means considered America an example to be imitated or a model of a future social structure."[7]

Six years after the book's publication, no country in the world exceeded the new Russian Republic's determination to reform along American lines.

"Everybody really understood that the Soviet era [was] coming to its close," recalled Alexei Arbatov, a member of Russia's parliament later in the 1990s. "So, they were looking for a model and they couldn't find a better model than the United States." Among them stood President Boris Yeltsin, who pointed in 1992 to American economic development as "a great example for today's Russian reformers and entrepreneurs." A few years earlier, academic institutes and think tanks in Moscow and Leningrad had already grown sufficiently bold to debate the features of various nations that might serve as archetypes for reform. Two participants in these discussions noted that "the social and government systems of the United States were by far the most popular ones."[8]

Public appeals to benefit from American practices centered initially on economic or technical endeavors.[9] Thus, in 1988 a *Pravda* correspondent described features of American telephones (speed dialing, conference calls, call forwarding, car phones, and so forth) in a tone of approval similar to that directed at *tekhnika* in America sixty years earlier. He expected readers to be impressed with the electronic conveniences common in the United States, and his was not the only article to duplicate early Bolshevik acclaim for Western technology. Echoing Lenin's praise for American agriculture, *Izvestiia* published a glowing description of an Iowa farm in 1989. The reporter spent twenty-one days with a family who grew corn and soy beans with techniques recommended by *Izvestiia* for Soviet agriculturists. Now, however, the American farmer's most striking equipment was not a tractor but his computers—one at home for keeping accounts and even helping his daughter with her homework and another on his tractor to enhance the precision of its operation. Perhaps this was all too much for the Soviet audience, reflected the family's guest, who anticipated "a reproach" from his readers: "Is there any sense in telling our own farmers transoceanic tales about 'computer-agronomists,' if we still don't have even a decent tractor-cultivator?"[10]

Sergei Plekhanov, assistant director of the Institute of U.S. and Canadian Studies in the Soviet Academy of Sciences, chose a historical perspective from which to welcome American *tekhnika*. Applauding the less xenophobic view of the United States that prevailed up to the early 1930s, he explained that it had been possible to condemn the "social vices of capitalism" without fostering "hatred or fear" of America. "In those years, for us, it was much more important to borrow as much American experience as possible in the area of organizing production and in the scientific-technical sphere. The idea of cooperation and the idea of competition ('To catch and surpass!') did not contradict each other." When published in the autumn of 1988, this no longer sounded radical. But Plekhanov had more in mind—an interest in

American "democratic traditions," which he claimed had also been shared by the first generation of Bolsheviks.[11]

Perhaps Plekhanov understood how dubious it was to extend Bolshevik approval beyond "capitalist" *tekhnika* to American politics. Lenin's comments contained little admiration for the New World's "democratic traditions," and Plekhanov may have invoked the Soviet pantheon simply to provide cover for his own interest in American political institutions. In any case, essays of this sort numbered among the most remarkable publications loosed by the freedoms of *glasnost*. Never before in the Soviet era had commentators ventured to praise American political practices and recommend them for adoption at home. Soon they would do so routinely.

A few months later the journal published by Plekhanov's institute advanced this line in an article titled "American Experience and Our Perestroika." Its author, Eduard Batalov, pointed out that ever since 1917 the Soviet Union had demonstrated a high regard for American science and technology, even during periods of rancorous relations between the two nations. But there were still people in the USSR, he complained, who saw nothing to learn from America's social-political experience, despite the fact that bourgeois civilization had much to offer in this sphere. Soviet propaganda had long declared socialism immune from a wide variety of ills, Batalov continued, but now one had to admit that many such afflictions—drug addiction, organized crime, pollution, alienation of the people from the government, and so forth—had survived. Therefore, careful investigation of the methods used to combat these problems in America and elsewhere "could be quite useful." The challenge, he concluded, "is not how to 'save' ourselves from foreign influence, but rather how to make our society more receptive to rational things practiced beyond our borders." Plekhanov agreed and left no doubt about it: "Authoritarian, bureaucratic socialism fears American democracy like the devil fears incense. The democratic, creative socialism that we have begun to build finds much of use in the democratic experience of America."[12]

For Batalov, "democratizing the organs of power and perfecting a system of elections to these organs" remained one of the Soviet Union's most vital goals. "Hasn't the time come," he asked, "to evaluate more objectively those mechanisms and models that Soviet critics of 'vaunted bourgeois democracy' have habitually scorned?"[13] Yes indeed, concurred Stanislav Kondrashov, a political commentator and international correspondent for *Izvestiia*. As the Soviet legislature discussed a law for the election of a president in 1990, Kondrashov drew on his observation of the political system in the United States to advocate "a strict separation of powers between the executive, legislative, and judicial branches [that] provides an essential equilibrium in running the state and protection from attempts to usurp power." Even more important, American experience had shown that democracy requires "the freedom of political parties and tendencies, on which the previously mentioned [executive, legislative, judicial] triad is in fact based."[14]

Two years before his rise to the Russian presidency, Boris Yeltsin showed himself of similar mind regarding foreign political examples:

> Well, "communist" is a word which, in my view, needs generally to be understood simply as a dream or an idea which one can constantly cherish, but only cherish—it cannot be used. What is needed is some sort of a new model of socialism which would be constructed taking account not only of the experience of socialist countries but also the experience of the USA, for instance, which has more than 200 years' experience of bourgeois democracy.[15]

Meanwhile, numerous American officials and commentators applauded the events transforming the Soviet Union and called on the U.S. government to assist Russia in acquiring a Western-style democracy and market economy. Individuals differed over the details of these institutions and the best methods for transplanting them in Russia, but some form of "democratic capitalism" dominated American recipes for reform. Outside government, the National Planning Association (composed of leaders from business, labor, academia, agriculture, and professional sectors) urged the Clinton administration to "take a key leadership position in helping the former communist republics make the transition from totalitarian to democratic and market-oriented societies."[16] Countless government publications backed this blueprint, including a "Focus on Russia" assessment from the State Department in 1994, which insisted that "immediate support for key market and democratic reforms in Russia and the other new independent states of the former Soviet Union is fundamental to a more secure world now and throughout the next century." Perhaps no official spoke more often in this vein than Deputy Secretary of State Strobe Talbott, as in his remarks to the House Foreign Affairs Committee that year: "Our approach has been to reinforce those trends in Russian political and economic life that together, we believe, constitute the essence of the great transformation underway in that country. They are democratization and privatization."[17]

The challenge of privatization—converting state enterprises into private businesses—represented the heart of Washington's strategy for promoting a market economy throughout Russia. By early 1995 Talbott reported to the Senate that privatization had spread to almost 100,000 firms accounting for 70 percent of Russian industry and 40 percent of the workforce. The United

States more than any other country, he added, had provided support to Russia for this program.[18] American participation ranged from devising privatization methods to paying foreign firms to help orchestrate auctions of state assets. Harvard University's Institute for International Development took the lead in channeling U.S. funds to the endeavor and in placing American consultants among the Russian reformers who formulated privatization decrees. One of these advisers, Jonathan Hay, even drafted some of the laws himself.[19]

In the autumn of 1992 the U.S. Agency for International Development granted the Sawyer Miller consulting firm a contract for more than $6 million to help Moscow's privatization officials sell their program to the Russian people. Working with the Madison Avenue firm of Young and Rubicam, the Sawyer Miller team produced brief advertisements that championed privatization and ran for months on television. Sawyer Miller also launched a media blitz for the program shortly before a national referendum on the government's economic policies in April 1993 and continued to organize rallies and concerts, billed as Privatization Days, in various cities.[20] The privatizers failed, as it turned out, to implement a policy of apparent benefit to many Russians, but this should not obscure the central point here, that the United States advocated the program and did much to see it commence.

American statements of support for privatization often mentioned assistance in other areas as well—foreign trade, tax policies, land ownership, and much else—that, taken together, seemed essential to producing a hospitable environment for fledgling private enterprises. A few examples of these market-oriented measures suffice to demonstrate the scope of American involvement. Russian reformers understood, for instance, that stock markets and commodity exchanges provided businesses a means to raise capital and trade products. Thus, in the early 1990s they sought Western experts, including advisers from the New York Stock Exchange, to help train Russian counterparts at new exchanges in Moscow and elsewhere. "Wall Street Wizards Give Soviets a Crash Course on Capitalism," proclaimed the *Wall Street Journal* during a tutorial conducted in 1990 by representatives of the Big Board. Their seminar, staged in Moscow through efforts of the Soviet State Bank and Ministry of Finance, aimed to illuminate the workings of financial markets. When the Leningrad Stock Exchange opened the following year, it oriented employees with assistance from Americans and Finns, while in Moscow the New York Mercantile Exchange agreed to train Russian oil brokers.[21]

In 1992 the president of the Federal Reserve Bank of New York, E. Gerald Corrigan, called a news conference to announce the formation of a Russian-American Bankers Forum, designed to help modernize the Russian banking system and enable it to provide services required in a market econ-omy. Even more than stock exchanges, Russian banking practices gripped the attention of American officials and businessmen, as demonstrated by the presence in the Bankers Forum of senior Federal Reserve officers and execu-tives of major American banks. Chaired jointly by Corrigan and Yuli Vorontsov (Russia's ambassador at the United Nations and an adviser to President Yeltsin), the forum applied itself in Moscow to drafting recom-mendations on retail banking and payment services, an interbank market, a system for third-party payments, and a market for government securities.[22] The United States also worked with European nations and Japan to render technical assistance to the Central Bank of Russia through the International Monetary Fund, the World Bank, and other organizations that sponsored workshops on managing the money supply, exchange-rate policy, bank su-pervision, and the like.[23]

Among its numerous activities, the Bankers Forum moved quickly to cre-ate an academy to train officers of Russian financial institutions. During the summer of 1993 approximately 250 men and women from the former Soviet Union arrived at Connecticut's Fairfield University to begin several weeks of study and observation. There they heard Vorontsov describe David Rocke-feller, former chairman of Chase Manhattan Bank, as "a very good example to follow in banking"—no longer a surprising remark in 1993, but unthink-able words for a Soviet official less than a decade earlier. After five weeks at Fairfield, the apprentices scattered across the United States to spend addi-tional time at individual banks before returning home. "We expect that you will become agents for change," Corrigan told them, with confidence that would weaken among Americans and Russians a few years later.[24]

The Fairfield venture represented but one of dozens of foreign programs established to educate Russians seeking new careers in a market economy. At the end of the 1980s—that is, even before the demise of the USSR and its socialist aspirations—some Soviet officials made headlines by traveling to the West for training in management techniques. The titles "Perestroika to Rely on Way of the West to Aid Its Managers," "We Need Yuppies in Moscow," and "Crash Courses in Capitalism for Ivan the Globe-Trotter" in-troduced articles in the *Wall Street Journal*, *Fortune*, and *Business Week*, re-spectively, between 1988 and 1990.[25] Within a few years, systematic training programs took root across the United States, and by the middle of the decade several thousand Russians had spent periods ranging from a few weeks to six months learning American techniques for operating enterprises in a market setting. According to a report at the end of 1994, a training project funded under the U.S. Freedom Support Act had hosted some three thousand visitors from the former Soviet republics and awaited a similar number in the year to come. They studied at American businesses, universities, government agencies, and nonprofit groups, as determined by their specialties. In similar fashion, the U.S. Department of Agriculture awarded Cochran Fellowships to Russians seeking Western experience in food industries. "They Learn in the U.S., They Buy from the U.S." proclaimed the title of an article in the journal *AgExporter,* revealing one source of American enthusiasm for these trips. By the end of 1997 the Special American Business Internship Training Program of the U.S. Commerce Department had provided American companies with funds to train several hundred Russian interns, while the U.S. Information Agency's "Business for Russia" program brought 350 Russians to eleven American cities for one-month stays during 1993–94. A thousand more were scheduled to arrive in 1995.[26]

All told, nearly 12,000 people from the newly independent states of the former Soviet Union traveled to the United States on training and exchange programs in 1994, surpassing the total of 5,400 in 1993. With 10,000 more expected in 1995, Strobe Talbott was able to inform the Senate that "we easily will have matched the 24,000 Europeans that the Marshall Plan brought over on exchanges after World War II."[27] While some of these guests came from countries other than Russia, and the Russian contingent itself did not focus exclusively on business skills, Talbott's data support the general conclusion that several thousand Russians received training in America designed to invigorate a market economy at home.

At the same time, smaller numbers of Americans set out for Russia to assist private ventures at close range. In 1993, dozens of Peace Corps volunteers provided advice on business techniques to Russian enterprises around the country and taught classes on stocks, bonds, business proposals, and other commercial topics. They even sponsored an international trade conference in Nizhnii-Novgorod, where Russian businessmen participated in seminars with executives from DuPont, Sprint, Apple Computer, and General Motors. The U.S. Agency for International Development funded diverse projects of this sort, including the placement of eight hundred American "Farmer-to-Farmer" volunteers in Russia during 1992–94 to offer guidance on marketing, processing, storage, and other agricultural problems facing their Russian peers. Nongovernmental groups, such as San Francisco's Center for Citizen Initiatives, also obtained grants from the Agency to train Russian entrepreneurs.[28]

Some American organizations promoted a free-enterprise economy directly through Russian educational institutions, especially business schools of a Western type. Several of these establishments received initial assistance and continuing administrative support from American universities, and within a few years teams from six of Moscow's business schools entered a competition conceived by the American Chamber of Commerce. Students received a problem in international business and then worked overnight to formulate a presentation with which to impress a panel of judges the next day. American Express, Coca-Cola, and Pratt & Whitney numbered among the event's sponsors. Even secondary-school pupils, from "all over Russia" according to the *New York Times* in 1997, received instruction from a translated version of the American Junior Achievement system of applied economics—the method that encourages students to learn about business through means that sometimes include forming their own small enterprises.[29]

While Americans viewed a free market as Russia's ticket to prosperity, they mustered still more passion for freedom of another sort—Russian political liberty—generally advanced under such labels as "democracy" and "civil rights." Here, much of the reform took place in the realm of law, as late Soviet and early Russian legislatures adopted hundreds of new measures, including provisions for jury trials, the right to a defense lawyer, and freedoms of speech, press, and religion.[30] Not only did this legislation win applause in the West, but it also drew on Western models and the recommendations of Western experts, as did drafts of the Russian Constitution itself.[31] The American Bar Association, for example, published frequent lists of judges, law professors, and lawyers from the United States who had furnished advice to Russian authors of the Constitution, the civil and criminal codes, and numerous laws of narrower scope.[32]

Beginning in 1992 the most prominent American role in bringing the new codes to life belonged to the Central and East European Law Initiative (CEELI), run by the American Bar Association with assistance from the Justice Department. In addition to commenting on draft legislation and advising Russian lawyers who wished to create bar associations for managing their own affairs, CEELI's staff and volunteers worked to devise strategies for putting new laws into practice. They responded to a request from officials in Nizhnii-Novgorod to help reorganize an enterprise according to the nation's new bankruptcy law, for instance, but their top priority remained the introduction of jury trials in Russia. "Early on," concurred Strobe Talbott, "we recognized that the revival of the jury trial in Russia, where it had been missing since 1917, would be one of the most important factors in the emergence of the rule of law in that country."[33]

The legislation that reintroduced jury trials in 1993 drew inspiration from the Anglo-American "adversarial" approach—in contrast to the continental "inquisitorial" system, in which a judge functions more as a prosecutor and plays an active role in ferreting out the facts of the case. The new law required judges to preside impartially, while defense and prosecution teams battled to sway a jury. So novel did this seem to officials that they felt it prudent to test the procedure in nine regions, including Moscow, Rostov-on-the-Don, and Saratov, where the first trial took place at the end of 1993. Defendants accused of serious crimes could put their cases to a jury, but only if their lawyers so requested. Many hesitated, uncertain of the new procedures and wary of arguing before panels of citizens. Thus the reform faced a road obstructed not only by officials who defended the traditional inquisitorial format but also by less hostile judges and lawyers naturally apprehensive over such a sweeping change in their profession. Even the most basic features of the new system seemed problematic, as a Virginia Supreme Court justice discovered: "I was having an informal lunch discussion with several Russian legislators when we were helping assess the Russian Constitution," she recalled. "The question of how you get juries came up, and I was beginning to explain how we select potential jury members from different lists. 'No, no,' interrupted my questioner. 'I mean, how do you get them to actually show up?'"[34]

Enter CEELI, whose personnel welcomed the first jury trials and encouraged their proliferation. Before long, summer programs transported small numbers of lawyers (sixteen in 1996) to the United States for classroom instruction and observation of American trials. Dubbed "train the trainers" workshops, these sessions prepared Russians to return home and teach trial skills to other lawyers. In Russia, CEELI sponsored workshops on trial strategies for hundreds of lawyers in regions already implementing the reform or poised to do so. Instruction often included mock trials and, as the years passed, CEELI turned more of the job over to Russians trained previously in the United States. Hoping to reach a much larger number of lawyers, CEELI's Moscow office set out with four Russian attorneys in 1997 to write the country's first criminal defense manual.[35]

Three years earlier, Americans and Russians had collaborated to write a jury-trial manual for judges, some of whom made use of the volume's sample jury instructions and questions for prospective jurors. Nothing threatened the reform as bluntly as the shortage of well-trained judges, and CEELI scurried to respond. Soon, Russian judges studied in the United States at the Federal Judicial Center in Washington, D.C., and at other sites, while hundreds more attended workshops around Russia to learn procedures appropriate in the new courtroom.[36] With considerable resolve, then, Americans unveiled projects to nurture adversarial trials in Russia. The task was formidable, however, and it remained to be seen whether the system would flourish in its new environment.

Meanwhile, dozens of American projects sought to promote "democracy" in other ways, starting with parliamentary elections. Toward this end, and the ultimate goal of a legislative body representing the views of the population, American government and private organizations attempted to advance the formation of viable political parties in Russia. They also helped orchestrate drives to encourage voter turnout, trained Russian teams of election monitors, and conducted seminars on campaign-coverage techniques for Russian journalists. In 1994 the new Russian Parliament began exchange visits with members of the U.S. Congress and received assistance from the Library of Congress in developing a modern research and information system. At the same time, the American Congressional Research Service supplied computers and books on legislative matters and offered tutorials for Russian legislators and their staffs on topics that included the drafting of bills. Later in the decade, Congress sponsored visits by thousands of young Russian politicians and officials to American towns for a look at government procedures and other events squeezed into ten-day tours.[37]

Washington did not drown these programs in funds—from a total of $3.3 billion committed by the end of 1994, only $2.2 billion had been expended. Over the period 1992–97, American bilateral aid to Russia amounted to $4.9 billion. Even with the addition of grants from other nations and loans channeled through the International Monetary Fund and the World Bank, the international contribution remained modest. It was also confusing, with funds announced but not released (because Russia could not meet certain economic conditions) and sometimes reported twice when transferred between aid packages. In absolute terms Russia received more money than other eastern European nations, but weighted according to the size of the country's economy, Russian receipts ranked near the bottom. According to one estimate, the new republic required a trillion dollars annually in the early 1990s to match the effect of capital transfers from western to eastern Germany at that time. With just a few billion dollars per year actually delivered, some critics charged that the volume of grants and loans would not foster significant improvement.[38]

American officials responded with a proverb encountered often in their speeches, articles, and testimony: "Give a man a fish, he'll eat for a day; teach him how to fish, and he'll eat forever." "From the beginning," Talbott explained to a House subcommittee in 1994, "our assistance efforts have assumed that advice and training, rather than cash transfers, are the most effective ways for us to support the whole spectrum of reform in the region. As the saying goes. . . ."[39] He and others did anticipate a large volume of Western funds flowing to eastern Europe, but not from the U.S. government.

They pointed to investment for profit by American businesses as the best source of financial resources necessary to remodel Russia.

Toward the end of the twentieth century, American companies established a more diverse and visible presence in Russia than ever before. As long as Gorbachev's central government could control the process, much of the commerce remained between American firms and the state in the area of heavy industry and high technology, as it had in 1930. Thus, joint-venture agreements signed between 1987 and 1990 included projects to produce or supply chemicals, semiconductors, automobile parts, satellite communication facilities, steel, and so forth.[40] But even then, consumer goods figured in some of the contracts, in part because Gorbachev hoped to demonstrate to the population that his reforms had brought them more to purchase. By the end of the decade, Coca-Cola had gained the right to enter the Soviet market, long monopolized by its rival PepsiCo, which in turn reached agreement on opening two Pizza Hut restaurants. Polaroid launched a retail store in Moscow; a Tambrands joint venture prepared to market tampons; Time-Warner planned a multiscreen theater; and American Express promoted itself by contributing two million dollars to help stage a musical, *Sophisticated Ladies*.[41]

During the 1990s, when the Soviet (and then Russian) central government grew poorer, American businesses found less to tempt them in transactions with state agencies. As in the early 1920s, the Kremlin lacked funds to purchase Western factories and other equipment in great number, but it could invite foreign enterprises to modernize the extraction of raw materials in return for profits realized later on sales abroad. The nation's oil industry required tens of billions of dollars in repairs, to say nothing of the cost of opening new fields, and only Western companies could furnish capital of this magnitude. Petroleum dwarfed all of Russia's other natural resources in the eyes of Western corporations, and they signed numerous exploration and production agreements with Russian officials. Exxon, Chevron, Mobil, Amoco, Texaco, and other American firms took the lead in these projects and announced plans to commit billions of dollars in the years to come. By 1998 a Russian press report estimated that the fuel and energy sector absorbed 60 percent of all American investment in the country.[42]

Western firms could also seek a profit by selling directly to Russian consumers, an activity nearly impossible previously. In the 1920s, a few foreign entrepreneurs had produced household goods at factories in the Soviet Union, but they could not open their own retail networks or set prices. The state's currency restrictions and monopoly on foreign trade placed even more severe constraints on retail distribution of imported goods, leaving the field empty of public shops featuring Western merchandise. If American goods circulated at all, they did so through illegal or at least informal channels. Not so in the 1990s. Gone was the government's foreign trade monopoly, together with the extensive restrictions on private commerce that had marked most of the Soviet era. Western goods appeared everywhere, providing one of the most visible signs of change for those familiar with shopping in Soviet times.

Along with Coca-Cola and Big Macs, dozens of other well-known American products surfaced in short order. Procter & Gamble detergent, Mars bars, Marlboros, Uncle Ben's rice, and much else familiar in the United States appeared in Russian stores. As meat production dropped, American hotdog sales in Russia soared from $122,000 in 1992 to more than $70 million in 1996. Chicken did even better, making Russia the largest export market for U.S. producers by the middle of the decade. Given that Americans preferred white meat, companies like Tyson Foods welcomed the opening of a large market in which customers favored dark pieces (dubbed *nozhki Busha* or Bush legs, after the Bush administration's initial encouragement of the exports). Sales to Russia jumped from $81 million in 1993 to $500 million two years later, a figure that could well be doubled by adding exports routed indirectly to avoid high tariffs. At the same time that Russians discovered Bush legs, they also noticed Avon cosmetics on store shelves. By 1995 Avon commenced full-scale direct sales and before long had hired sixteen thousand representatives in Moscow, St. Petersburg, and the Siberian city of Perm. The company expected revenue of $30 million in 1996, up more than 200 percent from the year before. Not to be outdone, Mary Kay brought its lipstick to Russia in 1993 and within three years had amassed a sales force of twenty-five thousand in Russia and other countries of the former Soviet Union. After selling the region's consumers $25 million worth of cosmetics in 1995, Mary Kay saw its sales triple by 1997 and its army of representatives reach sixty thousand. Direct marketers of other products followed, and even Tupperware opted in 1997 to test the Russian waters in St. Petersburg. "With the large number of households and significant under employment in Russia," concluded Tupperware's chairman, "we see this country as a great market opportunity and are investing time and training to build a strong sales force."[43]

No major foreign corporations advanced their products more tenaciously in Russia than American cigarette makers. Even after television commercials for cigarettes were banned in 1995, billboards and direct marketing continued the campaign. Unmoved by such findings as a 1997 World Health Organization report that nearly one-third of all male deaths in Russia stemmed from tobacco use, American companies sponsored concerts and other public events during which cigarettes were distributed free of charge. Russia beckoned as a vast tobacco market, the world's fourth largest, and mostly barren of American cigarettes before 1990. In that year the Soviet government asked Philip Morris and RJR Nabisco to supply 34 billion cigarettes in an effort to overcome the worst shortage in decades. Over the next few years American companies built or acquired factories in Russia and soon accounted for 40 percent of the market. Philip Morris's St. Petersburg facility turned out 3.1 billion cigarettes in 1997, up from 2 billion in 1996, but not enough to satisfy demand. The company then announced plans to build a new factory near St. Petersburg with an annual output of 25 billion. RJ Reynolds, whose St. Petersburg enterprise yielded 37 billion cigarettes in 1997, publicized its intention to expand production by investing another $120 million.[44]

American companies also entered Russia to sell services, including financial advice, legal counsel, and the use of credit cards. When Aeroflot, the national airline, planned to seek Western investors, the firm of Price Waterhouse prepared an audit of the company necessary to help meet disclosure requirements in the United States. At various times Goldman, Sachs & Company and J. P. Morgan helped the Russian government place its bonds on the international market, and in 1992 Russian authorities hired the American investigative firm of Kroll Associates to trace some $14 billion in hard currency and goods for which officials could not account. Major American advertising agencies opened offices in Moscow, and American consultants discovered a demand for marketing other "products" not for sale in stores. To this end, Boris Berezovsky, as deputy secretary of the National Security Council, hired Edelman Public Relations of Washington, D.C., to polish his image abroad, while, more discreetly, Boris Yeltsin's team engaged American political advisers during the 1996 presidential campaign.[45]

Western advertising quickly became a fact of life in Russia, with commercials for domestic and foreign products appearing routinely on television, radio, billboards, and mass transit, as well as in print. *Pravda*, the Communist Party's newspaper, invited Western companies in May 1990 to purchase space in the paper to hawk their wares—following the example set several months earlier by the principal government paper, *Izvestiia*. Three-quarters of the Russians surveyed across the country in 1995 responded "yes" to the question "Have you noticed any of the TV advertising for American products?" Half the sample added that they had purchased some of these items, most of which were unavailable just a few years before. Marketers dramatized the pace of change with promotions a world removed from the

Soviet environment. These included Coca-Cola's Coca-Shkola program (*shkola* meaning "school" in Russian), which sent students on tours of Coca-Cola's Moscow plant for what the company called an introduction to the "capitalist system." Just as surprising if viewed in reference to Soviet times, an American manufacturer of air-conditioning and heating equipment, York International Corporation, sought publicity through the work of a functionary from Stalin's day. Tikhon Khrennikov had gained notoriety in the West as head of the Soviet Composers' Union when he harassed the gifted but unorthodox composers Dmitry Shostakovich and Sergei Prokofiev. Perhaps that all seemed long ago in the winter of 1995–96 as Khrennikov, now 82, witnessed the music he composed for a new ballet, *Napoleon Bonaparte*, entertain packed houses at the Kremlin's Palace of Congresses, under the sponsorship of York International.[46]

Russian children studying "capitalism" at a Coca-Cola factory; a Stalin-era composer sponsored by an American corporation—much had changed since Soviet times, as visitors found in 1996 at a Russian air base outside Moscow. The Russian Army Choir sang "America the Beautiful" while officials unveiled a Soviet Tu-144 aircraft now decorated with the logos of Boeing, Rockwell International, and McDonnell Douglas—all American defense contractors "renting" the aircraft as a flying laboratory in which to test the feasibility of a new supersonic airliner.[47] Everywhere spectacles appeared in astounding contrast to Soviet practice. American bankers provided guidance on implementing a market economy, while political consultants from California joined Boris Yeltsin's election campaign. From school textbooks to assistance in guarding nuclear weapons, American hands seemed busy in areas recently of utmost sensitivity to party leaders.

Not everything had been altered, of course. Many in the new elite came from the old elite, and they presided over an economy that featured numerous privatized firms run by the same managers as before. Jury trials remained the exception. Yeltsin summoned tanks to settle a dispute with an elected parliament, while a significant minority of Russians pined for Soviet times. With every passing year, it seemed, support for the reforms and American advice eroded along with the standard of living, as noted in following chapters.

Nonetheless, nothing should obscure the fact that the Soviet era seemed remote after just a few years of rapid and fundamental transformation that began at the end of the 1980s. The U.S. ambassador to Russia, Thomas Pickering, pointed to one aspect of this change in his remarks at the Council on Foreign Relations in New York early in 1994. "Foreigners, foreign products, and foreign ideas are common in Russia today—a sharp contrast from a few years ago when most citizens had never even seen a person from the West. Most important, the fear of contact with foreigners, so pervasive in the old system, is a thing of the past." Something dramatic had certainly occurred, often with American participation. Yet Pickering hastened to advise his audience not to exaggerate the foreign role in these events.

> It is not the case, however, that foreigners define Russia's future, however much some may imagine they do. Russia is in a profound process of self-redefinition, with the emphasis on "self." Russians listen to what outsiders have to say, although they have become a bit impatient with what they refer to as "assistance tourism." They study foreign models of various kinds. They travel abroad to see how things are done in other countries. Then something happens which some foreign advisers had not anticipated: The Russians make up their own minds, based on their estimation of their needs in the context of their national traditions.[48]

Pickering's point must be emphasized here, in a book addressing American influence in Russia, for our focus carries the risk of creating an exaggerated sense of America's role. It was indeed the Russians (and non-Russians in diverse republics of the former Soviet Union) who decided to reform and opted to scour foreign experience. Russians demonstrated in the streets, elected leaders, and implemented new policies. When they embraced foreign products and practices, they often adapted them to suit domestic preferences, whether increasing the garlic in American hotdogs or crafting provisions of foreign documents into a unique constitution.

However, such qualifications leave ample room for the themes of this chapter. Russians themselves did choose to reform, but not by reviving a set of traditions seen as distinctly Russian and not by attempting to modify imports so extensively that they became unrecognizable. As the Soviet Union ruptured, observers and opinion polls described a widespread inferiority complex in which nearly anything domestic seemed woeful and prompted Russians to look abroad in many fields, including mass entertainment, education, politics, law, economics, and fashion. When they scrutinized foreign possibilities, they usually preferred Western rather than Asian, African, or South American practices—and of their Western options, they turned more often to America than to any other country.

All this invites comparison with the young Soviet Union as it took shape before World War II. Both the early Soviet state and the new Russian Republic of the 1990s emerged determined to remake society, and both ventures recruited the United States. In each case America seemed a showcase of certain features desired by the Kremlin's architects of transformation, and in each period American influences of other sorts, not central to official plans, left their mark on society, too. Sixty years apart, in other words, both Stalin and Yeltsin presided over "revolutions" that included vital features in which American ingredients figured prominently.

That said, the Stalinist upheaval of the early five-year plans also took place along several fronts where American experience was irrelevant or unnecessary: forced collectivization of the peasantry, elimination of private business in favor of a centralized "command economy," and mass death in labor camps, to name only three endeavors of the period. In only one area, the industrialization drive, did American expertise bear heavily on the course of events. Industrialization may have been Stalin's top priority, but the fact remains that he saw no need for wholesale American involvement in any other essential project of the day. Popular culture from the United States—jazz, dancing, and movies—did win millions of fans in the new Soviet state, but the seduction occurred in the 1920s, before Stalin's thunder shook the land.

American influence followed two stages over the ten years beginning in the mid-1920s. After the ravages of World War I, the civil war of 1918–20, and the Volga famine in 1921–22, the new Soviet regime found itself with a substantial economic challenge but few resources with which to obtain Western technology essential for industrial revival. Hope faded that the Russian Revolution, now half a decade removed, would incite revolutions in the West and thereby unlock assistance from new socialist states with more advanced economies. At the same time the party leadership did not feel it prudent or perhaps even possible to squeeze from its flock the labor and resources necessary for a dash to overtake Western economies. Officials might invite foreign companies to consider joint ventures, and they could urge citizens to acquire "American" diligence and efficiency, but for the most part they appeared to accept that industrial recovery would be an extended process marked by only scattered Western participation. The 1920s became, officially, a transition period, with the party prepared to tolerate certain unpalatable phenomena, including a modest rate of industrialization, until the passage of time brought more experience to the government and enlightenment to the population. Meanwhile American popular culture joined the ranks of activities (including domestic private trade) whose large followings elicited grumbling in party circles but did not trigger an offensive to cleanse society of the blights. Leaders advised patience until superior socialist practices could be perfected to win people over from the "bourgeois remnants" of a doomed epoch.

That time arrived at the end of the 1920s, sooner than many expected. Proclamations from the new Stalinist elite rebuked former associates for obstructing revolutionary progress and declared it possible, even essential, to abandon gradualist transition measures in order to industrialize at breakneck speed. Two considerations drove this decision: a desire to hasten the advent of socialism and a concern for national strength linked to closing the industrial gap with the West. Both factors yielded an expanding centralized state seeking more than ever to mobilize the population and focus its energies on the regime's goals. Along with much else tolerated in the 1920s, American mass entertainment now seemed a corrupting distraction, and it felt the wrath of a party prepared to purge society of toxins from the capitalist world. However, this same capitalist world, above all the United States, held the technical keys to the leaders' top priority, swift industrialization. As a result, most Soviet citizens lost direct contact with American popular culture at a time when the government opened the door and its treasury wider than ever to American corporations and engineers.

Compare this with the nature of American influence during the "Russian Revolution" of the late twentieth century. Certain similarities appear, especially with the 1920s. Then, as seventy years later, a disrupted economy lay in need of Western technology while denying leaders the funds to pay for it. During both periods, American cultural temptations circulated in considerable volume. So did the opinion that Russians should learn to work like Americans, and in this regard a commentator in 1992 went so far as to contrast American and Russian folk tales. Heroes in Russian stories, he contended, had celestial visions, endured long periods of suffering, or journeyed aimlessly to a miraculous outcome. The American hero did not wait for miracles. "He calculates, estimates, economizes, rationalizes. He is constantly in motion, in action. He looks for tasks, and tasks look for him. And he completes them, applying his exceptional strength, energy, and skill." After a good deal more in this vein, the author concluded that, "perhaps, having grasped such values as love of labor, efficiency, thrift, and enterprise, we will grow closer to the heroes of American fables, legends, and songs"—sounding much like those calling for "Russian-Americans" in the 1920s.[49]

For now, though, these resemblances pale before the contrasts that distinguish the two eras. One might begin by qualifying the comparisons just made. During the last decade of the century, American entertainment reached much farther than it did in the 1920s, when no one possessed a television and most people lived scattered across the country in peasant villages. Beyond that, extensive American influence on Russian officials in such areas as law and free-market economics finds scant parallel in the early Soviet period. Party leaders of the 1920s may have exhorted the multitude to master certain "American" work habits in combination with Russian revolutionary vision, but the goal remained a new society, superior to the West. By the early 1990s, reformers no longer spoke of eclipsing the West but of joining it. For these officials and pundits, Russia was not a progressive alternative to America. The outcome of the Cold War, and perhaps their own experiences in Soviet times, had demonstrated to their satisfaction the merit of the West, and they did not think of themselves as defending a socialist homeland from bourgeois contamination. They wanted to shed their Soviet clothes and don Western apparel off the rack without fussing over alterations. The West had won, and the sooner that Russia adopted the basics of Western economic, political, legal, and social systems, the sooner the country would enter the community of "normal," "civilized" lands. These sentiments find no speck of common ground with Bolshevik opinion.

In addition, Lenin and Stalin (and the tsars before them) regarded the centralized, autocratic state as the best means for carrying out major policies, including drives to borrow from the West and campaigns to resist Western influence. Thus, one of the most stunning features of the late twentieth century became the Russian struggle to reform without the dominant thrust of a powerful state to impel the transformation. Indeed, the *abolition* of an autocratic state stood as one of the central goals of the period. Never before in Russian history had officials relied as much on general self-interest, initiative, and even consent to yield the results they desired. Debate continues over the wisdom and longevity of this new course, but that only underscores the remarkable nature of the change.

If Russian officials in 1992 saw the United States differently than did their early Bolshevik predecessors, popular images of America changed less over the seventy years. Although the lack of comprehensive evidence from the 1920s prevents specificity, the weight of testimony regarding this sentiment suggests that many Russians, at both ends of the century, imagined the United States as a land of wealth and modern technology. Those raised during the Cold War might also fear or resent aggressive policies attributed to Washington, and they could well know more than most white Americans about the history of racial injustice in the United States. But these impressions did not necessarily dispel a sense of American prosperity and verve.

Nonetheless, riches, technology, and entertainment never tempted everyone to embrace the United States. If Russian reformers, including many prominent officials in the early 1990s, could join a large share of the population in regarding America as more advanced than Russia, they did not account for all opinion in the country. Other voices, muted at first, described the United States as little better than Viking pillagers and scarcely an attractive model for the East Slavs. As the decade progressed, this dissent grew louder and began to affect the course of domestic politics. These sentiments require attention, for they represent one of the factors that may yet steer post-Soviet Russia's relationship with America closer to features reminiscent of earlier years.

Notes

1. Serge A. Zenkovsky, ed., *Medieval Russia's Epics, Chronicles, and Tales* (New York: Dutton, 1974), 49–50.

2. George D. Holliday, *Technology Transfer to the USSR, 1928–1937 and 1966–1975: The Role of Western Technology in Soviet Economic Development* (Boulder, Colo.: Westview, 1979), 78–80 (the Kosygin quote is on 79); Mikhail Gorbachev, *Memoirs* (New York: Doubleday, 1995), 103.

3. Jerry F. Hough, *Russia and the West: Gorbachev and the Politics of Reform* (New York: Simon and Schuster, 1988), 186; *Pravda*, 5 October 1988, 4; Loren R. Graham, *Science in Russia and the Soviet Union: A Short History* (Cambridge: Cambridge University Press, 1993), 255–56; Michael Ellman and Vladimir Kontorovich, eds., *The Disintegration of the Soviet Economic System* (London: Routledge, 1992), 47; *Izvestiia*, 8 March 1989, 5.

4. Richard C. Schneider, "Privatization in One Country: Foreign Investment and the Russian Privatization Dynamic," *Hastings International and Comparative Law Review* 17, no. 4 (Summer 1994): 713; *New Times* (a Soviet weekly of world affairs), no. 13 (1989): 28. The parliamentarian making the comments was Fyodor Burlatsky.

5. Andrei Kozyrev, "Russia: A Chance for Survival," *Foreign Affairs* 71, no. 2 (Spring 1992): 8.

6. A. Kortunov and A. Nikitin, *The "American Model" on the Scales of History* (Moscow: Progress, 1985), 19, citing Ruhl J. Bartlett, ed., *The Record of American Diplomacy: Documents and Readings in the History of American Foreign Relations* (New York: Knopf, 1948), 387–88. For other examples of this outlook among Americans, see Walter A. McDougall, *Promised Land, Crusader State: The American Encounter with the World since 1776* (New York: Houghton Mifflin, 1997).

7. Kortunov and Nikitin, "American Model," 13.

8. Transcript of "America's Impact on Russia," a television program in the series *America's Defense Monitor*, first broadcast on 14 June 1998 by the Center for Defense Information; Deborah Anne Palmieri, ed., *Russia and the NIS in the World Economy: East-West Investment, Financing, and Trade* (Westport, Conn.: Praeger, 1994), 9; Eric Shiraev and Vladislav Zubok, *Anti-Americanism in Russia: From Stalin to Putin* (New York: Palgrave, 2000), 31.

9. Everette E. Dennis, George Gerbner, and Yassen N. Zassoursky, eds., *Beyond the Cold War: Soviet and American Media Images* (Newbury Park, Calif.: Sage, 1991), 28–29; William C. Brumfield, ed., *Reshaping Russian Architecture: Western Technology, Utopian Dreams* (Cambridge: Cambridge University Press, 1990), 66, note 60.

10. *Pravda*, 9 September 1988, 6; *Izvestiia*, 28 February 1989, 3. For a Soviet correspondent's praise of the American Automobile Association, which he joined while in the United States, see *Sovetskaia kul'tura*, 18 July 1987, 7.

11. *Moskovskie novosti*, 2 October 1988, 6.

12. Eduard Ia. Batalov, "Amerikanskii opyt i nasha perestroika. Sotsiologicheskie razmyshleniia," *SShA: ekonomika, politika, ideologiia*, no. 1 (1989): 4–5, 8; *Moskovskie novosti*, 2 October 1988, 6.

13. Batalov, "Amerikanskii opyt," 9.

14. *Izvestiia*, 9 March 1990, 3. See *Moskovskie novosti*, 2 October 1988, 6, for more remarks by Kondrashov in this vein. See *Pravda*, 6 December 1989, 5, for praise of the American jury system from a correspondent in New York.

15. *BBC Summary of World Broadcasts*, SU/0565, 19 September 1989, A1/3. See also Dennis et al., *Beyond the Cold War*, 96, 99, 108–109.

16. *An Economic Rehabilitation Corps for the Former Soviet Republics and Eastern Europe: A Policy Statement* (Washington, D.C.: National Planning Association, 1993), 1. See also Jeffrey Sachs, "The Grand Bargain," in *The Post-Soviet Economy: Soviet and Western Perspectives* (New York: St. Martin's, 1992), 209.

17. *U.S. Department of State Dispatch* 5, no. 1 (3 January 1994): 3; 5, no. 5 (31 January 1994): 39. See also 6, no. 12 (20 March 1995): 220; Thomas Carothers, "Democracy Promotion under Clinton," *Washington Quarterly* 18, no. 4 (Autumn 1995): 13.

18. *U.S. Department of State Dispatch* 6, no. 8 (20 February 1995): 123.

19. Janine R. Wedel, *Collision and Collusion: The Strange Case of Western Aid to Eastern Europe, 1989–1998* (New York: St. Martin's, 1998), 122, 131, 134, 141–42; Adil Rustomjee, "Role of Foreign Advisers in the Russian Privatization Program," from David Johnson's Russia List, #2300, 6 August 1998; John Lloyd, *Rebirth of a Nation: An Anatomy of Russia* (London: Michael Joseph, 1997), 247; Anders Åslund, *How Russia Became a Market Economy* (Washington, D.C.: Brookings Institution, 1995), 247.

20. *U.S. Department of State Dispatch* 5, no. 5 (31 January 1994): 40; 5, no. 23 (6 June 1994): 367; Karen LaFollette, "Massive Aid to Russia Won't Help," *USA Today* 122, no. 2586 (March 1994): 45; David Corn, "Sawyer, Miller Goes to Moscow: Propagandists to Power," *Nation* 257, no. 4 (26 July 1993): 139; Lynn D. Nelson and Irina Y. Kuzes, *Radical Reform in Yeltsin's Russia: Political, Economic, and Social Dimensions* (Armonk, N.Y.: Sharpe, 1995), 59. For a critical reaction to U.S.-produced television advertisements that promoted capitalism in Russia, see Dick Kirschten, "On the Rebound," *National Journal* 26, no. 22 (28 May 1994): 1239.

21. *U.S. Department of State Dispatch* 5, no. 23 (6 June 1994): 367; Palmieri, *Russia and the NIS*, 121, 124; *New York Times*, 5 August 1994; *Wall Street Journal*, 9 October 1990.

22. James R. Kraus, "Fed, U.S. Bankers Plan Assistance for Russia," *American Banker*, 22 June 1992, 1, 6; Susanna V. Pullen, "United States Foreign Banking and Investment Opportunities: Branching Out to the Russian Federation," *Transnational Lawyer* 8, no. 1 (Spring 1995): 164; *Wall Street Journal*, 22 June 1992.

23. J. B. Zulu et al., eds., *Central Banking Technical Assistance to Countries in Transition: Papers and Proceedings of Meeting of Donor and Recipient Central Banks and International Institutions* (Washington, D.C.: International Monetary Fund, 1994).

24. *Business Week*, 2 August 1993, 75; *Wall Street Journal*, 23 May 1994.

25. *Wall Street Journal*, 25 October 1988; *Fortune*, 20 November 1989; *Business Week*, 28 May 1990. See also "Industrialist Gives $4 Million to Duke to Re-Educate Soviet Business Managers," *Wall Street Journal*, 17 April 1989.

26. Amy Magaro Rubin, "Officials from Former Soviet Republics Study U.S. Management," *Chronicle of Higher Education* 41, no. 16 (14 December 1994): A44; Keith Scearce, "They Learn in the U.S., They Buy from the U.S.," *AgExporter* 6, no. 11 (November 1994): 12; "Funds Available to Train Potential Business Partners from the NIS," *Business America* 116, no. 8 (August 1995): 26–27; *U.S. Department of State Dispatch* 6, no. 8 (20 February 1995): 124; personal correspondence received from the Commerce Department, 10 December 1997; *New York Times*, 3 December 1994.

27. *U.S. Department of State Dispatch* 6, no. 8 (20 February 1995): 124.

28. *U.S. Department of State Dispatch* 5, no. 1 (3 January 1994): 3, 5; "Russia/Women in Business," Voice of America, 28 October 1997, from David Johnson's Russia List, #1320, 29 October 1997; "IEWS Russian Regional Report, 23 October 1997, Yekaterinburg," from David Johnson's Russia List, #1315, 25 October 1997.

29. "World Bank Study Ranks Russia's Top 20 Business Schools," from David Johnson's Russia List, #1394, 25 November 1997; Peter Ekman, "Moscow MBAs," from David Johnson's Russia List, #3226, 5 April 1999; *New York Times*, 9 February 1997.

30. Vladimir A. Kartashkin, "Human Rights and the Emergence of the State of the Rule of Law in the USSR," *Emory Law Journal* 40 (1991): 902; Gordon B. Smith, *Reforming the Russian Legal System* (Cambridge: Cambridge University Press, 1996), 231.

31. William W. Schwarzer, "Civil and Human Rights and the Courts under the New Constitution of the Russian Federation," *International Lawyer* 28, no. 3 (Fall 1994): 825, 832–33; Barbara A. Perry, "Constitutional Johnny Appleseeds: American Consultants and the Drafting of Foreign Constitutions," *Albany Law Review* 55, no. 3 (1992): 783–84; Kartashkin, "Human Rights," 895; Janet Key, "Old Countries, New Rights," *ABA Journal* 80, no. 5 (May 1994): 71; Oleg G. Rumyantsev, "The Present and Future of Russian Constitutional Order," *Harriman Review* 8, no. 2 (July 1995): 33, note 17.

32. Along with issues of *CEELI Update* from the 1990s, see *U.S. Department of State Dispatch* 5, no. 21 (23 May 1994): 337; 5, no. 23 (6 June 1994): 367. For more on American assistance with economic laws, see Key, "Old Countries," 68–69; *Assistance Programmes for Central and Eastern European Countries and the Former Soviet Union* (Paris: OECD, 1996), 64; Talbot D'Alemberte, "Our Eastern European Challenge," *ABA Journal* 78 (March 1992): 8; Jacqueline Lang Weaver, "The History and Organization of the Russian Petroleum Legislation Project at the University of Houston Law Center," *Houston Journal of International Law* 15, no. 2 (Winter–Spring 1993): 271–315.

33. Key, "Old Countries," 68–69; *U.S. Department of State Dispatch* 6, no. 8 (20 February 1995): 123.

34. Stephen C. Thaman, "Trial by Jury and the Constitutional Rights of the Accused in Russia," *East European Constitutional Review* 4, no. 1 (Winter 1995): 78–79; *CEELI Update* 6, no. 1 (Spring 1996): 27; *U.S. Department of State Dispatch* 5, no. 5 (31 January 1994): 38; Key, "Old Countries," 71.

35. *CEELI Update* 4, no. 1 (January–March 1994): 18; 5, no. 2 (Summer 1995): 22; 5, no. 3 (Fall 1995): 24; 6, no. 2 (Summer 1996): 1, 28–29; 6, no. 3 (Fall 1996): 24; 7, no. 2 (Summer 1997): 29.

36. *CEELI Update* 4, no. 1 (January–March 1994): 18; 4, no. 4 (Winter 1994): 1; 5, no. 3 (Fall 1995): 23; 6, no. 1 (Spring 1996): 28; 6, no. 2 (Summer 1996): 28, 30; Rubin, "Officials," A44.

37. *U.S. Department of State Dispatch* 5, no. 5 (31 January 1994): 38; 5, no. 14 (4 April 1994): 189; 5, no. 23 (6 June 1994): 367–68; James Voorhees, "A Footnote on Russian Fundamentals," from David Johnson's Russia List, #2446, 26 October 1998; Monica Ware, "Independent TV 'Opens the Skies' of Broadcasting," *Surviving Together* 12, no. 1 (Spring 1994): 18; "Exchange Program for Young Russian Leaders to Start Monday," Washington, 19 July 1999 (Itar-Tass), from David Johnson's Russia List, #3398, 19 July 1999.

38. *U.S. Department of State Dispatch* 5, no. 52 (26 December 1994): 847; Janine Wedel, "U.S. Aid Added to Russia's Woes," *San Francisco Chronicle* 3 September 1998, from David Johnson's Russia List, #2345, 3 September 1998; Edward P. Lazear, ed., *Economic Transition in Eastern Europe and Russia: Realities of Reform* (Stanford, Calif.: Hoover Institution Press, 1995), 145–46; Marie Lavigne, *The Economics of Transition: From Socialist Economy to Market Economy* (Basingstoke, England: Macmillan, 1995), 235, 237; Salvatore Zecchini, "The Role of International Financial Institutions in the Transition Process," *Journal of Comparative Economics* 20, no. 1 (February 1995): 119; Maurice R. Greenberg, "Privatizing Western Assistance to Russia," *Washington Quarterly* 17, no. 4 (Autumn 1994): 22.

39. *U.S. Department of State Dispatch* 5, no. 21 (23 May 1994): 337; Kirschten, "On the Rebound," 1240.

40. *Wall Street Journal*, 17 March 1988, 20 June 1988, 31 August 1988, 9 August 1989, 8 June 1990, 19 June 1990.

41. *Wall Street Journal*, 20 June 1988, 16 September 1988, 9 January 1989, 23 February 1989, 7 March 1990, 17 May 1990.

42. Kevin J. Vaughan, "Russia's Petroleum Industry: An Overview of Its Current Status, the Need for Foreign Investment, and Recent Legislation," *Law and Policy in International Business* 25, no. 2

(Winter 1994): 821–22; U.S. Department of State Dispatch 5, no. 1 (3 January 1994): 4; Alexander Ivashenko, "Larger Volumes of US Investments in Russian Economy to be Discussed during Regular Session of the Chernomyrdin-Gore Commission on March 10–12," Moscow, 6 March 1998 (RIA Novosti), from David Johnson's Russia List, #2100, 9 March 1998; Patrick Artisien-Maksimento and Yuri Adjubei, eds., Foreign Investment in Russia and Other Soviet Successor States (New York: St. Martin's, 1996), 150–56.

43. "The American Hot Dog Invades Russia and China and Takes on Different Forms," Washington, 1 December 1997 (PRNewswire), from David Johnson's Russia List, #1403, 2 December 1997; New York Times, 18 January 1996; 14 August 1996; Newsweek, 8 December 1997, 52; "Tupperware Begins Operations in Russia," Orlando, Fla., 24 November 1997 (PRNewswire), from David Johnson's Russia List, #1392, 25 November 1997.

44. Wall Street Journal, 14 September 1990; Independent (London), 22 October 1997; Anna Dolgov, "Russia's Friendly to Tobacco Cos.," Moscow, 28 February 1998 (AP), from David Johnson's Russia List, #2086, 1 March 1998; Adam Tanner, "Tobacco Giants Announce New Russian Investments," Moscow, 16 March 1998 (Reuters), from David Johnson's Russia List, #2112, 17 March 1998.

45. New York Times, 29 June 1997; 18 October 1998; Nezavisimaia gazeta, 14 November 1997, 1; William E. Butler, Russian Law (Oxford: Oxford University Press, 1999), 13; Kraus, "Fed, U.S. Bankers," 6; Wall Street Journal, 16 June 1989; 24 May 1990; 19 June 1990; Daniel R. Kempton and Richard M. Levine, "Soviet and Russian Relations with Foreign Corporations: The Case of Gold and Diamonds," Slavic Review 54, no. 1 (Spring 1995): 104–105; Stefan Hedlund, Russia's "Market" Economy: A Bad Case of Predatory Capitalism (London: UCL, 1999), 350; New York Times, 14 June 1997; Time, 15 July 1996, 28–37.

46. Ludmilla Gricenko Wells, "The Role of Advertising in the Soviet Union" (Ph. D. diss., University of Tennessee, 1992), 71–72; Wall Street Journal, 17 May 1990; Anatole Shub, What Russians Know and Think about America: A Survey in Summer 1995 (Washington, D.C.: United States Information Agency, 1995), 16–18; New York Times, 1 February 1996, 12 January 1997, 9 February 1997.

47. New York Times, 18 March 1996.

48. U.S. Department of State Dispatch 5, no. 8 (21 February 1994): 91.

49. Nezavisimaia gazeta, 22 May 1992, 8.

CHAPTER EIGHT

~

Counterstrike

Brother Slavs (and non-Slavs), in trading totalitarianism for democracy, haven't we just traded one bad thing for another?

—Alexander Lebed

But our woeful reformers, out of the whole wealth of world economic theories and practices, have adopted the one, "only true" monetarist theory of Milton Friedman, according to which it is enough for the government to refrain from giving anyone any money and from interfering in anything for everything to take care of itself.

—Gennady Zyuganov

In the winter of 1997–98 billboards around Moscow advertised new Yava Gold cigarettes by flaunting images of America. This alone scarcely merited attention, for invocations of the United States had recommended products to Russians for nearly a decade. Yava Gold, however, unveiled no Florida beaches or evenings on Broadway to attract customers. New York City did appear in a billboard display, but with a package of Yavas cruising overhead, escorted by the menacing slogan "counterstrike." Another panel showed a Russian cosmonaut painting the words Yava Gold on an American space station, accompanied again by the "counterstrike" caption under the picture. Something had changed, the advertisements declared. Rather than savor America's mystique by smoking Marlboros or Camels, people could purchase Yavas and strike back at the United States. Yava Gold's manufacturer—the

British-American Tobacco Company, as it turned out—sensed a shift in the public mood away from the lopsided favor shown to almost anything Western in the early 1990s. Certain other American companies also heeded the signs and chose Russian or even Soviet images for some products. Procter & Gamble reintroduced Mif, a detergent familiar in Soviet times, while RJ Reynolds summoned the memory of Peter the Great in naming a new cigarette Peter I. The package bore the nation's emblem, a double-headed eagle, and an appeal to those who "believe in the revival of the traditions and grandeur of the Russian lands." It became the company's most successful new brand since Camel.[1]

Native entrepreneurs, too, emphasized the domestic roots of their wares, none more flamboyantly or profitably than Vladimir Dovgan. His household merchandise—vodka, ketchup, tea, chocolate, toothpaste, and much else— appeared in shops and kiosks with labels that trumpeted a Russian provenance, even for those products actually imported. The mood also gripped Russia's political reformers, among them First Deputy Prime Minister Boris Nemtsov, who inaugurated a "Buy Russia" association in 1998 to promote Russian goods. The year before, President Yeltsin used a radio address to ask his audience: "Do you want to help Russian enterprises? Do you want us to stand on our own feet and work at full strength? Then I say to you, buy our goods, our Russian goods and you won't regret it."[2]

Whether or not Yeltsin moved any consumers with his advice, it no longer seemed pitiable to accentuate a commodity's Russian origin. Although Western products did not surrender all allure, and in numerous categories they remained the clear preference of Russians, their general appeal receded from the adoration of the early 1990s. Foreign chocolate candy, seemingly ubiquitous after the birth of the Russian Republic, plunged from four-fifths of the market in 1992 to roughly one-third by the end of 1997, as nostalgia and lower prices buoyed sales of Russian confectionery. The Mars Company's Snickers bar, extolled relentlessly in commercials at the beginning of the decade, endured ridicule and indignation a few years later as a symbol of pushy American merchandise that had worn out its welcome. "People are tired of the idea that Russia can't make anything of its own," concluded Sergei Kostin, host of the television show *National Interest*. "When they see nothing but Snickers bars, it reminds them of how low our country has sunk." Fighting to retain its market share, the Mars Company's locally incorporated subsidiary presented itself as a Russian firm that manufactured various sweets formulated for Russian palates.[3]

By the second half of the decade, the most popular radio station in Moscow played only Russian selections, primarily tunes from the Brezhnev period. "The audience is fed up with Western music," explained the station manager. "Fifteen-year-olds call in to request songs that were hits in the 1970s and 1980s." On television, in the guise of a New Year's program to welcome 1996, the nation's largest network broadcast a three-hour tribute to old Soviet musicals—upbeat films that had sought to paint a smile on the Stalin era. While such fare would not have drawn many viewers in 1991, the program's coproducer now felt confident. "Everyone is sick of American movies and tired of having an inferiority complex," he observed. "These old Soviet films are very sentimental and immensely popular." So it appeared the next year, too, when the station's second tribute to Soviet musicals captured nearly two-thirds of the viewing audience.[4]

Russia's romance with America had cooled. This could only be expected with the country seemingly swamped by American consultants and popular culture, especially in the absence of an economic recovery to validate the new course. Measures urged by foreign advisers and promoted by Russian reformers did not rush many people toward prosperity. Instead, year after year, the country sank farther below the comforts anticipated when officials first endorsed a Western blueprint at the birth of the Russian Republic. The enthusiasm for reform in those days now seemed ever more naïve.

If this false start toward Western affluence disheartened many Russians, there were others more troubled by the effort to cultivate a thirst for it at all. They saw the American standard of living as a hazard, rather than a goal, and worried about duplicating in Russia a consumer culture that encouraged its members to gauge their worth in terms of possessions. Alexander Yakovlev, one of Mikhail Gorbachev's key advisers, looked back over the period of reforms and acknowledged that Western democracy had won the *political* contest with the Soviet Union. But in other respects the verdict was not so clear, he noted, for "free societies such as America have made a disappointing use of their freedom. They seem to lack a system of moral checks and balances, and we in Russia are rapidly making the same mistake. We imitate mainly the cheap materialism." Another commentator, the political philosopher Alexander Panarin, argued in 1996 that the "insatiable greed of the consumer consciousness" fostered by Westernization threatened the ecology of the planet and, more immediately, the national traditions of Russia. Tradition imposes social obligations, he explained, while people in the grip of "mass consumer consciousness" resent responsibilities that limit self-gratification. Thus there "arises the danger that Westernization will acquire the character of borrowing mainly the worst aspects of the donor culture."[5]

Even the moderate voices of coauthors Vladimir Lukin and Anatoly Utkin lamented that competition from mass-cultural products of the West had devastated the Russian fine arts, contributing to a "deintellectualization of society." Movement toward the nationalist end of the political spectrum turned up sharper language, including a complaint by Alexander Rutskoi, the early ally and subsequent opponent of Boris Yeltsin: "Not only has the intelligentsia refrained from defending the fatherland, it has not protested against the cheapest Western 'kitsch' in [Russian] book stores or against 'colonial commodities' shown on TV." At the xenophobic extreme favored by such groups as Pamiat (Memory), a worker complained that young Russians displayed more interest in rock 'n' roll and Sylvester Stallone than in the heroes of Russian history. "All of these things in Western culture substitute for love of the motherland," he told a Pamiat meeting in 1987. "Right now there is a truly spiritual aggression by the West on our youth. And very often our TV and our press promote this."[6]

In short, Gorbachev's reforms nurtured more than "liberal" sentiments. The new freedom also left room for publications to attack Western influence, and some did so with growing alarm. Much of this criticism resembled previous Soviet condemnation, in both its tone and its view of American culture. In 1988, for instance, an article in Our Contemporary characterized rock 'n' roll as "a rather powerful narcotic, entirely comparable with cocaine, opium, and LSD," while two years later Pravda deplored the ruin of wholesome girls who ventured to large cities and succumbed to the temptation of "beauty contests [another Western import in the late 1980s], cafes, and video salons with erotic films." In terms reminiscent of the Cold War, Our Contemporary warned that Western intelligence agencies sought to subvert the Soviet economy by corrupting young people—the next generation of the labor force—through incessant exposure to rock 'n' roll and other forms of alien popular culture: "Today one can say that a musical war has been launched against the USSR."[7]

Although the new criticism of Western influence preserved some of the concerns expressed under Brezhnev, it developed a distinct personality during the Soviet Union's final years and the decade to come. For one thing, the rallying cry of socialism yielded top billing to defense of eternal "Russian" qualities and institutions. Among these native treasures numbered the Russian Orthodox Church, which even Pravda now praised occasionally as an antidote to Western toxins. Outrage over the foreign cultural invasion also revealed a greater degree of frustration and humiliation than in previous years. The nation brimmed with Western amusements as never before, and critics could no longer assume that the government would favor measures to stem the incursion. "Rock 'n' roll rings forth now in kindergartens, at polling places, and it accompanies people going to a demonstration at Lenin's tomb," snapped another article in Our Contemporary. "What next?"[8]

Although few in the West noticed *Our Contemporary*, other voices carried farther in the 1990s. General Alexander Lebed, whose political star had risen to the level of presidential contender by 1996, sounded a call of distress in his autobiography: "Some say that Western culture is a threat to Russian traditions—and I believe that is true. Unfortunately, Russia has become a refuse pit for low-grade Western art: action movies where thirty or forty people are killed in a variety of ways, or pornography, or other mass-produced, formulaic rubbish on television." The head of the new Communist Party, Gennady Zyuganov, agreed with his political rival Lebed on this point. "We face a progressive 'Americanization' of our culture," Zyuganov warned, "which is already dangerously deprived of national spirit. Most of our movie theaters show American films, predominantly containing pornography and violence."[9] Bolsheviks had complained in similar tones about Hollywood's influence during the 1920s, but in those years they championed "socialist" spirit rather than Zyuganov's "national" alternative.

Condemnation of American commercialism and popular culture had indeed appeared regularly in Soviet publications ever since the Revolution. So common were these themes that their presence after the demise of the Soviet Union might seem to be floating debris from the wreck of "communist propaganda," remnants of a defunct ideology yet to wash away. It stands to reason that the Soviet media's indictment of American society created the unflattering assessment of the United States retained by some commentators years after the red flag had disappeared over the Kremlin. Decades of Cold War propaganda did not vanish without a trace in Russia (or America) at the close of the twentieth century, and some Russians certainly clung to dark images of America promoted in the past by the Communist Party. But criticism of America need not equate with fondness for Brezhnev, Lenin, or even socialism. Distaste for Bolshevism coexisted comfortably in some minds with contempt for much of the "American dream," however implausible that might sound to Americans themselves.

The Soviet Union alienated hundreds of thousands of its inhabitants sufficiently to drive them to emigration or dissent. Here were people disinclined to prefer life at home to that which they encountered or imagined in the United States, yet their interest in America could turn to disappointment or exasperation. Alexander Solzhenitsyn comes first to mind, with his dismay over an American society that seemed to encourage citizens to indulge every material whim. In his Harvard commencement address of 1978, he assured the audience of his aversion for Soviet socialism. "But should someone ask me whether I would indicate the West such as it is today as a model for my country, frankly I would have to answer negatively." The United States and other Western nations had developed according to the following principle, he explained: "Governments are meant to serve man, and man lives to be free and to pursue happiness. . . . It has become possible to raise young people according to these ideals, leading them to physical splendor, happiness, possession of material goods, money, and leisure, to an almost unlimited freedom of enjoyment." But nothing loftier. "Everything beyond physical well-being and accumulation of material goods, all other human requirements and characteristics of a subtler and higher nature, were left outside the area of attention of state and social systems, as if human life did not have any superior sense. . . . Mere freedom does not in the least solve all the problems of human life and it even adds a number of new ones."[10]

Not all émigrés embraced the United States, in other words, and some joined Solzhenitsyn in publishing laments on the nature of American society. The newcomers discovered a land in which the natives appeared isolated from one another, unwilling or unable to share more than superficial conversation and sentiments. American "individualism" had led to a society of members busily walling themselves off from their neighbors, guarding their deepest feelings and their private property like one and the same. Perhaps they no longer possessed profound emotions, having surrendered to a passion for money and the latest fads. If so, this might explain the deplorable level of culture prevailing in the United States. "For us," an émigré writer informed a Russian audience in 1989, "the word 'book' is associated with the concept of serious literature, but when an American says 'book' he can mean a guide to how best to water his vegetable garden or how to put his money in the bank." Another writer confessed a wry nostalgia for the KGB because he could at least count on its officers to read his books carefully.[11]

Long before 1917, members of the Russian intelligentsia had disparaged the United States in similar tones, and not necessarily with any sympathy for Marxism. Fyodor Dostoyevsky imagined America to embody much of the worst of Western civilization: a nation of rootless individuals, intent on personal profit, where money and machinery had withered the soul. Commenting on St. Petersburg in 1873, he remarked sarcastically: "And here, at last, is the architecture of a modern, enormous hotel. This is business-like efficiency, Americanism, hundreds of rooms, a huge industrial establishment. Right away it is evident that we too have railways and have suddenly found ourselves to be business-like people." In notes to *The Possessed* he insisted that "mankind will still be able to live without America, without railroads, even without bread," while various passages in his novels compare flight to America with suicide or desertion of the Russian homeland. Thus in the epilogue to *The Brothers Karamazov*, Dmitry Karamazov betrays no relish for escaping the reach of Russian courts by "running away" to the United States: "Oh, I hate that America even now! And though they were all of them there marvellous engineers, or whatever it is they are there—to hell with them! They are not my own people, they're not my sort."[12]

Other prominent members of the Russian intelligentsia also saw more to reproach than to praise in the United States during the second half of the nineteenth century. Populist radicals favored socialism on the foundation of communal village institutions, believing that peasants had mastered socialism's essence through centuries of cooperation in coping with the hardships of rural life. If the tsar and his nobles could be overthrown, the countryside seemed ripe for socialist camaraderie. Remote from the urban, industrial socialism of Karl Marx, this was an idyll appropriate for "backward" Russia. Cities, railroads, competition and riches left the populists cold, and their vision for Russia bore less resemblance with each decade to industrializing America.

Even earlier, in the middle third of the century, a loose-knit group of Slavophiles had gained prominence with their own expectations for the peasant commune. They, like the populists later, imagined the peasants to be instinctively collectivist, inclined to share their burdens and their resources with one another. The Slavophiles viewed these rural practices as an opportunity to revive a traditional, patriarchal peasant society in which the Orthodox Church and a father tsar would participate to ensure the harmonious well-being of the collective. Such hopes for church and tsar demonstrated that more than just years separated the Slavophiles from populist zeal for revolution and socialism. Yet both camps agreed that America represented no model for them, mired as it was in problems they trusted could never take root among the Russian peasants.

Common themes abounded. Whether peering or traveling across the Atlantic, Slavophiles, populists, and various other observers formed impressions of a society driven by a lust for wealth. Amassing dollars and possessions amounted to the national religion of the United States, preventing the formation of spiritual bonds in what had failed to become a community. America was a market, not a homeland, with no profound traditions to unite a hodgepodge of immigrants and no worthy indigenous culture arising to supplant the tattered remains of European customs. Beneath the bustle in America, a Slavophile detected "the most petty life, cut off from everything that lifts the heart above personal profit, sunk in the work of egoism, and recognizing material comfort together with its subsidiary elements as the highest goal." Were he compelled "to exchange his great future" in Russia "for the one-sided life of the West," he would choose Germany, Italy, France, or even England over the United States, where he "would suffocate in this prose of factory relations, in this mechanism of selfish worry."[13]

As for American democracy, some Russian commentators included this "vessel of liberty" in their indictment. What good was freedom, they asked, without effective institutions and traditions for instilling socialist (populist) or Christian (Slavophile) values in the population? The American founding fathers had drafted documents that treated each citizen as an isolated individual, insulated by law from other citizens and encouraged to set out alone in "pursuit of happiness." These "freedoms" may have led many Americans to prosperity, but not to wisdom or harmony sufficient to prevent them from slaughtering one another, with the most modern technology, during the Civil War. Eventually, predicted another Slavophile in 1865, "an American state will be organized, without faith, without moral principles and ideals; it will either fall apart, from the unruliness of personal egoism and the lack of faith of the individuals, or it will coalesce into a horrible despotism of the New World."[14]

As America industrialized in earnest after the Civil War, references to rampant technology increased among Russian critics. Exploitation of workers, dehumanizing urban landscapes, and a fanatical emphasis on efficiency in all walks of life struck them as principal consequences of "modernization." When the populist author Vladimir Korolenko visited America in 1893, a tour of the Armour, Swift & Company slaughterhouse in Chicago left him pondering the robotic nature of the industry and the society itself.

> We had not even had time to express our desires when an elegantly dressed gentleman came out to meet us and, with the mechanical movements of an automaton, passed out printed cards to each of the arrivals [indicating that the company had slaughtered 90 million animals in 1892]. . . .
>
> The gentleman invited us to have a seat while he retired into an office, where a host of young men and women were busy calculating something and clicking away at the keys of their Remington typewriters. He probably entered us as statistics for his visitors' count. In the office clicking and whirring completely filled the air. "Ninety million head," I thought to myself involuntarily, "and each of these clicks marks one more death in that ninety million."[15]

Russians who embraced Marxism at the turn of the century exalted neither the Orthodox Church nor the peasant commune as alternatives to the bleak American spectacle, but they accepted most of the criticism aimed at the United States by their predecessors. In fact, when Maxim Gorky visited America in 1906 and published a group of sketches, Marxist repugnance for the United States reached a level of ferocity unrivaled by the most indignant Russians of previous generations. In his story "City of the Yellow Devil," Gorky set out to unmask the hollow, slavish quality of New Yorkers panting after money: "No inner freedom, no freedom of the spirit, shines in people's eyes. And this energy without freedom reminds you of the cold gleam of the knife that has not yet been dulled. It is the freedom of blind instruments in the hands of the Yellow Devil—Gold."[16]

In the raving metropolis, Gorky considered modern technology anything but the blessing that Marxists expected machines to become in their own hands.

> Locomotives crawl like huge worms, pulling cars behind them; automobile horns quack like fat geese; electricity wails sullenly; the stifling air is as saturated with thousands of roaring sounds as a sponge is with water. Pressed down against this dirty city, fouled by smoke, the air is motionless amidst the high soot-covered walls.

Life consisted of little more than the monotony of a day's work (for those with jobs) and the consumption of useless products hawked by ceaseless advertising: "Entire walls glitter with flaming words about beer, whiskey, soap, a new razor, hats, cigars, theaters. . . . People come at its call, buy trash they don't need, and watch spectacles that stupefy them." Not only did the city's brazen materialism create a spiritual void, it failed even to shield many of its inhabitants from privation. "The horror of poverty on the East Side," Gorky declared, "is more dismal than anything I know."[17]

Bolshevik thirst for American technology and Stalin's promotion of "American efficiency" are not anticipated in Gorky's chronicle. His hostility apparently flowed from diverse pools, ranging from a desire to rebut praise of America to pique at his eviction from a New York hotel upon discovery that he was lodging with a woman not his wife. In private correspondence and conversations about the United States, Gorky did manage compliments. "The most remarkable thing," recalled fellow writer Leonid Andreyev, "is that while in his stories and articles about America Gorky wrote nothing but the very worst that could be said about the country[,] he never told me anything but the very best about America."[18] Whatever Gorky may have related to Andreyev and written on occasion to friends, it was his published stories that Soviet officials canonized in decades to come. Even more than his attack on jazz, the American sketches enjoyed frequent reincarnation by the state press. As late as 1962, when Viktor Nekrasov found himself under fire for painting too complimentary a portrait of America, Soviet critics thought it best that he return to Gorky (and Mayakovsky) for instruction.[19]

Thus, some Russian grimaces at America persisted from the nineteenth century through the Soviet era and beyond. Images of self-centered individuals, obsessed with competition for possessions at the expense of other Americans (especially racial minorities and the poor in general), needed little reshaping to fit the views of Slavophiles, populists, Marxists, and a new range of critics at the onset of the twenty-first century. To be sure, other themes blossomed or withered along the way, in accordance with American development and prevailing notions in the Russian intelligentsia. Allegations that the United States sought to impose its ways on the rest of the world spread mainly in the twentieth century, along with American cultural, economic, and military influence. Russian nationalists made this charge in the 1990s as readily as Soviet ideologists before them, but it attracted less attention from Slavophiles or populists facing a remote, adolescent America in the nineteenth century. Also, Marxists differed from their predecessors by praising Western industrial technology and by arguing at the beginning of the twentieth century that Russia must proceed through the same historical stages as other nations (from feudalism to capitalism and on to socialism) rather than skip capitalism and veer off to a community of peasant collectivists, as the Slavophiles and populists had dreamed. In the Marxist telling, Russia lagged behind the West until the revolutionary events of 1917 vaulted the new Bolshevik state ahead of the capitalist pack. The Soviet Union and Western lands were all still traveling in the same direction, however, toward the socialist institutions essential for every nation to reach the ultimate goal of communism.

On this point—the question of similar paths of development—the most extreme critics of American influence in the 1990s resembled the Slavophiles and populists, who generally rejected the contention that Western values and institutions (liberal, Protestant, Catholic, or Marxist) could, or should, take root in Russia. Alexander Prokhanov, editor of the newspaper *Tomorrow*, declared that "President Yeltsin cannot make a decision without consulting his friend Bill Clinton. But Russians are not stupid. They see that the liberal idea will not work here." Numerous officials in the Orthodox Church and politicians close to the church decried American materialism's emphasis on earthly pleasures and hoped that such priorities would not spread in Russia at the end of the twentieth century. "These Protestant theologians are preaching that it is good to make a lot of money and God wants you to succeed monetarily," complained Vladimir Osipov of the Christian Democratic Movement. "They do not understand that such a philosophy is fundamentally alien to our beliefs." Even the leader of the new Communist Party, whose Bolshevik ancestors had reviled Orthodoxy along with other re-

ligions and placed Russia on the same historical course as the West, now concurred with the church's rebuff of Western models. "We are a communal nation, brought up on a thousand years of experience in mutual support and patriotic feeling," Zyuganov asserted. "And the West is trying to impose on us
their individualism and Protestant egotism. Some in the West would demand
that we live by rules that are completely alien to us, which we could never
accept."[20]

With the failure of reforms to meet their architects' expectations by the
mid-1990s, a growing assortment of intellectuals and politicians outside the
xenophobic segment of the political spectrum questioned the transplanting
of American institutions to Russia. Not all scorned Western society, and
some traced contemporary difficulties to deplorable aspects of Russian or Soviet history, but they all joined Alexander Panarin in challenging "the mechanical transfer of this [American political] system under the current conditions of our shattered society." Panarin could not side with reformers who
"attempt to convey to our soil the American political model, assuming that
its effectiveness is of an institutional character" and forgetting that the
American system "depends on many noninstitutional preconditions linked
to the peculiarities of history and culture in America."[21] Lukin and Utkin
agreed:

> Recent relations between East and West have revealed something that formerly
> was hidden by economic contradictions and (from 1917) by ideological dispute,
> namely: the West is a unique region with a unique civilization, and a country
> can't become part of it simply by renaming a general secretary a president, and
> by putting into a constitution a phrase about the separation of powers, and by
> declaring support for the rights of man and citizen. The experience of the 1990s
> has shown, more clearly perhaps than the previous era of confrontation, that
> Russia and the West exist in different zones of civilization, formed first of all by
> different historical experience. Being cut off from the West by two centuries of
> Mongol bondage, followed by two centuries of self-isolation, not undergoing
> the three crucial revolutions of the West—Renaissance, Reformation, and
> Enlightenment—Russia remained under the influence of its religion, history,
> and cruel historical experience, which created its own way of life, its own world
> view, its own civilization.[22]

Government leaders, too, began to question more often "the mechanistic
transfer of methods of Western economies to Russian soil." This approach,
continued Prime Minister Viktor Chernomyrdin in 1994, "does more harm
than good." In an address three years later, President Yeltsin declared that
"the country's continuing problems have been caused by the blind embrace

of the Western-style capitalist ideology and the disregard for traditional social values."[23]

If Western institutions were inappropriate for Russia, did this amount to
Russia's misfortune or blessing? Over the past two centuries, pessimists have
asserted on occasion that Russia's divergence from Western nations doomed
it to backwardness and despotism. More often, though, members of the intelligentsia who uncoupled their country from the West foresaw Russia making its own way toward a splendid future. According to a Slavophile poem,
while a "thick darkness is falling on the distant West," a bright Russian dawn
would follow: "Hear then the call of fate, spring up in a new radiance, awake,
oh somnolent East." In 1861 the Populist Nikolai Shelgunov complained:
"We have already been apes of the French and the Germans; are we now to
be apes of the English? . . . Why cannot Russia arrive at some new order unknown even to America? We not only can, we must."[24] Nearly identical
words issued in the 1990s from officials, intellectuals, and others roused by
nationalist instincts, including the film director Stanislav Govorukhin: "We
have become lackeys to Germany, to the West, especially to the U.S.," he
told an audience at one of his films. "We have to start doing it for ourselves
again." Zyuganov, the Communist Party head, remarked that the United
States could support liberal reformers in Russia as much as it pleased. "But it
won't bring them to power. They will disappear. And Russia will emerge
again," guided by its own lights.[25]

Once Russia had identified its special destination—one based on age-old
Orthodox and rural values, perhaps, or a newer "Eurasian" synthesis of West
and East—nationalists might opt to ignore Europe and America as much as
possible. Russia would need to defend itself from attack, but as long as the
West kept its distance, it remained of minor consequence. A few visionaries,
however, chose a messianic tone, contending that Russia could set an example for its unfortunate neighbors and thereby lead them to a magnificent new
stage of development. They argued, in effect, that while Russia found Western institutions inappropriate, Russian experience would be instructive for
the West and might well save the world.[26] Here unfurled the assumption that
diverse countries should indeed follow the same path—with Russia blazing
it—a view with some resemblance to Bolshevik assurances that the Soviet
Union would lead the world to socialism.

By no means all Russians who rejected Western models turned the tables
by presenting Russia as world savior. Slavophiles and populists focused more
on escaping the West than rescuing it. But if they occasionally suggested
recipes for Western salvation, the instructions required acceptance of the
Russian example. So, too, in the 1990s voices surfaced now and then advo-

cating a culture for Russia that was not only non-Western but that might also benefit all civilizations. When asked what Russia offered the West, Alexander Prokhanov replied: "Russia will keep producing for the world, and particularly the Western world, the idea of a subtle irrationalism, of a universal love, of pan-humanity. All ideas that do not exist in this one-dimensional and rather primitive America." According to Alexander Panarin, "if the future post-industrial society remains technology-centered, then most likely the world will remain American-centered," which has led humanity "to the dead-end of ecological catastrophe." The Western countries, feeling themselves victors in the Cold War, see no need to change their ways, he explained, but Russia in the aftermath of Soviet rule could appreciate criticism of both totalitarianism and techno-industrial society. Thus, Russia was better prepared than the West to shape a desirable community—a point to which Panarin returned with two concluding questions: "Will we find the courage and fervor at the end of the twentieth century to give rise to a civilized alternative, which we promised to the world at the century's beginning? Will the West find the wisdom to recognize the appropriateness of this alternative, to understand the prophetic character of Russian 'traditionalism'?"[27]

Russian thirst for Western models and guidance arose from assorted factors that included circumstances of brief duration at the end of the Soviet era. Gorbachev's policies yielded roughly four years of exposés about a society long accustomed to discourses on the inspiring panorama of Soviet history. People now listened day after day to chronicles of domestic problems (corruption, pollution, homeless children, prostitution, and much else) accompanied by disclosures that numerous projects of Stalin's period, previously concealed from the population or celebrated as triumphs of socialist construction, had led to the starvation, deportation, or death of millions. Thus, by the end of the 1980s new freedoms had discredited the Soviet system without conceiving a more prosperous variant of socialism. The declining standard of living and an uncertain future prompted Russians to seek guidance outside their ranks more readily than at any other juncture in the twentieth century.

Meanwhile, access to the West expanded. Travel, movies, publications, and television advertised a way of life largely prohibited just a few years before. Hard times at home and vivid impressions of Western affluence left Russians receptive to foreign leads, while the West itself, long an exotic and forbidden temptation, appeared suddenly at close range. This applied especially to the United States. As early as the 1920s no other nation had seemed more advanced to Russians, and the passing decades did not eliminate images of

American prowess in diverse endeavors. Nor did Americans shrink from interpreting contemporary events in eastern Europe and the Soviet Union as proof of their system's superiority and its desirability as a guide for others. This American confidence reinforced ebullient Russian expectations in 1991 for nearly everything that bore the label "Made in the USA."

It could not last. An extraordinary episode, the fall of the Soviet Union, had intensified the Russian appetite for Western standards, but the subsequent gorging led to indigestion. Privatization and other "market reforms" did not catapult Russia to prosperity or even maintain levels of consumption that most people had experienced prior to 1985. Whether the blame lay primarily with imprudent foreign advisers, faulty implementation by Russians, or unrealistic expectations for the pace of recovery, the fact remained that most Russians judged themselves worse off as the years passed. American guidance lost its magic aura, and subsequent elections placed parliament under the control of politicians apprehensive over Western influence. To survive politically, Yeltsin dismissed subordinates associated with privatization and spread the word that experiments with "market romanticism" would be curbed. As long as the economy floundered, American "medication" could strike Russians as useless or even as the cause of their distress. "Two years ago," reported the U.S. ambassador to Russia in 1994, "despite our protests, many Russians imagined we in the United States had all the answers; now they know we do not."[28]

For a time, however, at the close of the 1980s and the beginning of the next decade, those leery of the West appeared as cranks, sidestepped by history like monarchists after 1917. These nationalist intellectuals and die-hard devotees of the Soviet regime combined their hostility to popular culture from the United States with immediate suspicion regarding American-inspired economic activities in Russia. "Economic imperialism" had been the Soviet label for charges that American firms preferred impoverished nations with low labor costs and no pressure to improve local working conditions. Year after year, it was said, these countries served the West as little more than sources of cheap labor and raw materials. Citizens who managed to acquire advanced technical skills often disappeared from their native soil, drawn through the "brain drain" into the service of foreign corporations. Thus, concluded a Soviet account, the option offered to "economically weak agrarian or semi-industrial" nations "by the use of American recipes is not a path of independent development but that of perpetuating their status as raw-material appendages of none other but the United States."[29]

When this book appeared in 1985, the Soviet Union itself still seemed immune to exploitation at American hands. Just a few years later, though, the growing presence of American companies encouraged some critics to include Russia in the list of international capitalism's victims. All the familiar abuses, transported from Asia, Africa, and Central America, had now arrived, they insisted, to plague the homeland. Allegations included the use by Western corporations of equipment banned on environmental grounds in Europe or America and the looting of Russian raw materials. Joint ventures with Western companies created only "hyenas feasting on the energy of the Russian nation," thought Alexander Prokhanov.[30] Those who lamented the presence of American companies even before 1991 also wasted no time in questioning the motives of the U.S. government in supporting reform. So undesirable were Western economic recipes, concluded indignant critics, that Washington could only be offering "aid" with the intention of weakening Russia. "By now, it is probably obvious to all," wrote Zyuganov in 1993, "that this liberal model was made for Russia by special order. Only this model provided a blueprint for breaking up a great nuclear power into pieces that 'world civilization' could swallow without fear of choking." As the economy deteriorated in the 1990s, polls discovered similar suspicions spreading beyond xenophobic groups to more than 75 percent of those volunteering opinions by 1996. In the national poll of 1995, cited in previous chapters, 59 percent of the sample agreed with the statement that "the US is utilizing Russia's current weakness to reduce it to a second-rate power and producer of raw materials," while only 27 percent disagreed.[31]

That said, not all indications of America's image and influence turned sour. The same poll in which 59 percent of the respondents suspected American intentions regarding Russia's power and natural resources found that 58 percent *concurred* with the assertion that "the US usually plays a constructive role in world affairs."[32] Opinions also differed wildly when sorted by age, education, and other factors. Among those less than thirty years old, for example, 60 percent "liked" American popular music (24 percent did not), while 74 percent of those over fifty either "never listened" to or "disliked" such entertainment. The following question revealed a similar gulf between the two age groups on the issue of reform: "Some say American society offers a political and socioeconomic example for Russia. To what extent would you agree or disagree with that view?" Approximately 60 percent of the young agreed, and almost exactly the same share of the older voices did not.[33]

Such differences registered in earlier polls as well, and it makes no more sense to claim that all Russians craved Western baubles and advice in 1991 than it does to regard them at the end of the decade as uniformly hostile to American amusements and the goals of reform. Over time, though, certain views lost some of the confidence with which they had earlier reigned, while competing positions won broader support. Clearly, a shift took place during the 1990s away from an uncritical acceptance of nearly anything Western and toward a doubt that foreign solutions were entirely appropriate for Russia. Nationalist appeals in the arts and politics seemed less isolated or eccentric as the years passed, especially in the wake of Vladimir Zhirinovsky's surprising electoral showing at the end of 1993. "Russia's troubles have always come from the West, and today they are still coming from the West," he declared in 1996 and repeated in numerous variations throughout the decade. "Nothing but poor-quality food, poor-quality medicines, and bad advisers who are helping to rob our country quickly are coming from over there."[34]

Still, a New Year's Eve of Stalinist musicals is one thing, while voting for leadership characteristic of 1975 (or 1935) is something else. Zhirinovsky, for that matter, won enough votes to preserve a modest role in parliament for his party, but he ceased to figure prominently in discussions of political influence by the end of the century. For all his antics and those of other nationalist groups, it may be more remarkable that a decade of domestic disarray and international demotion did not produce an even louder call to abandon the nation's Western-inspired political and economic institutions. The nativist sentiments that have dominated this chapter have yet to entrance the entire population. Nor have they monopolized opinion on America in Russia's intellectual tradition. Educated audiences in the century before 1917 read not only the attacks of Slavophiles, Dostoevsky, and Gorky but also numerous accounts that looked more favorably on the United States. A diverse corps of visitors reached America, in other words, and some identified much to endorse. The authors did not achieve the renown of a Dostoevsky, but their articles and books won avid readers in sufficient number to vex Gorky and Dostoevsky himself.

American technology, for instance, a satanic horror in Gorky's "City of the Yellow Devil," dazzled many other travelers. From one end of the century to the other, reports echoed the travelogue of Pavel Svinin, secretary to a Russian diplomat in Philadelphia from 1811 to 1813. "The Americans," he informed Russian readers, "resorted to perfecting various machines, making them simpler and more convenient. In this matter they exhibited creative intelligence of a high order, and, where necessity was the mother of invention, their achievements were extraordinary. Mechanical inventions have completely replaced human hands in the United States."[35] Alexander Lakier, a former official in the Ministry of Justice who traveled through the New World in 1857, came away convinced that "every new mechanical technique, every discovery, is taken into account and applied to the matter at hand, so that nowhere do improvements spread so quickly as in America."[36]

Apart from initiative, energy, and technical cleverness in the United States, Russian observers detected social and political contrasts with Europe—to the Old World's disadvantage. Class distinctions appeared less pronounced than in France or Germany, to say nothing of Russia, where mannerisms, speech, and dress underscored social divisions. A Russian traveler taken with the velocity of American trains in the 1870s added that "there are no classes, private compartments, and so forth. Passengers are accommodated in identical large cars that resemble long waiting rooms very comfortably and sumptuously appointed with an excellent ventilation system." People were not cowed by "social betters" or officials. "The most complete freedom reigns in the car: No one shouts at you, no one points out places where you are permitted or not permitted to stand or sit, no one orders you to come aboard or get off."[37]

Some Russians praised the United States for promoting rather than smothering private enterprise and for protecting rather than trampling individual liberties. In 1904 the historian Pavel Mizhuev published an article, the "Birth of the Great Republic," in which he lauded the scope of popular sovereignty in the United States. No other democracy since antiquity, he declared, had preserved freedom for so long. "Thus, ever since Tocqueville, that is for 70 years, European publicists who are interested in popular freedom follow with rapt attention the vicissitudes of political life in this most remarkable democracy of modern times." Two years later Mizhuev authored a book on the rights of citizens, which a Russian law professor deemed instructive in 1991, when America again seemed a model for reformers. Constitutional safeguards might be suspended from time to time in European democracies, Mizhuev observed, but not in America. There "the people, besides being the source of power, are its only possessor in the full measure as well, while all bodies of authority possess only such authority as are granted to them by the sovereign people in accordance with the Constitution."[38]

Black Americans and union organizers saw a different nation (and their plight did not escape comment from visitors), but the point here is that literate Russians encountered admiration as well as criticism of the United States before 1917. Nativists advocated their favored course for Russia by claiming that America's example discredited the Western road, while other Russians described social and political institutions in the United States that they recommended between the lines for tsarist Russia. Each portrait of America validated a competing image of what Russia ought to be. This choice of options receded in Soviet times, but during the twentieth century's final decade, liberal and nativist views again seized the opportunity to confront each other openly, and for the same reason as before.

Less clear is the relevance of these arguments to broader public opinion. Disputes among intellectuals took place outside the world of the peasantry and did not shape the notions of golden America that lodged in many villages. Variations on the image of an exotic and glittering United States have survived in Russian society, despite decades of Soviet rebuttal, and it remains to be seen how present controversies will affect such fascination. When an émigré writer, Sasha Sokolov, confirmed to readers of a Soviet periodical in 1989 that the United States was "a fantastic country where there's absolutely everything," the thrust of his comments led elsewhere. He emphasized that "for all their prosperity Americans have forgotten about things that are no less important." In fact, Sokolov continued, "you know all those critical outbursts by Soviet journalists about the West? About spiritual poverty, about the power of the 'golden calf,' all those unflattering clichés. We didn't believe them," but those "Soviet journalists turned out to be right about many things."[39] So far, it does not appear that most Russians, whatever their thoughts on U.S. foreign policy, have linked America "where there's absolutely everything" with the desolate nation of "spiritual poverty" described by Sokolov and other critics. Both impressions exist, but the bulk of current evidence suggests that the first predominates in the wider population, as it did a century ago.

At the same time, however, belief in the existence of golden America need not sustain enthusiasm for democratic political institutions or market reforms *in Russia*. Given the disappointing results registered during the Russian Republic's initial decade, who can assume that prevailing conceptions of bounteous America will continue to yield support for "Western" measures? As never before, Russians are judging democracy and market mechanisms by the results attributed to them at home, and detractors can now blame social and economic distress on "foreign," American advice more effectively than the Politburo could saddle "Western imperialism" with problems endured at one time or another by Soviet citizens.[40]

Prosperity and social order may finally emerge to validate the reformers' visions and persuade most Russians to accept private enterprise and multiparty elections without a second thought. But this has not occurred yet, and in the meantime Russian intellectuals, politicians, and the general population continue to face "American questions" more directly than in any previous era. Should economic or political practices from the United States continue to serve as guides for any Russian reforms? Should Russians enjoy American popular culture? Is the American way attractive in the United States itself? As we have seen, numerous answers to these questions crystallized in different segments of society at various periods throughout the twentieth century. Now, early in the twenty-first, when virtually all Russians believe that recent American influence has been substantial, the questions—and answers—will remain as provocative as ever.

Notes

1. Stephanie Baker, "Russia: Entrepreneur Taps into 'Buy Russian' Mood," Moscow, 2 March 1998 (RFE/RL), from David Johnson's Russia List, #2094, 5 March 1998; Adam Tanner, "Tobacco Giants Announce New Russian Investments," Moscow, 16 March 1998 (Reuters), from David Johnson's Russia List, #2112, 17 March 1998; Baltimore Sun, 19 October 1997; Guy Chazan, "Russians Develop Preference for 'Homegrown' Products," Wall Street Journal, 15 January 2001, from David Johnson's Russia List, #5030, 16 January 2001; Amelia Gentleman, "Coke's Russian Invasion Fizzles Out," Observer (UK), 15 October 2000, from David Johnson's Russia List, #4580, 16 October 2000.

2. Baker, "Russia"; Chazan, "Russians Develop Preference."

3. U.S. News and World Report, 26 January 1998, 50, 52; Chicago Tribune, 23 November 1997; Sergei Kostin, quoted in Boston Globe, 15 December 1997.

4. New York Times, 30 December 1995; 12 January 1997; New York Times Magazine, 8 June 1997, 82.

5. Peter Klebnikov, "'Markeeting Imedge': American Popular Culture in the New Russia," World & I 7, no. 7 (July 1992): 642; V. V. Il'in, A. S. Panarin and A. S. Akhiezer, Reformy i kontrreformy v Rossii. Tsikly modernizatsionnogo protsessa (Moscow: Izdatel'stvo Moskovskogo universiteta, 1996), 261, 299.

6. V. P. Lukin and A. I. Utkin, Rossiia i zapad: Obshchnost' ili otchuzhdenie? (Moscow: SAMPO, 1995), 14; Izvestiia, 31 January 1992, 3; New York Times Magazine, 26 July 1987, 50.

7. V. Chistiakov and I. Sanachev, "Troianskii kon'," Nash sovremennik, no. 10 (1988): 130, 138; Pravda, 13 May 1990, 3.

8. Gun'ko, "Dve estetiki," Nash sovremennik, no. 10 (1988): 121; Pravda, 30 July 1992, 3.

9. Aleksandr Lebed', General Alexander Lebed: My Life and My Country (Washington, D.C.: Regnery, 1997), 372; Gennady Zyuganov, My Russia: The Political Autobiography of Gennady Zyuganov (Armonk, N.Y.: Sharpe, 1997), 12.

10. Alexander Solzhenitsyn, "The Exhausted West," Harvard Magazine, (July–August 1978): 22, 24–25.

11. Julian Graffy, "Émigré Experience of the West as Related to Soviet Journals," in Under Eastern Eyes: The West as Reflected in Recent Russian Emigre Writing, ed. Arnold McMillin (New York: St. Martin's, 1992), 132–35 (the quotation is on 135); New York Times, 9 October 1986.

12. F. M. Dostoevskii, Polnoe sobranie sochinenii v tridtsati tomakh (Leningrad: Nauka, 1972–1990), 11:233, Dostoevskii, Polnoe sobranie, 21:107; Fyodor Dostoyevsky, The Brothers Karamazov (Harmondsworth, England: Penguin, 1958), 2:899; Abbott Gleason, "Republic of Humbug: The Russian Nativist Critique of the United States, 1830–1930," American Quarterly 44, no. 1 (March 1992): 8–9.

13. Hans Rogger, "Amerikanizm and the Economic Development of Russia," Comparative Studies in Society and History 23, no. 3 (July 1981): 388; V. Shestakov, "Russkoe otkrytie Ameriki," in Vzaimodeistvie kul'tur SSSR i SShA XVIII–XX vv., ed. O. E. Tuganova (Moscow: Nauka, 1987), 26; Ivan Kireevskii, quoted in Nicholas V. Riasanovsky, Russia and the West in the Teaching of the Slavophiles (Gloucester, Mass.: P. Smith, 1965), 113.

14. Ivan Aksakov, quoted in Riasanovsky, Russia and the West, 114; Hans Rogger, "Russia and the Civil War," in Heard Round the World: The Impact Abroad of the Civil War, ed. Harold Hyman (New York: Knopf, 1969), 183, 240; Gleason, "Republic of Humbug," 7–8, 11–12.

15. Vladimir Korolenko, "Factory of Death: A Sketch" in America through Russian Eyes: 1874–1926, ed. and trans. Olga Peters Hasty and Susanne Fusso (New Haven, Conn.: Yale University Press, 1988),

87–88. See also Hans Rogger, "America in the Russian Mind—or Russian Discoveries of America," *Pacific Historical Review* 47, no. 1 (February 1978): 29–30; Gleason, "Republic of Humbug," 4.

16. Maxim Gorky, "City of the Yellow Devil," in Hasty and Fusso, *America through Russian Eyes*, 135.

17. Gorky, "City of the Yellow Devil," 133–40.

18. Richard Ruland, *America in Modern European Literature: From Image to Metaphor* (New York: New York University Press, 1976), 69. Regarding the diverse factors that helped shape Gorky's stories, see Charles Rougle, *Three Russians Consider America: America in the Works of Maxsim Gor'kij, Aleksandr Blok, and Vladimir Majakovskij* (Stockholm: Almqvist and Wiksell International, 1976).

19. See, for example, G. Lenobl', "Amerikanskie ocherki i pamflety Gor'kogo," *Zvezda*, no. 3 (1948): 82–89. On Nekrasov, Gorky, and Mayakovsky, see "Na perednii krai ideologicheskoi bor'by," *Voprosy literatury*, no. 4 (1963): 15.

20. *New York Times*, 2 May 1996; Klebnikov, "'Markeeting Imedge,'" 641; Zyuganov, *My Russia*, 15.

21. Il'in et al., *Reformy i kontrreformy*, 282–83. See also "Russian Clergyman Says Liberalism Not Always Best," Moscow, 26 January 1999 (Reuters), from David Johnson's Russia List, #3032, 27 January 1999; "Russia's Heritage Sets It Apart; 'Not for Us' Are Western Ways," *Star Tribune*, 29 October 1999, from David Johnson's Russia List, #3595, 30 October 1999; Zyuganov, *My Russia*, 73–74; L. I. Abalkin, [no title], *Voprosy ekonomiki*, no. 3 (March 1997): 4.

22. Lukin and Utkin, *Rossiia i zapad*, 142.

23. "Is Russian Democracy Doomed?" *Journal of Democracy* 5, no. 2 (April 1994): 16; Vladimir Shlapentokh, "Now That the Russian Inferiority Complex Has Faded, It Is Politically Correct in Moscow to Scold the West," 8 January 1998, from David Johnson's Russia List, #2008, 9 January 1998.

24. Riasanovsky, *Russia and the West*, 118; James H. Billington, *Mikhailovsky and Russian Populism* (Oxford: Clarendon, 1958), 47.

25. *New York Times Magazine*, 19 June 1994, 44, 52. See also Tim McDaniel, *The Agony of the Russian Idea* (Princeton, N.J.: Princeton University Press, 1996).

26. *Times* (London), 31 August 1998. An essay in the mainstream newspaper *Nezavisimaia gazeta* described Russia as "a country whose greatness is based on her spiritual, intellectual and moral potential. Only Russia, with her moral position in foreign policy, can oppose the American cowboy style in the international arena. If the U.S. is permitted to act alone, America herself, along with the whole Western civilization, will suffer." Vladimir Shlapentokh, "The Rise of Russian Anti-Americanism after September 2001: Envy as a Leading Factor." This unpublished paper was kindly provided to me by the author.

27. "Western Values Are Clichés," *Transitions* 4, no. 3 (August 1997): 76; Il'in et al., *Reformy i kontrreformy*, 368–69, 377, 391.

28. *U.S. Department of State Dispatch* 5, no. 8 (21 February 1994): 94. See also Edward P. Lazear, ed., *Economic Transition in Eastern Europe and Russia: Realities of Reform* (Stanford, Calif.: Hoover Institution Press, 1995), 146; Peter Truscott, *Russia First: Breaking with the West* (London: Tauris, 1997), 106; Richard C. Schneider, "Privatization in One Country: Foreign Investment and the Russian Privatization Dynamic," *Hastings International and Comparative Law Review* 17, no. 4 (Summer 1994): 700; "Is Russian Democracy Doomed?," 14–15; Suzanne Massie, "To the Russian People, We're Ugly Americans," *Surviving Together* 12, no. 1 (Spring 1994): 6; Eric Shiraev and Vladislav Zubok, *Anti-Americanism in Russia: From Stalin to Putin* (New York: Palgrave, 2000).

29. A. Kortunov and A. Nikitin, *The "American Model" on the Scales of History* (Moscow: Progress, 1985), 183, 188, 190.

30. *Environmental Opposition to Foreign Investment in the USSR* (Washington, D.C.: United States Information Agency, 1989), 10–11; Daniel R. Kempton and Richard M. Levine. "Soviet and Russian Relations with Foreign Corporations: The Case of Gold and Diamonds," *Slavic Review* 54, no. 1

(Spring 1995): 104; "Russia Has Become a Klondike for International Fund Speculators," *Russian Press Digest*, 31 October 1997, from David Johnson's Russia List, #1327, 1 November 1997; Boris Kagarlitsky, "America, Please Leave Us Alone to Solve Our Problems," from David Johnson's Russia List, #2450, 28 October 1998; *New York Times*, 2 May 1996.

31. Zyuganov, *My Russia*, 45; Truscott, *Russia First*, 13; Jerry F. Hough, *Democratization and Revolution in the USSR, 1985–1991* (Washington, D.C.: Brookings Institution Press, 1997), 519; Anatole Shub, *Russian Public Opinions of the U.S. Divide Mainly along Generational Lines* (Washington, D.C.: United States Information Agency, 1996), 3.

32. Anatole Shub, *What Russians Know and Think about America: A Survey in Summer 1995* (Washington, D.C.: United States Information Agency, 1995), 22.

33. Shub, *What Russians Know and Think about America*, 12, 21.

34. Shiraev and Zubok, *Anti-Americanism*, 69.

35. Avrahm Yarmolinsky, *Picturesque United States of America 1811, 1812, 1813. Being a Memoir on Paul Svinin, Russian Diplomatic Officer, Artist, and Author. Containing Copious Excerpts from His Account of His Travels in America with Fifty-two Reproductions of Water Colors in His Own Sketch-book* (New York: William Edwin Rudge, 1930), 7.

36. Aleksandr Lakier, *A Russian Looks at America: The Journey of Aleksandr Borisovich Lakier in 1857*, edited by Arnold Schrier (Chicago: University of Chicago Press, 1979), 81.

37. Lakier, *A Russian Looks at America*, 98; Hasty and Fusso, *America through Russian Eyes*, 62.

38. P. G. Mizhuev, "Zarozhdenie velikoi respubliki," *Russkaia mysl'*, no. 4 (1904): 126; Vladimir A. Kartashkin, "Human Rights and the Emergence of the State of the Rule of Law in the USSR," *Emory Law Journal* 40 (1991): 889, citing P. Mizhuev, *Prava cheloveka i grazhdanina* (1906), 104.

39. Graffy, "Émigré Experience," 133.

40. Diverse voices in Russia and the West have linked Russian hardship to reforms "made in America." See, for example, the transcript of "America's Impact on Russia," a television program in the series *America's Defense Monitor*, first broadcast on 14 June 1998 by the Center for Defense Information; *New York Times*, 1 September 1998; 16 June 1999; *Washington Times*, 24 September 1998; "Mayor Luzhkov Criticizes US Economic Advisers for Crisis," Moscow, 8 December 1998 (Interfax-Moscow), from David Johnson's Russia List, #2515, 12 December 1998; Fritz Ermarth, "Seeing Russia Plain," from David Johnson's Russia List, #3323, 4 June 1999; Alexei Arbatov, "Natsional'naia ideia i natsional'naia bezopasnost'," *Mirovaia ekonomika i mezhdunarodnye otnosheniia*, no. 6 (1998): 8.

CONCLUSION

~

Gud-bai Amerika?

For the first time in history we have the chance to expand the reach of democracy and economic progress across the whole of Europe and to the far reaches of the world.

—Bill Clinton

It will not happen soon, if it ever happens at all, that Russia will become the second edition of, say, the U.S. or Britain in which liberal values have deep historic traditions. Our state and its institutes and structures have always played an exceptionally important role in the life of the country and its people. For Russians a strong state is not an anomaly which should be got rid of.

—Vladimir Putin

In 1893, long before he thought much about Russia, Theodore Dreiser was chosen to accompany a group of twenty schoolteachers to the Chicago World's Fair. He reacted with mixed emotions. The teachers had won a popularity contest sponsored by the St. Louis *Republic,* and Dreiser, a young reporter for the paper, received an assignment to file stories describing their reactions to the exposition. He relished the trip to Chicago, where he had lived for a time, but not the responsibility of guiding a flock of schoolmarms on the tour. However, his pulse quickened when he met the group on the train and discovered the "state's best teachers" to be young women, several of whom he found irresistibly attractive. No longer annoyed by the assignment, he flirted with his charges from beginning to end of their two-week excursion, and in at least one instance reached the point of kisses on a lonely beach. Among the targets of his ardor was Sara White, "a simple country girl," she told him, unwilling to hold his hand at the fair, let alone kiss him, and whom he would later marry.[1]

As Dreiser strolled through the fairgrounds, he let his eyes wander beyond the teachers often enough to appreciate the breathtaking spectacle. The setting (planned to celebrate the four-hundredth anniversary of Columbus's voyages) evoked the grandeur of Athens, he wrote in the *Republic:* "One can understand . . . why the Grecians were proud and how it came that men could mediate the sublime philosophy that characterized the mythic age." At night, when the fair closed, "the great enthusiastic mass tramped its way out and rejoiced that it had been fortunate enough of all the world's children to have seen such a display."[2] Photographs reveal an array of buildings that would still be imposing today. The principal structures, designed in Roman, Romanesque, and Renaissance styles, were finished with a substance that simulated white marble and prompted many to refer to the complex as the "White City." Fourteen main exhibit halls and some two hundred other facilities, arranged over an attractive site in Jackson Park, provided roughly three times the roofed space available at the Paris Exposition, which had introduced the Eiffel Tower in 1889. After sundown, the White City's buildings continued to dazzle crowds under electric lights that would soon alter the appearance of metropolises in the twentieth century. A British journalist said of the panorama, "Nothing that I have ever seen in Paris, in London, in St. Petersburg, or in Rome, could equal the effect produced by the illumination of these great white palaces that autumn night." The fair consumed three times more electric lighting power than the entire city of Chicago and ten times more than the Paris Exposition four years earlier. L. Frank Baum's walk through the lustrous realm reportedly helped inspire him to create the Emerald City of Oz, while the French novelist Paul Bourget professed himself "struck dumb . . . with wonderment" at the "dream city" he surveyed. All the way from New Zealand came another visitor, who left the fair "feeling assured that if I lived to the age of some of the most ancient patriarchs I could never again have a chance of beholding its superior or even its equal."[3]

How things had changed for the United States. Early in the century, as Great Britain led the world into the Industrial Revolution, Americans themselves journeyed across the Atlantic to study mechanical wonders in the mother country. Moncure Robinson made the trip in 1825 to inspect canals and returned a convert to the new gospel of railroads. His letters disclose an awe over British industrial vitality that anticipated the reaction of visitors to the United States several decades later: "New buildings & Manufactories are springing up every where whilst every new scheme abroad is put into operation with English Capital. What a wonderful country." Great Britain's efforts to preserve this technical leadership drew Americans, along with entrepreneurs and governments from continental Europe, into industrial espionage. If no nation has worked harder than the United States in recent decades to prevent the piracy of intellectual property and block the flow of technology to certain regions, this was not the case 150 years earlier.[4]

A quarter-century after Robinson's exclamation, the luster of the machine age still belonged mainly to Great Britain. At London's Crystal Palace exhibition in 1851, America won attention for firearms, vulcanized rubber, agricultural machinery, and a handful of other products, but European accomplishments dwarfed the contribution from the New World. Exhibits from the United States numbered no more than six hundred in a sea of fifteen thousand, and of the 170 Council Medals awarded, Americans received only five. If this harvest of awards seemed paltry, the modest recognition of American achievements served at least to close the fair on a more encouraging note for the United States than it had begun. American participants had not even been able to fill the display space they had requested and found themselves ridiculed in the British press. The English satirical paper *Punch* imagined that gaps in America's presentation might be plugged by supplementary shipments of such items as "the leg of a Multiplication Table" and "the tremendous Wooden Style that separates the American from the English Fields of Literature." In short, there was no denying the fact that, as Horace Greeley put it, America still had more to learn than to teach. According to the *Illustrated London News*, "there are very few of their [American] manufactures which they could hope to sell here. American manufactures of the same kind as those exported from Europe could only be sent as a matter of curiosity by a Government organization. Private individuals seldom take such useless trouble." Two years later, when New York staged a world's fair modeled on the Crystal Palace exhibition, Europeans largely ignored it.[5]

Over the next two decades, however, the United States began to cut a larger figure at international expositions, and did so with growing confidence. By the Philadelphia World's Fair of 1876, celebrating the nation's centennial, no one expected a second century to pass before America made its weight felt abroad. Under the heading "The Centennial's Lesson to Foreigners," a French visitor's assessment included an italicized prediction: "*America will learn to dispense more and more with Europe, and Europe cannot dispense with her. It is veritably like another England rising on the shores beyond the ocean, and menacing old England in all her markets.*" Indeed, commented the British statesman William Gladstone two years later, "there can hardly be a doubt as between the America and the England of the future that the daughter, at some no very distant time, whether fairer or less fair, will be unquestionably yet stronger than the mother."[6]

Such declarations may have sounded premature in 1876, but seventeen years later, at the Chicago World's Fair, many Americans took them in stride. Among those brimming with confidence stood President Grover Cleveland, who delivered an opening address and then pressed a button to send electricity coursing through the fair. In his remarks, Cleveland did not shrink from praising "the stupendous results of American enterprise and activity" and "the magnificent evidences of American skill and intelligence." According to the Chicago Tribune, it was not "idle boasting" when he "called the attention of foreign nations to the fact that 'we not only exhibit the unparalleled advancement and wonderful accomplishments of a young nation, but we have also built the magnificent fabric of a popular government whose grand proportions are seen throughout the world.'"[7] An American journalist, writing in 1901, regretted that "in the last few years we have attained a place [among other nations] that has, perhaps, made us too boastful." But even he did not let modesty inhibit his description of Chicago's fair. "In the mechanical arts and sciences we had, for the most part, no superiors; and in many respects we led easily. . . . Our mechanical pole is longer than that of any other nation, and we knock the most persimmons."[8]

Scores of Russians witnessed these fruits of industrial advancement. "Even the previous world's fairs in Europe cannot compare with the Columbian Exposition," reported the commissioner general of the Russian delegation sent to Chicago. "Here was displayed in full force the productive power of the American people. In particular there advanced to the forefront the engineering, machine-building and architectural successes of the New World." The tsarist government dispatched numerous experts to study Western technology at the fair, and they were joined by tourists, including Peter Tverskoi, whose description of America for Russian readers has already come to our attention. As he roamed the machinery hall, Tverskoi recognized that "undisputed superiority belongs to the United States. It was necessary to see this exhibition in order to fully grasp all this economy of human labor, all this inventiveness in saving human labor and increasing productivity in practically all branches of activity, that contemporary American machinery has achieved."[9]

Meanwhile the principal Russian exhibit, inside the Manufactures and Liberal Arts Building, treated visitors to displays of precious furs, silverware, dishes, bronzes, carpets, amber, silks, satin, and other elegant wares. By all accounts, the pavilion attracted numerous Americans to admire the ornate handiwork of Russian craftsmen. Perhaps it occurred to some of these spectators, as it did to various Russian visitors and Soviet scholars thereafter, that the applause for Russian baubles could not carry far through the din produced by the age of machinery. The White City celebrated railroads and electricity more than mosaics and gilt furniture, leaving Russia's luxury goods to sparkle in a void created by the near absence of any contribution to the advanced technology showcased beside Lake Michigan. In the machinery hall, Tverskoi observed, "there is no Russian section, as if Russia did not exist on the face of the earth. The official catalog does mention a few insignificant Russian exhibits, but they are stuck in some inaccessible corner, and I could not even find them."[10]

At the formal opening of the Russian exhibit on 5 June 1893, Bishop Nikolai of the Russian Orthodox Church complained that "everyone admires the progress of the Americans; everyone marvels at the prosperity of the citizens here, while, on the contrary, when they speak or write about our fatherland, they have trouble finding words to describe its worst qualities." If these pundits developed a more sophisticated understanding of the two civilizations, he explained, they would discover "nothing special at which to be astonished in America and no reason to criticize Russia." As Bishop Nikolai lamented, however, his views did not prevail among Russians who contemplated Chicago's fair. Whatever their thoughts about Russian civilization, they expected to find much worth learning at the Columbian Exposition. Two years earlier, in 1891, the minister of finance advised Tsar Alexander III that Russian industrialists would indeed benefit from study of the exhibits in Chicago and there "receive very useful information for the development of various branches of Russian manufacturing." Several days before the fair opened, the *Chicago Tribune* reported a remark by one of the Russian commissioners that "the Czar anticipates good results for Russia from the Exposition, as it will lead to the importation of American machinery, railway appliances, and agricultural implements much needed in European Russia."[11]

As for the leading countries of Europe, declared a Russian economist shortly after the fair, the spectacle in Chicago chilled them as an indication of their expiring preeminence:

In the course of over two thousand years European culture set the tone for the whole world; but now they fearfully await the moment when America will leave old Europe behind in the main branches of industry. One of the contemporary German publicists notes with despair, "culture, like the sun, moves from east to west. From Babylon, Athens, Rome, it passed to London and Paris, and now is moving across the Atlantic ocean to New York and Chicago." The exposition in Chicago can offer, perhaps, still greater grounds for such gloomy conclusions.[12]

Thereafter, those who favored the economic modernization of Russia might well concur with the renowned chemist Dmitry Mendeleev, who in 1899 advocated "catching up with America" as a national goal. The United States soon became the premier symbol of an industrial juggernaut—so much so that in 1913 Alexander Blok chose the title "New America" for a poem about the birth of a Russian nation that would be propelled to unprecedented heights by the vitality characteristic of young civilizations. Two years later, the bulletin of the Society for Promoting Friendly Relations between Russia and America, founded by an assortment of Russian businessmen, politicians, and scholars, advised that their homeland could attain the standing of a great power only by emulating American industrial practices, not the less ambitious methods of western Europe.[13] In similar fashion, Nikolai Borodin (an engineer who twenty-two years earlier had attended the Columbian Exposition) described Europeans as lacking the industrial vision that was characteristic of America and that, some day, Russia would share. Adventuresome men descended from the heroes of James Fenimore Cooper and Mayne Reid propelled industry in the United States, he asserted, thereby creating an American entrepreneur who "astonishes the world by the boldness of his undertakings and the genius with which these are carried out, as well as by their breadth of scale, one that is unknown in Europe, but more comprehensible and close only to us Russians."[14]

If confidence in Russia's economic potential eluded visitors to Chicago in 1893, many who toured the Soviet pavilion at the New York World's Fair in 1939 formed a different impression of the nation's aptitude. Industrial accomplishments of the early five-year plans filled the exhibit halls and provided grounds for Soviet claims that the "world of the future" could be glimpsed in the East. By 1958, in Brussels, those on hand for the initial fair of the postwar era had reason to believe that Soviet technological aspirations had been realized. No longer a quaint repository for amber, furs, and other baubles as Russia had seemed to crowds in Jackson Park sixty-five years earlier, the Soviet Union presented itself convincingly in Brussels as a modern power of the first rank. The nation's representatives, like American commentators in Chicago for the Columbian Exposition, described the display as proof of their society's eminence—and they had much to celebrate. Crowds marveled at Soviet depictions of the world's first atomic station, the largest synchrophasotron, the first jets for civilian use, computer equipment, and a good deal more—while in the background, throughout the exhibit, pulsed the "beep . . . beep . . . beep" of a signal from Sputnik I, the world's pioneer of the space age.[15]

"Standing in the throng of visitors to the Soviet pavilion, you feel considerable patriotic pride in our socialist homeland, firmly holding a leading role in scientific and technical progress," reported *Pravda.* "Everywhere is heard exclamations of astonishment, approval, and delight." Soviet newspapers quoted enthusiastic messages left in the visitors' book, including the remarks of an American impressed by "the high level of development of Soviet industry." Over at the neighboring American pavilion, noted *Pravda,* officials chose to introduce the American way of life by greeting crowds with a fashion show. Perhaps such pageants attracted some interest, the paper granted, but "many visitors, especially our Soviet tourists, are disappointed by the skimpy display of technical novelties" provided by the United States. Although *Pravda* may have underestimated the appeal of American attire (and popular culture in general), tens of thousands of people did flock to the Soviet exhibits on opening day, prompting *Izvestiia* to declare that "the success of the Soviet pavilion is already evident. The majority of Belgian and foreign newspapers say so."[16]

Among these journalists numbered a *New York Times* correspondent, Howard Taubman, who described the Russians in Brussels as "confident and optimistic, fresh from such scientific triumphs as the launching of their sputniks. . . . They are showing their big machines." Taubman himself found the exhibits heavy-handed, but he allowed that they disseminated an image of spirited resolve and progress: "On this key question—the all-important one of aim—the Russians outstrip us. Like it or not, we must face up to the fact." While some visitors resisted Soviet ebullience, concluded Taubman, "many cannot help but be impressed and perhaps overwhelmed by this representation of a huge and powerful nation." More quietly, the U.S. Information Agency also expressed concern, as in a confidential report that "the U.S. exhibit at the Brussels Fair was outranked in audience preference by several of its competitors and in particular by the presentation of the Soviet Union." "Catch and surpass" no longer appeared a hopeless slogan, and Nikita Khrushchev said as much to an audience in Hollywood the following year: "When Ford helped us build the Gorky Automobile Plant, we ruined quite a few machines before learning to make automobiles. But now we, your ex-pupils, have sent a rocket into outer space and a Soviet pennant has now reached the moon. Not bad pupils, are we?"[17]

At the beginning of the twentieth century, who could have anticipated this new Soviet state that posed as a technological showcase for the world?

With speed of the sort relished by modernist poets, another superpower had soared to join America. Now, Moscow proclaimed, the United States no longer eclipsed all others—an assertion that seemed plausible in many corners of the world. Even in the United States, by the end of Dwight Eisenhower's presidency experts in the Central Intelligence Agency and other offices described a robust Soviet economy growing at roughly three times the annual rate of its American rival.[18] Surely no one in attendance at the Brussels Fair felt confident that within a few decades the Soviet giant would lie in fragments, dismissed near and far as a land of economic stagnation.

Yet, as early as the 1960s, leaders in Moscow voiced a need to obtain larger infusions of technology from abroad, and their efforts in this regard gained more notice with every decade.[19] In 1985, shortly after Mikhail Gorbachev became the Soviet Union's final leader, officials invited American engineers from the Ford Motor Company and USX, a steel company, to consider the feasibility of modernizing the plants at Gorky and Magnitogorsk, built with American assistance half a century before. In each case the engineers were surprised to discover how little the layout of the factories had changed since the 1930s. Even some of the original manufacturing equipment remained in service until the 1970s at Gorky, which Ford engineers dubbed a museum to the art of automotive assembly.[20] Outside certain narrow sectors of the economy, the Soviet Union could not match Western innovation, and the cry of "catch and surpass" rang ever more hollow.

Toward the end of his life, Khrushchev himself conceded to a tape recorder that "there is apparently some great defect in our system." Despite the nation's multitude of scientists and engineers, "we still need to buy the best things abroad." "It makes you think," he added, and it also left him "saddened and envious." How could this have happened? The Soviet Union had mounted Herculean campaigns and celebrated substantial accomplishments during the fifty-two years since the October Revolution, yet the Kremlin had not kept pace with the world's most advanced countries—including adversaries defeated in World War II. "We have no cause to brag about our technology and science," Khrushchev concluded. "Our scientists know, probably better than I do, how we are being propped up by scientists from the capitalist countries."[21]

For centuries, Russian rulers have launched periodic drives to overtake the West, sometimes with sacrifices and achievements of astonishing scale. The problem with such campaigns in the past (from the state's point of view) has been the nation's inability to sustain technological advancement following a massive dose of foreign expertise. Even the most dramatic surges under Peter the Great and Stalin eventually left the nation peering into the distance again at the backs of fleeter rivals. Yegor Gaidar, prime minister during the period of the most ambitious Western-inspired reforms in the early 1990s, said as much after President Yeltsin dismissed him from the government:

> Russia's race for a place in the civilized world recalls Achilles' chase after the tortoise—through superhuman effort, Russia would manage to "catch up and overtake," especially in military technology. Yet the world would "unnoticeably" but steadily move on, and again after disgraceful and torturous setbacks the country would "regroup for a leap" and make another lurch, and everything would be repeated.[22]

Why did these modernization efforts fail to keep pace with foreign standards? Many countries, including the United States, have borrowed from more advanced outsiders, and some mastered their acquisitions sufficiently to become successful in the eyes of other ascendant states. This was the confident expectation of early Soviet leaders, but it crumbled in disappointment. Explanations for the Russian (and especially Soviet) frustration generally boil down to a common theme: an autocratic government, the driving force in the developmental surges, tended in the longer run to retard innovation. The centralized state may have been effective at channeling resources into a few top-priority endeavors, but its structure inhibited creativity, or the application of creativity, elsewhere. With decision making monopolized by a relatively small number of people, economic advancement depended more than elsewhere on these officials identifying and advocating promising alternatives to established methods—which did not happen often enough in Russia or the Soviet Union. Leaders meddling in complex scientific or economic projects could do more harm than good by stifling auspicious options whose merits lay beyond their ken.[23]

Indeed, the system tended to encourage suspicion of departures from the tried and true. A safe recipe for success centered on fulfilling (or appearing to fulfill) the existing plan with familiar techniques that would not focus attention on oneself in the event of disappointing results. In most areas of endeavor, the Soviet system provided scant competitive pressure to spur innovation and productivity, as people had little fear of losing markets or jobs. Apart from fields of vital importance to the state (military projects and international athletics, for example), where the government bestowed what rewards it could for successful competition, prevailing incentives pointed people away from novel initiatives. Even when talented researchers devised new theories and techniques, the tenuous links between research and production frustrated diffusion of ideas. Researchers did their jobs (and fulfilled plans) by dreaming up theories or prototypes. After that, they did not promote their discoveries, and factory directors rarely chanced failure by embracing unusual methods—if they learned about them at all. Incentives to attempt the unconventional remained more widespread among the nation's foreign rivals.

The reforms of the 1990s may be seen as another attempt to close the gap through more fundamental Westernization than anything previously attempted in Russia or the Soviet Union. Initial results satisfied no one, and within a few years many American observers joined Russians in expressing their disappointment, often placing primary responsibility on formulas hatched in the United States. "We were so supremely confident in what we were saying," concluded Deborah Anne Palmieri, president of the Russian-American Chamber of Commerce in the wake of the bank and currency crisis of August 1998. "Guess what? It didn't work." Stephen Cohen of New York University maintained that "ever since the US government launched an inherently doomed crusade seven years ago to transform post-Communist Russia into a replica of the American system, it has been only a matter of time before that missionary arrogance led to disaster and clamorous shouts of 'Who lost Russia?'" Duke University's Jerry Hough, another prominent political scientist, saw things in a similar light. "The real scandal," he argued, "is that the corruption [in Russia], much of which has been 'legal,' is the logical consequence of the policy the West imposed on Russia as a condition of its aid."[24]

Even those who attributed the economic disarray to Russian shortcomings—the nation's leaders, perhaps, or the legacy of Soviet practices—concluded, in the words of Harvard's Marshall Goldman, that "the patient is dying." Strobe Talbott himself, while not prepared to write off the patient or lambaste the doctors, voiced regret to an audience at Oxford University in 2000 that Russia's current "lawlessness" has, "quite literally, given a bad name to democracy, reform, the free market, even liberty itself."[25] Boris Yeltsin, too, confessed disappointment over the course of events. His poignant resignation address on the last day of the century asked Russians "to forgive me for not fulfilling some hopes of those people who believed that we would be able to jump from the grey, stagnating, totalitarian past into a bright, rich and civilised future in one go. I myself believed in this. But it could not be done in one fell swoop. In some respects I was too naive."[26]

Did this amount to a eulogy for the reforms? Yeltsin had not repudiated the goals of a democratic political system and an economy with a substantial private sector; nor did his successor, Vladimir Putin. Both men insisted, as Yeltsin put it a year earlier, that "there is no other path for Russia."[27] Some ongoing programs even recalled the heyday of reform, as thousands of Russian politicians, officials, and judges continued to make American-sponsored visits designed to study life and government in the United States of the twenty-first century. Talks between Presidents Putin and Bush in the spring of 2002 yielded a joint statement endorsing "government-supported exchange programs" through which "more than 50,000 Russian students, scientists, legislators and others have been hosted by families and communities in all 50 American states" over the past decade. During 2001 alone "about 1,000 Russian entrepreneurs visited the United States to exchange experience and develop mutually profitable ties with their American hosts," the two presidents noted, before expressing their approval that "these business exchanges are set to increase significantly this year."[28]

Back in Russia, the financial crisis of August 1998 chastened American firms but did not drive most of them from the country. Within a few months, McDonald's had revived efforts to enlarge its Russian network, which already included forty-five restaurants in greater Moscow alone. By the early twenty-first century, the chain extended far into the provinces, as headquarters developed plans to add some two dozen outlets each year. The original establishment, whose line of patrons awaiting "holy communion" had so upset Alexander Rutskoi, remained the busiest in the world. Meanwhile, the Ford Motor Company entered a new stage in its long relationship with the land of tsars, commissars, and presidents. Toward the end of 2002, not far from St. Petersburg, it became the first foreign automaker to own as well as build an assembly plant in the Russian Republic.[29]

As for consumption of American popular culture, nothing suggested that most Russians had reached the point of indigestion, whatever the pain registered by some critics. Hollywood blockbusters still dominated Russian theaters in the summer of 2002, with one Russian director complaining that distributors in his country showed no interest at all in domestic movies. "They tell us: Learn to film like they do in America!"—much as others had urged in the 1920s. Even on television, where considerations of cost drove Russians to watch most of their movies, fully a third of the total shown in 1999 were American. Sitcoms and cartoons from the United States also remained prominent, as did American music. Britney Spears, the Backstreet Boys, and other American performers continued to figure in Russian MTV's top-twenty countdown, prompting one observer to marvel in 2001 that "even kids in villages I visit are fans" of Spears. She added that "many of the top pop and rock people here have videos that include footage of trips to America. This appears to be a sign of having made it."[30] The fact that such things—exchange visits of politicians and entrepreneurs, along with American popular culture's broad floodplain—attracted far less comment abroad than they did in the early 1990s could be taken as a measure of progress by supporters of Westernization. The remarkable had become routine.

Still, there was no pretending that the zeal for reform, so palpable in 1992, continued to animate many people a decade later. Russian journalists and politicians were now more likely to complain about American arrogance than to rhapsodize over an American model. The new measures and institutions cherished by reformers at the close of the Soviet era had not come to life with the ease or the results they had expected. Goals and strategies that made sense in America (and some that did not) often failed to take root and flourish in Russia. The jury system, despite years of effort to transplant it from the United States, functioned in only 422 Russian cases as late as 1999 and in only nine of eighty-nine administrative regions by 2002. Privatization enriched a few and satisfied almost no one else, while a Russian banker, brimming with suggestions acquired during a period of training in America, heard colleagues balk after her return: "Forget about all this. This is Russia, not the U.S."[31] As Yeltsin acknowledged upon resigning, the road to prosperity had not appeared so tortuous at the outset of his presidency, when hopes soared that Russia could absorb Western ways expeditiously and then share in the affluence of the United States and other wealthy nations.

As early as the eighteenth century, a small number of Russians looked to America and thought more of politics than economics. They included Alexander Radishchev, a passionate critic of Russian serfdom who did not let his abhorrence of slavery in the former British colonies prevent him from writing an *Ode to Liberty* (1783), lauding America's freedom as a goal for Russia:

> To thee, epic land,
> Toward thee my burning soul strives,
> Where Liberty lay trampled,
> Bent with the yoke of oppression;
> Have your rejoicing! but we suffer here!
> What you have, indeed, is what we thirst for;
> Your example has revealed the dream.
> I am not party to your glory—
> But, since at least my spirit is free,
> Would that your shores could cover my ashes![32]

Even a Russian tsar, Alexander I (1801–25), showed an interest in American constitutional provisions. Writing to President Thomas Jefferson in 1804, he noted that "at all times I nourished a very high esteem for your nation which knew well enough how to use its independence particularly by giving itself a free and wise constitution which insures the happiness of all and that of every one in particular."³³ Two years later, when thanking Jefferson for some materials on the American constitution, he emphasized the seriousness of his intent to enact reform in Russia. "It is very satisfying for me to be able to add to the testimony of my own conscience, the fairness with which you consider my intentions, and this feeling should be for you a sure guarantee that these intentions will never change. If they should be crowned with the success towards which my most serious efforts are directed, it is partly in your approval that I shall seek my reward."³⁴ Alexander's sentiments did not confine themselves to private correspondence. They moved him on occasion to allow prominent officials to draft constitutional documents for Russia that drew on American precedent, especially in sections concerned with the separation of powers, federalism, and civil liberties.³⁵

In the end, though, Alexander could not bring himself to accept measures that would limit his own authority, and the constitutional propositions languished without his signature. Frustration over the stunting of reforms led a small number of noble conspirators to rebel in December 1825, after Alexander's death. Some had served as officers in the war with Napoleon (1812–15), during which Alexander appeared to promise new freedoms if the nation rallied to defeat the French conqueror. Marching from Moscow to Paris with the Russian army, the officers witnessed Western liberties that surpassed the meager rights of the population back home. When the war ended and Alexander excluded Russia from those countries he permitted to enact constitutions, liberal hopes wilted. The awkward insurrection in St. Petersburg and southern Russia collapsed almost at once, but the subsequent investigation of these "Decembrists" by the government of the next tsar, Nicholas I, proved more tenacious—and showed the United States among the Decembrists' inspirations.

During the years before their rebellion, future Decembrists met frequently to discuss political events in Europe and America. Their ideas and their militancy stemmed from diverse sources, not always related to the United States, but references to America do reside in the documents they left behind. Respect for George Washington, Benjamin Franklin, and other founding fathers merged with more specific interest in constitutional provisions devised in the United States. "A constant topic of conversation among us," asserted a participant in southern Russia, "was that the American Constitution is the best model for Russia." Not all agreed, of course, but the most famous of the Decembrists' draft constitutions, prepared by Nikita Muravev of the St. Petersburg circle, drew numerous features directly from the American example. Once the rebellion had been crushed, Nicholas I and his officials interrogated the Decembrists to discover what had led them to such an outrage. Here, too, references to America mingled with other factors described by the prisoners in response to such questions as: "When and from where did you acquire liberal ideals?" Pavel Pestel, leader of the southern Decembrists, replied by attributing his republicanism to a list of influences ranging from the cruel nature of Russian serfdom to the work of European political philosophers and the course of European history. To this he added that "all newspapers and books praised so much the increase of happiness in the United States of America, ascribing it to their political system, that I took it to be clear proof of the superiority of the republican form of government."[36]

Decembrist admiration for the United States as a land of political liberties arose decades before anyone thought of America as a model of industrial advancement. But even in the early twentieth century, when Russian impressions of America centered more on wealth and technology, the nation's small corps of liberals eyed American freedoms with interest reminiscent of the Decembrists. A few months after the outbreak of revolution drove Nicholas II from the throne in 1917, Prince Georgii Lvov, head of the new Provisional Government, declared that "for decades of darkness and oppression America has been our ideal of freedom and intellectual and material development; rather, not our ideal, for we had considered it unattainable, but a remote fairy tale of happiness." Now, he continued, Russia had matched America's level of freedom in a single leap and could set out on "the slower but not impossible task to overtake her in education, material progress, culture, and respect for order. We are on the right track." Shortly after the United States became the first nation to formally recognize the Provisional Government, its new foreign minister, Pavel Miliukov, responded to the Americans: "I have been more than once in your country and may bear witness that the ideals which are represented by the Provisional Government are the same as underlie the existence of your own country. I hope that this great change which has come to Russia will do much to bring us closer together than we have ever been before."[37]

The American ambassador radiated optimism on this score as he cabled from the Russian capital at the passing of the monarchy: "The six days between last Sunday and this have witnessed the most amazing revolution . . . the practical realization of that principle of government which we have championed and advocated." A few months thereafter, in words similar to those chosen seventy-five years later by others in the State Department, he added: "The Russian people have been in a dream or a drunk and are now beginning to awaken or sober up. I have never despaired of their ability to organize a Government on proper lines if guided and assisted by us." So thought former secretary of state Elihu Root, who led an American delegation to Russia in the summer of 1917. "Please say to the president," he reported, "that we have found here an infant class in the art of being free containing 170 million people and they need to be supplied with kindergarten material; they are sincere, kindly good people, but confused and dazed." President Woodrow Wilson could not have been surprised at this communication, for he had already advised Congress that Russia "was always known by those who knew it best to have been always in fact democratic at heart."[38] Now it seemed (as it would again in the early 1990s) that Russia's government might look to the United States as a political model as well as an industrial leader.

Several months later, a tide of revolution swept away the feeble Provisional Government and deposited a new Bolshevik regime with no zest for "bourgeois democracy." Most of the remaining twentieth century appeared as infertile for Russian liberal aspirations as had the nineteenth. In 1979 the *New York Times* bureau chief in Moscow, David Shipler, declared that while "a great infatuation has developed for the material goods and popular styles of the United States, . . . deeply rooted values that have prevailed since Czarist times foster a mystical respect for central authority, a yearning for order and unanimity, a distaste for disagreement and diversity, a dread of any turmoil of ideas." As a result, "Western ideas of democracy remain alien, incomprehensible and unattractive to broad masses of Russians." More specifically, "the Moscow teenagers who sport dungaree jackets with American flags sewn on the sleeves are rarely enchanted with American-style elections. The millions who listen to the Voice of America seldom see virtue in a free press. Many more risk imprisonment for illegal dealing in American goods than are willing to face jail for advocating free speech." Hope had faded that the proliferation of exchange programs with Western nations in the 1970s "would open the Soviet Union," Shipler concluded, in a tone that discouraged any optimism over democracy's potential in Russia.[39]

At the time of Shipler's assessment, Western observers tended to accept claims that Soviet officials and the general population had long craved American technology and popular culture, respectively, but had shown little interest in democracy. No one in 1979 foresaw Gorbachev's reforms, less than ten years away, to say nothing of the Russian Republic that followed. These developments have encouraged scholars to credit exchange programs and other Western contact with more potency than Shipler supposed in "opening" the Soviet Union to the United States and the West.[40] But did this "opening" reveal a thirst for democracy, which Shipler felt the nature of Russian history had discouraged?

Scholarly debate persisted throughout the 1990s and into the following century on numerous themes regarding democratization—the proper democratic model, for instance, and the grounds for considering Russia a democracy at one point or another since 1991.[41] The more basic issue, central in Shipler's comments, remained the question of whether the Russian people *desired* democracy (taken to mean freedom of speech and other civil liberties together with the right to periodically elect government officials). Some opinions updated Shipler's doubt in this regard, notably the contribution from sociologist Tim McDaniel in his *Agony of the Russian Idea* (1996): "No social groups or political forces committed to economic and political Westernization or able to carry out such a project ever matured within the Communist system, nor do they exist now." McDaniel disputed claims that "the broad masses want a peaceful transition to a Western-type society and that they are ready to make temporary sacrifices for this goal," finding it "more accurate to say that, although there are polar extremes of committed democrats and staunch Communists, the painful transition period has created an overall mood of skepticism and uncertainty about all political ideologies, institutions, and leaders." According to Grigory Vainshtein of the Institute of World Economy and International Relations in Moscow, "ordinary Russian citizens perceive the absurdities and defects of the current political system as characteristic of genuine democracy. In this environment, the democratic idea turns out to be increasingly discredited."[42]

Vainshtein reached his conclusion by 1994, but others clung longer to optimism regarding Russian desires. No one did so more steadfastly than Strobe Talbott, who in 1995 informed the Senate that "a strong democracy" combined with respect for "human and civil rights" are "the wishes of the great majority of the people of Russia." Two years later Jerry Hough took a different tack by arguing that "in fact, the Russian people strongly supported democratization after 1989. When they finally turned against the 'democrats,' their responses in public opinion surveys made it clear they were rejecting authoritarian dictatorship masquerading as democracy, not democracy itself." By the beginning of the twenty-first century, a pair of scholars felt compelled to warn against the formation of "a new conventional wisdom" holding that disappointment with the reforms of the 1990s had "fueled mass disenchantment with democratic norms and brought authoritarianism back into repute." The two, Timothy Colton and Michael McFaul, allowed that "Russian democratic institutions are performing miserably, . . . especially since Putin's ascent to power," but the problems, they contended, "are not caused by, or for that matter consistently reinforced by, popular attitudes toward democracy." Russians may "in many ways share our negative assessment of the way their national institutions work," but "it would be wrong to jump to the conclusion that they single-mindedly spurn democratic values and ideas per se."[43]

Although the debate will continue, few would dispute that voting rights and civil liberties unthinkable during Shipler's watch took root in Russia and survived an initial decade of economic hardship. If nothing else, "democracy" developed more resilience than it enjoyed in 1917. But how long it could last without prosperity, or at least optimism, reaching much of the population remained a question often asked, and impossible to answer, during the Russian Republic's infancy. Analysts could only add that in the face of intractable disarray, Russians would not be the first to turn their hopes to an authoritarian remedy.

Whichever direction Russia moves along the authoritarian-democratic spectrum, various forms of American influence will continue to affect the country's development. A democratic Russia would share much of the general European intake of American exports—popular culture, especially, but with American practices gradually more evident as well in law, business, political consulting, and other areas. Unlike smaller European states, however, a prosperous and democratic Russia would also desire an international standing on par with the superpower across the Atlantic, ensuring that the theme of America as measuring stick and rival would emerge in new guise from the Soviet rubble. Something besides "communist aggression" would have to explain the persistence of certain tensions previously associated with the Cold War.

Should Russia steer toward autocracy, the nation would experience a voyage with more similarities to its past, and the issue of American influence would acquire a stronger resemblance to patterns of Soviet and tsarist vintage. Beyond competition with the United States, expected to some degree from any revived Russian state, an authoritarian regime would face a question posed often since the Muscovite centuries that preceded Peter the Great: Does contact with the West strengthen or weaken the country? In other words, could Moscow work with foreign governments, businesses, and experts to obtain the equipment and technical knowledge necessary to compete internationally without at the same time opening doors to Western toxins—political principles, religions, cultural pursuits, and so forth—that would threaten the essence of the state and society prized by its leaders? Past experience predicts frustration for officials determined to confine Western influence to narrow channels.

If an autocratic Russian government's appetite for American technical expertise swelled in the twenty-first century, its tolerance would diminish not only for Western political and economic doctrines but also for American popular culture. Officials anywhere commonly resist the intrusion of an opponent's culture, and even America's NATO allies complain on occasion (some more loudly than others) about the Americanization of European languages and patterns of life. An authoritarian government can exist while enduring a good deal of foreign popular culture, as did the Soviet Union in the 1920s, but the more the United States is cast as a rival, and the bolder grows Russian talk of competition, the more discomforting would become the continued appeal of American amusements and symbols. The Soviet experience does not tell a successor autocracy how to respond. Instead it reveals complications awaiting an official antidote to American movies, television, music, magazines, and clothing. Repression would diminish the visibility of these products but not their attraction and would restore the aura of independence or defiance they conveyed before 1991. Even the use of English expressions—a target of President Putin's Russian Language Council in 2000 and of occasional legislation thereafter—would acquire new significance if the government ever revealed a sustained determination to ban such words.[44]

Late in the Soviet era a Russian rock group, Nautilus Pompilus, performed the hit "Farewell Letter," whose refrain begins *"Gud-bai Amerika"*:

> Good bye America—oh!
> Where I have never been
> Good bye forever
> Take a banjo and play farewell to me.
>
> Your washed out jeans
> Became too small for me
> We were taught for so long
> To love your forbidden fruits
> Good by, America—oh
> Where I will never be.[45]

The song bids farewell to the America that existed for youths growing up in the Soviet Union during the decades following World War II—an inaccessible America whose blue jeans, records, and other black-market treasures enticed Russians and spurred them to imagine a wondrous and remote land. Now, with the real United States in reach and Soviet cultural prohibitions dismantled, the mythical America of the Soviet counterculture has evaporated. There remains in the song only a nostalgic remembrance of an earlier age's forbidden images and pleasures, no longer off-limits and thus stripped of a symbolism that had aroused Russians for generations.

Americas of the imagination persist around the world, fulfilling a human need to believe in the existence of a locale free of familiar problems. On occasion the fabled images have also motivated people to labor tirelessly in their homelands, seeking to match or exceed the achievements they fancied in the New World. Others departed for the United States or emigrated "internally" by finding solace in the supposed existence of a promised land outside their own. Throughout the twentieth century, despite frequent broadcast of America's shortcomings, the spell survived in many countries and complicated efforts of Soviet rulers to mobilize their own people. In a new Russian homeland whose previous government appropriated much of the nation's resources striving to catch and surpass that shimmering America, another forced march to do so might eventually serve to renew the distant glow and recall the attraction of Nautilus Pompilus's forbidden fruit.

In 1871 Grand Duke Alexei, the fourth son of Tsar Alexander II, arrived in New York aboard the Russian warship *Svetlana*. He may not have desired this opportunity to visit America, for it had been arranged to separate him from a lover. She was Alexandra Zhukovskaia, daughter of his father's former tutor, and thus inappropriate as a wife for a member of the august Romanov family. Rumors circulated that the young couple had married secretly in Italy the previous year, but if so the marriage was not recognized in Russia and was soon annulled. As a precaution, Alexander ordered his son off to tour the world on the *Svetlana*, which brought him to New York harbor and the first of many grand receptions in the American cities on his itinerary. In Washington, D.C., President Grant struck Alexei as ill-mannered, but Alexei bore the meeting with a civility that served him well on numerous tours of waterworks, factories, and stockyards scheduled by eager civic leaders from Boston to Denver and Milwaukee to New Orleans. The pace may have tired Alexei on occasion, and he was certainly puzzled by the American republic's enthusiasm for foreign royalty, but he also enjoyed some of the outings planned by his hosts. Travel through the Wild West, which included several days of buffalo hunting with General Custer, Buffalo Bill, and a group of Sioux braves, remained a high point of the tour. In the end, Alexei felt moved to inform others in his party that the United States and Russia shared a variety of physical features responsible for a similarity in the character of the two peoples.[46]

He was not the first Russian to reach this conclusion. During the presidency of James Madison, a Russian diplomatic secretary surmised that "there are no two countries more alike than Russia and the United States," and this opinion survived both the Russian Revolution and the fall of the Soviet Union. In 1984 the writer Ales Adamovich decided that "if there is a people that resembles us more than any other it is the Americans," while eleven years later a new Russian millionaire insisted that "Russians feel closer to Americans than Europeans." Pitirim Sorokin, a Russian-American sociologist, asserted during World War II that the continental expanse of the two countries "favors broad mental horizons, vast perspectives, freedom from a narrow and meticulously calculated mentality, from the parsimonious policy in the economic, political, and sociocultural fields so common in the case of the small powers." Others, including a deputy editor of the newspaper *Izvestiia*, compared traits of individual Russians and Americans: "Both are generous and carefree. An Englishman will never talk to a stranger on a train. But you start talking to an American after a minute. After 20 minutes you're friends, and after 40 minutes you're drinking together. Russians are the same." A trip to San Francisco late in the Soviet era convinced a *Pravda* correspondent that "even though our two peoples are separated by the Pacific Ocean, they are in essence very similar to one another—in their broadness of nature, native wit, zeal for work, and love of their country."[47]

Belief in an affinity with America intensified following the collapse of the Soviet Union, when a Western market economy and democracy became Russia's goal. Neither the Soviet nor tsarist regimes had ever desired such an outcome, yet no nation seemed more eager than Russia in 1991 to follow a path into the Western community recommended by the United States. The two nations now shared economic and political objectives as well as the physical and psychological traits often claimed before. Thus, as Nautilus Pompilus bid *gud-bai* to one mythic America, another candidate, this time in the guise of a friend and benefactor, rushed to take its place. Prosperity appeared within reach, no longer forbidden and abstract. Amid deteriorating conditions in the Soviet Union, America became the hot ticket—indeed, the escape ticket in "American Boy," a popular song of the day, describing the desire of a Russian woman to find an American lover and emigrate to the land of plenty. Never in the Soviet period had the obstacles to such liaisons been lower, and she hoped to capitalize.

> (*Chorus, sung in English*)
> American boy, American joy
> American boy for all this time
> American boy, I'll go away with you
> I'll go away with you,
> Moscow goodbye

(in Russian)
We have no happiness in our private lives
We come to no purpose in our years
Somewhere my prince is across the border
I wait for you, come fast to me

(Chorus)
I am a simple Russian girl
I have never been outside the country
Don't sleep in America, my boy
Come and take me, that's all
I will cry and laugh when I sit in your Mercedes.
I will be swimming in riches.
American boy, American joy. . . .[48]

America had become a tangible oasis or savior fast approaching, an image that surfaced in the Russian media during the extraordinary beginning of the twentieth century's final decade.

Within a few years, though, pop music produced a response titled "Mother, I Love a Russian." Now American boys did not interest the singer, who dismissed her mother's nagging advice to marry someone from the United States: "Mama, what good are these States to us? / Mama, here one can live well too." And the refrain: "Mama, everything's all right; what do we need these States for?"[49]

By the summer of 2000 the popular Russian movie *Brother 2* not only saw the United States as unnecessary, it reveled in contempt for golden America and emphasized the point through ironic use of the *"Gud-bai Amerika"* refrain. An American villain in *Brother 2* swindles a Russian hockey player in Chicago, prompting a group of Russians to set out for the United States to avenge the injustice. After doing so in a manner that left no question about the director's debt to Hollywood action films, the heroes board a plane to return home. In parting, one of them aims an obscene gesture at an American official, and the soundtrack signals the movie's end with *"Gud-bai Amerika,"* no longer suggesting any of the nostalgia intended originally by Nautilus Pompilus.[50]

Russian infatuation with America faded during the 1990s, but did this mean that most (or many) Russians turned hostile toward Americans and the United States? The evidence is mixed, with an answer depending much on the wording of a question and the month in which it was asked. Many commentators, Western and domestic, argued that Russians en masse blamed the United States for misguided economic advice or even intentional efforts to weaken Russia.[51] This analysis cannot be dismissed, and it has found support in some polls, as noted in chapter 8. Yet opinion remained volatile in the

1990s, and more Russians tended to pin responsibility for economic setbacks on their own officials when questioned by pollsters during the winter of 1998–99. While displaying little favor for foreign investment in Russia, they most often cited President Yeltsin personally or the Russian government in general as the authors of their hardship. Only 1 percent named foreigners or foreign capital. Three years later, another airing of the question "Who is to blame for Russia's misfortunes and setbacks in the 1990s?" found people choosing such options as Gorbachev, Yeltsin, organized crime, the bureaucratic elite, and even "ourselves" far more often than "the United States, US imperialism."[52]

Surges of animosity toward the United States rose more readily from such events as NATO's expansion into eastern Europe, its bombing of Yugoslavia, Western criticism of Russian campaigns in Chechnya, spats over protectionism, and Russian frustration at the 2002 Olympic Games in Salt Lake City. Polls conducted during these periods, especially the bombing of Serbia, revealed widespread "dislike" of the United States that reached nearly three-quarters of the sample population in the spring of 1999.[53] More recently, though, the spikes of resentment subsided in national surveys, which also indicated that most Russians continued to distinguish between American foreign policy on the one hand and, on the other, American people and their country abstracted from the arena of international competition. When asked by the All-Russian Public Opinion Research Center in February 2000, "What is your attitude to the American people in general?" 78 percent responded favorably, while no more than 10 percent characterized their opinion as negative. Even the question "What is your attitude to the United States?"—more likely to trigger feelings about American behavior abroad—found 66 percent of the sample prepared to answer "good" or "mostly good," with only 22 percent choosing "bad" or "mostly bad."[54]

Over the decade after 1991, polls did detect a reduction in the percentage of Russians who selected the most enthusiastic responses to questions about the United States, but a majority remained positively inclined. "Fairly good," if not "very good," prevailed. "In the final analysis," declared Sergei Karaganov, chairman of the Council on Foreign and Defense Policy in Moscow, "most Russians do not particularly like the American government, but rather like America."[55] Candid responses during the Brezhnev era would probably have revealed comparable sentiments in much of the population.

Just as Russians tend to differentiate between the U.S. government and the American people, they do not appear to link disappointing results of American-inspired economic reforms in Russia with a conclusion that this

failure unmasks the American way *in America*. That is, the polls do not support an assertion that many Russians interpret the distress they witness at
home as a revelation of blights in American society transported to Russia for
all to see. Among those surveyed in 2001 on their images of America, fewer
people (a total of 16 percent) cited negative options of any sort, including
"Russian enemy, primitive ideology, low level of culture, drugs, and sex,"
than specified "a strong economy and a high standard of living" (26 percent).
A joke told at the end of the century—"Everything the Communists told us
about communism was a complete and utter lie. Unfortunately, everything
the Communists told us about capitalism turned out to be true"—speaks
more about circumstances at home than in the United States.[56] If American
life has dismayed some in the Russian intelligentsia ever since the nineteenth century, their fellow citizens have more often imagined an America
containing much to tempt them. Were popular opinion of living conditions
in the United States to grow dark, it would indeed be a historic change—and
one not confirmed to date by credible evidence.

Wherever Russians place the blame for their current hardship, it seems
likely that this plight will enhance the comparative perception of a wealthy
America. Russian newspapers sometimes convey this impression regardless of
their editorial inclinations, as in the following examples: (1) reports in January 2000 on the refusal of half the Don Cossack Song and Dance Ensemble
to return to Russia after an international tour because members expected to
earn much more by staying in America; (2) publication of statistics showing
an expanding gap between per capita income in the two countries, with the
American figure ten times larger than the Russian; and (3) a story on Russian women who travel to work as maids in the United States, where lavish
pay (compared to earnings back home) and numerous labor-saving appliances are said to make life easy.[57] Such articles play a role not unlike that of
newspaper stories 100 years earlier in shaping Russian images of an opulent
land over the sea.

Nevertheless, sentiment appears stronger now in Russia than a decade ago
that the nation should find its own path. America may be rich, this opinion
holds, but Russia must walk for itself in the way it knows best. Vladimir Putin
left no doubt in his millennium message at the end of 1999:

> The experience of the 90s vividly shows that our country's genuine renewal
> without any excessive costs cannot be assured by a mere experimentation in
> Russian conditions with abstract models and schemes taken from foreign text-
> books. The mechanical copying of other nations' experience will not guaran-
> tee success, either. Every country, Russia included, has to search for its own way

of renewal. We have not been very successful in this respect thus far. Only in the past year or the past two years we have started groping for our road and our model of transformation.[58]

But what road should that be? A few days after his electoral victory in 1996, President Yeltsin remarked: "In Russian history of the 20th century there were various periods—monarchism, totalitarianism, perestroika and, finally, a democratic path of development. Each [previous] stage had its ideology. We have none." His concern led to the formation of a committee in 1997 to devise a "national idea"—which the members proved unable to formulate. The following year Igor Chubais, an eminent scholar (and older brother of Anatoly, the leading advocate of privatization in Russia), commented that no one supposed any longer that Russia was the Soviet Union or the Russian empire of the tsars. Moreover, "we understand that we are not western Europe. But then who are we? Until we have developed a new identity we cannot conduct serious, reasonable, logical, consistent policies."[59] At a ceremony in June 2000, marking the tenth anniversary of the Russian Republic's declaration of sovereignty within the Soviet Union, President Putin agreed with a previous speaker that "there can be no great state without an idea and Russia is a great state." Consequently, he continued, there had to be a national idea for Russia. "We must all simply become aware of what that idea is."[60]

During his first months of prominence in 1999–2000, Putin insisted on numerous occasions that Russia's destiny incorporated much from the West. In London, he told an interviewer that "I cannot imagine my own country in isolation from Europe and what we often call the civilized world," while the excerpt above from his Millennium message continues with the following sentence: "We can pin hopes for a worthy future only if we prove capable of combining the universal principles of a market economy and democracy with Russian realities." As for the "Russian realities" that should play a part in the country's revival, Putin exalted the Orthodox Church at times, but more often—and more ominously for Western observers, if not for most Russians to date—he identified forceful government as a vital feature of Russia's heritage. "In general, Russia has from the very start developed as a super-centralised state," he explained in a book prepared before the presidential election of March 2000. "It is part of its genetic code, its tradition, the mentality of its people." If such remarks suggested to some a Russian predisposition to authoritarian rule, Putin has continued to endorse a different objective, the one he reiterated in his state-of-the-nation address to the Russian parliament in April 2002. "Our aims remain the same," he advised the deputies assembled in the Kremlin's Marble Hall: "to develop democracy in Russia; to establish a civilized market and a law-based state."[61]

It remains to be seen how devoted Putin will be to his avowed goal of nurturing democracy and a market economy by means of strengthening the authority of the central government. Some critics have argued that the means will become the ends, or even that Putin's praise of market economics and democracy serves mainly to camouflage sterner intentions. Be that as it may, no one has questioned his determination on another matter, namely the challenge of overcoming the economic chasm between Russia and the most advanced countries. His millennium message warned of peril if the gap were not closed:

> Russia is in the midst of one of the most difficult periods in its history. For the first time in the past 200–300 years, it is facing a real threat of sliding to the second, and possibly even third, echelon of world states. We are running out of time left for removing this threat. We must strain all intellectual, physical and moral forces of the nation. We need coordinated creative work. Nobody will do it for us.[62]

Earlier, during the autumn of 1999, this theme appeared repeatedly in Putin's speeches and interviews. "We must stop the process of our being left behind by the economically developed nations of the world, and find the path which will allow us to take up a suitable place in the ranks of leading nations in the 21st century," he told a Russian journalist in Moscow, using the same words he had chosen the previous week in the far-eastern city of Khabarovsk. The following March, at a presentation of prizes in the fine arts, he seized an opportunity to remind the gathering that "competition in the world is very tough and if we fail to realise that we must be effective, successful and competitive, we will be very rapidly lagging behind and losing positions and the result may be so sad that we cannot even visualise the consequences." Subsequent years witnessed no muting of Putin's concern, as evident in his 2002 state-of-the-nation address: "For Russia to remain a significant and fully-fledged member of the world community and for her to be a strong competitor, our economy must grow at a much faster rate, for otherwise we shall lose all the time, whilst our opportunities in the politics and economy of the world will shrink."[63]

Along with this emergency to catch up with the advanced countries of the world, Putin's thoughts contain other points that have figured in previous chapters. He has argued, for instance, that only the importation of resources from abroad will enable Russia to overtake the leading countries as rapidly as necessary: "Frankly speaking, the rise [of Russia] would be long and painful without foreign capital. But we have no time for this. Consequently, we must do our best to attract foreign capital to the country." In addition, America remains the most compelling measuring stick by which to gauge Russia's progress or stagnation, as Putin's millennium message made clear. The document furnishes perspective on Russia's condition by citing the accomplishments of several countries, but the United States endures as the paramount standard of comparison.[64]

Two years later, both the comparison and the gap assumed an overtly military aspect as Russians weighed the apparent U.S. success in Afghanistan against their own stalled campaign in Chechnya. To be sure, newspaper articles with such titles as "Yankee, Go to Chechnya! Russia Has Been Shown How to Fight a War" did not obscure Russian fears that America had acquired a peremptory attitude toward the rest of the world.[65] But "one has to admit," General Leonid Ivashov told a reporter, "that Americans displayed quite a powerful performance in Afghanistan. Today we can play only a secondary role in this country." Some articles described the U.S. military's technological superiority in terms that recalled Lenin's comments about the American economy early in the twentieth century. Then as now, observers could find the United States troubling—a capitalist exploiter or global bully—but the vaunted *tekhnika* still contrasted with Russia's plight. A journalist formerly employed by the daily newspaper of the Soviet armed forces concluded that new American weapons and tactics in Afghanistan "show that, even if Russian military reform is successful, Russia will still end up with armed forces capable of winning a past but not a future war." At about the same time, parliamentary member Andrei Kokoshin described American defense spending as designed in part "to ensure a technological breakthrough in the military sphere in order to surge far ahead of NATO allies, Russia, China and India and create a situation where these countries would be unable to catch up with the USA in the next 25–30 years."[66]

Meanwhile, Putin faces difficult choices between options whose results, recently and long ago, have been troubling. An autocratic government could well restore the nation's power with hothouse speed, but the undertaking would doubtless create obstacles to future progress as it did in the Soviet Union and tsarist Russia. A democracy might succeed in freeing Russia from the centuries-long pattern of periodic binge-borrowing of foreign practices, but this journey to sustainable preeminence could be long, with no guarantee of success even then. Whatever the choice, global circumstances early in the twentieth-first century confront any Russian president with a Western world in general and a United States in particular that provide an example to copy or at least a level of performance to overtake. As Putin emphasized during his state-of-the-nation address in 2002, "best practice worldwide" must serve as Russia's goal "in everything, in business, science, sport, in the rate of economic growth, in the quality of the work of the state apparatus and the professionalism of the decisions which we all take." He added, in words recalling the "catch and surpass" slogans of an earlier time, that "only then, when we not merely match up to this best practice in the world, but create it ourselves, only then will we genuinely have an opportunity to become rich and strong."[67]

For the indefinite future, though, America will continue to shape much of what is taken for "best practice" simply by existing as the world's lone superpower and thus the standard of comparison most credible to Russian leaders. Less clear is the aspect of the United States that Putin and his successors will deem of primary importance. Military power? A civil society with democratic politics? A massive economy sustaining prosperity beyond that enjoyed by most Russians? To date, Putin has avoided talk of military rivalry with other nations, preferring the tone he adopted before the Russian parliament in the summer of 2000: "The only realistic choice for Russia is the choice to be a strong country, strong and confident in its strength, strong not in spite of the world community, not against other strong states, but together with them."[68] Still, the global activity of America's military and Putin's own experiences during a period that included the Soviet Union's achievement and subsequent loss of martial parity with the United States suggest that his "strong country" would require a formidable military. He and subsequent leaders may seek patiently to restore the nation's power within the current bounds of "managed democracy," or, in the manner of tsars and general secretaries, they may opt once again to accelerate the pace by imposing sacrifices and restrictions on the population. The greater the impositions, however, the more vital becomes a source of inspiration to replace the once-promising socialist vision of 1917. Otherwise, Putin's memory of the late Soviet era should remind him that coercion in the absence of a compelling "national idea" will leave popular imaginations susceptible to tantalizing images of a "land where I have never been" and, eventually, subvert the loudest official proclamations of triumph.

Notes

1. W. A. Swanberg, *Dreiser* (New York: Scribner, 1965), 47–49; Richard Lingeman, *Theodore Dreiser: An American Journey* (New York: Wiley, 1993), 68–70.

2. Lingeman, *Theodore Dreiser*, 69–70.

3. Arnold Lewis, *An Early Encounter with Tomorrow: Europeans, Chicago's Loop, and the World's Columbian Exposition* (Urbana: University of Illinois Press, 1997), 167; Norman Bolotin and Christine

Laing, *The Chicago World's Fair of 1893: The World's Columbian Exposition* (Washington, D.C.: Preservation, 1992), 20, 44, 158; P. I. Glukhovskoi, *Otchet general'nago kommisara russkago otdela vsemirnoi kolumbovoi vystavki v Chikago* (St. Petersburg: V. Kirshbaum, 1895), 21; Paul Bourget, quoted in Robert Muccigrosso, *Celebrating the New World: Chicago's Columbian Exposition of 1893* (Chicago: Ivan R. Dee, 1993), 179; William Cronon, *Nature's Metropolis: Chicago and the Great West* (New York: Norton, 1991), 342, 367.

4. Darwin H. Stapleton, *The Transfer of Early Industrial Technologies to America* (Philadelphia: American Philosophical Society, 1987), 21–24, 122–23, 134; David J. Jeremy, *Transatlantic Industrial Revolution: The Diffusion of Textile Technologies between Britain and America, 1790–1830s* (Cambridge, Mass.: MIT Press, 1981), 138, 176, 257.

5. Marcus Cunliffe, *In Search of America: Transatlantic Essays, 1951–1990* (Westport, Conn.: Greenwood, 1991), 231–33, 235, 237, 243; Merle Curti, "America at the World Fairs, 1851–1893," *American Historical Review* 55, no. 4 (July 1950): 840; Muccigrosso, *Celebrating the New World*, 8.

6. Curti, "America at the World Fairs"; L. Simonin, *A French View of the Grand International Exposition of 1876* (Philadelphia: Claxton, Remsen & Haffelfinger, 1877), 68–69; Donald W. White, *The American Century: The Rise and Decline of the United States as a World Power* (New Haven, Conn.: Yale University Press, 1996), 22.

7. *Chicago Tribune*, 2 May 1893, 12.

8. Joseph M. Rogers, "Lessons from International Exhibitions," *Forum* 32, no. 4 (December 1901): 502, 508.

9. Glukhovskoi, *Otchet general'nago kommisara*, 142; P. A. Tverskoi, *Ocherki Severo-Amerikanskikh Soedinennykh Shtatov* (St. Petersburg: Tipografiia I. N. Skorokhodova, 1895), 448–49.

10. A. S. Sokolov, "Rossiia na vsemirnoi vystavke v Chikago v 1893 g.," *Amerikanskii ezhegodnik* (1984): 157–59; Tverskoi, *Ocherki*, 450. For descriptions of the Russian exhibit, see "Czar Land Treasure," *Chicago Tribune*, 24 July 1893, 8; "Russia's Exhibit," *Sunday Inter Ocean*, 2 July 1893, 13.

11. Glukhovskoi, *Otchet general'nago kommisara*, 107–8; Sokolov, "Rossiia na vsemirnoi vystavke," 154; *Chicago Tribune*, 19 April 1893, 13.

12. A. I. Chuprov, quoted in Robert V. Allen, *Russia Looks at America: The View to 1917* (Washington, D.C.: Library of Congress; Government Printing Office, 1988), 207.

13. Hans Rogger, "America in the Russian Mind—or Russian Discoveries of America," *Pacific Historical Review* 47, no. 1 (February 1978): 43; Hans Rogger, "*Amerikanizm* and the Economic Development of Russia," *Comparative Studies in Society and History* 23, no. 3 (July 1981): 410–11; Charles Rougle, *Three Russians Consider America: America in the Works of Maxsim Gor'kij, Aleksandr Blok, and Vladimir Majakovskij* (Stockholm: Almqvist and Wiksell International, 1976), 86, 95–96; Hans Rogger, "America Enters the Twentieth Century: The View from Russia," in *Felder und Vorfelder russischer Geschichte*, ed. Inge Auerbach et al. (Freiburg, West Germany: Rombach, 1985), 172.

14. Allen, *Russia Looks at America*, 226.

15. *Pravda*, 17 April 1958, 6; 18 April 1958, 6. *Izvestiia*, 18 April 1958, 3; Robert W. Rydell and Nancy Gwinn, *Fair Representations: World's Fairs and the Modern World* (Amsterdam: VU University Press, 1994), 168–69.

16. *Pravda*, 18 April 1958, 6; 19 April 1958, 6; 25 April 1958, 6. *Izvestiia*, 18 April 1958, 3.

17. *New York Times Magazine*, 1 June 1958, 11, 14; Robert W. Rydell, *World of Fairs: The Century-of-Progress Expositions* (Chicago: University of Chicago Press, 1993), 211; N. S. Khrushchev, *Khrushchev in America* (New York: Crosscurrents, 1960), 107.

18. Aleksandr Fursenko and Timothy Naftali, "*One Hell of a Gamble*": *Khrushchev, Castro, and Kennedy, 1958–1964* (New York: Norton, 1997), 77.

19. See, for example, Bruce Parrott, ed., *Trade, Technology, and Soviet-American Relations* (Bloomington: Indiana University Press, 1985), 36, 120; Seyom Brown, *New Forces in World Politics* (Washington, D.C.: Brookings Institution, 1974), 67–68; John R. Thomas and Ursula M. Kruse-Vaucienne,

eds., *Soviet Science and Technology: Domestic and Foreign Perspectives* (Washington, D.C.: George Washington University, 1977).

20. Loren R. Graham, *Science in Russia and the Soviet Union: A Short History* (Cambridge: Cambridge University Press, 1993), 256.

21. Nikita S. Khrushchev, *Khrushchev Remembers: The Glasnost Tapes* (Boston: Little, Brown, 1990), 93–94.

22. Serge Schmemann, *Echoes of a Native Land: Two Centuries of a Russian Village* (New York: Vintage, 1997), 153–54.

23. For a sampling of scholarly comments on Russian and Soviet problems with technological innovation and diffusion, see Joseph Bradley, *Guns for the Tsar: American Technology and the Small Arms Industry in Nineteenth-Century Russia* (Dekalb: Northern Illinois University Press, 1990), 186–87; Thomas and Kruse-Vaucienne, *Soviet Science and Technology*; Kendall E. Bailes, *Technology and Society under Lenin and Stalin: Origins of the Soviet Technical Intelligentsia, 1917–1941* (Princeton, N.J.: Princeton University Press, 1978), chapter 13; Graham, *Science in Russia and the Soviet Union*, 201, 251-60.

24. Michael Lelyveld, "Corporate US Rethinks Free Market for Russia," *Journal of Commerce*, 3 September 1998, from David Johnson's Russia List, #2343, 3 September 1998; Stephen Cohen, "'Who Lost Russia?'" *Nation*, 12 October 1998, from David Johnson's Russia List, #2397, 25 September 1998; Jerry Hough, "West Shares Blame for Scandal," *Los Angeles Times*, 23 September 1999, from David Johnson's Russia List, #3520, 23 September 1999.

25. Marshall Goldman, quoted in *New York Times*, 30 August 1998; Deputy Secretary of State Strobe Talbott's lecture at Oxford University, 20 January 2000, from David Johnson's Russia List, #4065, 25 January 2000. See also "Conference Summary. 'Russia: What Went Wrong? Which Way Now?'" (conference organized by the Jamestown Foundation, 9–10 June 1999), from David Johnson's Russia List, #3408, 26 July 1999; "U.S. Assistance for Market Reforms: Foreign Aid Failures in Russia and the Former Soviet Bloc," *Cato Institute Policy Analysis*, no. 338, 22 March 1999, from David Johnson's Russia List, #3107, 24 March 1999.

26. "Yeltsin's Resignation Statement," Moscow, 31 December 1999 (Reuters), from David Johnson's Russia List, #3717, 31 December 1999.

27. Vladimir Isachenkov, "Yeltsin Vows to Continue Reforms," Moscow, 29 December 1998 (AP), from David Johnson's Russia List, #2536, 30 December 1998.

28. "Exchange Program for Young Russian Leaders to Start Monday," Washington, D.C., 19 July 1999 (Itar-Tass), from David Johnson's Russia List, #3398, 19 July 1999; "2,600 Russian Political Leaders to Visit U.S. in 2002 as Part of Center for Russian Leadership Development Open World Program," Washington, D.C., 3 December 2001 (PRNewswire), from David Johnson's Russia List, #5579, 4 December 2001; "The Russians Are Coming . . . to Like U.S. Practices," *American Banker*, 3 January 2002, from David Johnson's Russia List, #6003, 3 January 2002; "Joint Statement by President George W. Bush and President Vladimir V. Putin on U.S.–Russian People-to-People Contacts," White House, 24 May 2002, from David Johnson's Russia List, #6270, 24 May 2002.

29. Elisaveta Konstantinova, "Foreign Firms Stay in Russia Despite Crisis," Moscow, 14 October 1998 (Reuters), from David Johnson's Russia List, #2429, 14 October 1998; "McDonald's Plans Russia Investment," Moscow, 15 February 1999 (UPI), from David Johnson's Russia List, #3055, 16 February 1999; Bill Keller, "Arise, Ye Prisoners of Starvation," *New York Times*, 23 February 2002, from David Johnson's Russia List, #6094, 23 February 2002; Mark McDonald, "US Automakers Starting New Revolution in Russia," Vsevolozhsk, 25 November 2002 (Knight Ridder Newspapers), from David Johnson's Russia List, #6574, 27 November 2002.

30. Clara Ferreira-Marques, "Russian Film Industry Battles Hollywood Goliath," 17 June 2002 (Reuters), from David Johnson's Russia List, #6313, 11 June 2002; Daniil Dondurei, "An Average Russian Sees 180 Films a Year," *Vremia novosti*, 25 April 2000, from David Johnson's Russia List,

#4292, 10 May 2000; Peter Rutland, "Russian Film and Television: Making a Slow Comeback," *Transitions Online* (forthcoming), from David Johnson's Russia List, #4422, 25 July 2000; Sarah Lindemann, "Pop Culture in Russia: An Update," from David Johnson's Russia List, #5083, 9 February 2001.

31. *Wall Street Journal*, 23 May 1994. Also see Stefan Hedlund, *Russia's "Market" Economy: A Bad Case of Predatory Capitalism* (London: UCL, 1999); Anne Williamson, "An Inconvenient History," 1 September 1999 (WorldNetDaily.com), from David Johnson's Russia List, #3477, 2 September 1999. Regarding judicial reform, see "Stronger Judicial System Is Russia's Priority for 2000," Moscow, 30 January 2000 (Itar-Tass), from David Johnson's Russia List, #4080, 31 January 2000; "Can Foreign Aid Promote the Rule of Law? Reflections on the Russian Experience" (seminar at the Woodrow Wilson International Center for Scholars, Washington, D.C., 15 April 1999), from David Johnson's Russia List, #3359, 24 June 1999; Masha Gessen, "A Matter of Justice," *U.S. News and World Report*, 20 November 2000, from David Johnson's Russia List, #4641, 18 November 2000; "Trial by Jury to Be Introduced in All Parts of Russia by Next Year," Moscow, 28 January 2002 (Itar-Tass), from David Johnson's Russia List, #6045, 28 January 2002; "Reforming Russia's Courts," *East European Constitutional Review* 11, nos. 1–2 (Winter–Spring 2002), excerpt from David Johnson's Russia List, #6277, 29 May 2002.

32. Allison Blakely, "American Influences on Russian Reformist Thought in the Era of the French Revolution," *Russian Review* 52, no. 4 (October 1993): 451.

33. Max M. Laserson, *The American Impact on Russia—Diplomatic, and Ideological—1784–1917* (New York: Macmillan, 1950), 83.

34. Laserson, *American Impact*, 83–84.

35. George Vernadsky, "Reforms under Czar Alexander I: French and American Influences," *Review of Politics* 9 (1947): 57–61; Laserson, *American Impact*, 84–90.

36. N. N. Bolkhovitinov, "Dekabristy i Amerika," *Voprosy istorii*, no. 4 (1974): 91–94, 96; V. Shestakov, "Russkoe otkrytie Ameriki," in *Vzaimodeistvie kul'tur SSSR i SShA XVIII–XX vv.*, ed. O. E. Tuganova (Moscow: Nauka, 1987), 22–23; G. G. Krichevskii, "'Konstitutsionnyi proekt' Nikity Murav'eva i Amerikanskie konstitutsii," *Izvestiia akademii nauk SSSR. Seriia istorii i filosofii*, no. 6 (1945): 397–406; Marc Raeff, *The Decembrist Movement* (Englewood Cliffs, N.J.: Prentice Hall, 1966), 54.

37. Frederick L. Schuman, *American Policy toward Russia since 1917* (New York: International, 1928), 45; Laserson, *American Impact*, 397.

38. *Papers Relating to the Foreign Relations of the United States: 1918, Russia* (Washington, D.C.: Government Printing Office, 1931), 1:5–6; David C. Engerman, "America, Russia, and the Romance of Economic Development" (Ph.D. diss., University of California at Berkeley, 1998), 207; Elihu Root, quoted in Engerman, "America, Russia," 191; Woodrow Wilson, quoted in John Lewis Gaddis, *Russia, the Soviet Union, and the United States: An Interpretive History*, 2d ed. (New York: McGraw-Hill, 1990), 57.

39. *New York Times*, 14 June 1979.

40. See chapter 6.

41. Numerous sources cited in previous chapters provide a sense of the contending positions. Also, David Johnson's Russia List continues to host periodic debates on these topics (and on other goals of the reformers, including the question of whether Russia's economy is now governed predominantly by market forces).

42. Tim McDaniel, *The Agony of the Russian Idea* (Princeton, N.J.: Princeton University Press, 1996), 5, 169; Grigory Vainshtein, "Totalitarian Public Consciousness in a Post-Totalitarian Society: The Russian Case in the General Context of Post-Communist Developments," *Communist and Post-Communist Studies* 27, no. 3 (September 1994): 256.

43. *U.S. Department of State Dispatch* 6, no. 8 (20 February 1995): 121; Jerry F. Hough, *Democratization and Revolution in the USSR, 1985–1991* (Washington, D.C.: Brookings Institution Press,

1997), 496; Timothy Colton and Michael McFaul, "Are Russians Undemocratic?," working paper no. 20 (excerpt), from David Johnson's Russia List, #5294, 12 June 2001. James Gibson of Washington University analyzed a series of polls taken in 1996, 1998, and 2000 and concluded that "findings concerning support for democracy were mixed. Support for many democratic freedoms was expressed by large majorities that remained quite stable over time. Thus 85–95 per cent supported equality before the law and the right to privacy, while 70–80 per cent supported freedom of speech, publication, and religion and the right to protest. However, freedom of association had support from only 50–60 per cent. A competitive multi-party system was also not very popular. Only a third of the sample agreed that party competition strengthened the political system, with a similar proportion saying that Russia needed one-party rule. The idea of outlawing all political parties appealed to 50–55 per cent." Stephen Shenfield, ed., "Do Russians Believe in Democracy?" in *JRL Research and Analytical Supplement*, from David Johnson's Russia List, #5425, 4 September 2001. See also tables 7, 8, and 9 under the heading "Democracy: Russian Way" in Georgy Ilyichev, "Decade of Russian Reforms through the Eyes of Sociologists," *Izvestiia*, no. 66 [no date], from David Johnson's Russia List, #6227, 7 May 2002.

44. Alice Lagnado, "Putin to Purge Russian Tongue of Foreign Elements," *Times* (London), 1 May 2001, from David Johnson's Russia List, #5233, 1 May 2001; Oksana Yablokova, "Government Moves to Purify Russian," *Moscow Times*, 27 June 2001, from David Johnson's Russia List, #5325, 27 June 2001; Fred Weir, "Russian Lawmakers Try to Stomp Out Foreign Slang," *Christian Science Monitor*, 4 June 2002, from David Johnson's Russia List, #6287, 4 June 2002.

45. Svetlana Boym, *Common Places: Mythologies of Everyday Life in Russia* (Cambridge, Mass.: Harvard University Press, 1994), 119–20. The complete text of the song ("Poslednee pis'mo") is available in Russian at the website of Nautilus Pompilus at http://www.nautilus.ru/ (accessed June 2000).

46. Allen, *Russia Looks at America*, 234–36; John Van der Kiste, *The Romanovs 1818–1959: Alexander II of Russia and His Family* (Stroud, England: Sutton, 1998), 55–57; Alexandre Tarsaïdzé, *Czars and Presidents: The Story of a Forgotten Friendship* (New York: McDowell, Obolensky, 1958), 269–81.

47. Shestakov, "Russkoe otkrytie Ameriki," 21; Mitsuko Shimomura, *America through the Eyes of Soviet People* (Moscow: Novosti, 1988), 8, 30; *Vogue* (February 1995): 77; Pitirim A. Sorokin, *Russia and the United States* (New York: Dutton, 1944), 28. *Pravda*, 24 May 1988, 4; 1 February 1996, 4.

48. Lyrics in Walter L. Hixson, *Witness to Disintegration: Provincial Life in the Last Year of the USSR* (Hanover, N.H.: University Press of New England, 1993), 6.

49. I am grateful to Julia Friedman for informing me of this song and the lyrics quoted here.

50. David Filipov, "Russian Shoot-'em-up Pokes Holes in an America Once Revered," *Boston Globe*, 3 June 2000, from David Johnson's Russia List, #4344, 3 June 2000.

51. See, for example, Georgy Arbatov, "Cold War May Become a Reality Yet Again," *Nezavisimaia gazeta*, 17 June 1998, from David Johnson's Russia List, #2233, 22 June 1998; remarks by former secretary of state James Baker, *Meeting Report: Kennan Institute for Advanced Russian Studies* 17, nos. 1–2 (1999); Tatyana Matsuk, "War or Peace? The Reasons for and Possible Consequences of Anti-Western Feeling in Russia," *Jamestown Foundation Prism*, 23 April 1999, from David Johnson's Russia List, #3257, 25 April 1999; Donna Smith, "U.S. Lawmakers Warned of Russia Corruption Dangers," Washington, D.C. (Reuters), from David Johnson's Russia List, #3517, 22 September 1999 (quoting former CIA director James Woolsey).

52. Steven Grant, *Is Economic Reform in Russia Dead?* (Washington, D.C.: United States Information Agency, 1999), 2–4; "Poll: Russians Oppose US Investment," Moscow, 2 July 1999 (AP), from David Johnson's Russia List, #3376, 3 July 1999; Ilyichev, "Decade of Russian Reforms."

53. "Russian Poll Shows US Out of Favor," Moscow, 16 April 1999 (UPI), from David Johnson's Russia List, #3243, 17 April 1999; "Anti-Western Feeling Grows in Russia over Chechnya," Moscow,

12 November 1999 (AFP), from David Johnson's Russia List, #3622, 13 November 1999; "New Poll Shows Russians View West as Hostile," Moscow, 23 November 1999 (Reuters), from David Johnson's Russia List, #3640, 23 November 1999; Anatole Shub, *Many Russians Still Admire America, But More and More Disapprove of U.S. Foreign Policies* (Washington, D.C.: United States Information Agency, 1999); Boris Kagarlitsky, "Roots of Anti-Americanism," *Moscow Times,* 9 April 2002, from David Johnson's Russia List, #6174, 9 April 2002; Eric Shiraev and Vladislav Zubok, *Anti-Americanism in Russia: From Stalin to Putin* (New York: Palgrave, 2000).

54. "Russians No Longer Bitter towards US over Kosovo," Moscow, 2 September 1999 (Reuters), from David Johnson's Russia List, #3479, 3 September 1999; Vitaly Golovachev, "Is the Cold War a Thing of the Past?" *Trud,* 7 March 2000, from David Johnson's Russia List, #4153, 8 March 2000; "Russians Are Positive about the USA but Negative about the Creation of the American ABM System," Moscow, 2 June 2000 (Interfax), from David Johnson's Russia List, #4344, 3 June 2000; Vladimir Shlapentokh, "Russian Attitudes toward America: A Split between the Ruling Class and the Masses," from David Johnson's Russia List, #5188, 5 April 2001.

55. Aleksei Levinson, "Fairly Good: What Do Russians Really Think of the United States?" *Ezhenedel'nyi zhurnal,* no. 19 (May 2002), from David Johnson's Russia List, #6268, 24 May 2002; Sergei Karaganov, "The Trouble with the U.S.: It's Just Too Darn Big," *Newsweek International,* 31 January 2000, from David Johnson's Russia List, #4075, 28 January 2000.

56. Shlapentokh, "Russian Attitudes"; "Anti-Americanism in Russia—Misunderstanding and Myth," Strana.ru, 16 June 2001, from David Johnson's Russia List, #5303, 15 June 2001; Michael Dobbs and Paul Blustein, "Lost Illusions about Russia: U.S. Backers of Ill-Fated Reforms Now Portrayed as Naive," *Washington Post,* 12 September 1999, from David Johnson's Russia List, #3495, 12 September 1999.

57. "Cossack Singers and Dancers Choose Not to Come Back from America," *Trud,* 13 January 2000, from David Johnson's Russia List, #4040, 16 January 2000; Vitaly Golovachev, "Humiliation," *Trud,* 18 June 1998, from David Johnson's Russia List, #2229, 19 June 1998; Anna Blundy, "Russians Lured by Promise of US Servitude," *Times* (London), 12 January 1999, from David Johnson's Russia List, #3012, 12 January 1999 (regarding maids—descriptions of reports and advertisements in Russian newspapers).

58. Vladimir Putin, "Russia at the Turn of the Millennium," at www.pravitelstvo.gov.ru/english/statVP_engl_1.html (accessed December 1999).

59. Boris Yeltsin, quoted in the *Baltimore Sun,* 8 December 1997; John Thornhill, "Chubais: A Crisis of Ideas Is the Real Trouble," *Financial Times* (UK), 3 October 1998, from David Johnson's Russia List, #2412, 5 October 1998; *New York Times,* 31 March 1998.

60. "President Putin on the Idea That Makes Russia Great," Moscow, 12 June 2000 (NTV International, from BBC Monitoring), from David Johnson's Russia List, #4365, 13 June 2000.

61. *New York Times Magazine,* 19 March 2000, 64; "Putin Hopes Orthodox Christianity Will Strengthen Russia," Moscow, 6 January 2000 (Interfax), from David Johnson's Russia List, #4017, 7 January 2000; Oleg Shchedrov, "Central Power in Russia's Genes, Putin Says," Moscow, 13 March 2000 (Reuters), from David Johnson's Russia List, #4167, 14 March 2000; "Russian President's Address to Federal Assembly," 8 July 2000 (BBC Monitoring), from David Johnson's Russia List, #4391, 9 July 2000; "Full Text of Putin Annual State-of-the-Nation Address," 18 April 2002 (BBC Monitoring), from David Johnson's Russia List, #6195, 19 April 2002.

62. Putin, "Russia at the Turn of the Millennium." See also "Russian President's Address to Federal Assembly."

63. For the comments made a week apart, see "Putin—Russian Economy Not to Remain Transitional," Khabarovsk, 27 October 1999 (Interfax), from David Johnson's Russia List, #3593, 29 October 1999; "Russian PM Says Russia Stuck in Transition," Moscow, 6 November 1999 (Reuters), from David Johnson's Russia List, #3610, 7 November 1999. For the other quotations, see "Putin: Russia

Has Not Much Time to Overcome Lag," Moscow, 1 March 2000 (Itar-Tass), from David Johnson's Russia List, #4141, 1 March 2000; "Full Text of Putin Annual State-of-the-Nation Address."

64. Putin, "Russia at the Turn of the Millennium."

65. For article titles of this sort, see Vladimir Georgiev, "Yankee, Go to Chechnya! Russia Has Been Shown How to Fight a War," *Nezavisimaia gazeta*, 25 January 2002, from David Johnson's Russia List, #6040, 26 January 2002; Said Bitsoyev, "How We Fight Wars—and How They Do It," *Novye Izvestiia*, 28 December 2001, from David Johnson's Russia List, #5618, 28 December 2001; Alexander Golts, "Afghan Lessons for Russian Generals," *Russia Journal*, 25–31 January 2002, from David Johnson's Russia List, #6040, 26 January 2002.

66. Igor Torbakov, "Russia Worries That Afghan Success Will Prompt US Unilateralism," *Eurasia Insight*, 2 January 2002, from David Johnson's Russia List, #6003, 3 January 2002; Golts, "Afghan Lessons"; "Ex-Secretary of Russia's Security Council on the Afghan Campaign," *Vremya MN*, no. 33, 2002, from David Johnson's Russia List, #6092, 22 February 2002.

67. "Full Text of Putin Annual State-of-the-Nation Address."

68. "Russian President's Address to Federal Assembly."

Index

About the Author

Alan M. Ball is associate professor of history at Marquette University. He is the author of two previous books on Russian history.